UK Accounting Standards
A Quick Reference Guide

Dedicated to the memory of my father

PUBLISHING

UK Accounting Standards
A Quick Reference Guide

Robert J. Kirk

ELSEVIER

AMSTERDAM   BOSTON   HEIDELBERG   LONDON   NEW YORK   OXFORD
PARIS   SAN DIEGO   SAN FRANCISCO   SINGAPORE   SYDNEY   TOKYO

CIMA Publishing
An imprint of Elsevier
Linacre House, Jordan Hill, Oxford OX2 8DP
30 Corporate Drive, Burlington, MA 01803

First published 2005

British Library Cataloguing in Publication Data
A catalogue record for this book is available from the British Library

ISBN 0 7506 6474 6

For information on all CIMA publications visit our website at
www.cimapublishing.com

Typeset by Newgen Imaging Systems (P) Ltd, Chennai, India
Printed and bound in Great Britain by Biddles Ltd, Kings Lynn, Norfolk

**Working together to grow
libraries in developing countries**

www.elsevier.com | www.bookaid.org | www.sabre.org

ELSEVIER   BOOK AID
International   Sabre Foundation

Contents

About the author

Robert J. Kirk BSc (Econ) FCA CPA qualified as a chartered accountant in 1976. He trained in Belfast with Price Waterhouse & Co., and subsequently spent 2 years in industry in a subsidiary of Shell (UK) and 4 further years in practice. In 1980 he was appointed a director of a private teaching college in Dublin where he specialized in the teaching of professional accounting subjects. He later moved into the university sector, and is currently Professor of Financial Reporting in the School of Accounting at the University of Ulster.

He has been lecturing on the CIMA Mastercourses presentations *Recent Accounting Standards* and *Accounting Standards in Depth* since 1985. He has also presented continuing professional education courses for the Institute of Chartered Accountants in Ireland over the same period.

His publications to date, in addition to numerous professional journal articles, include two books on company law in Northern Ireland, co-authorship with University College Dublin of the first Survey of Irish Published Accounts, a joint publication with Coopers & Lybrand on the legislation enacting the 7th European Directive into UK legislation and two Financial Reporting publications for the CIMA Study Packs.

Preface

The pace of development in financial reporting has accelerated sharply during the last few years, especially since the advent of the Accounting Standards Board (ASB) in 1990. The pace of progress shows no sign of abating and it has become increasingly difficult for the professionally qualified accountant to keep abreast of the changes.

UK Accounting Standards: A Quick Reference Guide examines the standards in a unique and detailed way and it has been written with a broad readership in mind. Each chapter includes a brief summary of the relevant accounting standards in force together with the proposed changes contained within the exposure drafts. A selection of illustrative examples are included which attempt to cover most of the major problem areas that practitioners are likely to encounter.

The book commences with an introduction to the standard-setting process. As well as looking at the development of the ASB it examines the conceptual framework behind the practice of financial accounting and, in particular, the Statement of Principles. It also incorporates the likely switch that companies will face in moving towards complying with international accounting standards in the near future. The next three chapters cover the key accounting problems in the balance sheet, i.e. tangible fixed assets, intangible assets and stocks and work in progress. Chapters 5 and 6 concentrate on the profit and loss account and in particular the effects of taxation and disclosure of earnings per share. Chapter 7 covers the important area of liquidity and viability by examining cash flow statements, and Chapter 8 picks up difficult pensions accounting problems as well as segmental reporting and post balance sheet events, provisions and contingencies.

The longest chapter (Chapter 9) is reserved for the accounting aspects of groups and this encapsulates accounting for acquisitions, mergers and associated undertakings. Chapter 10 concentrates on foreign currency translation, and Chapter 11 sweeps up recent developments in financial reporting.

The intention of the book is that the reader will feel comfortable with basic numerical application, on an understanding of the underlying theory and on presentation of financial statements under the current regulatory framework.

Introduction

Introduction to Standard-Setting Process

The first Statement of Standard Accounting Practice (SSAP) was published in 1970 in the United Kingdom. Prior to this, there were relatively few financial reporting requirements for companies. It was the highly publicised scandals of the late 1960s, such as the GEC takeover of AEI, that brought the need for more extensive regulations and the setting up of a standard-setting body.

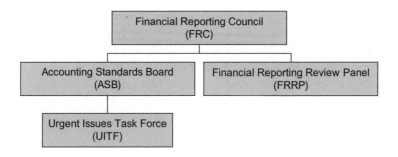

The Financial Reporting Council (FRC)

The FRC was set up to ensure that the standard-setting process works relatively smoothly. The role of the FRC is basically both a funding and a human resources one. They have to find approximately £3.5m to fund the operation each year and they are responsible for appointing the main personnel in the standard-setting process. In addition, they have an overall responsibility for overlooking the whole process. Membership contains both members of the profession and those who are concerned with the use, preparation and interpretation of financial statements. Once a year they publish a Review of the previous calendar year and it can be downloaded from its website www.frc.org.uk. The FRC could be described as the 'House of Lords' of the standard-setting system.

The Accounting Standards Board (ASB)

The 'House of Commons' of the new system is the main standard setter, the ASB. The ASB has ten members and is responsible for issuing standards on its own authority in the United Kingdom. To date they have published 19 Financial Reporting Standards (FRSs) as well as taking on board all the remaining nine SSAPs. However, since the emergence of the International Accounting Standards Board (IASB) in April 2001 the ASB has agreed not to issue any further standards unless these are the same as those promulgated by the IASB. It will become more like a district society rather than a major standard-setter. However, their technical resources will be used by the IASB to develop future world standards.

Standards in the past were developed by first identifying a topic from the ASB's own research or from external sources. A programme of initial consultation was then initiated which would lead to the publication of a discussion paper or consultation paper. Once that has been circulated any comments are reviewed and eventually an exposure draft is issued (known as a FRED), which outlines the intended contents of the new or revised standard. The FRED is then exposed for public comment for 3–6 months and again comments are analysed and that will result in a modified document which will eventually be published as a full Financial Reporting Standard. A list of all extant documents is provided at the end of the chapter.

The Financial Reporting Review Panel (FRRP)

Under the Companies Act 1989 large private and all listed and public interest entities are subject to review by the FRRP. They must state in writing whether or not their accounts have been prepared in accordance with applicable standards and provide details of any material departures from those standards and the reasons for them.

The Panel have investigated over 400 entities since they were set up in 1990 and have published more than 75 public press releases giving information as to the wrongdoings of the company investigated and how that company has agreed to amend their financial statements. If a company refuses to agree to the findings of the Panel they can be brought to Court and fined for non-compliance. To date (October 2004) no company has taken on the Panel and all cases have resulted in voluntary compliance by the companies concerned.

The Panel obtain their information from three sources:

1. Qualified audit reports
2. Adverse press comment
3. Whistleblowing.

Surprisingly, very few cases are discovered by qualified audit reports and most of the cases come from the latter two sources. In particular, a monthly publication, *Company Reporting*, which has a database of more than 500 companies, provides a rich vein of material for the Panel. They also have a special Whistleblowers Corner on their website www.companyreporting.com.uk in which they encourage users to complain about non-compliance with standards.

The Panel has been a reactive force over the first 12 years of their existence but they have now decided to increase their resources in the near future to introduce a more pro-active approach. In some cases the Panel has caused companies to republish their financial statements and force the Directors to pay for those republications. One of the worst cases was the case of the Wiggins Group Plc, who had to rip up 5 years' published financial statements (years ended 31 March 1996 to 2000) and reissue them. Instead of revealing 5 years increasing profit performance the revised accounts reveal 5 years' increasing losses! The company had failed to comply with a number of accounting standards as well as not complying with company legislation.

The new IASB is considering the setting up of an international Review Panel to investigate multi-national compliance with IFRSs.

The Urgent Issues Task Force (UITF)

The UITF is a sub-committee of the ASB and its role is to act as a firefighter, to ensure that any holes in existing accounting standards are covered and to ensure that any new creative accounting technique is quickly addressed. Over the first 12 years of its life it has issued 38 abstracts or consensus pronouncements. Some of these will only be temporary as they will be replaced by a more fully thought out standard in the future. However, there are still some that were issued 10 years ago that are still in exitence today. A full list of extant abstracts is provided in Chapter 10.

Other Sub-Committees

Committee on Accounting for Smaller Entities (CASE)

This sub-committee was set up to concentrate on the development and periodic revision of the *Financial Reporting Standard for Smaller Entities (FRSSE)*. That standard, which has been updated on four occasions (last in June 2002), has been designed to exempt the vast majority of limited companies from compliance with the full set of accounting standards and instead gives them the opportunity to comply with a single comprehensive standard containing the measurement and disclosure requirements that are considered most relevant to smaller entities.

In March 2004 the ASB, after advice from CASE, published a Discussion Paper *A One Stop Shop Financial Reporting Standard for Smaller Entities (FRSSE)*. This document incorporates both legal and accounting standards requirements within the one document. Currently small companies are defined in companies legislation as having a turnover not greater than £2.8m, gross assets of no more than £1.4m and up to 50 employees but these are currently being revised.

Public Sector and Not for Profit Committee

Treasury and the public sector have been committed to introducing resource accounting into the public service over the last 10 years and to introduce as much as possible of private sector accounting. In June 2003 the body recommended to the ASB the publication of a Discussion Paper *Statement of Principles for Public Benefit Entities* in which the original principles were tailored to meet the needs of the public sector. In particular, instead of investors being made the main user, funders and financial supporters are recognised and there are differences in how assets and liabilities might be defined. Overall, however, the principles are largely the same. The Committee also overviews the publication of any revised Statement of Recommended Practice (SORP) on Charities.

Financial Sector and Other Special Industries Committee

This body has the responsibility of reviewing SORPs developed for specific industries and sectors.

Authority of Accounting Standards

The ASB issued a *Foreword to Accounting Standards* in June 1993 in which it set out the authority, scope and application of accounting standards.

Authority

1. FRSs and SSAPs are 'accounting standards' for the purpose of the Companies Act 1985. The Act requires the financial statements of large companies to publicly state whether they have been prepared in accordance with applicable accounting standards and to provide particulars of any material departures from those standards and the reasons for them.
2. Members of the professional accounting bodies are expected to observe accounting standards whether acting as preparers or auditors of financial information.
3. If accountants act as Directors the onus on them is to ensure that the existence and purpose of accounting standards are fully understood by fellow directors.

The accountancy profession itself has the sanction of bringing disciplinary action against any of their members who have failed to observe accounting standards or to ensure adequate disclosure of significant departures from standards. In extreme cases members could be excluded from membership.

Scope

Applicable to all financial statements intending to provide a true and fair view of the state of a company's affairs at the balance sheet date and of its profit and loss for the financial period.

Authority

Accounting standards need not be applied to immaterial items but they should be applied to group statements which include overseas subsidiaries.

UK Standards and International Standards

The International Accounting Standards Committee (IASC) was set up in 1973 to promulgate international standards with the objective of harmonising standards on a world-wide basis. Generally these were ignored by the UK but a major decision was taken by the European Commission that all consolidated accounts of listed companies within the European Union must be prepared under these international standards for all accounting periods ending on or after 1 January 2005. In 2001 the IASC was disbanded and replaced by a new body, the International Accounting Standards Board (IASB).

The UK Government has announced, in a Department of Trade and Industry (DTI) Consultation Document published in March 2004 *Modernisation of Accounting Directives/IAS Infrastructure*, details of how non-listed companies in the UK can opt to adopt international rather than national standards as from the 1 January 2005.

The ASB has also agreed to harmonise its standards in line with international require-ments. However, this process will take some years to occur and the ASB has agreed to evolve its standards slowly in that direction. In March 2004 they made a commitment to amend three standards before 1 January 2005. These standards will see the replacement of SSAP 17 *Accounting for Post Balance Sheet Events*, FRS 8 *Related Party Transactions* and FRS 14 *Earnings per Share* with IAS 10, IAS 24 and IAS 33 respectively.

There are major new topics still to be introduced, both on an international and national front in the near future. Already IFRS 2 *Share Based Payment* has been published (March 2004) and this will be incorporated as FRS 20 in early Spring 2004 into UK reporting. This will require a fair value to be measured at the date of grant of share options and that to be charged to profit and loss over the vesting period. In addition, IFRS 3 *Business Combinations* will require all business combinations to be accounted for as acquisitions as merger accounting will be banned. Goodwill will have to be treated as a permanent asset with no amortisation but with a requirement for an annual impairment review of the good-will. It is likely that many entities will try to reclassify goodwill as other intangibles as the amortisation rules will still apply to those assets. IFRS 5 *Disposal of Non Current Assets and Presentation of Discontinued Operations* (March 2004) will eventually have to be adopted as a national standard and this will require all assets and disposal groups which are classified as 'held for sale' to be transferred to current assets and recorded at the lower of their book value and recoverable amount. It will also introduce a much 'softer' definition of a discon-tinued operation which could lead to a plethora of discontinued operations being disclosed in company accounts. For insurance companies IFRS 4 *Insurance Contracts* will not revo-lutionise accounting for insurance contracts but it will bring some consistency in choosing the most appropriate policies.

There are still major political obstacles to overcome before international standards, *in toto*, become acceptable in all countries. In France, President Chirac has written to the president of the EC about the 'nefarious economic consequences' of introducing IAS 39 *Financial Instruments: Recognition and Measurement*, particularly the need for fair value financial instruments and to record all gains and losses in the profit and loss account.

List of Extant Financial Reporting Standards and International Standards

UK Accounting Standards SSAPs and FRSs	International Accounting Standards IFRSs and IASs
SSAP 4 Accounting for Government Grants	IAS 20 Accounting for Government Grants and Disclosure of Government Assistance
SSAP 5 Accounting for Value Added Tax	—
SSAP 9 Stocks and Long Term Contracts	IAS 2 Inventories
	IAS 11 Construction and Service Contracts
SSAP 13 Accounting for Research and Development	IAS 38 Intangible Assets
SSAP 17 Accounting for Post Balance Sheet Events	IAS 10 Events After the Balance Sheet Date
SSAP 19 Investment Properties	IAS 40 Investment Properties
SSAP 20 Foreign Currency Translation	IAS 21 The Effect of Changes in Foreign Exchange Rates
	IAS 29 Financial Reporting in Hyperinflationary Economies
SSAP 21 Accounting for Leases and Hire Purchase Contracts	IAS 17 Leases
SSAP 25 Segmental Reporting	IAS 14 Segment Reporting
FRS 1 Cash Flow Statements	IAS 7 Cash Flow Statements
FRS 2 Accounting for Subsidiary Undertakings	IAS 27 Consolidated Financial Statements
FRS 3 Reporting Financial Performance	IAS 8 Net Profit or Loss for the Period, Errors and Changes in Accounting Policies
	IAS 35 Discontinuing Operations
FRS 4 Capital Instruments	IAS 39 Financial Instruments: Recognition and Measurement
FRS 5 Reporting the Substance of Transactions	—
FRS 6 Acquisitions and Mergers	IFRS 3 Business Combinations
FRS 7 Fair Values in Acquisition Accounting	IFRS 3 Business Combinations
FRS 8 Related Party Disclosures	IAS 24 Related Party Disclosures
FRS 9 Associates and Joint Ventures	IAS 28 Investments in Associates
	IAS 31 Financial Reporting of Interests in Joint Ventures

FRS 10 Goodwill and Intangible Assets	IFRS 3 Business Combinations
FRS 11 Impairments of Fixed Assets and Goodwill	IAS 36 Impairment of Assets
FRS 12 Provisions, Contingent Liabilities and Contingent Assets	IAS 37 Provisions, Contingent Liabilities and Contingent Assets
FRS 13 Derivatives and Other Financial Instruments: Disclosures	IAS 32 Financial Instruments: Disclosure and Presentation
FRS 14 Earnings Per Share	IAS 33 Earnings Per Share
FRS 15 Tangible Fixed Assets	IAS 16 Property, Plant and Equipment
	IAS 23 Borrowing Costs
FRS 16 Current Tax	IAS 12 Income Taxes
FRS 17 Retirement Benefits	IAS 19 Employee Benefits
FRS 18 Accounting Policies	IAS 1 Presentation of Financial Statements
	IAS 8 Net Profit or Loss for the Period, Errors and Changes in Accounting Policies
FRS 19 Deferred Tax	IAS 12 Income Taxes
FRS 20 Share Based Payment	IFRS 2 Share Based Payment
FRS 21	
FRS 5 Reporting the Substance of Transactions: Revenue Recognition (AN G)	IAS 18 Revenue Recognition
SORP Retirement Benefit Plans	IAS 26 Accounting and Reporting by Retirement Benefit Plans
–	IAS 30 Disclosures in the Financial Statements of Banks and Similar Financial Institutions
SBP Interim Accounts	IAS 34 Interim Financial Reporting
–	IAS 41 Agriculture
–	IFRS 1 First Time Application of Financial Reporting Standards

1

The regulatory framework and the standard-setting process

1.1 Statement of Principles (December 1999)

Background

One of the main problems that has faced the standard-setting bodies in their quest to develop authoritative accounting standards was their failure to publish standards which have been consistent with each other. There has been no firm foundation on which they could be built, apart from the four fundamental concepts listed in SSAP 2. As a result the actual standards have been produced in an *ad hoc* manner with very little logical thought behind their publication. The Statement of Principles is an attempt to put this right by introducing, in a series of eight chapters, the core principles that should govern financial reporting.

Chapter 1: Objective of financial statements

This chapter argues that although there are several users of financial reporting the main user of the Annual Report is the shareholder and therefore the information should largely be directed towards his/her needs. These needs are twofold – to ensure the reporting entity has performed adequately (the stewardship function) and to ensure that the shareholder has sufficient information on which to make decisions about their future investment (i.e. the decision-making function). In order to provide information which would be helpful to users it is recommended that the entity provide information about the *financial position, performance* and *financial adaptability* of the organisation.

Chapter 2: The reporting entity

This short chapter recognises that there are two types of entity that should be publishing final accounts – the single entity and the group entity. However, the statement also requires any entity, where there is a legitimate demand for financial accounting information, to publish financial statements for their users. This would include clubs, partnerships, sole traders, charities, etc., as well as limited companies.

Chapter 3: Qualitative characteristics

This chapter identifies the key primary qualitative characteristics that should make the information in the Annual Report useful to users. There are four, two relating to the content of the Report and two in relation to its presentation.

Relevance

The information must be relevant, i.e. be up to date and current and be actually used by the reader.

Reliability

The reader must have faith in the information provided and it must be free from material error and represent faithfully what it is supposed to represent.

These two characteristics tend to come into conflict since relevance would favour the adoption of current subjective values whereas reliability would gravitate towards the adoption of historic and more objective costs. Where the two do clash the Accounting Standards Board (ASB) favours relevance.

Comparability

This is in reality the former consistency concept of SSAP 2 and insists that information must be comparable from period to period and within like items in the same period. However, it also requires sufficient disclosure for a user to appreciate the significance of transactions.

Understandability

This concept insists that the information being provided by the reporting entity be presented in such a way that it is as understandable as possible to the user. However, this does not mean that it is so simple that the information being provided becomes meaningless.

Chapter 4: The elements of financial statements

This chapter contains the key elements in a set of financial statements. It defines the balance sheet elements first and then argues that the profit and loss should pick up any residuals, for example a gain is either an increase in an asset or a decrease in a liability. The main definitions are as follows.

Balance sheet

- Asset: 'Rights or other access to future economic benefits controlled by the entity as a result of a past transaction or event.'
- Liability: 'Obligation of an entity to transfer economic benefits as a result of a past transaction or event.'
- Ownership interest: 'The residual amount found by deducting all of the entity's liabilities from all of the entity's assets.'

Profit and loss

- Gains and losses: 'Gains are increases in ownership interest, other than those relating to contributions to owners and losses are decreases in ownership interest, other than those relating to distributions to owners.'

Clearly this chapter puts the balance sheet on a pedestal with its concentration on getting the assets and liabilities right first before looking at the profit and loss. This represents a cultural swing for the UK from its current profit and loss and accruals based preference. The accruals concept is now clearly downgraded in importance in that expenditure cannot be matched against future income unless it can meet the definition of an asset in the first place. Similarly the prudence concept has been given a 'knock', as a liability can only be created if there is either a legal or constructive obligation in place. A mere intention to expend monies in the future is not sufficient on its own.

Chapter 5: Recognition in financial statements

Even if a transaction meets the definition of an asset/liability it will not be recorded on the balance sheet unless it meets the two recognition criteria or tests found in Chapter 5:

(i)   Is there sufficient evidence that a change in assets or liabilities has occurred?; and
(ii) Can it be measured at cost or value with sufficient reliability?

If these cannot be passed initially then the transactions must be written off directly to profit and loss. If one of the criteria is subsequently failed then the asset/liability must be removed or derecognised from the balance sheet. It is possible that the asset/liability will need to be remeasured where there is sufficient evidence that the amount has changed, and the new amount must be measured with sufficient reliability (see FRS 5 and the use of the linked presentation approach for factored debts).

Chapter 6: Measurement in financial statements

This chapter investigates the adoption of historic costs against that of current values when evaluating assets and liabilities. The original draft chapter took the view that it would be essential long term for companies to maintain their capital in real terms and this therefore would require the use of current values in measuring assets and liabilities. However, this section was particularly heavily criticised by Lord Hanson and Ernst and Young, who saw this as a test bed for academic theories and not answering practical needs. As a result the final draft now permits reporting entities to choose either historic cost or current value, whichever would be most appropriate to a particular entity's needs to provide a true and fair view.

Chapter 7: Presentation of financial information

As promised in Chapter 1, Chapter 7 agrees that, in order to meet the needs of users, the following primary statements should be published.

(a)   statement of financial performance;
(b)   balance sheet; and
(c)   cash flow statement.

It also suggests that additional supplementary information would be useful but is not core to the problem. This should include 5- or 10-year summaries, financial highlights, operating and financial reviews and the use of graphs, etc.

Chapter 8: Accounting for interests in other entities

This chapter provides the theoretical background to group reporting. It looks at the influence or control that one entity might hold over another as crucial in determining how to account for that investment in its financial statements. If it has little or no influence, a trade investment should be recorded; if significant influence but not control, then an associated or joint venture relationship is said to be set up and finally if it controls the other entity then it should be fully consolidated, either as a legal subsidiary (FRS 2) or as a quasi-subsidiary (FRS 5).

In addition, Chapter 8 also investigates the two major methods of reporting business combinations – via merger or via acquisition accounting. Merger accounting should only occur if there is a genuine pooling of interests and both parties go forward as one single entity as if they had always been the one entity. However, it should be rarely adopted in practice and instead acquisition accounting should be applied in the majority of combinations. This requires the adoption of fair value reporting and the consequent calculation of goodwill.

Summary

The final draft of this statement was published in late 1999 in the form of a statement of best practice which will form the cornerstone of all future standard-setting procedures. However, it has also resulted in the withdrawal of SSAP 2 *Disclosure of Accounting Policies* as that document only covered some of the fundamental concepts in financial reporting and did not look at the overall conceptual framework. It was subsequently replaced, in December 2000, by FRS 18 *Accounting Policies*.

In June 2003 a separate *Statement of Principles for Public Benefit Entities* was published to meet the needs of the public sector and charities. Currently it is still in draft form but it concentrates on funders and financial supporters as being the main users rather than shareholders and it has slightly different objectives as a result. However, the main thrust of ensuring that assets and liabilities are reported first before matching income and expenses is retained.

1.2   FRS 18 *Accounting Policies* (December 2000)

Key points

(i)   Removal of fundamental accounting concepts (FAB 4) from the standard and their inclusion instead in the Statement of Principles

SSAP 2 picked up four of many possible broad basic assumptions which are assumed to underlie the preparation of financial statements. They are not referred to specifically in the annual accounts but they are assumed to exist because of their general applicability. The four concepts are:

- going concern;
- accruals;
- consistency;
- prudence.

Going concern

The enterprise is assumed to continue in operational existence for the foreseeable future, i.e. there is no intention to liquidate the reporting entity. Under FRS 18 this is still treated as a cornerstone of the measurement process (see Chapter 6 of Statement of Principles).

Accruals

The 'matching principle', i.e. costs and revenues, should only be recognised in the profit and loss account when they are incurred or earned, not when they are paid or received, and matched so far as possible with each other so far as can be justifiably assumed.

Under SSAP 2, the concept emphasised the profit and loss account as the primary document in the annual report. On the publication of the Statement of Principles this concept is downgraded in that an accrual/prepayment can only be created if it meets the definition respectively of liabilities and assets contained in the Statement of Principles. This ensures that the preparation of the balance sheet is paramount in arriving at a true and fair view of performance. No longer will deliberate smoothing of profits be permitted by the carry-forward of 'spurious' prepayments/accruals.

Consistency

There must be consistency in accounting treatment of like items within the same accounting period as well as from one period to another. This is still a primary qualitative characteristic in financial reporting and, when allied to disclosure of accounting policies, should provide comparable information both across reporting entities and over time.

Prudence

Profits and revenues must not be anticipated in the financial statements and must only be recorded if ultimately realisable in cash. However, losses and expenses should be recorded as soon as the reporting entity becomes aware of them, whether or not the amounts are known with certainty. The Statement of Principles and FRS 18 agree that a degree of caution must be exercised when assessing the values of uncertain assets and liabilities but it must not be taken too far. Both emphasise the need to exercise more prudence in relation to the value of assets rather than liabilities. Excessive provisions are no longer acceptable.

The Statement of Principles insists that before a liability may be established there must be a genuine legal or constructive obligation. Similarly, accruals is being slightly relegated in that no matching will be permitted until an asset or liability is established in the first place on the balance sheet. The balance sheet will therefore become the primary statement with residuals being positioned in the profit and loss account, making that document more volatile than it has been in the past.

(ii) Accounting bases are dropped

There are a number of possible options (bases) for applying the fundamental accounting concepts to specific accounting issues and, in particular, on the decision as to which transactions result in revenues/expenses and therefore recognised in the profit and loss account and assets/liabilities which should be recorded on the balance sheet.

A number of specific issues should illustrate the point: Should research and development expenditure be written off as an expense or carried forward as an asset? Should stocks be valued on the basis of first in first out (FIFO) or last in first out (LIFO)?

The main objective of the standard-setting operation is to reduce the number of bases available to preparers of financial statements. Most accounting standards now only permit one or two options to be adopted as the reporting entity's accounting policy for each material group of transactions.

FRS 18 has dropped this definition as it was felt to be unclear as to the difference between an accounting base and an accounting policy. Instead a new definition of estimation techniques is introduced.

(iii) Introduction of a new definition of an accounting policy as:

'Principles, bases, conventions, rules and practices applied by an entity that specify how the effects of transactions and other events are to be reflected in its financial statements through

(i)   recognising,
(ii) selecting measurement bases for, and
(iii) presenting

assets, liabilities, gains, losses and changes to shareholders' funds.'

(iv) Introduction of a new definition of estimation techniques as:

'Methods adopted by an entity to arrive at estimated monetary amounts, corresponding to the measurement bases selected, for assets, liabilities, gains, losses and changes to shareholders' funds. They implement the measurement aspects of accounting policies and include, for example, methods of depreciation and estimates of proportion of trade debts not recoverable.'

(v) Explanation of the difference between a change in accounting policy and a change in estimation technique

A change in accounting policy can occur if any of the following are changed.

• Change in recognition, e.g. from a policy of non-discounting deferred tax to one of discounting;

- Change in measurement base for fungible assets, e.g. stocks from FIFO to weighted average;
- Change in presentation, e.g. administration expense to cost of sales.

(vi)   Disclosure of accounting policies

The end product of FRS 18 is to ensure that the directors provide a clear explanation of the specific accounting policies adopted by a reporting entity as being significant in providing a true and fair view. Only those which are material or critical in determining profits or losses should be disclosed by way of note. The note should help readers interpret the financial statements and provide them with a better understanding of why the reported results in one company might differ from those of another. The following are required to be disclosed.

- Description of each material accounting policy adopted;
- Description of significant estimation techniques;
- Details of any changes to accounting policies including a brief description of:

  Why a new policy is more appropriate;
  The effects of prior period adjustments on the preceding period – as per FRS 3;
  The effects of a change in accounting policy on the current period's performance;
  The effect of a change to estimation techniques on current results.

- Where the going concern is in doubt:

  Any material uncertainties of which the directors are aware that may cast doubt on the ability of the reporting entity to continue as a going concern;
  If the foreseeable future is restricted to under one year, that fact should be disclosed;
  If the accounts are not prepared under the going concern, that fact and the reasons for an alternative basis, including basis adopted, should be provided, e.g. break-up.

- True and fair override – disclosure:

  A clear, unambiguous statement that a departure from an accounting standard is essential for a true and fair view;
  A statement of what the normal accounting treatment would require;
  A statement of why the normal treatment would not provide a true and fair view;
  A description of how the position differs from the standard – with quantification unless it cannot be reasonably quantified.

- Where a choice exists across estimation techniques, an entity should select the most appropriate in providing a true and fair view. Any changes, however, should not be treated as prior period adjustments unless:

  (i)   they represent a correction of a fundamental error; or
  (ii) another accounting standard or UITF abstract requires the change to be treated as a prior period adjustment.

Application in published accounts

An example of the application of the standard in relation to disclosure of accounting policies is provided by the accounts of BT for their 2003 financial statements:

British Telecommunications Plc   Year Ended 31 March 2003

Accounting Policies

I Basis of preparation of the financial statements

The financial statements are prepared under the historic cost convention and in accordance with accounting standards and the provisions of the Companies Act 1985. The group financial statements consolidate those of the company and all of its subsidiary undertakings. Where the financial statements of subsidiary undertakings, associates and joint ventures do not conform with the group's accounting policies, appropriate adjustments are made on consolidation in order to present the group financial statements on a consistent basis. The principal subsidiary undertakings' financial years are all co-terminous with those of the company.

The preparation of financial statements requires management to make estimates and assumptions that affect the reported amounts of assets and liabilities and disclosure of contingent assets and liabilities at the date of the financial statements and the reported amounts of income and expenditure during the reporting period. Actual results could differ from those estimates. Estimates are used principally when accounting for interconnect income, provision for doubtful debts, payments to telecommunication operators, depreciation, goodwill amortisation and impairment, employee pension schemes, provisions for liabilities and charges and taxes.

II Turnover

Group turnover net of discounts, which excludes value added tax and other sales taxes, comprises the value of services provided and equipment sales by group undertakings, excluding those between them.

Total turnover is group turnover with the group's share of its associates' and joint ventures' turnover, excluding the group's share of transactions between the group and its principal joint venture, Concert BV.

Turnover from calls is recognised in the group profit and loss account at the time the call is made over the group's networks. Turnover from rentals is recognised evenly over the period to which the charges relate. Turnover from equipment sales is recognised at the point of sale. Prepaid call card sales are deferred until the customer uses the stored value in the card to pay for the relevant calls. Turnover arising from the provision of other services, including maintenance contracts, is recognised evenly over the periods in which the customer is provided with the service. Turnover from installation and connection activities is recognised in the same period as the related costs. Turnover from classified directories, mainly comprising advertising revenue, is recognised in the group profit and loss account upon completion of delivery.

III Research and development

Expenditure on research and development is written off as incurred.

IV Leases

Operating lease rentals are charged against the profit and loss account on a straight line basis over the lease period except where the contractual payment terms are considered to be a more systematic and appropriate basis.

V Interest

Interest payable, including that related to financing the construction of tangible fixed assets, is written off as incurred. Discounts or premiums and expenses on the issue of debt securities are amortised over the term of the related security and included within interest payable. Premiums payable on early redemptions of debt securities, in lieu of future interest costs, are written off when paid.

VI Foreign currencies

On consolidation, assets and liabilities of foreign undertakings are translated into sterling at year-end exchange rates. The results of foreign undertakings are translated into sterling at average rates of exchange for the year.

Exchange differences arising from the retranslation at year-end exchange rates of the net investment in foreign undertakings, less exchange differences on borrowings which finance or provide a hedge against those undertakings, are taken to reserves and are reported in the statement of total recognised gains and losses.

All other exchange gains or losses are dealt with through the profit and loss account.

VII Intangibles

(a) *Goodwill.* Goodwill, arising from the purchase of subsidiary undertakings and interests in associates and joint ventures, represents the excess of the fair value of the purchase consideration over the fair value of the net assets acquired.

For acquisitions completed on or after 1 April 1998, the goodwill arising is capitalised as an intangible asset or, if arising in respect of an associate or joint venture, recorded as part of the related investment. In most cases, the goodwill is amortised on a straight-line basis from the time of acquisition over its useful economic life. The economic life is normally presumed to be a maximum of 20 years.

For acquisitions on or before 31 March 1998, the goodwill is written off on acquisition against group reserves.

If an undertaking is subsequently divested, the appropriate unamortised goodwill or goodwill written off to reserves is dealt with through the profit and loss account in the period of disposal as part of the gain or loss on divestment.

(b) *Other intangibles.* Licence fees paid to governments, which permit telecommunication activities to be operated for defined periods, are amortised from the later of the start of the licence period or launch of service to the end of the licence period on a straight-line basis.

VIII Tangible fixed assets

Tangible fixed assets are stated at historical cost less depreciation.

(a) *Cost.* Cost in the case of network services includes contractors' charges and payments on account, materials, direct labour and directly attributable overheads.

(b) *Depreciation.* Depreciation is provided on tangible fixed assets on a straight-line basis from the time they are available for use, so as to write off their costs over their estimated useful lives taking into account any expected residual values. No depreciation is provided on freehold land.

The lives assigned to other significant tangible fixed assets are:

Freehold buildings	40 years
Leasehold land and buildings	Unexpired portion of lease or 40 years, whichever is the shorter
Transmission equipment:	
duct	25 years
cable	3 to 25 years
radio and repeater equipment	2 to 25 years
Exchange equipment	2 to 13 years
Computers and office equipment	2 to 6 years
Payphones, other network equipment, motor vehicles and cableships	2 to 20 years
Software	2 to 5 years

IX Fixed asset investments

Investments in subsidiary undertakings, associates and joint ventures are stated in the balance sheet of the company at cost less amounts written off. Amounts denominated in foreign currency are translated into sterling at year-end exchange rates.

Investments in associates and joint ventures are stated in the group balance sheet at the group's share of their net assets, together with any attributable unamortised goodwill on acquisitions arising on or after 1 April 1998.

The group's share of profits less losses of associates and joint ventures is included in the group profit and loss account.

Investments in other participating interests and other investments are stated at cost less amounts written off.

X Asset impairment

Intangible and tangible fixed assets are tested for impairment when an event that might affect asset values has occurred. Goodwill is also reviewed for impairment at the end of the first financial year after acquisition.

An impairment is recognised to the extent that the carrying amount cannot be recovered either by selling the asset or by the discounted future cash flows from operating the assets.

XI Stocks

Stocks mainly comprise items of equipment, held for sale or rental, consumable items and work in progress on long-term contracts.

Equipment held and consumable items are stated at the lower of cost and estimated net realisable value, after provisions for obsolescence.

Work in progress on long-term contracts is stated at cost, after deducting payments on account, less provisions for any foreseeable losses.

XII Debtors

Debtors are stated in the balance sheet at estimated net realisable value. Net realisable value is the invoiced amount less provisions for bad and doubtful debtors. Provisions are made specifically against debtors where there is evidence of a dispute or an inability to pay. An additional provision is made based on an analysis of balances by age, previous losses experienced and general economic conditions.

XIII Redundancy costs

Redundancy or leaver costs arising from periodic reviews of staff levels are charged against profit in the year in which the group is demonstrably committed to the employees leaving the group.

If the estimated cost of providing incremental pension benefits in respect of employees leaving the group exceeds the total accounting surplus based on the latest actuarial valuation of the group's pension scheme and the amount of the provision for pension liabilities on the balance sheet, then the excess estimated costs are charged against profit in the year in which the employees agree to leave the group, within redundancy or leaver costs.

XIV Pension scheme

The group operates a funded defined benefit pension scheme, which is independent of the group's finances, for the substantial majority of its employees. Actuarial valuations of the main scheme are carried out by an independent actuary as determined by the trustees at intervals of not more than 3 years, to determine the rates of contribution payable. The pension cost is determined on the advice of the company's actuary, having regard to the results of these valuations. In any intervening years, the actuaries review the continuing appropriateness of the contribution rates.

The cost of providing pensions is charged against profits over employees' working lives with the group using the projected unit method. Variations from this regular cost are allocated on a straight-line basis over the average remaining service lives of current employees to the extent that these variations do not relate to the estimated cost of providing incremental pension benefits in the circumstances described in XIII above.

Interest is accounted for on the provision or prepayment in the balance sheet which results from differences between amounts recognised as pension costs and amounts funded. The regular pension cost, variations from the regular pension cost, described above, and interest are all charged within staff costs.

The group also operates defined contribution pension schemes and the profit and loss account is charged with the contributions payable.

XV Taxation

Full provision is made for deferred taxation on all timing differences which have arisen but have not reversed at the balance sheet date. Deferred tax assets are recognised to the extent that it is regarded as more likely than not that there will be taxable profits from which the underlying timing differences can be deducted. No deferred tax is provided in respect of any future remittance of earnings of foreign subsidiaries or associates where no commitment has been made to remit such earnings. The deferred tax balances are not discounted.

XVI Financial instruments

(a) *Debt instruments.* Debt instruments are stated at the amount of net proceeds adjusted to amortise any discount evenly over the term of the debt, and further adjusted for the effect of currency swaps acting as hedges.

(b) *Derivative financial instruments.* The group uses derivative financial instruments to reduce exposure to foreign exchange risks and interest rate movements. The group does not hold or issue derivative financial instruments for financial trading purposes.

Criteria to qualify for hedge accounting

The group considers its derivative financial instruments to be hedges when certain criteria are met. For foreign currency derivatives, the instrument must be related to actual foreign currency assets or liabilities or a probable commitment and whose characteristics have been identified. It must involve the same currency or similar currencies as the hedged item and must also reduce the risk of foreign currency exchange movements on the group's operations. For interest rate derivatives, the instrument must be related to assets or liabilities or a probable commitment, such as a future bond issue, and must also change the interest rate or the nature of the interest rate by converting a fixed rate to a variable rate or vice versa.

Accounting for derivative financial instruments

Principal amounts underlying currency swaps are revalued at exchange rates ruling at the date of the group balance sheet and, to the extent that they are not related to debt instruments, are included in debtors or creditors.

Interest differentials, under interest rate swap agreements used to vary the amounts and periods for which interest rates on borrowings are fixed, are recognised by adjustment of interest payable.

The forward exchange contracts used to change the currency mix of net debt are revalued to balance sheet rates with net unrealised gains and losses being shown as part of debtors, creditors, or as part of net debt. The difference between spot and forward rate for these contracts is recognised as part of net interest payable over the term of the contract.

> The forward exchange contracts hedging transaction exposures are revalued at the prevailing forward rate on the balance sheet date with net unrealised gains and losses being shown as debtors and creditors.
>
> Instruments that form hedges against future fixed-rate bond issues are marked to market. Gains or losses are deferred until the bond is issued when they are recognised evenly over the term of the bond.

Consultation Paper (May 2002)

The ASB issued the full text of an amended international accounting standard, IAS 1 *Presentation of Financial Statements,* which will eventually replace FRS 18, but probably not before 2006. The ASB is not prepared to issue IAS 1 for a number of reasons, particularly the state of the current project on financial reporting which could fundamentally change the layout of the performance statement and the need to change the Companies Act. The most significant change proposed by the IASB in the context of UK reporting is that IAS 1 sets out the overriding requirement that financial statements should 'present fairly' the financial position, financial performance and cash flows of an entity whereas the UK insists on providing a 'true and fair view'. The ASB want to be sure there are no fundamental differences between the two concepts.

There are also important changes to the layout and structure of the balance sheet, particularly the need to include both current and non-current assets separately and not solely within current assets.

1.3   FRS 5 *Reporting the Substance of Transactions* (April 1994, amended December 1994, September 1998 and November 2003)

Background

FRS 5 is probably one of the most important standards developed by the ASB. It was designed to prevent the growth of off-balance sheet financing schemes in this country by insisting that reporting entities always report the substance or commercial reality of their transactions rather than their strict legal form.

Off balance sheet schemes developed in the 1970s as a method of reducing gearing ratios by ensuring that certain debts were held off the balance sheet. A simple example should suffice:

ABC plc is a distillery which manufactures long-term maturing stocks which require 10 years to mature before being bottled and sold to their customers. All the material, labour and overhead costs, however, must be paid for immediately. This would normally result in substantial amounts of borrowing being required to finance the manufacturing process. However, many distillers have got round this by legally selling the whisky to their financial institutions (ABC for £100) with a double option both to repurchase and for the banks to sell the whisky back to the distiller at the end of the 10-year period of maturation (for £180).

This double option will always be exercised since, if the price of whisky falls, the bank will certainly offload the whisky, whereas if the price rises then the distiller will always want to take advantage of taking up the profit. In effect the substance of the arrangement is that it is a finance agreement, not a sale.

Legal form

Year 1

Dr	Bank	£100	
Cr	Stocks		£100

Sale of whisky to bank

Year 10

Dr	Stocks	£180	
Cr	Bank		£180

Repurchase of whisky in 10 years at a cost of £180

Substance

Year 1

Dr	Bank	£100	
Cr	Loan		£100

Cash received is really a loan

Years 1 to 10

Dr	Profit and loss or stocks	£8	
Cr	Loan		£8

Annual interest charge over 10 years

Year 10

Dr	Loan	£180	
Cr	Bank		£180

Repayment of loan in 10 years' time

By the end of the 1980s the number of off balance sheet schemes had grown so numerous that one commentator was prompted to say that financial statements were now being prepared in such a way that they were 'only being economic with the truth'.

The ASB decided to address the issue in two ways:

(i)   They would go for an all-out global attack on all off balance sheet finance schemes rather than tackling each one individually. In a tax analogy it was only when the decision in *Furniss v Dawson* stated that all tax schemes designed deliberately to avoid tax were illegal that the growth in tax avoidance schemes came to a halt.

(ii) They needed to ensure that the balance sheet was fairly presented and that therefore all off balance sheet liabilities were reinstated. Mere disclosure by itself would not be sufficient.

Key issues

The standard has been built on the general principle that all transactions should be recorded according to their substance and not necessarily their legal form. For most transactions this is not a problem since their substance and legal form are one and the same. It is only when the legal profession has deliberately introduced additional clauses into invoices, agreements, etc., and has succeeded in divorcing or splitting the two concepts, that FRS 5 becomes particularly important.

Although FRS 5 is 150 pages long, there are a number of key rules which are at the heart of the standard:

(i)   In applying substance the accountant must ask himself/herself whether a particular transaction results in the creation of a new asset/liability or a change in the existing assets/liabilities.

To answer that question it is first necessary to define what an asset or liability represents.

- An asset represents 'rights or other access to future economic benefits controlled by the entity as a result of a past transaction or event'.
- A liability represents 'an obligation to transfer economic benefits as a result of a past transaction or event'.

(ii)   Once an asset/liability has been identified then before it can be placed on the balance sheet it must pass the two recognition tests included in the Statement of Principles, i.e.

- Can the asset/liability's value or cost be measured with sufficient reliability?
- Is there sufficient evidence that there will be future economic benefits flowing into or out of the business?

Only if both of these recognition tests can be accomplished may an asset/liability be recorded on the balance sheet.

(iii)   Particularly in relation to the creation of an asset, risk is a significant indicator of the party that should record the asset on its books as the ultimate risks and rewards usually belong to that party. The distiller above provides a clear example of this.

(iv)   If a subsequent transaction occurs then an asset previously recognised on the balance sheet will have to be derecognised if it can no longer meet the recognition criteria in (ii) above but if a subsequent transaction has no impact on (ii) above then the asset should remain on the balance sheet.

In certain defined situations a third possibility exists. This is where finance received from a third party is linked to a specific asset and the risk is being shared between the two parties involved. In that situation a 'linked presentation' approach may be adopted whereby any monies received from the third party are deducted on the face of the balance sheet from the asset indicating both the maximum benefit to be derived and also the potential risk. However, in general, one must never net off assets against liabilities and thus there are fairly strict rules attached before the technique may be adopted.

An example is provided below:

ABC plc have sold £500 of goods to a variety of customers on credit and these have been recorded correctly in debtors and in sales. The company has now decided to enter into a factoring arrangement with a financial institution and is interested in the impact of various options on their balance sheet. The three options are:

(i)   Sell off the debts in full, with no recourse for the factor for bad debts;

(ii)   Sell off the debts in full, but enable the factoring company to charge ABC plc in full for any bad debts not collected;

(iii) The factor company will pay 80 per cent of the monies immediately on account but will only pay up the remaining 20 per cent provided they can collect sufficient debts. The company in effect has a maximum bad debt liability for that 20 per cent.

(i)		£	£
Dr	Bank	480	
	Finance costs	20	
	Cr Debtors		500

The asset is transferred as no further risk to ABC plc

(ii)			
Dr	Bank	490	
	Finance costs (say)	10	
	Cr Loan		500

This is really a loan as the risk remains fully with ABC plc

(iii)			
Dr	Bank	400	
	Cr Payment on account		400

Balance sheet extract		
Debtors	500	
Less: payment on account	400	
		100

The asset of £500 remains on the balance sheet as the risk of non-payment is on this figure, but the maximum benefit can only be the £100 outstanding.

Other points

Disclosure

This is not regarded as significant by FRS 5 since the main objective was to 'get the balance sheet right'. Nevertheless these complex transactions are different from normal and therefore further details should be disclosed in order for the reader to fully appreciate their importance. This may even apply if the transaction does not occur until the following accounting period.

Quasi-subsidiary

This is a special-purpose vehicle which, although not meeting the strict legal definition of a subsidiary, is in effect controlled by the reporting entity and gives rise to the same benefits as a legal subsidiary. It should therefore also be consolidated. Two listed companies were caught by non-compliance with this aspect of the standard and have had to amend their financial statements to incorporate their quasi-subsidiaries within the group accounts (Associated Nursing Services plc and Kensington Group plc – see www.uitf.org.uk).

Application notes

There are a number of application notes provided at the back of the accounting standard which provide the accountant with more precise details on how to apply the general concept of substance to those specific situations. There were initially five notes but a sixth was published in September 1998 dealing with the accounting treatment of private finance initiatives which, in theory, should result in most public sector organisations having to include both the capital expenditure and their associated 'loan' from the private sector participants, on the balance sheet. In addition a seventh note was added in November 2003 as a 'stop gap' measure to bring some regulation into the reporting of revenue recognition.

In particular it defines a 'right to consideration' or debtor rather than defining revenue thus concentrating on getting the balance sheet right. For the debtor to be incorporated on balance sheet an entity must perform by delivering the goods or providing the service. If a customer pays in advance any monies received should be treated as creditors until the work is performed when it will be transferred to revenue. The application note also provides guidance on how those basic principles could be applied to the specific issues of long-term contracts, sale with rights of return, agency/principal relationships, the separation and linking of contractual arrangements and bill and hold arrangements.

The first five notes cover the following subjects:

- Consignment stocks;
- Sale and repurchase of stock;
- Factoring of debts;
- Securitised assets;
- Loan transfers.

The following examples illustrate how to apply the doctrine of substance to some of the more popular application notes. There is also an example provided of a quasi-subsidiary:

Example – Lambeg Plc (sale and possible repurchase)

Lambeg plc sells land to a property investment company, Hilden plc. The sale price is £20 million and the current market value is £30 million. Lambeg plc can buy the land back at any time in the next five years for the original selling price plus an annual commission of 1 per cent above the current bank base rate. Hilden plc cannot require Lambeg plc to buy the land back at any time.

The accountant of Lambeg plc proposes to treat this transaction as a sale in the financial statements.

Suggested solution – Lambeg Plc

Lambeg plc has the option of buying the land back at any time in the next 5 years but is not compelled to do so, and therefore is protected from any collapse in the value of the land below £20 million. This risk has therefore been transferred to Hilden plc in return for the commission of 1 per cent above the current bank base rate. However, Lambeg plc has retained the benefits of ownership and can also benefit from any increase in the value of the land by exercising its option. At the time of the agreement, both parties must have anticipated that the option would be exercised. Lambeg plc would presumably not sell the land at below the current market price. Hilden plc must have anticipated that any profit from the contract would be derived from the receipt of the 'commission' payment from Lambeg plc. It is unlikely that the land value would fall below one third of its present value and therefore the degree of risk transferred to Hilden plc is quite minimal. The essence of the contract is effectively a loan of £20 million secured on the land held by Lambeg plc. Accounting practice would dictate that the commercial reality of the transaction reflected a financing deal rather than the legal form of a sale.

	DR	Bank	£20m	
	CR	Loan		£20m
Not	DR	Bank	£20m	
	CR	Disposal of land		£20m

Example – Moira Plc (consignment stock)

A car manufacturer, Moira plc, supplies cars to a car dealer, Lurgan Ltd, on the following terms. Lurgan Ltd has to pay a monthly fee of £100 per car for the privilege of displaying it in its showroom and also is responsible for insuring the cars. When a car is sold to a customer, Lurgan Ltd has to pay Moira plc the factory price of the car when it was first supplied. Lurgan Ltd can only return the cars to Moira plc on the payment of a fixed penalty charge of 10 per cent of the cost of the car. Lurgan Ltd has to pay the factory price for the cars if they remain unsold within a 4-month period. Moira plc cannot demand the return of the cars from Lurgan Ltd.

The accountant of Lurgan Ltd proposes to treat the cars unsold for less than 4 months as the property of Moira plc and not show them as stock in the financial statements.

Suggested solution – Moira Plc

The main problem surrounding this example is the determination of the substance of the agreement. The accountant has to determine whether Lurgan Ltd has bought the cars or whether they are on loan from Moira plc.

There are certain factors which point toward the treatment of the cars as stock of Lurgan Ltd. Lurgan Ltd has to pay a monthly rental fee of £100 per car and after 4 months has to pay for the cars if they are unsold. This could be regarded as a financing agreement as Lurgan Ltd is effectively being charged interest by Moira plc which is varying with the length of time for which Lurgan Ltd hold the stock. Lurgan Ltd is also bearing any risk of slow movement of the cars. The purchase price of the car is fixed at the price when the car was first supplied. Thus any price increases in the product are avoided by Lurgan Ltd, which would indicate that there is a contract for the sale of goods. Lurgan Ltd has to insure the cars and is partially suffering some of the risks of ownership of the vehicles.

Moira plc cannot demand the return of cars from Lurgan Ltd and therefore has no control over the assets.

A fixed penalty charge of 10 per cent of the cost of the car is chargeable to Lurgan Ltd if cars remain unsold; therefore the risks of ownership are with Lurgan Ltd. The double entry should therefore be:

```
DR      Stocks      £xxx
   CR               Loan        £xxx
```

Example – Claudy Plc (factoring of debts)

Claudy plc supplied large industrial and commercial customers direct on 3-month credit terms. On 1 November 2002 it entered into an agreement with Keady plc whereby it transferred title to the debtors to that company subject to a reduction for bad debts based on Claudy plc's past experience and in return received an immediate payment of 90 per cent of the net debtor total plus rights to a future sum, the amount of which depended on whether and when the debtors paid. Keady plc had the right of recourse against Claudy plc for any additional losses up to an agreed maximum amount.

The position at the year end, 31 October 2003, was that title had been transferred to debtors with an invoice value of £15m less a bad debt provision of £600,000 and Claudy plc was subject under the agreement to a maximum potential debit of £200,000 to cover losses.

Suggested solution – Claudy Plc (using linked presentation)

The transaction appears to satisfy the criteria set out in FRS 5 for linked presentation in that the finance will be repaid only from the proceeds generated by the specific item it finances and there is no possibility of any claim on the entity being established other than against funds generated by that item and there is no provision whereby the entity may either keep the item on repayment of the finance or reacquire it at any time. The accounting treatment for linked presentation is as follows:

	£m	£m
Current assets		
Receivables subject to financing arrangements		
Gross receivables		
(after providing £600,000 for bad debts)	14.40	
Less: non-returnable proceeds		
90% of net debtors £14.4m	(12.96)	1.44
Current asset: Cash		12.96

Example – Larne Plc (quasi-subsidiary)

On 1 December 2002 Larne plc sold a factory that it owned in Scotland to Inter plc, a wholly owned subsidiary of Offshore Banking plc, for £10m. The factory had a book value of £8.5m. Inter plc was financed by a loan of £10m from Offshore Banking plc. Larne plc was paid a fee by Inter plc to continue to operate the factory, such fee representing the balance of profit remaining after Inter plc paid its parent company loan interest set at a level that represented current interest rates. If there was an operating loss, then Larne plc would be charged a fee that would cover the operating losses and interest payable.

For the year ended 31 October 2003 the fee paid to Larne plc amounted to £3m and the loan interest paid by Inter plc amounted to £1.5m.

Suggested solution – Larne Plc

The arrangement with Inter plc has been structured so that it does not meet the legal definition of a subsidiary within the provisions of FRS 2, para 14. However, the commercial effect is no different from that which would result were Inter plc to be a subsidiary of Larne plc and under FRS 5 it falls to be treated as a quasi-subsidiary. As Sir David Tweedie stated on the introduction of FRS 5: 'if it looks like a duck, talks and waddles like a duck, then duck account it!'

Under FRS 5, the factory will appear as an asset in Larne plc's consolidated accounts. Its value will be reduced to £8.5m, being its cost to the group and the profit on disposal will be cancelled out; the fee will be cancelled as an intra-group transaction; the loan interest will appear as £1.5m in the consolidated profit and loss account; and the loan of £10m will appear as a creditor in the consolidated balance sheet.

Example – Debt factoring

During the most recent financial year (ended 31 August 2003), the company entered into a debt factoring arrangement with F plc. The main terms of the agreement are as follows:

(1)   On the first day of every month S Ltd transfers (by assignment) all its trade debts to F plc, subject to credit approval by F plc for each debt transferred by S Ltd.
(2)   At the time of transfer of the debtors to F plc, S Ltd receives a payment from F plc of 70 per cent of the gross amount of the transferred debts. The

payment is debited by F plc to a factoring account which is maintained in the books of F plc.

(3) Following transfer of the debts, F plc collects payments from debtors and performs any necessary follow-up work.

(4) After collection by F plc, the cash received from the debtor is credited to the factoring account in the books of F plc.

(5) F plc handles all aspects of the collection of the debts of S Ltd in return for a monthly charge of 1 per cent of the total value of the debts transferred at the beginning of that month. The amount is debited to the factoring account in the books of F plc.

(6) Any debts not collected by F plc within 90 days of transfer are regarded as bad debts by F plc and reassigned to S Ltd. The cash previously advanced by F plc in respect of bad debts is recovered from S Ltd. The recovery is only possible out of the proceeds of other debtors which have been assigned to S Ltd. For example if, in a particular month, S Ltd assigned trade debts having a value of £10,000 and a debt of £500 was identified as bad, then the amounts advanced by F plc to S Ltd would be £6,650 [70% × £10,000 − 70% × £500].

(7) On a monthly basis F plc debits the factoring account with an interest charge which is calculated on a daily basis on the balance on the factoring account.

(8) At the end of every quarter, F plc pays over to S Ltd a sum representing any credit balance on its factoring account with S Ltd at that time.

Suggested solution – debt factoring

Taking each aspect of the agreement in turn:

1. Transfer of debt to F plc, subject to credit approval – possibility of risks attaching to F plc.
2. Receipt of 70 per cent of gross debts – is it non-returnable? If so, could be a linked presentation.
3. F plc collects the debts – possible transfer.
4./5. F plc credits cash to factoring account of F plc and handles all aspects of cash collection.
6. F plc has full recovery of bad debts even though only receivable from debts outstanding – evidence of a full recourse agreement.

On the balance of the terms of the agreement it would appear that the original selling company has full recourse for all bad debts and therefore still retains the risks over the debts. Legal title may have passed to F plc but the economic control over the asset still rests with S Ltd. As such the debtors should remain on the balance sheet and the finance received treated as a loan until such time as the debtors are cleared by F plc.

Financial Reporting Review Panel

Associated Nursing Services Plc (April 1997)

The ANS accounts for March 1995 and 1996 were under review by the Panel and one of matters concerned quasi-subsidiaries. ANS had entered into joint ventures with two partners and treated these as associated undertakings in 1995 and 1996. Although the Board was 'deadlocked' in one company the Panel took the view that the operating and financial policies were under the control of ANS and thus ANS had control. In the second case the underlying agreements also were substantially predetermined and thus it was also under ANS's control. Under FRS 5 they therefore were quasi-subsidiaries and should have been consolidated. ANS has now agreed to apply that concept.

Kensington Group Plc (February 2003)

The matter at issue was the method of complying with FRS 5 *Reporting the Substance of Transactions*, when using a linked presentation in respect of the securitisation of mortgages in the context of the requirements of the Companies Act 1985. The matter was highlighted by the fact that the financial statements for 2000 and 2001 both purport to comply with relevant accounting requirements while adopting a different accounting treatment for the securitisation companies (SPVs), the vehicles through which the company securitises its mortgage portfolio.

The Panel satisfied itself that the 2001 financial statements were consistent with the Companies Act 1985, including applicable accounting standards, particularly FRS 5, as to the manner in which the SPVs are included in the consolidated accounts as quasi-subsidiaries.

Where an entity is considered a quasi-subsidiary, FRS 5 requires that the assets, liabilities, profits, losses and cashflows are included in the group financial statements in the same way as if they were those of a subsidiary. Where certain tests are satisfied, as in Kensington's case, the treatment should be modified and the quasi-subsidiary should be included in the consolidated financial statements using a linked presentation.

The Panel concluded that Kensington's 2000 accounting treatment of its SPVs did not comply with FRS 5 to the extent that, in the original 2000 accounts, the SPVs had not been fully consolidated in the consolidated balance sheet and cash flow statement, using a linked presentation, as required by FRS 5.

The directors accepted the Panel's view in respect of the accounting for SPVs in the 2000 financial statements, and in Kensington's November 2002 report and accounts, they clarified that the SPVs should have been included in the 2000 consolidated balance sheet and cash flow statement just as they were in the 2001 accounts.

Application in published accounts

The first application provides an example of an entity which is controlled by a parent company but is not a legal subsidiary, being consolidated as a quasi-subsidiary under FRS 5.

1.   Quasi-Subsidiary

Man Group Plc   Year Ended 31 March 2003   Investment Fund Provider

33. Quasi-subsidiary

The Group has one quasi-subsidiary, Forester Limited, which is consolidated into the Group for accounting purposes but is not a member of the Group. Forester Limited was incorporated in Guernsey as a company limited by shares on 1 November 2002. All its issued shares are held for, and on behalf of, Guernsey Trust Company Limited. On 12 November 2002, Forester Limited issued exchangeable bonds (details in note 19) which indirectly provided the Group with additional funding. The summary accounts of Forester Limited from its incorporation (1 November 2002) to 31 March 2003 are set out below:

Balance sheet at 31 March 2003	2003
	£'000
Investments in Man Group subsidiaries	396,500
Debtors	8
Cash at bank	717
Creditors: amounts falling due within 1 year	(5,832)
Creditors: amounts falling due in more than 1 year	
– exchangeable bonds	(390,700)
– other	(682)
Net assets	11
Share capital and reserves	11

Profit and loss account	2003
For period 1 November 2002 to 31 March 2003	£'000
Operating expenses	(35)
Net interest income	46
Profit before tax	11
Taxation	–
Profit for period	11

There were no recognised gains and losses other than the profit for the financial year.

	2003
	£'000
Cash flow statement	
For the period 1 November 2002 to 31 March 2003	
Cash inflow from operating activities	18
Capital expenditure and financial investment	(389,445)
Net cash inflow	(389,427)
Financing	390,144
Increase in cash	717

The next two examples incorporate application of the latest application note on revenue recognition which has caused several companies to reasssess their policies for recognising revenue in the financial statements. In particular, the disclose note of Pearson plc also provides evidence of compliance with the new agency/principal rules introduced by the application note:

2.   Revenue Recognition Application Note G

Debenhams Plc   Year Ended 31 August 2003 Department Stores

The financial review discloses that the ASBs proposed application note on revenue recognition to FRS 5 'Reporting the substance of transactions' may result in income from concession sales being recorded on a net basis instead of the current gross basis which, Debenhams states, is in line with other retailers. The application note, which becomes effective for accounting periods ending on or after 23 December 2003 requires that, where a department store provides space for concessionaires to sell products and receives a fixed amount of rental income, it should not include within its turnover the value of the concessionaire's sales (para. G71).

Pearson Plc   Year Ended 31 December 2003   Book Publishers

Notes to the Accounts (Extract)

1.   Accounting Policies

Accounting policies have been consistently applied and the amendment to FRS 5 – Application Note G 'Revenue Recognition' has been applied in respect of multiple element arrangements as set out in note 1d below. The impact of this revision has not given rise to a material adjustment to these financial statements.

d. Sales – Sales represent the amount of goods and services, net of value added tax and other sales taxes, and excluding trade discounts and anticipated returns, provided for external customers and associates.

Revenue from the sale of books is recognised when the goods are shipped. Anticipated returns are based primarily on historical return rates.

Circulation and advertising revenue is recognised when the newspaper or other publication is published. Subscription revenue is recognised on a straight-line basis over the life of the subscription.

Where a contractual arrangement consists of two or more separate elements that can be supplied to customers either on a stand-alone basis or as an optional extra, such as the provision of supplementary materials with textbooks, revenue is recognised for each element as if it were an individual contractual arrangement.

Revenue from long-term contracts, such as contracts to process qualifying tests for individual professions and government departments, is recognised over the contract term based on the percentage of services provided during the period, compared to the total estimated services to be provided over the entire contract. Losses on contracts are recognised in the period in which the loss first becomes foreseeable. Contract losses are determined to be the amount by which estimated direct and indirect costs of the contract exceed the estimated total revenues that will be generated by the contract.

On certain contracts, where the Group acts as agent, only commissions and fees receivable for services rendered are recognised as revenue. Any third party costs incurred on behalf of the principal that are rechargeable under the contractual arrangements are not included in revenue.

One of the most difficult issues is deciding when the linked presentation approach may be adopted. It usually occurs in the factoring of debts but the final example in the chapter provided below recognises that it can be adapted to both loan transfers and securitised assets:

3.   Linked Presentation

The Paragon Group of Companies Plc   Year Ended 30 September 2003

Balance Sheet Extract

	Notes	£m	£m
Fixed Assets			
Intangible assets			
Negative goodwill	18		(18.8)
Tangible assets	19		4.2
Investments			
Assets subject to non recourse finance	20	2,361.6	
Non-recourse finance	20	(2,285.3)	
		76.3	
Loans to customers	21	3,051.3	
Own shares	22	10.8	
			3,138.4
			3,123.8

Notes Extract

Note 20 Assets Subject to Non-Recourse Finance

Prior to its acquisition by the group certain loans originated by Britannic Money plc (now Mortgage Trust Limited) had been sold to companies ultimately beneficially owned by charitable trusts, which had raised non-recourse finance to fund these purchases. The group is not obliged to support any losses of these companies and does not intend to do so. This is clearly stated in the terms and conditions under which the finance was raised, which provide that the finance providers will receive interest and repayment of principal only to the extent that sufficient funds are generated by the mortgage portfolios acquired by each company.

CHAPTER

2

Asset valuation: accounting for tangible fixed assets

2.1 FRS 15 *Tangible Fixed Assets* (February 1999)

Background

The ASC developed an accounting standard on depreciation, SSAP 12 *Accounting for Depreciation*, before defining precisely what a tangible fixed asset was. The ASB has remedied this by publishing FRS 15 *Tangible Fixed Assets*, which has developed rules on how to initially cost tangible assets but also when and how to revalue them. It also incorporates all the old rules in SSAP 12 on depreciation. However, SSAP 19 *Accounting for Investment Properties* has been expressly excluded from the standard and is therefore still extant.

SSAP 12 introduced compulsory depreciation, for the first time, for all tangible fixed assets having a finite useful life.

Definitions

- *Tangible fixed asset.* Has physical substance and held for use in the production and supply of goods or services, for rental to others or for administrative purposes on a continuing basis in the reporting entity's activities.
- *Depreciation.* The measure of the cost or revalued amount of the economic benefits of the tangible fixed asset that have been consumed during the period. It includes the wearing out, using up or other reduction in the useful economic life of a tangible fixed asset whether arising from use, effluxion of time or obsolescence through either changes in technology or demand for the goods and services produced by the asset.

Accounting treatment

Initial measurement

Whether acquired or self-constructed, a tangible fixed asset should initially be recorded at cost. Only those costs that are directly attributable to bringing an asset into *working condition* for its *intended use* are permitted to be capitalised. Capitalisation of costs is also only permitted for the period in which activities are in progress.

Capitalisation of interest is permitted but the policy must be applied consistently and all finance costs directly attributable to the construction of a tangible fixed asset should be capitalised, provided that they do not exceed the total finance costs incurred during the period.

The amount recognised should not exceed an asset's recoverable amount.

Subsequent expenditure should normally be expensed (maintenance) but may be capitalised if either:

(i)   a component of an asset has been treated as a separate asset and is now replaced or restored, e.g. Ryanair's splitting up of aircraft into different components and BAA's policy of separating runway surfaces from runway beds; or

(ii) where the expenditure enhances the economic benefits of the asset in excess of the original assessed standard of performance; or

(iii) it relates to a major overhaul or inspection whose benefits have already been consumed in the depreciation charge.

Valuation

Tangible fixed assets should be revalued only if the company adopts such a policy. If it does then all assets of the same class should be revalued.

If an asset is revalued, the following must be carried out:

Non-specialised properties	– full valuation every 5 years, an interim in year 3 and a further valuation in years 1, 2 and 4 if there has been a material change in value during those years;
	– full valuation on a rolling basis over 5 years, with interim if material change in value, of a portfolio of similar assets;
	– should be valued on an existing use basis (EUV).
Specialised properties	– with same frequency as for non-specialised properties;
	– should be valued on a depreciated replacement cost basis (DRC).
Surplus properties	– the same frequency as for other buildings;
	– valued on an open market value (OMV) basis.

Revaluation gains should be recognised in the statement of total recognised gains and losses (STRGL) unless they reverse a revaluation loss previously recognised in the profit and loss, in which case they should be credited to the profit and loss account.

Revaluation losses due to a consumption of economic benefits should be recognised in the profit and loss account. However, other revaluation losses should be recognised in the STRGL to the extent that they reverse previous gains in the STRGL but thereafter they must be charged to profit and loss unless their value in use is greater than their replacement cost, in which case the loss should be recognised in the STRGL to the extent that their value in use exceeds their recoverable amounts.

There is no change to the requirement of FRS 3 that profits and losses on disposal be charged/credited to profit and loss as the difference between the proceeds and the assets' carrying values.

There are specific disclosures required for revalued assets re the valuation, particularly the names of the valuers, their qualifications and the date of the last valuation.

Depreciation

Tangible fixed assets must be depreciated on a systematic basis over their economic useful lives. Depreciation is treated as an expense in the profit and loss account.

Where a tangible fixed asset comprises two or more major components with substantially different useful economic lives, each component should be treated as a separate asset.

The allocation depends on three factors:

(i)   the cost (purchase or acquisition) or valuation of the fixed asset;
(ii) the expected economic useful life of the asset;
(iii) the estimated residual value of the asset at the end of its useful life.

- *The cost or valuation of the fixed asset.* Assets may be incorporated on the balance sheet at their original cost or at market value but the depreciation charge must be consistent with that value, i.e. if revalued then the depreciation charge must be based on the revalued amount and not on original cost. All of the charge must be recorded in the profit and loss account.
- *The expected economic useful life of the asset.* The expected economic useful life depends on the nature of the asset, e.g. leasehold property has a finite life and therefore should be written off over a predetermined life; quarries/mines are depleted by extraction and should be depreciated as the quarries/mines reserves are consumed; plant and machinery tends to wear out and deteriorate physically and should be written off over a relatively short life; and computer equipment is made both technically and market obsolete very quickly with the advent of new software and hardware and therefore should be written off over a very short life.
- *The estimated residual value of the asset at the end of its useful life.* The residual values must only be estimated using prices prevailing at the date of acquisition or revaluation. They must never be revalued.

Subsequent developments

- *Revision of useful economic life.* This should be reviewed on a regular basis and, if necessary, the life of the fixed asset adjusted to recognise depreciation over the asset's remaining economic useful life.
- *Change in method of depreciation.* The method of depreciation can be changed if it would present a truer and fairer view of the financial statements. The net book value should be written off over its estimated remaining useful life. This is not a change in accounting policy but merely a change in estimate and therefore no prior year adjustment is required. FRS 15 encourages the use of fairly simplistic methods of depreciation – straight line and

reducing balance – and only encourages other more complicated methods if they would clearly provide a truer and fairer view of the financial statements. Currently an exposure draft is outstanding which is proposing to ban the adoption of interest-based methods of depreciation on the grounds that they charge too much depreciation to later years.

• *Policy of non-depreciation.* All tangible fixed assets should be depreciated, per FRS 15, with the exception of land. Even buildings are expected to be depreciated over their economic useful lives with the exception of investment properties. There has grown up a practice, however, of non-depreciation of certain buildings which interface with the public, e.g. supermarkets, hotels, public houses, etc. This policy was confirmed by the Financial Reporting Review Panel in the test case of Forte plc. However, it was subsequently rejected, for industrial buildings, by the Panel in the case of SEP Industrial Holdings plc. FRS 15, however, still permits this policy but insists that an annual impairment review be carried out (under FRS 11) on such assets to ensure that they are not recorded above their recoverable amount. That has led to many companies reverting back to a policy of depreciation. Groupe Chez Gerard plc, however, wrongly treated that change as a change in policy – it is clearly regarded as a change in estimate under FRS 18 and must be recorded within profit and loss performance, and not treated as a change in accounting policy. In addition, under renewals accounting, certain infrastructure assets may still avoid depreciation completely as long as the assets are in a stable state and a clear programme of planned maintenance is evident.

If subsequent expenditure is incurred on a tangible fixed asset this does not obviate the need to charge depreciation. However, where the remaining useful life of an asset is greater than 50 years or where the depreciation charge is immaterial, due to its long useful life or high residual value, then it should be subject to an impairment review at the end of each reporting period in accordance with FRS 11.

Where the residual value is material, it should be reviewed annually to take account of technological changes but residual values may not be adjusted for price changes.

Specific disclosures are required with regard to depreciation policies and changes in those policies and, in particular, a tangible fixed asset schedule should be published giving details of the full movement for the year in cost/value and in accumulated depreciation.

Transitional provisions

On the introduction of FRS 15, revalued assets could be:

(i) retained at their current book value at the date of effectance of FRS 15 (subject to an impairment review under FRS 11); or

(ii) the asset values could be restated to historical cost less accumulated depreciation to date, as a change in accounting policy.

Generally most companies that revert back to cost, on first adoption of FRS 15, opt for the first option.

Depreciation should be allocated to charge a fair proportion of the cost or valuation of a fixed asset, to each accounting period as the asset is consumed, i.e. the accruals objective.

Disclosure requirements

For each major class of depreciable asset the following should be disclosed:

 (i)   the depreciation methods adopted;
 (ii)   the useful economic lives or the depreciation rates adopted;
 (iii) the total depreciation charged for the period; and
 (iv)   the gross amount of depreciable assets and related accumulated depreciation.

FRED 29 *Property, Plant and Equipment; Borrowing Costs* (May 2002)

This FRED is part of the convergence project of the ASB to link in with the IASB. FRED 29 will result in the implementation of IAS 16 *Property, Plant and Equipment* and IAS 23 *Borrowing Costs* into UK reporting. FRED 29 is similar to FRS 15 in most respects but there are a number of significant differences. These are:

(1)   FRED 29 requires exchanges of assets to be recorded at fair value – FRS 15 was silent on the issue;

(2)   FRED 29 requires residual values to be upgraded for inflation but FRS 15 only permits residual values to be based on prices existing at the date of acquisition of the fixed asset. This could lead to a resurgance in revaluation as there is no requirement for an annual impairment review in these circumstances;

(3)   FRED 29 does not address renewals accounting at all, so many of the utility companies may be forced to restart depreciation of their water mains, transmission lines, railway lines, etc.;

(4)   FRED 29 adopts a fair value rather than FRS 15's current value approach if entities adopt revaluation. One practical impact is that where the open market value is greater than its existing use value then open market value (OMV) would be adopted under FRED 29;

(5)   FRED 29 provides very little advice on the frequency of revaluations. There is no requirement for a qualified external valuer and it merely requires more frequent valuations where there are significant and volatile changes in fair values. There is no 5-yearly compulsory valuation;

(6)   FRED 29 requires revaluation losses to be charged against equity to the extent of previous revaluation surpluses. However, FRS 15 requires losses caused by a consumption of economic benefits to be expensed to profit and loss regardless of previous surpluses. This change, together with the reduction in frequency of revaluations could also help the resurgence of the policy of revaluation;

(7)   FRED 29 extends capitalisation of interest costs to inventories as well as to fixed assets;

(8)   FRED 29 requires any temporary investment income received from borrowed funds to be netted off the actual borrowing costs capitalised.

The FRED is likely to result in the implementation of IAS 16 and IAS 23 in the next few years into UK reporting.

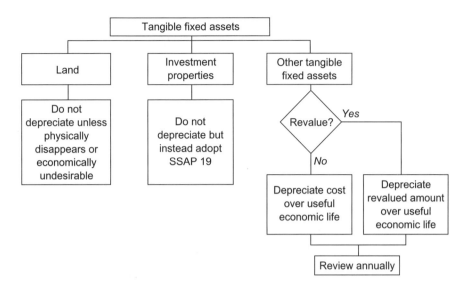

Figure 2.1 Summary.

The example below simply illustrates the preparation of a Fixed Assets schedule but it does incorporate the process of revaluing property on the balance sheet. The example also illustrates the calculation of depreciation for the year using a monthly rather than annual approach.

Example – Jupiter Ltd (Tangible fixed asset note)

You are the financial accountant of Jupiter Ltd, a company in the electronics industry, whose accounting reference date is 31 October, and you have been provided with the following information in respect of its fixed assets:

	On 1 November 2002		
	Cost	Accumulated depreciation	Total depreciable life (years)
	£'000	£'000	
Land	60	nil	–
Freehold buildings			
Factory	150	30	50
Salesroom	180	30	45
Plant and machinery	475	365	10
Computer equipment	295	85	4
Furniture and fittings	100	40	5
Motor vehicles	50	35	4

None of these assets will be fully depreciated by 31 October 2003.

During the year, C Starr, a chartered surveyor, was engaged to value the properties at an open market value for existing use. His valuations as on 1 November 2002 were as follows:

	£'000
Land	400
Factory	240
Salesroom	150
Additions during the year were:	
Plant	100
Computer	8
Motor vehicles	28

The only disposals were cars which cost £6,000 and which had accumulated depreciation at 1 November 2002 of £5,000.

All purchases and disposals took place on 1 May 2003. All depreciation is charged on a straight-line basis from the date of acquisition to the date of sale.

Suggested solution – Jupiter Ltd

(a) Notes to the accounts
  Tangible fixed assets

	Freehold land and buildings £'000	Plant and machinery £'000	Fixtures and fittings £'000	Motor vehicles £'000
Cost/valuation				
Balance 1. 11. 02	390	770	100	50
Additions	–	108	–	28
Disposals	–	–	–	(6)
Revaluations	400	–	–	–
Balance 31. 10. 03	790	878	100	72
Depreciation				
Balance 1. 11. 02	60	450	40	35
Charge for year (W1)	10	127.25	20	15.25
Disposals (W2)	–	–	–	(5.75)
Revaluations	(60)	–	–	–
	10	577.25	60	44.5
Net book value at 31. 10. 03	780	300.75	40	27.5
Net book value at 31. 10. 02	330	320	60	15

Freehold land and buildings were revalued during the year by C Starr, chartered surveyor, at an open market valuation on an existing use basis.

Revalued tangible fixed assets

There is considerable inconsistency in the treatment of revaluations of fixed assets in annual company reports. Revaluations are permitted under the Companies Act 1985 and, until the advent of FRS 15, they were actively encouraged by the ASC/ASB. At present, revaluation is purely optional and tends to be adopted almost exclusively for land and buildings.

The main reason for revaluing land and buildings is that these assets are held for a long period, have long estimated useful lives and are usually appreciating in value. Also, the original cost is completely out of touch with the true value of the asset. This results in net assets being understated and possibly makes the company more susceptible to an unwanted takeover bid.

Revaluation under FRS 15 will result in an increased depreciation charge as it is important to match the charge to profit and loss with the related value in the balance sheet. The charge to profit and loss should be based on the carrying value of the asset (either cost or revaluation). Thus as asset values rise, so will depreciation charges. This provision was adopted to prevent the so-called Woolworth split depreciation policy. Here all the revaluation surplus went to the balance sheet, with only historical cost depreciation being charged against profits, any excess being debited direct to the revaluation reserve. Another advantage of regular revaluations would be to make the directors more aware of the value of the assets being used by the company. If the value is less than open market value, it may be sensible to dispose of the asset.

The arguments against revaluation are put forward in FRS 15. Revaluations are not transaction-based and therefore any value placed on the assets is subjective and should not be included under historical cost accounting.

Another argument against revaluation is its inconsistency in application. It appears that only assets which are appreciating are revalued and those depreciating are quietly ignored. FRS 15 now insists that, while not overly in favour of revaluation, if revaluation is to continue then directors must decide which classes of assets are to be revalued. They must then revalue all the assets within that class at least once every 5 years, albeit possibly on a rolling basis.

Even with this possible amendment there will still be a loss in comparability between companies. This must detract from the usefulness of the accounts for decision-making. FRS 3 has introduced a specific note to the accounts, a 'note of historical cost profits and losses', to ensure comparability between revaluing companies and historical cost based companies.

One of the major problems in adopting revaluation is how to account for the sale of revalued assets. FRS 15 has taken the view that if a company revalues an asset then that figure becomes its book value for all subsequent events, i.e. profit/loss on disposal will be calculated as the difference between the proceeds of sale and the revalued net book figure. Any balance remaining on revaluation reserve relating to that asset is now realised and must be transferred to the profit and loss account via an intra-reserve transfer.

The ASB in Chapter 6 of the Statement of Principles has opted for a long-term 'current value' revaluation policy for assets. In the interim the discussion paper

The Role of Valuation in Financial Reporting (March 1993) proposed compulsory valuation for properties, quoted investments and commodities. However, FRS 15 *Tangible Fixed Assets* permits revaluation of certain classes of fixed asset, so long as these are updated at least once every 5 years.

Workings

W1 Calculation of depreciation charge for the year

	£000
Factory	
£240,000 ÷ 40 years (asset 30/150 or 20% expired to 1. 11. 02)	6
Salesroom	
£150,000 ÷ 37.5 years (asset 30/180 or 1/6 expired to 1. 11. 02)	4
	10

Depreciation amortised evenly over the asset's remaining useful life

Plant and machinery	
Balance 1. 11. 02	
£475,000 ÷ 10 years	47.5
Additions (assume mid-year)	
£100,000 ÷ 10 years × 1/2	5.0
	52.5

Computer equipment	£000
Balance 1. 11. 02	
£295,000 ÷ 4 years	73.75
Additions (assume mid-year)	
£8,000 ÷ 4 years × 1/2	1
	74.75

Furniture and fittings	
Balance 1. 11. 02	
£100,000 ÷ 5 years	20

Motor vehicles	
Balance 1. 11. 02 less disposal	
£44,000 ÷ 4 years	11
Disposal (mid-year)	
£6,000 ÷ 4 years × 1/2	0.75
Additions (mid-year)	
£28,000 ÷ 4 years × 1/2	3.5
	15.25

W2 Calculation of accumulated depreciation on motor vehicle sold

	£000
Balance 1. 11. 02	5
Charge to the date of disposal (W1)	0.75
	5.75

The second example examines the possibility of capitalising interest as part of fixed assets rather than expensing it all through the profit and loss account. In particular, it illustrates when that process may be justified and when it should not be adopted:

Example – Ballyclare Ltd (Capitalisation of interest)

Ballyclare Ltd, a retailing company with many high street shops, is considering a major expansion incorporating two distinct initiatives.

First, it is proposing to build a major new store which it will finance partly by bank borrowings and partly through existing cash resources. There will be substantial external and imputed interest costs both while the store is being built and on the stocks held once the store opens.

Secondly, it is planning to start a credit card operation for its customers. The credit card debtors and the associated borrowings from Newtown Bank Ltd will be accounted for by a new company, Doagh Ltd, which will have a share capital of £100. Ballyclare Ltd will hold 50 per cent of the share capital but will bear 100 per cent of the bad debt risk; the balance of share capital will be held by Newtown Bank Ltd. The present proposal is that Doagh Ltd will be accounted for on an equity basis in the Ballyclare Ltd group consolidation at the amount invested in its share capital plus attributable retained earnings.

Suggested solution – Ballyclare Ltd

Capitalisation of interest
Under the Companies Act 1985, Sch. 4, it is permitted to include as part of the production cost of an asset:

(1)   a reasonable proportion of the costs incurred by the company which are only indirectly attributable to the production of that asset; and
(2)   interest on capital borrowed to finance the production of that asset, to the extent that it accrues in respect of the period of production.

The main arguments advanced in support of this capitalisation are as follows:

(1)   Interest incurred as a consequence of a decision to acquire an asset is not intrinsically different from other costs that are commonly capitalised. If an asset requires a period of time to bring it to the condition and location necessary for its intended use, any interest incurred during that period as a result of expenditure on the asset is part of the cost of acquisition (IAS 23).
(2)   A better matching of income and expenditure is achieved, in that interest incurred with a view to future benefits is carried forward to be expensed in the periods expected to benefit. A failure to capitalise would reduce current earnings artificially and not give a representative view of the benefits of the acquisition.

(3)   It results in greater comparability between companies constructing assets and those buying similar completed assets. Any purchase price would normally include interest as the vendor would wish to recover all costs, including interest, on pricing the asset.

The main arguments advanced against capitalisation are as follows:

(1)   Interest is incurred in support of the whole of the activities of the company. Any attempt to associate borrowing costs with a particular asset would be arbitrary.
(2)   Capitalisation results in the same type of asset having a different carrying value, depending on the particular method of financing adopted by the enterprise.
(3)   Treating interest as an expense leads to comparable information from period to period and provides a better indication of the future cash flows of an enterprise. Interest fluctuates with the amount of capital borrowed and with interest rates, not with asset acquisition.

In Ballyclare's specific circumstances, examination of FRS 15 reveals a number of specific conditions which should be applied:

(1)   Where an entity's accounting policy is to capitalise borrowing costs, only those which are directly atttributable to the construction of a tangible fixed asset should be capitalised.
(2)   The amount capitalised should not exceed the amount of borrowing costs incurred during the period.
(3)   Capitalisation should commence only when:
•   borrowing costs are being incurred;
•   expenditure on the asset is being incurred; and
•   activity is in progress in getting the asset ready for use.
(4)   Capitalisation should be suspended during extended periods in which activity is not taking place.
(5)   Capitalisation should cease when all activities are complete. If the asset is built in parts, then capitalisation should cease on completion of each part.
(6)   A weighted average of borrowing costs may be adopted, but no notional borrowing costs are to be included.

It is certainly fair to capitalise interest as the store is being built because this will bring the asset to its intended location and condition and thus ensure comparability between self-built and acquired stores. This has been adopted by most retail stores and hotel groups in the UK and Ireland, e.g. Marks and Spencer, Sainsbury, Jurys Hotel Group.

    An additional problem is whether or not interest can be imputed to the balance sheet value for stock as the cost of financing those stocks once the store opens. This policy is common for stocks which mature over a long period of time (e.g. whisky), or for long-term work in progress when financing costs are a material element of total cost. However, the costs must be concerned with improving the condition of that stock. In Ballyclare's case this seems unlikely as the stocks would not change in condition once they have arrived in the store, while stock turnover should be fast enough to make any interest cost immaterial.

Accounting treatment of Doagh Ltd

Ballyclare's plan is to set up a credit card operation for its customers in line with other major department stores. A new company, Doagh Ltd, will be set up with a share capital of £100. Ballyclare Ltd will hold 50 per cent of the share capital but will bear 100 per cent of the bad debt risk. The other 50 per cent will be financed by Newtown Bank Ltd.

This could be argued to be an off balance sheet finance arrangement since it is proposed that Doagh Ltd should be accounted for on an equity basis. Before the Companies Act 1989, FRS 2 and the ASB's Interim Statement on consolidation, this would have been defined as a 'controlled non-subsidiary'. This is a company which, although not fulfilling the Companies Act definition of a subsidiary, is directly or indirectly controlled by and is a source of benefits or risks for the reporting enterprise and its subsidiaries that are in substance no different from those that would arise if the vehicle was a subsidiary.

Under the new legislation, if it could be argued that Ballyclare Ltd held 'dominant influence' over the affairs of Doagh Ltd, or had exercised significant influence so that both businesses were being operated on a 'unified basis', then legally Doagh Ltd would be a subsidiary. As such, Doagh Ltd would be a legal subsidiary of Ballyclare and should be consolidated in full. This would ensure that the commercial substance of the transaction was being recorded and not its legal form. Undoubtedly companies which previously have excluded their finance subsidiaries are now bringing them back into the fold for consolidation. There would also be no excuse for exclusion on the grounds of dissimilar activities, since the legislation and FRS 2 no longer permit exclusion unless it would destroy the true and fair view of the financial statements.

In addition, FRS 5 *Reporting the Substance of Transactions* requires that any special-purpose vehicle that is under the control of another party, even if not a legal subsidiary, be consolidated as a quasi-subsidiary.

The third example looks at what could legitimately be capitalised initially as cost for a fixed asset. As can be seen from the example the FRS does permit a fairly broad range of costs so long as they can be justified in bringing the asset to its present working condition and location:

Example – Dunloy Plc (Initial measurement)

Dunloy plc has recently purchased an item of plant from Armoy plc, the details of which are:

	£	£
Basic list price of plant		240,000
trade discount applicable		12.5% on list price

Ancillary costs:

shipping and handling costs		2,750
estimated pre-production testing		12,500
maintenance contract for 3 years		24,000
site preparation costs		
electrical cable installation	14,000	
concrete reinforcement	4,500	
own labour costs	7,500	26,000

Dunloy plc paid for the plant (excluding the ancillary costs) within 4 weeks of order, thereby obtaining an early settlement discount of 3 per cent.

Dunloy plc had incorrectly specified the power loading of the original electrical cable to be installed by the contractor. The cost of correcting this error of £6,000 is included in the above figure of £14,000.

The plant is expected to last for 10 years. At the end of this period there will be compulsory costs of £15,000 to dismantle the plant and £3,000 to restore the site to its original-use condition.

Suggested solution – Dunloy Plc

Initial cost of plant purchased from Armoy plc

	£	£
Basic list price of plant	240,000	
Less trade discount (12.5%)	(30,000)	
		210,000
Shipping and handling costs		2,750
Pre-production testing		12,500
Site preparation costs		
Electrical cable installation (14,000 − 6,000 abnormal)	8,000	
Concrete reinforcement	4,500	
Own labour costs	7,500	
		20,000
Dismantling and restoration costs (15,000 + 3,000)		18,000
Initial cost of plant		263,250

Note: Abnormal costs of rectifying the power loading cannot be included as they would not normally be incurred in getting the asset to its intended location and working condition. Cash discounts of 3 per cent should be treated as administration or selling costs and may not be included as part of fixed assets. Maintenance costs are a revenue cost although a case may be made for deferring two thirds as advance payments on account – as a prepayment but not as part of a fixed asset.

Financial reporting review panel

Forte group Plc (February 1992)

Prompted by Austin Mitchell MP, the group was investigated over its treatment of capitalisation of interest, expenses on IT projects and the lack of depreciation on long leasehold properties. The Panel accepted the explanation of both its directors and its auditor Price Waterhouse although it was agreed that more information should be provided in the future over its policy of non-depreciation.

This appeared to give blanket approval to the policy of non-depreciation of properties which were maintained up to a sufficient state of repair. This needs to be contrasted with the next case.

SEP Industrial Holdings Plc (October 1992)

Non-depreciation of freehold properties was raised in a qualified audit report. The Panel was not satisfied with a non-depreciation policy as these were industrial buildings. The directors agreed to depreciate these properties in the future.

Wyevale Garden Centres Plc (September 2001)

The company did not provide any depreciation on short-leasehold properties until the last 10 years of the lease; thereafter the depreciable amount was written off over the remainder of the lease's useful life. Nor did it provide depreciation on plant and equipment until the year after the year of acquisition. Neither policy complied with FRS 15 *Tangible Fixed Assets* since neither resulted in depreciation charges being incurred throughout the assets' useful lives.

A prior year adjustment has now been incurred to increase depreciation by £722,000 for leasehold properties and £99,000 for plant.

Groupe Chez Gerard Plc (September 2001)

In common with most companies in the restaurant leisure sector, the company had not provided depreciation for leasehold property or long leaseholds on the grounds that the buildings were being maintained to a high standard. Any depreciation was argued to be immaterial as residual values were approximate to book values.

The company reviewed its policies and recommended depreciation over a 50-year period and leasehold over the lease period. They were adjusted via prior year adjustments, as changes in accounting policy opening reserves were reduced by £1.2m. Of this £723,000 represented depreciation on improvements to leasehold properties and £489,000 to freehold properties. This led to an increase of £477,000 in exceptional profits made on the sale and leaseback of the properties when they were sold later in the year.

Under FRS 15, however, depreciation should be charged prospectively over the remaining useful lives of the assets. It is a change in useful life, i.e. an accounting estimate, not a change in accounting policy.

Northgate Plc (July 2001)

Vehicle-related bonuses were recorded as deferred income and then released to turnover over the anticipated holding period of the vehicle category to which they related. Under FRS 15 the bonuses should have been credited against the purchase price of the vehicles thus reducing the depreciation charge.

Application in published accounts

The example, BAA plc, was chosen to illustrate the wide variety of possible tangible fixed assets, to illustrate both the company's depreciation policy and the compilation of a fixed assets schedule. However, it also reveals BAA having to break up their runways into two assets and accelerate the depreciation on the runway surfaces to replace their former 'income smoothing' provision for the maintenance of the runways. This is because FRS 12 *Provisions, Contingent Liabilities and Contingent Assets* forbids the creation of a liability that fails to meet a legal or constructive obligation.

BAA Plc   Year Ended 31 March 2003

Accounting Policies (Extract)
Tangible fixed assets

1.   Operational assets

Terminal complexes, airfield assets, plant and equipment, rail assets, and Group occupied properties are stated at cost less accumulated depreciation. Assets in the course of construction are stated at cost less provision for impairment. It is assumed that projects in early planning stages will receive the consents necessary to achieve a successful outcome. Assets in the course of construction are transferred to completed assets when substantially all the activities necessary to get the asset ready for use are complete. Where appropriate, cost includes interest, own labour costs of construction-related project management and directly attributable overheads.

3.   Depreciation

Depreciation is provided on operational assets, other than land, to write off the cost of the assets less estimated residual value, by equal instalments over their expected useful lives as set out in the table on page 55.

Fixed asset lives

Terminal building, pier and satellite structures	20–60 years
Terminal fixtures and fittings	5–20 years
Airport plant and equipment	
Baggage systems	15 years
Screening equipment	7 years
Lifts, escalators and travelators	25 years
Tunnels, bridges and subways	50–100 years
Runway surfaces	10–15 years
Runway bases	100 years
Taxiways and aprons	50 years
Airport transit systems	
Rolling stock	20 years
Track	50 years
Railways	
Rolling stock	8–40 years
Tunnels	100 years
Track metalwork	5–10 years

Track bases	50 years
Signalling and electrification work	40 years
Motor vehicles	4–8 years
Office equipment	5–10 years
Computer equipment	4–5 years
Computer software	3–7 years
Short leasehold properties	Over period of the lease

Notes to the Accounts (Extract)

17   Tangible Fixed Assets (Extract)

(a)   Operational Assets

Group	Note	Terminal complexes	Airfields	Plant and equipment	Other land and buildings	Rail	Assets in the course of construction	Total
		£m	£m	£m	£m	£m	£m	£m
Balance								
1 April 2002		3,379	591	483	109	634	856	6,052
Foreign exchange translation differences		2	–	1	(1)	–	–	2
Additions		5	–	16	1	–	939	961
Reclassification		–	–	(2)	5	–	(3)	–
Transfers from/(to) investment properties	12(b)	–	–	–	9	–	(125)	(116)
Transfers to completed assets		282	53	25	(12)	3	(351)	–
Interest capitalised		–	–	–	–	–	31	31
Disposals		(10)	(5)	(29)	(2)	–	–	(46)
Balance 31 March 2003		3,658	639	494	109	637	1,347	6,884
Depreciation								
Balance								
1 April 2002		1,178	137	258	24	77	–	1,674
Foreign exchange translation differences		1	–	–	(1)	–	–	–
Charge for the year		152	17	61	5	22	–	257
Reclassification		1	(1)	(2)	2	–	–	–
Disposals		(3)	(5)	(26)	(2)	–	–	(36)
Balance 31 March 2003		1,329	148	291	28	99	–	1,895
Net book value 31 March 2003								
Net book value		2,329	491	203	81	538	1,347	4,989
31 March 2002		2,201	454	225	85	557	856	4,378

Assets in the course of construction (excluding capitalised interest) include £896 million (2002: £377 million) in respect of Terminal 5 at Heathrow Airport for which planning consent was given in November 2001. The Board formally approved this project to proceed on 27 March 2003. Included within the additional Terminal 5 capital expenditure of £519 million during the year is £187 million for the acquisition of land for the construction of Terminal 5. The operational assets employed by the vendor of this land have to be relocated and the acquisition cost represents the present value of the estimated deferred payments to be made over the next 35 years to the vendor in compensation for relocation. The present value of deferred consideration is included within other provisions in the balance sheet (see note 21).

Other land and buildings are freehold except for certain short leasehold properties with a net book value of £3 million (2002: £4 million).

2.2   SSAP 19 *Accounting for Investment Properties* (January 1975, revised July 1994)

Background

On the issue of SSAP 12, an accounting standard for the first time made it compulsory to depreciate buildings. This would have had a dramatic impact on the earnings per share of investment property companies, most of whose investment was tied up in buildings. As a result of that industry's intensive lobbying of the ASC, the ASC were persuaded to introduce a specific accounting standard for investment properties that would enable those properties to be exempt from the requirement to depreciate. There is no particular theoretical justification for the standard apart from the dubious argument that these properties are different in that they are being used for investment purposes rather than for operational purposes in the reporting entity. The standard, however, is general in that it applies to all investment properties not just the investment property industry itself.

Definition

*   *Investment properties.* 'Interests in land/buildings in which the construction work has been completed and which are held for their investment potential with any rental income being received at arm's length.'

There are exceptions to the above definition:

(i)   properties owned and occupied by a company for its own purposes;
(ii)   properties let to and occupied by another group company.

Accounting treatment

(1)   Investment properties must *not* be depreciated.
(2)   Investment properties must be valued at their *open market value*.

(3)   The valuation need not be carried out by qualified or independent valuers but SSAP 19 requires disclosure of the names of the valuers, their bases of valuation and whether or not the valuer is an officer or employee of the company.

(4)   The increase/decrease in value of an investment property should be taken to a separate investment property revaluation reserve but not the profit and loss.

      If a deficit on revaluation, however, exceeds the balance on the investment property revaluation reserve then the difference should be charged directly to the profit and loss account.

(5)   The balances on both the investment property and investment property revaluation reserve should be displayed prominently in the financial statements.

(6)   SSAP 19 was amended in 1994 to ensure that changes in the value of investment properties are shown in the statement of total recognised gains and losses with the exception that deficits on individual investment properties that are expected to be permanent should be charged to profit and loss.

Subsequent developments

The IASC published a new international accounting standard, IAS 40 *Investment Properties* (March 2000), which is largely in line with SSAP 19. The standard may therefore be incorporated in a revision of FRS 15 at some stage in the future. However, it does provide an option not to revalue and to stay at cost and also if the revaluation model is adopted then any revaluation gains/losses are recorded within income and are not recorded in reserves. The ASB are particularly unhappy about this option. These changes are contained in an ASB Consultation Paper (May 2002) which is unlikely to see light in the UK as a standard before 2007.

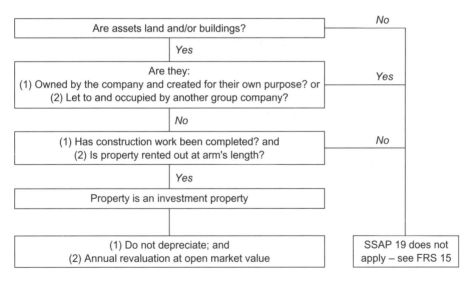

Figure 2.2   Summary.

The illustration below looks at a number of properties and examines SSAP 19 to see whether or not they could be classified as investment properties.

Example – Carrick Plc (Investment property)

Carrick plc owns three identical properties, North, South and East. North is used as the head office of Carrick plc. South is let to, and is occupied by, a subsidiary. East is let to, and is occupied by, an associate company. A fourth property, West, is leased by Carrick plc and the unexpired term on the lease is 15 years. West is let to, and is occupied by, a company outside the group.

Which, if any, of these properties is likely to be an investment property of Carrick plc and what additional information may be necessary for a final decision?

Suggested solution – Carrick Plc

SSAP 19 defines an investment property as an interest in land and/or buildings:

(1)   in respect of which construction work and development has been completed; and
(2)   which is held for its investment potential, with any rental income being negotiated at arm's length.

However, excluded from the definition are:

(1)   properties owned and occupied by a company for its own purposes and not for investment purposes;
(2)   properties let to and occupied by another member of the group.

These criteria can be applied to the individual properties of Carrick plc.

(1)   North is used as the head office of the group, therefore under exclusion (1) it would not be an investment property and would be accounted for under the rules of FRS 15.
(2)   South is let to and occupied by a subsidiary, therefore under exclusion (2) it would not be an investment property.
(3)   East is let to an associated company, but not part of the group. The property would appear to meet the definition of an investment property. Additional information required would include details of market rent to ensure that the asset is held for its investment potential.
(4)   West is let to an outside company at an arm's-length rental over a period of 15 years, being the unexpired period of the lease. This would appear to be an investment property.
(b)   FRS 15 requires that all fixed assets, including buildings but not land, should be depreciated over their estimated useful economic life. This is regardless of the market value of those assets which may well be increasing.

SSAP 19, however, emphasises the concept of current values in determining the balance sheet valuation of investment properties. Paragraph 13 emphasises that changes in the value of investment properties should not go through the profit and loss account but should be disclosed as a movement in an investment revaluation reserve. FRS 15 is not applicable and SSAP 19 states that investment properties should not be subject to periodic depreciation charges. The only exception to this rule are those leasehold properties whose unexpired terms are 20 years or less.

The application of these principles would have the following effect:

(1)   North and South are not investment properties, therefore they should both be depreciated as per FRS 15. The value of land and buildings should be separated because no depreciation is charged on land. The cost or revalued amounts for buildings should be depreciated over their estimated useful lives.

(2)   East is an investment property, therefore no depreciation should be charged. The asset should be shown at open market value in the balance sheet.

(3)   West is an investment property but the lease has less than 20 years to run. Therefore its revalued amount should be depreciated in accordance with FRS 15 over the remaining 15 years of life of the lease.

Application in published accounts

Again, BAA plc has been chosen to represent a typical disclosure of an accounting policy re investment properties in order to comply with SSAP 19.

BAA Plc Year Ended 31 March 2003

Accounting Policies (Extract)
Tangible fixed assets

2.   Investment properties

Fully completed properties let to, and operated by, third parties and held for long-term retention, including those at airport locations, are accounted for as investment properties and valued at the balance sheet date at open market value. All investment properties are revalued annually by the directors and by external valuers at least once every 5 years. Any surplus or deficit on revaluation is transferred to revaluation reserve except that deficits below original cost, which are expected to be permanent, are charged to the profit and loss account. Profits or losses arising from the sale of investment properties are calculated by reference to carrying value and treated as exceptional items. Profits are recognised on completion.

   In accordance with SSAP 19 *Accounting for Investment Properties*, no depreciation is provided in respect of freehold or long leasehold investment properties. This is a departure from the Companies Act 1985, which requires all properties to be depreciated. Such properties are not held for consumption but for investment, and the

Depreciation is only one among many factors reflected in the annual valuation of properties and accordingly the amount of depreciation, which might otherwise have been charged, cannot be separately identified or quantified. The directors consider that this policy results in the accounts giving a true and fair view.

The second example, taken from an investment property company covers both a typical accounting note on those properties but also a fixed asset schedule which complies with the disclosure requirements of SSAP 19.

Liberty International Plc Year Ended 31 December 2003

Principal Accounting policies (Extract)

Completed investment properties

Completed investment properties are professionally valued on a market basis by external valuers at the balance sheet date. Surpluses and deficits arising during the year are reflected in the revaluation reserve.

Investment properties under development

Investment properties under development and land are included in the balance sheet at cost. Provision is made where necessary for any anticipated valuation deficiencies arising on completion. Cost includes interest and other attributable outgoings, except in the case of properties and land where no development is imminent, in which case no interest is included. On completion investment properties under development are transferred to completed investment properties.

Notes to the Accounts (Extract)

Note 9 Investment properties

	Freehold	Leasehold over 50 years	Leasehold under 50 years	Total
	£m	£m	£m	£m
Completed properties at external valuation:				
At 31 December 2002	2,482.2	1,837.5	4.4	4,324.1
Additions, including transfers from joint ventures	59.8	9.5	–	69.3
Disposals, including transfers to joint ventures	(12.6)	–	–	(12.6)
Foreign exchange fluctuations	(17.8)	–	–	(17.8)
Reclassification – completed developments	7.3	–	–	7.3
Reclassification – trading properties	(2.3)	–	–	(2.3)
Amortisation	–	–	(1.0)	(1.0)
Surplus/(deficit) on valuation	147.2	(3.6)	(0.2)	143.4
At 31 December 2003	**2,663.8**	**1,843.4**	**3.2**	**4,510.4**

Properties under development at cost:				
At 31 December 2002 (including £2.0 million capitalised interest)	53.1	19.1	–	72.2
Additions	7.8	42.1	–	49.9
Reclassification – completed developments	(7.3)	–	–	(7.3)
At 31 December 2003 (including £3.9 million capitalised interest)	**53.6**	**61.2**	–	**114.8**
Investment properties				
At 31 December 2003	**2,717.4**	**1,904.6**	**3.2**	**4,605.2**
At 31 December 2002	2,535.3	1,856.6	4.4	4,396.3

	UK	US	Total
	£m	£m	£m
Geographical analysis	**4,433.1**	**192.1**	**4,625.2**

The group's interest in completed investment properties, including those held through joint ventures, were valued as at 31 December 2003 by external valuers in accordance with the Appraisal and Valuation Manual of RICS, which became effective on 1 May 2003, on the basis of market value. Market value represents the figure that would appear in a hypothetical contract of sale between a willing buyer and a willing seller. Market value is estimated without regard to costs of sale or purchase and thus values reported at 31 December 2003 no longer include purchasers' costs. At 31 December 2002 the open market value of investment properties included £208.1 million of purchasers' costs, in effect reflecting the theoretical replacement value. This change in valuation basis constitutes a change in estimation technique.

In the UK, properties were valued by either DTZ Debenham Thorpe Tie Leung Chartered Surveyors, Matthews and Goodman, Chartered Surveyors or CB Richard Ellis, Chartered Surveyors. In the US properties were valued by Jones Lang Lasalle.

The historical cost of completed investment properties was £2,617.6 million (2002 – £2,562.4 million). In accordance with the group's accounting policy and SSAP 19, no depreciation has been charged in respect of freehold or long leasehold investment properties. The effect of this departure from the Companies Act 1985 has not been quantified because it is impracticable and, in the opinion of the directors, would be misleading.

Included in properties under development is £40 million, being the initial payment in respect of the development of the shopping centre at Chapelfield, Norwich (see note 30).

2.3 SSAP 4 *Accounting for Government Grants* (April 1974, revised July 1990, amended October 1992)

Key points

Grants are receivable from many local, national and European sources. These grants are used to create more employment, to train more people and possibly also to help purchase capital equipment. Grants may often fit into one of two categories:

(i)   Revenue based, e.g. training grants; and
(ii) Capital based, e.g. purchase of new plant and machinery.

There are others that represent a mixture of the two and there is therefore a need to apportion the grant between the two categories. The key issue in the accounting standard is its requirement to follow the accruals concept, i.e. to match as closely as possible the value of the grant against the expenditure to which it relates, whether it be revenue- or capital-based.

Under the prudence concept, however, revenue and profits must not be anticipated, i.e. the grant must be virtually assured before it can be recorded in the financial statements.

Occasionally a grant is received in arrears of the expenditure undertaken. In this case it is too late to match and therefore SSAP 4 insists that the grant be recorded immediately as an income in the profit and loss account. Also, if a grant has to be repaid then it should be recorded as a liability on the balance sheet and also debited immediately to profit and loss.

Capital-based grants have been recorded in two separate ways by reporting entities:

(i)   The net of cost method – the cost of the fixed asset has been reduced by the amount of the grant and the annual depreciation charge reduced accordingly;
(ii) The deferred credit method – the grant is recorded initially in a 'capital grants reserve', held outside shareholders' funds, with a portion being credited to profit and loss annually.

The ASC took legal advice at the time of the issue of the revised version of the standard, in 1990, and the opinion given was that it was illegal to adopt the first method under the Companies Act 1985 on the grounds that it resulted in an unacceptable netting of assets against liabilities. Limited companies are therefore advised to opt for the alternative deferred credit approach.

The main disclosures required in the standard are:

(i)   the accounting policy adopted;
(ii)   the effects of the grants on the current period's results and financial position; and
(iii) the nature of any other government assistance received.

Purpose

The purpose of SSAP 4 is to ensure that the accruals concept, in particular, has been applied to accounting for all forms of government grants received, whether they be local, national, European or even quasi-government based. It requires the same accounting treatment for both revenue- and capital-based grants and since it has been revised it has become more flexible and can cope with the wide variety of new grants available. Previously it was geared up almost exclusively to capital-based grants.

Application

(1) Job creation grant
£100,000 to create 100 jobs in 4 years.

The jobs have been created as follows:

Year		Profit and loss (grant released) £
1	20	20,000
2	30	30,000
3	20	20,000
4	10	10,000
	80	80,000

The £20,000 in the deferred grants reserve is now effectively a liability as it will have to be paid back to Government. It should therefore be transferred from the deferred grants reserve to current liabilities.

(2)   Purchase of equipment £80,000 with attached grant of 20 per cent and estimated useful life of 4 years

Net of cost method		**Deferred credit method**	
Cost	£80,000	Cost	£80,000
Grant (20%)	£16,000	Capital grants reserve*	£16,000
	£64,000		
Depreciation straight line over 4 years	£16,000 p.a.		£20,000 p.a.
Release of grant to profit and loss			£(4,000) p.a.

*Recorded on the balance sheet outside shareholders' funds.

Currently SSAP 4 is very similar to the international accounting standard IAS 20 *Accounting for Grants and Disclosure of Government Assistance* but it is likely that IAS 20 will be changed in order to bring it closer to the IASB's conceptual framework. New Zealand is currently preparing an international draft standard which will probably require all capital-based grants to be recorded immediately in income and not spread over the useful life of the fixed assets.

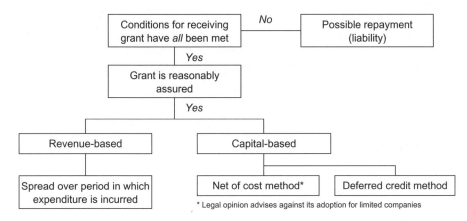

Figure 2.3   Summary.

Financial reporting review panel

London Underground Ltd (September 2000)

This case was in breach of SSAP 4 *Accounting for Government Grants* in respect of the accounts of London Underground Limited for the year ended 31 March 1999. The principal item requiring adjustment was the company's treatment of non-repayable grants from the Government, receivable via its parent entity, London Regional Transport and other grants received from third parties to fund specific tangible fixed assets. SSAP 4 requires that such grants and other forms of assistance made as a contribution towards expenditure on fixed assets be treated as deferred income, and accordingly be taken into account in determining net assets. The company however, credited the grants received for infrastructure to a capital grant reserve as it was not repayable and was in respect of non-depreciable assets. Grants received in respect of depreciable assets were similarly credited to a capital account for internal consistency and also because this treatment was required by the Secretary of State in the accounts of London Regional Transport.

The Panel did not accept that the lack of a depreciation charge in respect of infrastructure assets precluded the company from treating the grant in accordance with the requirements of SSAP 4. The directors now concur with the Panel's view and, in their March 2000 accounts reclassified all grants received as deferred income and accordingly took account of such amounts in determining net assets. The 1999 comparatives were adjusted accordingly and reduce both total capital employed and net assets from £7,628 million to £2,722 million.

Application in published accounts

The example below illustrates the normal accounting policy disclosed by companies receiving capital-based grants and treating them as deferred income to be released to profit and loss as income as the assets to which they relate are depreciated.

Henlys Group Plc Year Ended 30 September 2003 Bus and Coach Manufacturer

The company discloses receipt of Government grants in the period. Following along the lines of SSAP 4 *Accounting for Government Grants*, Henlys' accounting policies note states that grants relating to tangible fixed assets are treated as deferred income and released to the profit and loss account over the expected life of the asset concerned (para. 15). In a note, as a deduction from operating expenses, Henlys discloses £0.9 million release of Government Grants.

2.4   FRS 11 *Impairment of Fixed Assets and Goodwill* (July 1998)

Background

In July 1998 the Accounting Standards Board (ASB) published FRS 11 *Impairment of Fixed Assets and Goodwill*, which sets out the main principles and methodology for accounting for the impairment of both fixed assets and goodwill.

It incorporates all fixed assets with the exception of investment properties, Employee Share Option Plans (ESOP) shares, exploration costs and derivatives.

Prior to the publication of FRS 11 the only rules that preceded the standard were those contained in company legislation, which insists that assets be reduced to their recoverable amount if a permanent diminution occurs in the value of a fixed asset. The distinction between a temporary and a permanent diminution, however, has now been removed by the introduction of FRS 11 and now all sudden impairments in the value of fixed assets must be recognised immediately.

Key issues

How do you recognise an impairment?

Impairment is a sudden diminution in the value of a fixed asset over and above the normal wear and tear or reduction in the use of an asset value recognised by depreciation. How, therefore, does one recognise that an impairment has occurred?

FRS 11 provides a number of examples of indicators that might suggest that an impairment has occurred. These include:

(i)   a current operating loss or history of past or prospect of future losses;
(ii)   evidence of obsolescence or physical damage of an asset;
(iii)   a sudden drop in the market value of a fixed asset or a significant reorganisation;
(iv)   significant increase in market rates of interest.

The list provided in FRS 11 is not meant to be exhaustive. Ultimately the decision as to whether an impairment has arisen will rest with the subjective opinion of the directors. If they are not aware of any sign of impairment then the standard can be put back on the bookshelf for another year. However, there will still be a need to review asset lives even if no impairment has occurred.

However, there are three exceptions to the above which will require an annual impairment review. These are:

(i)   Life of goodwill in excess of normal maximum of 20 years under FRS 10;
(ii)   Life of buildings in excess of 50 years; and
(iii)   Infinite life of buildings with zero depreciation charges.

How do you calculate an impairment?

Assets should preferably be reviewed on an individual basis for impairment. Initially the net book value (NBV) of the asset should be compared to its net realisable value (NRV) and if the latter is greater then no impairment can have occurred. If no suitable NRV can be found then the net present value (NPV) must always be initially calculated.

However, if a reliable NRV is found and is found to be lower than the asset's carrying value (NBV) then the NPV must be calculated for that asset and the asset reduced to its recoverable amount (i.e. the higher of its NRV and NPV).

An example should help to illustrate the calculation.

EXAMPLE 1

Net book value (NBV)	£100	
Net realisable value (NRV)	£80	Higher value £90 (NPV)
Net present value (NPV)	£90	

The impairment is therefore £10.

Normally a simple estimate may be sufficient to demonstrate that the recoverable amount is greater than the asset's NBV and therefore no impairment has occurred.

Tax must also be incorporated into the calculation of both NPV and NRV.

EXAMPLE 2

Net book value (NBV)	£100	
Net realisable value (NRV) £100 − deferred tax £30	£70	Higher value £70 (NRV)
Net present value (NPV) £110 − deferred tax £45	£65	

The impairment is therefore £30.

How is NRV calculated?

The NRV should be calculated as the market value of fixed assets which is traded on an active market less any direct selling costs.

How is NPV calculated?

This is the more complicated of the recoverable values. The NPV should be valued on an individual asset basis, if practicable, but if not then it should be calculated at the level of the *income generating unit* (IGU).

An *income generating unit* is a group of assets, liabilities and goodwill whose income is independent of other income streams (both directly involved plus a reasonable proportion of common net assets).

On some occasions it may be acceptable to group a number of IGUs together especially if they are not regarded as material.

An IGU could be represented by a brand name, separate product, service, etc., and is likely to follow the way in which the management team monitors the different lines of the business.

Central assets and working capital needs to be apportioned across the IGUs on a logical and systematic basis:

EXAMPLE 3

IGU	A	B	C	Total
	£m	£m	£m	£m
Direct net assets	250	200	150	600
Common assets	10	8	6	24
Total	260	208	156	624

- If impairment in IGU 'A' then the NPV of A should be compared with £260m NBV and not £250m. However, the NPV should also incorporate outflows associated with common assets.

- If it is not possible to meaningfully apportion certain central assets across IGUs they may be excluded but an additional impairment review will then become necessary on the whole business. In this example the NPV of A would initially be compared to the NBV of £250 but a second test would need to be computed to compare the NPV of the whole business with the NBV of £624 m.

The cash flows that should be projected should be based on reasonable and supportable assumptions based on a reporting entity's own budget plans and forecasts which should not normally exceed 5 years. Any cash flows post that period should not exceed a steady or declining growth rate for the country as a whole.

However, this may be rebuttable in exceptional circumstances.

Another key issue is the determination of an appropriate discount rate to adopt. FRS 11 recommends the use of an implicit rate in a similar market transaction or a weighted average cost of capital (WACC) so long as it is adjusted for the specific risks attached to the IGU. A final possibility is the adoption of a WACC taken from a similar listed company but also adjusted for the specific risks attached to the IGU.

How is an impairment loss allocated in an IGU?

If the NBV of the net assets in the IGU exceed their recoverable amount (i.e. their net present value or net realisable value) then an impairment loss must be allocated in the specific order of:

(i)   goodwill;
(ii) intangible assets (but not below their NRV);
(iii) tangible assets on a *pro rata* basis (but not reduced below their NRV).

EXAMPLE 4

		Total	(i) Goodwill	(ii) Intangible assets	(iii) Tangible assets
		£m	£m	£m	£m
IGU 'A'	NBV	260	50	60	150
	NPV	180			
	Loss	80	(50)	(10)	(20)
	Restated values		Nil	50 (NRV)	130

Where an acquired business is, however, merged with existing operations it will be necessary to calculate a notional figure for internal goodwill at the date of acquisition of the existing business and therefore any subsequent impairments should be allocated *pro rata* to notional and purchased goodwill.

EXAMPLE 5

	£m	
Acquired business	60	(£40m net assets, £20m goodwill)
Existing business	150	(NPV at date of acquisition £150m plus internal goodwill £50m)

5 years	Combined business	115	(NBV £105m plus £10m purchased goodwill)
	Notional goodwill	25	(£50m × 50% not yet amortised)
		140	
	Value in use (NPV)	119	
	Impairment	21	
	Allocated:		
	2/7 × £21m	£6m	impairment loss to purchased goodwill
	5/7 × £21m	£15m	impairment loss charged notionally to internal goodwill

However, if the NPV is £98m then the impairment loss is £42m. After deducting total inherent and purchased goodwill of £35m, a further £7m must be allocated to intangible and tangible assets.

In subsequent periods the actual cash flows achieved should be compared with those forecasted and if the actual flows are materially less than those forecasted then the original impairment test should be re-performed using the actual data, and any impairment loss recognised.

Can a previous impairment loss be reversed?

A restoration of past impairment losses should be recognised where the recoverable amount of an asset has increased due to a change in economic conditions. However, this should only occur when an external event has caused the impairment and subsequent events clearly and demonstrably have reversed the effects of that event in a way not foreseen in the original impairment calculations.

In which performance document should the impairment be recognised?

Impairment losses should be recognised in the profit and loss account unless arising on a previously revalued fixed asset. In the latter case they are recognised in the statement of total recognised gains and losses until the NBV of the asset falls below its depreciated historical cost value and subsequently to the profit and loss account. However if the impairment has been caused by a consumption of economic benefits the whole impairment loss should be charged to the profit and loss account.

What disclosure must be provided for impairments?

(1) Impairment losses should be disclosed separately on the face of the profit and loss account as an *exceptional item* but within operating profit.

(2) The loss should be included as part of accumulated depreciation or, if revalued, included within the revalued carrying amount.

(3) The discount rate should be disclosed if the impairment has been calculated with reference to an asset's value in use.

(4) If an impairment loss is reversed, the reason for the reversal should be disclosed.

(5) If the steady state or declining growth rate period occurs more than 5 years away then the justification for that period must be disclosed and if the growth rates are greater than the long-term average for the country as a whole then details of the growth rates adopted and reasons for their adoption should be provided.

Date of effectance

This is treated as standard accounting practice for accounting periods ending on or after 23 December 1998. However, any impairment losses recognised for the first time will not be treated as a change in accounting policy. They are merely regarded as changes in accounting estimates as it has always been a principle that fixed assets be recorded no higher than their recoverable amount.

Summary

FRS 11 has introduced quite complex calculations to be incorporated into the impairment review. Effectively all impairment reviews will require the calculation of net present values even if there are reliable net realisable values available. Assets must not be reduced below their recoverable value, i.e. the higher of their net realisable and net present values.

This has all emerged from the Statement of Principles, which has now placed greater emphasis on the use of up-to-date relevant information rather than out-of-date although more reliable historical cost data.

The impairment review is only required if either there are indications of a sudden impairment occurring in a reporting entity's fixed assets or on an annual basis if

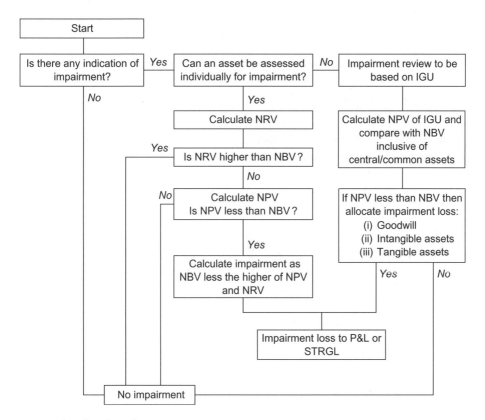

Figure 2.4   Flowchart: the impairment review.

goodwill/intangible assets have a life exceeding 20 years. In addition, entities with a nil depreciation policy on their buildings or operating a life in excess of 50 years should carry out the test on an annual basis.

The illustrations below provide examples of how to calculate impairment. The first illustrates impairment on a previous acquisition and how to allocate the loss across the various assets acquired in the strict order of goodwill first, then intangibles and finally tangible assets on a pro rata basis. The second covers the calculation of an impairment loss in an income generating unit and the final example, an additional calculation of impairment but tied to making a decision as to which performance statement the impairment should be charged.

Example – Mourne Group (Calculation of impairment loss [1])

Mourne Group prepares financial statements to 31 December each year. On 31 December 2002 assets of Binian Ltd at that date were £1.8 million and Mourne paid £2m to acquire the entity. It is the policy of the Mourne Group to amortise goodwill over 20 years. The amortisation of the goodwill of Binian Ltd commenced in 2003. Binian Ltd made a loss in 2003 and at 31 December 2003 the net assets of Binian Ltd – based on fair values at 1 January 2003 – were as follows:

	£'000
Capitalised development expenditure	200
Tangible fixed assets	1,300
Net current assets	250
	1,750

An impairment review at 31 December 2003 indicated that the value in use of Binian Ltd at that date was £1.5 million. The capitalised development expenditure has no ascertainable external market value.

Suggested solution – Mourne Group

Calculation of the impairment review loss of Binian Ltd

On 31 December 2002		
Fair value of purchase consideration		£2.0m
Fair value of net assets acquired		1.8m
Goodwill on acquisition		0.2m
On 31 December 2003		
Net book value	(£1.75m + £0.19 goodwill)	£1.94m
Net present value	(given)	1.50m
Impairment		0.44m

Allocation of impairment review loss

	Net book value	Impairment loss	Net present value
Goodwill	£0.19m	£(0.19)m	Nil
Capitalised development expenditure	0.20m	(0.20)m	Nil
Tangible fixed assets	1.30m	(0.05)m	£1.25m
Net current assets	0.25m		0.25m
	£1.94m	£(0.44)m	£1.50m

The journal entry should be as follows:

			£	£
Dr		Profit and loss account	0.44m	
	Cr	Goodwill		£0.19m
		Development expenditure		0.20m
		Tangible fixed assets		0.05m

The charge is to profit and loss account as it is due to operating problems and not to external factors.

Example – Ahoghill Ltd (Calculation of impairment loss [2])

Ahoghill Ltd has an income generating unit comprising the following assets at net book value at 31 May 2004:

	£
Goodwill	80
Intangible assets	70
Tangible assets	180

The net realisable value and value in use of the unit at the same date are £240m and £230m respectively. The intangible asset has a readily ascertainable net realisable value of £60m.

Suggested solution – Ahoghill Ltd

Ahoghill Ltd – Income generating unit

	£m	£m
Net book value		330
Net realisable value	240	
Value in use	230	
Higher of NRV and NPV		240
Impairment loss		(90)

Allocation of loss

	Total	Goodwill	Intangible assets	Tangible assets
	£m	£m	£m	£m
Net book value	330	80	70	180
Recoverable amount	240			
Impairment	(90)	(80)	(10)	Nil

The balance sheet will now be restated showing intangible assets valued at £60m and tangible assets at £180m, i.e. a total of £240m.

Example – Gracehill Ltd (Calculation of impairment loss [3])

Gracehill Ltd has been profitably manufacturing 'Bingos' for some years but technology developments suggest that the machinery involved will become obsolete in the foreseeable future in its present use. The directors of the company estimate that the present manufacturing process can continue for another 4 years after 30 June 2003. For the record the net book value of the machinery at 30 June 2003 may not be fully recoverable.

The following information relating to the machinery is available at 30 June 2003:

(a)   Net book value £5.9m (accumulated depreciation £2.8m). Depreciation for the year ended 30 June 2003 was £0.5m.

(b)   Saleable value on the open market – £2.5m with associated selling costs of £100,000.

(c)   Projections prepared by management show that net cash inflows of £1.6m per annum for the next 4 years should be obtained as a result of the machinery's continued use while its net realisable value at the end of 4 years would be immaterial. The discount rate implicit in market transactions of similar assets is 7 per cent. The appropriate present value factor is 0.8468.

Suggested solution – Gracehill Ltd

Gracehill Ltd	£m	£m
Net book value (NBV)		5.9
Net realisable value		
Saleable value	2.5	
Associated selling costs	(0.1)	
	2.4	
Net present value		
Present value of future cash flows		
(£1.6m × 4 years = £6.4m × 0.8468)	5.42	
Higher of NRV and NPV		5.42
Impairment loss		(0.48)

Because the impairment is caused by operating problems the full loss must be charged to profit and loss and the net assets reduced by £0.48m.

Dr	Profit and loss	£0.48m
Cr	Fixed assets	£0.48m

The impairment should be included within the accumulated depreciation part of the fixed assets' schedule as a separate depreciation charge. Thus the cost will remain at £8.7m and the accumulated depreciation increased from £2.8m to £3.28m, leaving the book value at £5.42m. If the asset had been revalued then the movement would have been recorded at the top of the fixed assets schedule as part of the cost/revalued movement.

Application in published accounts

Included below are a number of disclosures of recent impairments. As most of the information in the calculation is not disclosed in the published accounts there is usually only a paragraph or two in the notes describing the amount of the write off, the discount rates adopted and the cause of the impairment. You will note the wide variety of different rates adopted in practice which are supposed to take into account the specific risks involved within the assets concerned.

Abbey National Plc   Year Ended 31 December 2002   Banking

Abbey recognises a goodwill impairment of some £1.1 billion, primarily in respect of three businesses, with £604 million relating to Scottish Provident, £357 million to First National, and £149 million to Cater Tyndall. Following FRS 11, the impairment for each business is based on a comparison of carrying value and recoverable amount represented by value in use (para. 14). In relation to Scottish Provident, cash flow projections are for a 3-year period to December 2005 discounted at a rate of 8.2 per cent on a post tax basis. The growth rates used are 3.9 per cent and 5 per cent for the forecast period and terminal value respectively. Using an average growth rate of 8.7 per cent, the First National impairment is based on cash flow projections for a 5-year period to December 2007 including a terminal value. These cash flows are discounted at a rate of 7.6 per cent on a post tax basis. There is no disclosure of discount or growth rates for Cater Tyndall although Abbey states that it is expected to be loss-making over the period to December 2005.

Anglo American Plc   Year Ended 31 December 2002   Gold Mining

Two years ago, Anglo impaired in full an investment in a copper/gold project in Brazil and the impairment of $46 million was classified as an exceptional item. This year, Anglo has disposed of the project for consideration of $51 million and discloses that the sale price indicated a reversal of the conditions that resulted in the original impairment. This follows FRS 11 which states that, if after an impairment loss has been recognised the recoverable amount of the tangible fixed asset increases, the resulting reversal of the impairment loss should be recognised (para. 56). The impairment reversal is treated as an operating exceptional item but is more than offset by a write-down of investments of $30 million and other impairments of $97 million. After reversal of the original impairment, Anglo recognises a gain on disposal of $5 million, which is classified as a non-operating exceptional item.

In addition to the gain on disposal, Anglo recognises as non-operating exceptionals a further $93 million net profit on disposal of other fixed assets and a charge of $34 million on termination of a business. Following FRS 3 *Reporting Financial Performance*, these non-operating amounts are disclosed separately on the face of the profit and loss account after operating profit and before interest (para. 20).

Granada Plc   Year Ended 30 September 2002   Television

In addition to the £250 million goodwill impairment Granada recognises also £138 million of other exceptional items during the year. Of this, £120 million is in relation to joint ventures with £104 million in respect of a loss on the cessation of ITVDigital with the remainder being in relation to the reorganisation of a continuing joint venture. The loss on cessation is treated as a non-operating exceptional item and, following FRS 3 *Reporting Financial Performance*, is disclosed on the face of the profit and loss account after operating profit and before interest (para. 20). Of the other exceptional items, £10 million is in relation to a stock write-off with a further £4 million being in relation to exit costs from a business and the remainder being in respect of reorganisation costs.

British Airways Plc   Year Ended 31 March 2003   Airline Operator

Following the announcement that its Concorde fleet is to be retired at the end of October 2003, BA recognises an impairment charge of £58 million in relation to capitalised engineering and inventory costs. Recognition of the fixed asset impairment follows FRS 11, which states that an impairment review should be carried out if events or changes in circumstances indicate that the carrying value of the fixed asset may not be recoverable (para. 8). Additionally, an impairment of £26 million is recognised in relation to the write-down of Concorde's stock. This is in accordance with SSAP 9 *Stocks and Long-Term Contracts*, which states that, if there is no reasonable expectation of sufficient future revenue to cover the cost of stock, the irrecoverable cost should be charged to revenue in the year under review (para. 1). The total impairment charge of £84 million is recognised as an exceptional operating charge on the face of the profit and loss account.

Stagecoach Group Plc Year Ended 30 April 2002 Provision of Public Transport

Following the events of 11 September 2001 and consequent lack of demand, a £9.7 million impairment is recognised reducing the carrying value of approximately 330 vehicles which are no longer revenue generating. Following FRS 11 the impairment is included within cumulative depreciation [para. 68(a)].

Stagecoach has committed also to the sale or closure of a number of businesses in the USA, raising a £9.9 million exceptional provision in this respect. Of this, £8.2 million has been utilised during the year. Stagecoach discloses that the provision consists of a write-down of assets including goodwill, together with termination payments and other closure costs and relates to obligations which exist at the balance sheet date. During the year, further business disposals were made with an aggregate £4.8 million profit being recognised. Following FRS 3 *Reporting Financial Performance*, this profit is disclosed separately on the face of the profit and loss account, as a non-operating exceptional item, after operating profit and before interest (para. 20). A £0.5 million profit on the disposal of property is disclosed also on the face of the profit and loss account.

Asset valuation: accounting for intangible assets

3.1 SSAP 13 *Research and Development* (December 1977, revised January 1989)

Key points

Research and development expenditure is essential to the future survival of most manufacturing companies. However, it is highly speculative in nature with extreme uncertainty surrounding the likely level of future revenue emanating from that expenditure. The two theoretical concepts underlying the development of an acceptable accounting standard are prudence and accruals. The former would favour the immediate write-off of such expenditure to profit and loss while the latter would require deferral of such expenditure to be matched against future revenues. Under the Statement of Principles it would appear that research and development would probably fail to meet the recognition tests contained in Chapter 5 of that document and therefore have to be immediately expensed to profit and loss.

Definitions

- *Pure research* – experimental or theoretical work undertaken primarily to acquire new scientific or technological knowledge for its own sake, i.e. 'stab in the dark'.
- *Applied research* – original or critical investigation undertaken to gain new scientific or technical knowledge and directed towards a specific aim, i.e. 'know where one is going but haven't got there yet'.
- *Development* – use of scientific or technical knowledge to produce new or substantially improved materials, devices, products or services prior to the commencement of commercial production, i.e. 'a viable product, etc., has been produced that will be commercially successful'.

There are obviously grey areas between the three definitions but if there appears to be some form of innovation rather than mere routine then it should be included as research and development. SSAP 13 provides a list of examples which should be either included or excluded from the definition of research and development but it is far from being comprehensive.

Accounting treatment – initial

(i) Pure or applied research should be written off immediately to profit and loss.

(ii) Development expenditure should be written off immediately to profit and loss, unless it meets all five criteria below, in which case it *may* be either capitalised or expensed.

- There is a clearly defined project;
- The related expenditure is separately identifiable;
- The outcome has been assessed with reasonable certainty as to
  its technical feasibility, and
  its ultimate commercial viability;
- The total development costs plus all further costs and any selling and distribution expenditure are expected to be exceeded by related future sales;
- There are adequate resources, especially working capital, to complete the project. If one project is capitalised then that policy must be followed consistently for all other development projects.

(iii) The cost of fixed assets purchased or constructed for use in research and development should be capitalised and amortised over their economic useful lives. However, any depreciation incurred during the research and development phase should be included as part of the overall research and development expenditure.

(iv) Market research may never be capitalised but must instead be written off to profit and loss.

(v) Any research and development undertaken on behalf of a third party which is fully reimbursed by that third party is not regarded as part of research and development and must be incorporated as work in progress instead.

Subsequent amortisation of capitalised development costs

Once development has been capitalised it must be subsequently amortised to profit and loss on the commencement of commercial production. SSAP 13 requires that the process be carried out on a systematic basis to each accounting period benefiting from the sales or use of the product/service. Similarly, to other fixed assets this period of write-off should be reviewed and revised, if necessary, on a regular basis to reflect current conditions and, if considered irrecoverable, it should be written down on a project-by-project basis.

Disclosure in the financial statements

(1) The movements in the deferred development expenditure account.

(2) The total amounts of research and development expensed in the profit and loss account, separately analysed between the amounts expended in the current year and the amortisation of deferred development expenditure.
(*Note*: This particular requirement is only for plc's and large companies greater than ten times the size of a medium-sized company for filing purposes at Companies Office.)

(3)   The expenditure should be separately disclosed on the balance sheet as part of intangible fixed assets.
(4)   The accounting policy for research and development, if material.

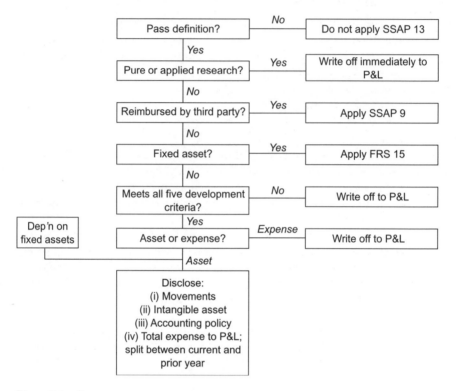

Figure 3.1   Summary.

The following example looks at a number of projects and requires the reader to distinguish contracts governed by SSAP 13 from those governed by the long-term contracts section of SSAP 9 *Stocks and Work in Progress*. Examples of both are provided and the reader is required to adjust the financial statements in order to comply with those standards.

Example – Cleaver Plc

Cleaver plc is a company involved in the design and manufacture of aircraft. During the year ended 31 March 2002, the company had commenced the following projects:

(A)   *Project Alpha* involves research into the development of a lightweight material for use in the construction of aircraft. To date, costs of £175,000 have been incurred but so far the material developed has proved too weak.

(B)   *Project Beta* involves the construction of three aircraft for a major airline at a total contract price of £75 million. Costs incurred to 31 March 2004 amounted to £21 million, and payments on account received, relating to £20 million of those costs, amounted to £24 million. It is estimated that the contract will cost another £40 million to complete.

(C)   *Project Gamma* involves the development of a new engine for an overseas customer for a total contract price of £7 million. The total cost of the project is estimated to be £5 million. Only £1.4 million had been incurred to 31 March 2004. Payments on account, relating to those costs, of £2.4 million have been received.

(D)   *Project Delta* involves the refurbishment of a fleet of ten aircraft for another airline. The total contract price is £30 million. To 31 March 2004, costs of £24 million have been incurred, and, because of materials shortage, it is estimated that it will cost another £12 million to complete. Although £20 million had been invoiced to 31 March 2004, relating to costs incurred to that date, only £19 million had been received at that date.

(E)   *Project Epsilon* commenced in February 2004 involving the production of light aircraft for a flying school for a total contract price of £18.2 million. Costs incurred to 31 March 2004 amounted to £1 million of a total estimated contract cost of £17 million. Invoices raised to 31 March 2004 amounted to £3 million of which £2.6 million had been received by that date.

Suggested solution – Cleaver Plc

Project Alpha

This is an item of applied research as the project is directed towards a specific outcome but that outcome has not reached the stage of producing a viable product. Under SSAP 13, therefore, the cost of £175,000 should be written off to the profit and loss account and the amount disclosed in the notes to the financial statements along with other research and development immediately written off.

Project Beta

This is a long-term contract on which a profit of £14m is expected on completion. A formula based on cost to date over expected cost would suggest (21/61 or a third complete) so £25m could be taken as turnover at this stage. The progress payment is deducted from turnover leaving a net debtor of £1m. Sales of £25m and matching cost of sales of £21m are included within normal sales and cost of sales for the period. (See appendix.)

Project Gamma

This is a long-term contract on which a profit of £2m (£7m − £5m) is expected on completion. A formula based on the cost to date over expected cost would suggest (1.4/5 × £2m) that £560,000 of the final profit can be taken to date. Sales of £1.96m and cost of sales of £1.4m will be recorded. Accordingly these amounts will be transferred from the contract account to the final profit and loss account and the balance of £440,000 will be carried forward as a creditor.

Project Delta

This a long-term contract with an expected loss of £6m on completion. This loss must be provided for immediately under the prudence convention. The loss on the contract will be debited to the profit and loss account via turnover of £20m and cost of sales £24m − £4m is recorded in the ledgers, so a provision for future losses of £2m should now be made to increase the cost of sales to £26m. Debtors of £1m would also appear in the balance sheet because the client has not yet paid all the invoices raised on this project.

Project Epsilon

This contract is at an early stage and it is too soon to take profit on the grounds of prudence, and of not being able to ascertain an eventual profit at this stage. The cost to date (£1m) is work in progress, but set off against the £3m invoiced to the client gives a net creditor for payments on account, and the £0.4m unpaid as a debtor.

Under SSAP 9, profits taken before completion of these long-term contracts must be based on prudent estimates of the profitable completion of the work, with reference to the rate of profitability for various parts of the contract.

Cleaver Plc – profit and loss account for year ended 31 March 2004

	£m
Turnover (25 + 1.96 + 20)	46.96
Costs (21 + 1.4 + 24)	46.40
	0.56
Provision for foreseeable losses	(2.00)
Loss on contracts	(1.44)
Research costs written off	(0.175)
Operating loss	(1.615)

Workings

Project Beta	£m	£m
Total price		75
Costs to date	21	
Costs to complete	40	61
Estimated total profit		14

WIP

	£m		£m
Total cost	21	Cost of sales	21

Profit and loss

	£m		£m
Cost of sales	21	Sales	25

Debtors

	£m		£m
Sales	25	Bank	24
		Balance c/d	1
	25		25
Balance b/d	1		

Profit to record	£m
1/3 costs completed ∴ 1/3 turnover	25
Less costs of sales	21
Profit to date	4

Balance sheet
Sales: £25m − £24m on account = £1m debtor

Project Gamma

	£m
Total price	7
Total cost	5
Estimated total profit	2

WIP

	£m		£m
Total cost	1.4	Cost of sales	1.4

Contract profit and loss

	£m		£m
Cost of sales	1.4	Sales	1.96
		(1.4/5.0 × 7m)	

Debtors

	£m		£m
Sales	1.96	Bank	2.40
Balance c/d	0.44		
	2.40		2.40

Project Delta

	£m		£m
Total price			30
Costs to date	24		
Costs to complete	12		36
Estimated total loss			(6)

WIP

	£m			£m
Total cost	24		Cost	24

Contract profit and loss

	£m			£m
Cost	24		Sales	20
Provision for foreseeable losses	2			

Debtors

	£m			£m
Sales	20		Bank	19
			Balance c/d	1
	20			20
Balance b/d	1			

Project Epsilon

WIP

	£m			£m
Total cost	1		Balance c/d	1
Balance b/d	1			

Contract profit and loss

	£m			£m
Cost	–		Sales	–

Debtors

	£m			£m
Balance	2.6		Bank	2.6

Cleaver plc – balance sheet at 31 March 2004

The provision for profit in suspense will appear on the balance sheet under 'provisions and liabilities' – a deduction from assets which is not part of shareholders' funds.

Provision for future losses of £2m.
Creditors for progress payments on account = £0.44m + 2.6m = £3.04m
Stocks and work in progress £1m
Debtors (1 + 1) = £2m

The second example also requires a decision to be made as to whether or not various projects meet the definition of development expenditure and therefore may be capitalised under SSAP 13 but it also requires knowledge of how to amortise any previously capitalised exapenditure.

Example – Cadogan Plc

Cadogan plc has an extensive research facility involved in the research, development and promotion of various projects. Information regarding the research department's activities for the year ended 31 July 2004 is given below:

(1)   £750,000 spent on a new gas ionising plant. Such plant is highly specialised and has minimal scrap value due to contamination. It has an expected life of 10 years and came into use from 1 July 2004.

(2)   A contract was entered into with a cosmetics group on a cost plus 25 per cent basis to develop a kiss-proof lipstick. So far Cadogan plc has incurred costs of £90,000 and has received £25,000 on account. Further costs of £35,000 to complete the contract are expected before 31 July 2005. The balance of the contract price is to be settled on completion.

(3)   Dr Zod, a nuclear physicist, was employed at a cost of £25,000 to conduct investigations into sub-atomic wave motions. The work is vital to the future success of several current projects.

(4)   £250,000 has been spent on the research and development of a new audio product. Forty per cent is attributable to development. The product will not be marketable until 2006. Further total costs of some £400,000 are estimated, but financial backing is available from institutions and there are no doubts over the technical feasibility of the product. It is expected to have the same impact on home entertainment as television.

(5)   Wallop, a new low-alcohol beverage, was launched on 1 February 2004 with an expected market life of 4 years. During the year £20,000 was spent on advertising. Development expenditure brought forward amounted to £300,000.

Suggested solution – Cadogan Plc

New gas ionising plant, £750,000

This is a fixed asset which should be capitalised and subsequently depreciated over its estimated useful life. However, if the asset is used specifically for development, then the depreciation charge may form part of overall development costs. No information is available concerning its use during 2004; thus it can be assumed it is not used on qualifying development projects and depreciation should be written off to the profit and loss account. With a life of 10 years and a charge for 1 month, depreciation should be £6,250 (£750,000 $\times$ 1/10 $\times$ 1/12) and the net book value is £743,750.

Development of kiss-proof lipstick

Although this is research expenditure, it is a contract with a third party to provide that party with a service, albeit on a contract exceeding 1 year. It thus falls under SSAP 9's definition of a long-term contract. As such it is not part of development expenditure under SSAP 13. Turnover should be recorded on the basis of work carried out to date and cost of sales should be matched to the same period of time. As this is a straightforward cost plus 25 per cent contract, then cost of sales would be fairly charged at £90,000 and turnover at £90,000 × 125% = £112,500. As payments on account amount to £25,000 to date, then debtors would be recorded at £87,500 (£112,500 − £25,000). No amount would be recorded as work in progress. However, if a more conservative view is taken of the profit to date, the turnover and related cost of sales can be reduced, thus creating a balance of costs not transferred to cost of sales, i.e. work in progress.

Employment of Dr Zod, £25,000

Dr Zod is a nuclear physicist and is probably an expert in the field of sub-atomic wave motions. However, the annual salary must be regarded as an expense unless it can be matched to a specific successful development project. If such a project cannot be identified then the cost of £25,000 should be written off straight to the profit and loss account.

New audio product, £250,000

This product would appear to meet the five qualifying conditions to enable development expenditure to be capitalised under SSAP 13. However, only 40 per cent (£100,000) is in respect of development and £150,000 will need to be written off immediately to the profit and loss account. The £100,000 may be carried forward in the balance sheet as an intangible asset, as well as the expected £400,000 when it is spent in future years. Assuming that £500,000 is eventually capitalised, this should be amortised to accounting periods on a systematic basis by reference to the periods over which it is expected that the new audio product will be sold. This could be on the basis of either time or units sold.

Wallop advertising (£20,000) and development costs (£300,000)

Development costs of £300,000 have already been capitalised in prior years. Amortisation should commence on 1 February 2004, the date of commencement of commercial production. With an expected market life of 4 years, annual amortisation will be £75,000 per annum assuming a straight-line allocation. For 2004, 6 months should be charged, i.e. £37,500. Development costs would be stated at £262,500 under intangible assets in the balance sheet. In addition, the movement for the year should be disclosed in the notes to the accounts. The advertising expenditure of £20,000 could be carried forward as an asset, provided that it meets the requirements of FRS 5, i.e. it is probable that future revenues will result from the expenditure and the asset has a cost or value which can be sufficiently reliably measured (general recognition tests). It would then be subsequently amortised to the profit and loss account over the period from which future benefits will derive. However, prudence would probably dictate an immediate write-off. For plc's and public interest bodies, this expenditure fits under the heading of *investment for the future* and should be disclosed in the *Operating and Financial Review*.

Financial Reporting Review Panel

Sinclair Montrose Heathcare Plc (February 2000)

The group had capitalised £3,482,000 development costs, under SSAP 13. The directors have now accepted that these costs should have been written off immediately to profit and loss. The costs related to the marketing and advertising costs incurred in developing its Medicentre brand. This has turned a profit of £840,000 into a loss of £1,933,000 for the year and reduced net assets from £9,153,000 to £5,714,000.

Wiggins Group Plc (March 2001)

The Panel's initial concern was in respect of expenditure of approximately £1 million which, in the 1999 accounts, was stated to be capitalised as an intangible fixed asset in accordance with SSAP 13. In the Panel's opinion the nature of the expenditure did not properly qualify as development expenditure and should accordingly have been written off against profits for that year. The directors did not accept the Panel's view, but without discussing their proposed course of action with the Panel, they decided to apply a new accounting policy in their 2000 accounts, reclassifying the same expenditure as 'start up costs', treating it as a prepayment within debtors and carrying it forward in current assets. They also revised the 1999 comparative figures to reflect the new policy. In the 2000 accounts, the total figure carried forward was in fact £3 million, being the £1 million brought forward from 1999 and a further £2 million of similar expenditure incurred in the year ended 31 March 2000. The latter amount was not disclosed in the 2000 accounts sent to shareholders.

Approximately 1 month before the company issued its preliminary announcement for 2000, the UITF issued Abstract 24 *Accounting for Start Up Costs* which proscribed the carrying forward of such costs and required them to be recognised as an expense when incurred. The Abstract stated, 'The accounting treatment required by this consensus should be adopted in financial statements relating to accounting periods ending on or after 23 July 2000 although earlier adoption is encouraged'. The company argued that since the company's relevant accounting period ended on 31 March 2000 it could disregard the Abstract in selecting an appropriate accounting policy. In the Panel's view, however, it was totally inappropriate for a company to adopt a new policy that it knew had already been proscribed, even if the prohibition was expressed as applying only to subsequent periods. In the Panel's view, the policy was neither 'appropriate' nor 'preferable'. The Panel was also of the view that the adoption of the policy did not comply with the legal requirement for accounting policies to be applied consistently. The company knew at the time that the new policy would have to change again in the following year, giving rise to three accounting policies for one type of expenditure within a 3-year period.

The Panel accepted that consistency of accounting policies is more usually applied by comparing the present with the past but is of the view that expected future changes should also be considered when seeking to comply with the Act. Accordingly, in the Panel's view, it was not appropriate for the company to adopt a new accounting policy that it knew would have to be withdrawn in the next accounting period as it would be prohibited by the new accounting requirement.

The company later put forward a second argument as justification for the change in policy in the 2000 accounts: that some of the expenditure reported as having been incurred in

1999 had in fact been incurred in 1998 and carried forward as a prepayment in that year's accounts. It maintained therefore that, in its 1998 accounts, the company had an accounting policy, albeit not disclosed to shareholders for reasons of non-materiality, for carrying forward such start-up costs in prepayments and that, in its 2000 accounts, the company was merely reverting to its earlier policy. The Panel noted that, if that were indeed the case, there were further errors in the 1999 accounts (in particular Note 9, Intangible Fixed Assets, and the cash flow statement and notes), which clearly showed all the expenditure as having been incurred in 1999. A small amount of the original £1 million had indeed been incurred in 1998 and included within prepayments in the 1998 accounts, but the Panel concluded on the evidence that this had not been because of an accounting policy adopted by the company in respect of start-up costs but because, at that time, it had been considered recoverable from a third party. The Panel did not accept this second argument as justifying the change of policy made in the 2000 accounts.

The company accepted that the accounting treatment in both the 1999 and 2000 accounts was incorrect and, in its revised accounts, £2 million was written off against the 2000 profit and loss account and £1 million against prior years.

Finelot Plc (January 2003)

The matter at issue was the capitalisation of £966,000 costs as development expenditure under SSAP 13. SSAP 13 defines development as: 'Use of scientific or technical knowledge in order to produce new or substantially improved materials, devices, products or services, to install new processes or systems prior to the commencement of commercial production or commercial applications, or to improving substantially those already produced or installed'.

Subject to satisfying a number of other qualifying criteria under the standard, development costs may be capitalised and amortised over the period in which the product or service is expected to be sold or used. All other research and development costs should be written off in the year of expenditure.

During the year, the company paid a third party £966,000 to carry out pre-production work for a new lifestyle magazine. In the Panel's opinion, the work that was conducted, which included concept design and establishing distribution and marketing networks, did not include a substantial element of 'scientific or technical' knowledge in the sense that was intended by SSAP 13.

In the Panel's view, therefore, the costs incurred were not for 'development' as defined within SSAP 13. Nor did they satisfy the criteria for recognition as an asset under any other relevant accounting standard. Therefore, the costs should have been written off as incurred, as required by UITF Abstract 24 *Accounting for Start-Up Costs* in such circumstances.

The directors accepted the Panel's findings and, in their July 2002 preliminary statement, wrote off the amount in full by way of prior year adjustment.

Application in published accounts

One of the main reasons for the development of SSAP 13 was the collapse of Rolls Royce in the 1970s after having met major teething problems in the development of the RB 211 aircraft engine. It is therefore useful to look at their current policy in which both certification and application engineering costs are capitalised but developments costs are written off immediately. The Intangible Fixed Assets schedule is also provided to illustrate the movement during the year.

Rolls Royce Plc Year Ended 31 December 2003   Aerospace Engineering

Research and development

The charge to the profit and loss account consists of research and development expenditure incurred in the year, excluding known recoverable costs on contracts, contributions to shared engineering programmes and application engineering. Application engineering expenditure, incurred in the adaptation of existing technology to new products, is capitalised and amortised over the programme life, up to a maximum of 10 years, where both the technical and commercial risks are considered to be sufficiently low.

9. Intangible fixed assets

	Goodwill £m	Certification costs £m	Application engineering £m	Total £m
Cost				
At 1 January 2003	937	144	37	1,118
Exchange adjustments	15	–	–	15
Additions	8	31	6	45
At 31 December 2003	960	175	43	1,178
Accumulated amortisation				
At 1 January 2003	151	99	–	250
Exchange adjustments	2	–	–	2
Provided during the year	48	15	–	63
At 31 December 2003	201	114	–	315
Net book value at 31 December 2003	759	61	43	863
Net book value at 31 December 2002	786	45	37	868

The second example, Merrydown plc as well as capitalising development expenditure, includes capitalised brands on the balance sheet. The company has also changed its accounting treatment to a direct write-off policy of development from the current year. This seems to be a recent trend and probably reflects the view that the US treatment, of not permitting development as an asset, is likely to prevail in world accounting.

Merrydown Plc Year ended 31 March 2003 Manufacture of cider and soft drinks

Accounting Policies (Extract)

Research and Development expenditure

It was previously the group's policy, in line with SSAP 13 *Accounting for Research & Development*, to capitalise the cost of development expenditure where the directors were confident future recoverability could be reasonably foreseen. The accounting policy has been reviewed in view of recent guidance on the relevant reporting standards and the practice of other drinks companies. The directors have considered the appropriateness of this accounting treatment in the current year and have determined that it is now more appropriate to write off development expenditure in the year in which it is incurred. This represents a change in accounting policy and as such has been accounted for as a prior year adjustment. Previously reported figures for the year ended 31 March 2002 have been restated accordingly.

Notes to the financial statements (Extract)

9. Intangible fixed assets

Group and Company

	Purchased Brand	Development costs	Total
Cost	£'000	£'000	£'000
At 1 April 2002 (as previously stated)	7,350	112	7,462
Prior year adjustment	–	(112)	(112)
At 1 April 2002 (as restated)	7,350	–	7,350
At 31 March 2003	7,350	–	7,350
Amortisation			
At 1 April 2002 and 31 March 2003	2,389	–	2,389
Net book value			
At 31 March 2003	4,961	–	4,961
At 31 March 2002 (as restated)	4,961	–	4,961

The purchased brand cost relates to the purchase of the manufacturing, distribution and selling rights to the Schloer brand and determined it to have an indefinite economic life due to the strength and durability of the brand coupled with Merrydown's commitment to developing and enhancing its value. Accordingly it has not been amortised with effect from 1 October 1999. The net book value at 31 March 2003 has been and will be subject to an annual impairment review.

If the new accounting policy for research and development had not been adopted in the current year, this year's profit before taxation would have been £67,000 higher (2002: £112,000 higher). The associated tax charge for 2003 would have been £20,000 higher (2002: £33,000 higher). The net effect on profits attributable to shareholders, net assets and profit and loss reserve in 2003 would have been £126,000 higher (2002: £79,000 higher).

3.2   SSAP 21 *Accounting for Leases and Hire Purchase Contracts* (August 1984, amended February 1997)

Background

This was the first accounting standard to implement the concept of substance taking precedence over legal form by ensuring that lessees who have leased their plant and machinery in such a way that they effectively control the use of those assets over substantially all of their economic useful lives, should in fact capitalise those assets.

Legally, a lease will always result in legal ownership staying with the lessor whereas, under a hire purchase agreement, title will eventually pass to the hire purchasee, by exercise of an option to purchase the asset.

Prior to SSAP 21 many companies had switched from outright purchase to leasing, on the grounds of both improved cash flow and, more importantly, the avoidance of the inclusion of certain loans on the balance sheet thus improving their gearing ratio. It was a form of 'off balance sheet financing'.

Definitions

- *Operating leases.* Lessee rents the asset for a short period of time, certainly less than the asset's useful economic life. Lessor retains most of the risks and returns. There is usually more than one user of the asset over its useful economic life.
- *Finance leases.* The lessor obtains sufficient monies to not only repay the cost of buying the fixed asset but to earn a sufficient return on their investment. The lessee usually bears all the risks and rewards including any maintenance costs. There is usually a secondary rental period at a nominal rental to enable the lessee to hold on to the asset for as long as it requires.

In practice the distinction between the two types of lease is very grey and the IASB is currently working with the FASB in the US to develop a world standard that will abolish operating leases, as it has been felt for many years that preparers have deliberately tried to manipulate leases to try to ensure that the vast bulk are defined as operating.

Accounting treatment – lessee

- *Finance lease initial.* Should be capitalised to ensure that the substance of the transaction is disclosed. It is the 'rights in the asset' not the asset itself which is being capitalised. A liability should be created for all future rental payments or at least the capital repayment thereof. Any difference between the total rentals to be paid and the fair value of the asset acquired must be recorded as finance charges in suspense.
- *Finance lease (annually).* Should charge the rentals against the overall liability if initially recorded gross. If recorded net then the rentals will have to be apportioned between finance charges for the period and the repayment of capital. The finance charge must be apportioned to the profit and loss in such a way that it ensures a constant periodic rate of charge on the outstanding obligations for each accounting period.
- *Operating lease.* All rentals payable should be charged on a straight-line basis to the profit and loss leases account.

Accounting treatment – lessor

The accounting treatment should be a mirror of that adopted for lessees, in order to ensure consistency of accounting treatment in the financial statements.

Finance leases should therefore be recorded in 'debtors' for the amount of the net investment in the lease made up of the minimum lease payments plus any residual value less any government grants receivable and less any finance charges allocated to future periods.

Operating leases should be capitalised with any rental income being credited directly to profit and loss.

Sundry issues

Sale and leaseback

Any profit/loss arising from a sale and leaseback transaction which results in the creation of a finance lease should be deferred and amortised in the lessee's books over the shorter of the lease term and the useful life of the asset. If the lease is operating then the profit/loss should be recognised immediately, provided that the transaction is at fair value.

Manufacturer or dealer lessor

Where leasing is used as a means of marketing products, a manufacturer/dealer should not recognise a selling profit under an operating lease at all and in the case of a finance lease it should be restricted to the excess of the fair value of the asset over the manufacturer/dealer's net costs after grants.

Disclosure in the financial statements

Lessee

- *Operating lease.* Disclose the amounts committed for next year split between land and buildings and other. These should also be analysed according to when the commitment expires, i.e. within 1 year, between 2 and 5 years and over 5 years.

- *Finance lease*. Disclose the value of leased assets included in tangible fixed assets either in a separate column or as a footnote. The total obligations should be split between those falling due within 1 year, between 2 and 5 years and over 5 years. The finance charge for the year should also be disclosed.

Lessor

- *Operating lease*. Disclose the gross cost and accumulated depreciation of assets held for rental.
- *Finance lease*. Disclose the net investment, i.e. at their minimum lease payments plus residual values less grants and finance costs allocated to future periods in the finance lease at each balance sheet date. Disclose the cost of assets acquired for the purpose of letting under either a finance lease or hire purchase agreement. Disclose the accounting policy adopted.

Consultation paper (May 2002)

In May 2002 the ASB published a Consultative Paper which incorporated some minor changes being made to IAS 17 *Leases*. However, because leasing is expected to undergo a more fundamental review, the ASB has decided not to implement the revised IAS 17 at present. A Discussion Paper was published in December 1999 that has put forward the suggestion that all operating leases be capitalised in the books of the user, not the legal owner. That has posed a controversial issue and we await the final outcome over the next few years. It could have dramatic consequences not only for gearing ratios of lessees but for the leasing industry itself.

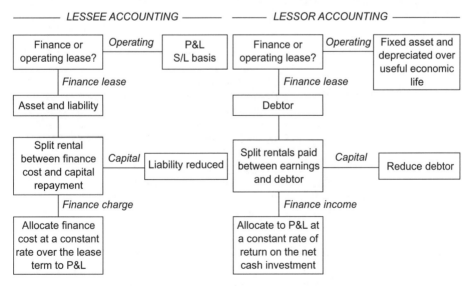

Figure 3.2 Summary.

The example below is a straightforward illustration of how to account for a sale and leaseback situation.

Example – Farset Ltd

Farset Ltd prepares financial statements to 31 March each year. On 1 April 2003, Farset Ltd sold a freehold property to another company, Lagan plc. Farset Ltd had purchased the property for £500,000 on 1 April 1995 and had charged total depreciation of £60,000 on the property for the period 1 April 1995 to 31 March 2005. Lagan plc paid £850,000 for the property on 1 April 2005, at which date its true market value was £550,000.

From 1 April 2005 the property was leased back by Farset Ltd on a 10-year operating lease for annual rentals (payable in arrears) of £100,000. A normal annual rental for such a property would have been £50,000.

Lagan plc is a financial institution which, on 1 April 2003, charged interest of 10.56 per cent per annum on 10-year fixed-rate loans.

Suggested solution – Farset Ltd

Journal entries to record the sale of property to Lagan plc and the payment of the first rental

Date				£	£
1 April 2005	Dr		Bank account	850,000	
		Cr	Loan account		300,000
			Disposal of property account		550,000
	being the sale of property at market value				
	Dr		Disposal of property account	500,000	
		Cr	Property		500,000
	being the cost of property sold transferred to disposal of property account				
	Dr		Accumulated depreciation – property	60,000	
		Cr	Disposal of property account		60,000
	being accumulated depreciation on property sold				
	Dr		Disposal of property account	110,000	
		Cr	Profit and loss account		110,000
	being profit on disposal of property				

These journal entries record the sale and disposal of property to/from Lagan plc in accordance with the requirements of FRS 5. The profit on sale is the difference between the fair value of the property and its carrying value at the date of sale.

			£	£
31 March 2006	Dr	Profit and loss account (leasing charges)	50,000	
		(interest 10.56% × £300,000)	31,680	
		Loan account		
		(Capital repaid £50,000 − £31,680)	18,320	
	Cr	Bank account		100,000

being the first rental payment to Lagan plc, which is a combination of an operating lease and a repayment of interest and capital on the loan.

The rental repayment reveals the recording of the substance of the sale and lease-back transaction undertaken by Lagan plc, which is a combination of an operating lease rental (for the continued use of the property) and the repayment of interest and capital on the loan.

The next example, illustrates the three types of agreement likely to be effected by SSAP 21 – the operating lease, the finance lease and the hire purchase agreement and requires the reader to apply SSAP 21 in the eyes of a lessee to all three situations. The actuarial method of allocating finance lease costs has been adopted as the company was able to derive its implicit rate of interest:

Example – Hinch Ltd

Hinch Ltd manufactures 'Poteen' and to improve efficiency has scrapped all its existing plant and replaced it as follows:

(1) On 1 December 2003 Hinch Ltd agreed to rent an 'Imperial Distiller' from Mick & Gerry at a cost of £1,500 per month payable in advance. The agreement is terminable at three months' notice by either party.

(2) On 1 June 2004 Hinch Ltd entered into an agreement with Saintfield for the lease of a 'Potillier'. Terms included:

(a) neither party could cancel;

(b) Hinch Ltd is to have responsibility for maintenance;

(c) six instalments of £7,500 are payable half-yearly in advance.

The cash price of a 'Potillier' on 1 June 2004 was £40,000 and the machine is considered to have a residual value of £5,000 at the end of a 5-year life. The rate of interest implicit in the lease is 5 per cent semi-annually.

(3)   A 'Finn McCool' was bought on 1 September 2004 from Causeway Ltd. The price of £120,000 is payable in ten equal quarterly instalments starting 1 September 2004.

A 'Finn McCool' is expected to have negligible value at the end of its 12-year life.

Other than the above items no amounts were unpaid at 30 November 2004. Hinch Ltd uses a straight-line basis for depreciation from the date of purchase.

Suggested solution – Hinch Ltd

Profit on ordinary activities before taxation

Profit on ordinary activities before taxation is after charging the following:

	£
Depreciation (£4,000 + £2,500)	6,500
Hire of plant and machinery	18,000
Finance charges	1,625

Tangible fixed assets

	Plant and machinery £
Cost	
Balance at 1.12.03	xxx
Additions	160,000
Disposals	(xxx)
Balance at 30.11.04	xxx
Accumulated depreciation	
Balance at 1.12.03	xxx
Charge for the year	6,500
Disposals	(xxx)
Balance at 30.11.04	xxx
Net book value at 30.11.04	xxx

Included within plant and machinery are assets held under finance leases £36,000.

Creditors: amounts falling due within 1 year

	£
Obligations under finance lease	13,669
Other loans	48,000

Creditors: amounts falling due after 1 year

	£
Obligations under finance lease	20,456
Other loans	60,000

Obligations under finance leases

	£
Amounts falling due:	
within one year (2 × £7,500)	15,000
between two and five years (3 × £7,500)	22,500
	37,500
Finance charges in suspense	
(5,000 − 1,625)	3,375
	34,125

Commitments under operating leases

Annual commitments under operating leases terminable at 3 months' notice	£18,000

Workings

Imperial Distiller

The agreement is terminable at 3 months' notice by either party and would therefore probably constitute an operating lease since the risks and rewards of ownership still rest with the lessor. The payments during the year (12 × £1,500 = £18,000) should be written off through the profit and loss account.

Potillier

This could constitute a finance lease as it would appear that the present value of the minimum lease payments of £45,000 would at least cover the fair value of the machine costing £40,000.

In addition the contract is non-cancellable and the lessee has responsibility for maintenance, indicating that the risks have passed to the lessee.

	£
Finance lease rentals 6 × £7,500	45,000
Cash price 1.6.04	40,000
Finance charge	5,000

	Opening balance £	Paid £	Liability £	Finance charge (5%) £	Closing balance £
30.11.04	40,000	7,500	32,500	1,625	34,125
31.05.05	34,125	7,500	26,625	1,331	27,956
30.11.05	27,956	7,500	20,456	1,023	21,479
31.05.06	21,479	7,500	13,979	698	14,677
30.11.06	14,677	7,500	7,177	323	7,500
1.12.07	7,500	7,500			

At 30.11.04 the balance sheet liability will be:

	£
Current: £7,500 × 2 = £15,000 − £1,331 =	13,669
Long-term: £7,500 × 3 = £22,500 − £2,044 =	20,456

The profit and loss account charges will be:

	£
Finance charge	1,625
Depreciation (£40,000 ÷ 5 yr × 1/2 yr)	4,000

Note: We must assume that the secondary period for the lease exceeds 2 years and therefore the useful life is less than the lease term for the Potillier. The residual value of £5,000 has been ignored in calculating the depreciation charge.

Finn McCool

This asset was purchased on 1 September 2004 and the quarterly instalments merely indicate a hire purchase agreement. The asset must be capitalised at £120,000 and the liability recorded at the same price, assuming that the loan is interest-free.

The liability will be reduced by the instalments paid over the ten quarters.

	£
Total payments due	120,000
Paid 1.9.04	12,000
Due at 30.11.04	108,000

Split between current liabilities (4 × £12,000 = £48,000) and long-term liabilities (£60,000). Depreciation £120,000 ÷ 12 yr × 1/4 yr = £2,500.

The third example takes SSAP 21 from a lessor's point of view and requires the lessor to spread its finance lease income over the net cash investment in the lease:

Example – Lessor Plc

Lessor plc leases plant (cost £50,000) to Lessee Ltd for 4 years from 1 January 2003 at a rental of £8,000 per half-year, payable in advance. Corporation tax is 35 per cent, and capital allowances on the plant are 25 per cent per annum, reducing balance basis. The rate of return (post-tax) on the lessor's net cash investment is 5.4 per cent per half year. The plant is assumed to have no residual value at the end of the lease term. Corporation tax is payable 12 months after the year end (31 December).

Suggested Solution – Lessor Plc

Financial statements

Profit and loss account (extracts) for years ended 31 December

	2003 £	2004 £	2005 £
Rental income	16,000	16,000	16,000
Capital repaid (bal. figure)	9,498	11,508	13,529
Profit before tax (W2)	6,502	4,492	2,471
Taxation (bal. figure)	2,276	1,572	865
Net profit (W1 & 2)	4,226	2,920	1,606

Balance sheet (extracts) as at 31 December

Assets	2003 £	2004 £	2005 £
Net investment in finance lease	40,502	28,994	15,465
Deferred taxation (W3)	–	–	1,970

Note: £50,000 – £9,498 = £40,502 – £11,508 = £28,994, £28,994 – £13,529 = £15,465

Liabilities	2003 £	2004 £	2005 £
Current tax (W1)	1,225	2,319	3,139
Deferred tax (W3)	1,051	304	–

Periodic rate of return on average net investment

	2003 £	2004 £	2005 £
Profits before taxation	6,502	4,492	2,471
Average net cash investment			
2000 (42,000 + 36,268 ÷ 2)	39,134		
2001 (30,226 + 23,858 ÷ 2)		27,042	
2002 (18,371 + 11,363 ÷ 2)			14,867
Percentage return	16.6%	16.6%	16.6%

Workings

(1) Calculation of rate of return

Period	Net cash investment	Rental received	Tax effect	Average net cash inv.	Rate of return (5.4%)	Closing balance
	£	£	£	£	£	£
1	50,000	(8,000)		42,000	2,268	44,268
2	44,268	(8,000)		36,268	1,958	38,226
3	38,226	(8,000)		30,226	1,632	31,858
4	31,858	(8,000)		23,858	1,288	25,146
5	25,146	(8,000)	1,225	18,371	992	19,363
6	19,363	(8,000)		11,363	614	11,977
7	11,977	(8,000)	2,319	6,296	340	6,636
8	6,636	(8,000)				

Tax	Rentals	Capital allowances (25%)	Taxable profits	Corp'n tax (35%)
	£	£	£	£
2003	16,000	12,500	3,500	1,225
2004	16,000	9,375	6,625	2,319
2005	16,000	7,031	8,969	3,139
2006	16,000	5,273	10,727	3,754

(2) Calculation of annual profit

		Net		Gross
2003	£2,268 + £1,958 =	£4,226	× 100/65 =	£6,502
2004	£1,632 + £1,288 =	£2,920	× 100/65 =	£4,492
2005	£992 + £614 =	£1,606	× 100/65 =	£2,471

(3) Calculation of deferred taxation

	2003	2004	2005
	£	£	£
Tax charge per profit and loss	2,276	1,572	865
Corporation tax	1,225	2,319	3,139
Transfer to/(from) deferred tax	1,051	(747)	(2,274)

The fourth example is a more complicated lessor illustration requiring disclosure of the main extracts in the lessor's profit and loss account and balance sheets to be provided. The income is also spread using the net cash investment method:

Example – Dungiven Clothes Plc

Dungiven Clothes plc manufactures a machine that prints on sports shirts at a cost of £126,000. It either sells the machine for £160,748 cash or leases the machine on a 3-year lease.

Lease with Limavady Shirts Plc

On 1 January 2004 Dungiven Clothes plc entered into a 3-year non-cancellable lease with Limavady Shirts plc on the following terms:

(1) Lease rentals were £56,000 payable annually in advance.
(2) Initial direct costs of £8,400 incurred in commission and legal fees were borne by Dungiven Clothes plc and charged to the profit and loss account on a systematic basis.
(3) There was a guaranteed residual value of £28,000.
(4) The interest rate implicit in the lease with Limavady Shirts plc was 18 per cent.

Transaction with Strabane Sales Ltd

On 1 January 2004 Dungiven Clothes plc entered into an arrangement with Strabane Sales Ltd. Strabane Sales Ltd had purchased a machine from Dungiven Clothes plc but, having run into cash-flow problems, the company arranged a sale and leaseback of the machine to Dungiven Clothes plc. The arrangement was that Strabane Sales Ltd sold the machine to Dungiven Clothes plc for £124,575 and immediately leased it back for 4-years at a rental of £37,500 payable yearly in advance. At the time of the sale the book value of the machine was £75,000 which was arrived at after the provision of depreciation on the company's normal straight-line basis. It was agreed that the machine should revert to Dungiven Clothes plc at the end of the 4-year period when its scrap value was estimated to be nil. The lease is non-cancellable and Dungiven Clothes plc are reasonably confident that the lease payments will be met. The interest rate implicit in the lease with Strabane Sales was 14 per cent. Tax is ignored and therefore the net cash investment in the lease is equivalent to the net investment.

Suggested solution – Dungiven Clothes Plc

Limavady Shirts Plc

Entries in the profit and loss account of Dungiven Clothes Plc

Profit and loss account for the year ended 31 December 2004

	£
Sales	160,748
Less cost of sales	126,000
Gross profit	34,748
Interest receivable under finance lease	18,855
Lease expenses (1/3 × £8,400)	2,800

(ii)   Entries in the balance sheet of Dungiven Clothes plc

Balance sheet as at 31 December	2005 £	2004 £
Current assets		
Amount receivable under finance lease	51,772	43,831
Prepayments	2,800	5,600
Non-current assets		
Amount receivable under finance lease	28,000	79,772

Workings

	£	£
Gross investment in lease		
Rentals 3 years @ £56,000 pa	168,000	
Guaranteed residual value	28,000	
		196,000
Net investment in lease		
Minimum lease payments (present value)		
£56,000 × (1.00 + 0.848 + 0.718)	143,696	
£28,000 × 0.609	17,052	
		160,748
Total finance income		35,252

Allocation of total finance income

Year	Opening net investment £	Lease payments £	Net investment outstanding £	Interest income 18% £	Reduction in net investment £	Closing net investment £
2004	160,748	56,000	104,748	18,855	37,145	123,603
2005	123,603	56,000	67,603	12,169	43,831	79,772
2006	79,772	56,000	23,772	4,228	51,772	28,000

Strabane Sales Ltd

			£	£
(1)	Dr	Bank	124,575	
	Cr	Plant and machinery		75,000
		Deferred income		49,575

Being sale of machine back to leasing company at a price of £124,575.

(2)   Dr   Paid under finance lease   124,575
      Cr   Finance lease obligation   124,575
      Being recording of loan received from the leasing company on leaseback of machine.

(3)   Dr   Finance lease obligation   37,500
      Cr   Bank   37,500
      Being annual rental of £37,500 payable annually in advance.

(4)   Dr   Finance lease interest   12,191
      Cr   Finance lease obligation   12,191
      Being the annual interest on the capital amount outstanding of (£124,575 − £37,500) × 14%.

(5)   Dr   Depreciation – profit and loss   31,144
      Cr   Accumulated depreciation   31,144
      Being the annual depreciation charge £124,575 ÷ 4 years on a straight-line basis.

(6)   Dr   Deferred income   12,394
      Cr   Profit on sale and leaseback   12,394
      Being overall profit on sale and leaseback of machine spread evenly over the leaseback period of 4 years.

Workings

	£
Sales price to Strabane Sales Ltd	124,575
Net book value at date of sale	75,000
Capital gain	49,575

The lease entered into with Dungiven Clothes plc is a finance lease. Therefore, in accordance with SSAP 21, para. 49, the profit on sale should be recorded and spread over the shorter of the life of the asset or the lease term, to provide an annual gain of £12,394. Depreciation is based on the same scenario and is also spread over 4 years in this case.

Application in published accounts

Vanco plc provides a good accounting policy note on its finance lease agreements. It has changed its policy from straight line to a sum of the digits approach and gives a detailed explanation of why the latter method was regarded as most appropriate. The notes to the balance sheet are also provided showing the breakdown of liabilities to be repaid in future years, broken down between 2 and 5 years and over 5 years. An illustration of the operating lease disclosures required by SSAP 21 is also provided in a separate note:

Vanco Plc   Year Ended 31 January 2003   Provision of Network Facilities

Vanco changed its policy, in January 2002, in relation to finance lease interest. Finance charges are allocated now to the profit and loss account on the sum of digits basis whereas in the past they were expensed on a straight-line basis. The company disclosed that the change had been made to ensure full compliance with SSAP 21. SSAP 21 states that the total finance charge under a finance lease should be allocated to accounting periods during the lease term so as to produce a constant periodic rate of charge on the remaining balance of the obligation for each accounting period, or a reasonable approximation thereto (para. 35). The guidance notes state that there are three ways of achieving this: actuarial method; sum of digits method; and straight-line method, with the actuarial method giving the most accurate result (para. 20). The sum of digits method is regarded as an acceptable approximation to the actuarial method provided the lease term is not very long and interest rates are not very high (para. 28). Therefore it depends on the leases entered into whether the sum of digits method ensures full compliance with SSAP 21.

Accounting Policies (Extract)

Leased assets

Fixed assets held under finance leases or hire purchase agreements are capitalised and depreciated over their expected useful lives. Finance charges are allocated to the profit and loss account on a sum of the digits basis.

Notes to the accounts (Extract ignoring company balances)

21. Creditors: Amounts falling due after more than 1 year

	2003 Group £	2002 Group £
Due in more than 1 year but not more than 2 years		
Bank loans	950,000	504,722
Other loans	308,206	117,520
Obligations under finance leases and hire purchase agreements	2,905,682	1,800,870
	4,163,888	2,423,112

Due in more than 2 years but not more than 5 years

Bank loans	3,100,000	1,032,767
Other loans	410,222	90,114
Obligations under finance leases and hire purchase agreements	2,118,356	1,470,802
	5,628,578	2,593,683
Total due within 1 to 5 years	9,792,466	5,016,795

30. Operating lease commitments

At 31 January 2003, the Group was committed to making the following payments during the next year in respect of operating leases:

	2003		2002	
	Land and buildings £	Other £	Land and buildings £	Other £
Leases which expire:				
Within 1 year	–	120,154	8,587	66,413
Within 2 to 5 years	945,766	584,592	350,667	405,564
After 5 years	113,263	–	299,818	–
	1,059,029	704,746	659,072	471,977

The company had no operating lease commitments at 31 January 2003 (2002: £nil)

3.3 FRS 10 *Goodwill and Intangible Assets* (December 1997)

Background

The subject of goodwill has been one of the most controversial topics in financial reporting. The accounting profession has been split down the middle in the United Kingdom between those who argue that goodwill is a once-off acquisition cost and should therefore be written off immediately to reserves and those that would argue that it is an asset that should be capitalised and subsequently amortised through the profit and loss account. There are also several variants of each approach.

Even the ASB itself was split 50:50 on the issue when it released a discussion paper, in December 1993, on the subject. Respondents to that paper came out with a small majority in favour of the asset-based approach and as a result a working paper was published in June 1995 as a basis for discussion at a public hearing held in London in September of that year. Although not conclusive the ASB felt that sufficient due process had occurred to enable it to drive forward with the asset approach. Internationally also the IASC (now the IASB) and the FASB in the USA have only accepted that accounting treatment. FRED 12 and subsequently FRS 10 have therefore been drafted to ensure the enforcement of capitalisation of goodwill as an asset on the balance sheet.

Accounting treatment – initial recognition

Goodwill

Not a normal asset but a *bridge*, between the cost of an investment in another entity and the value of the net assets acquired. It is part of a larger asset, i.e. the total investment, for which management should remain accountable.

Purchased goodwill – should be capitalised as an asset.

Internal goodwill – should *not* be recognised as no transaction has occurred.

Intangible assets

Must have control over the future economic benefits via either custody or legal rights – there is a wide spectrum from those which are clearly separable, e.g. patents, to those that are closely aligned with goodwill, e.g. brands.

Accounting, however, should be aligned between the two types of asset.

Purchased intangible assets – should be capitalised as an asset.

Internally generated intangible assets – only capitalised, provided that there is a readily ascertainable market for those assets.

Accounting treatment – subsequent amortisation

Goodwill

Should be systematically amortised over the asset's useful economic life, on a straight-line basis.

There is a rebuttable presumption that the maximum life of goodwill will be 20 years. If this is rebutted, goodwill must be expected, however, to be capable of being continually measured.

Intangible assets

Should be treated identically to goodwill.

Accounting treatment – impairment

All fixed assets must be carried on the balance sheet at the lower of their cost and recoverable value. In order to verify that this is the case an impairment review needs to be carried out.

If the amortisation period is less than 20 years then the review need only take place at the end of the first full financial year post recognition. Subsequently this will only take place if events clearly have occurred to suggest that the carrying value may not be recoverable in full.

If the amortisation period exceeds 20 years or is argued to be infinite, then the impairment review is required annually.

The process should be performed in accordance with FRS 11. In year 1 the review may be performed in two stages:

(a)   identify the initial impairment by comparing post-acquisition performance with pre-acquisition forecasts; and

(b)   perform a full review via FRS 11 only if the initial review indicates that the carrying value may not be recoverable.

Accounting treatment – restoration of past losses and revaluations

Restoration. Only permitted if the original factor causing the loss has been reversed. Any reversal due to the internal generation of goodwill and not the cause of the impairment should not be reinstated.

Revaluation. Goodwill may never be revalued but intangible assets can be, provided that all assets of the same class are revalued and should ensure that the values are close to market value.

Negative goodwill

Need to test the fair value of assets first to ensure that the assets are not overstated. Negative goodwill should be recorded immediately below positive goodwill, on the face of the balance sheet, followed by the subtitle of the net amount. It should be credited to profit and loss as the non-monetary assets acquired are sold or depreciated.

Disclosures

The main disclosures are:

(i)   The bases of valuation of the intangible assets;
(ii)   If the 20-year life for goodwill is rebutted, the grounds should be disclosed for the rebuttal;
(iii) The movement in the intangible fixed asset schedule;
(iv) The method of amortisation and the reasons for method adopted, if not straight-line;
(v)   Period over which the negative goodwill is being credited to profit and loss.

Transitional

Normally, if a company has previously written off goodwill to reserves, this would represent a change in accounting policy and would be applicable to approximately 95 per cent of all previous acquisitions. However, FRS 10 forgives reporting entities for 'their sins of the past' and only requires capitalisation of all future acquisitions when the standard is effective from 23 December 1998 and thereafter. However, it is permissible to reinstate goodwill of previous acquisitions, if desired, but this is highly unlikely to happen in most cases although Reuters plc did implement that policy for their December 1997 financial statements.

If the negative goodwill reserve approach has been adopted in the past this should now be netted off against other reserves to avoid the confusion of having two goodwill figures in two different places on the balance sheet.

Future changes

The FASB in the USA has published FAS 141, which has effectively banned the use of merger accounting in the USA, and FAS 142, which requires reporting entities to include goodwill as a permanent asset on the balance sheet, albeit with annual impairment reviews for sudden impairments in their values. The IASB has now also committed itself to similar changes and have issued ED 3 *Business Combinations* (now published as IFRS 3) that will require an adjustment to FRS 10 over the next few years along those lines.

The example below illustrates the calculation of goodwill under FRS 10 and how that asset is subsequently amortised over its estimated useful life. The linkages with FRS 11 *Impairment of Intangible Assets and Goodwill*, where the life exceeds 20 years, are also covered:

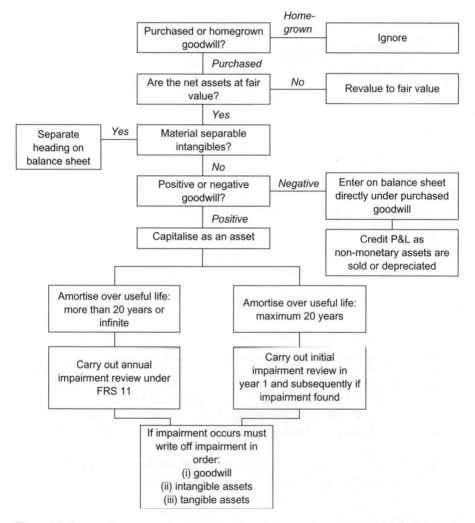

Figure 3.3 Summary.

Example – Inver Plc

Inver plc has a number of subsidiaries. The accounting date of Inver plc and all its subsidiaries is 30 April. On 1 May 2003, Inver plc purchased 80 per cent of the issued equity shares of Clare Ltd. This purchase made Clare Ltd a subsidiary of Inver plc from 1 May 2003. Inver plc made a cash payment of £31 million for the shares in Clare Ltd. On 1 May 2003, the net assets which were included in the balance sheet of Clare Ltd had a fair value to Inver plc of £30 million. Clare Ltd sells a well-known branded product and has taken steps to protect itself legally against unauthorised use of the brand name. A reliable estimate of the value of this brand to the Inver Group is £3 million. It is further considered that the value of the brand can be maintained or even increased for the foreseeable future. The value of the brand is not included in the balance sheet of Clare Ltd.

For the purposes of preparing the consolidated financial statements, the directors of Inver plc wish to ensure that the charge to the profit and loss account for the amortisation of intangible fixed assets is kept to a minimum. They estimate that the useful economic life of the purchased goodwill (or premium on acquisition) of Clare Ltd is 40 years.

Suggested solution – Inver Plc

Charge for amortisation of goodwill for the year ended 30 April 2004

Calculation of the goodwill acquired on the acquisition of Clare Ltd at 1 May 2003

	£'000	£'000
Fair value of the purchase consideration		31,000
Fair value of the net assets acquired		
Net assets included at balance sheet at fair value	30,000	
Brand name acquired not included in net assets	3,000	
	33,000	
Group share (80%)		26,400
Purchased goodwill		4,600

Calculation of annual amortisation charge for goodwill on the acquisition of Clare Ltd

Useful economic life of goodwill	40 years
Amortisation (straight-line approach)	£4.6m ÷ 40 years = £115,000 per annum

However, as the life exceeds the normal maximum life of 20 years permitted by FRS 10 the company must undergo an annual impairment review to ensure that the asset has not been impaired. This will be calculated in accordance with the rules in FRS 11 *Impairment of Fixed Assets and Goodwill*.

In addition the purchased brand name of £3m will also have to be amortised over its economic useful life. This should also not normally exceed 20 years. If the life does exceed 20 years then the annual impairment review process must take place, under FRS 11.

The second example is a more complicated version of the first, requiring a knowledge of FRS 7 *Fair Values in Acquisition Accounting* in the calculation of goodwill (see Chapter 9) as well as linking that standard with the requirements of FRS 10 to separate out intangibles with a market value and the need to subsequently amortise both over their estimated expected future useful lives.

Example – Kilkeel Plc

Kilkeel plc acquired 80 per cent of the ordinary share capital of Rostrevor plc on 31 May 2004. The balance sheet of Rostrevor plc at 31 May 2004 was:

Rostrevor Plc – balance sheet at 31 May 2004

	£'000
Fixed assets	
Intangible assets	6,020
Tangible assets	38,300
	44,320
Current assets	
Stocks	21,600
Debtors	23,200
Cash	8,800
	53,600
Creditors: amounts falling due within 1 year	24,000
Net current assets	29,600
Total assets less current liabilities	73,920
Creditors: amounts falling due after more than 1 year	12,100
Provision for liabilities and charges	886
Accruals and deferred income	
Deferred government grants	2,700
	58,234

Capital reserves	
Called-up share capital (Ordinary shares of £1)	10,000
Share premium account	5,570
Profit and loss account	42,664
	58,234

Additional information relating to the above balance sheet:

(i)   The intangible assets of Rostrevor plc were brand names currently utilised by the company. The directors felt that they were worth £7 million but there was no readily ascertainable market value at the balance sheet date, nor any information to verify the directors' estimated value.

(ii) The provisional market value of the land and buildings was £20 million at 31 May 2004. This valuation had again been determined by the directors. A valuer's report received on 30 November 2004 stated the market value of land and buildings to be £23 million as at 31 May 2004. The depreciated replacement cost of the remainder of the tangible fixed assets was £18 million at 31 May 2004, net of government grants.

(iii) The replacement cost of stocks was estimated at £25 million and its net realisable value was deemed to be £20 million. Debtors and creditors due within 1 year are stated at the amounts expected to be received and paid.

(iv) Creditors amounts falling due after more than 1 year was a long-term loan with a bank. The initial loan on 1 June 2003 was £11 million at a fixed interest rate of 10 per cent per annum. The total amount of the interest is to be paid at the end of the loan period on 31 May 2007. The current bank lending rate is 7 per cent per annum.

(v)   The provision for liabilities and charges relates to costs of reorganisation of Rostrevor plc. This provision had been set up by the directors of Rostrevor plc prior to the offer by Kilkeel plc and the reorganisation would have taken place even if Kilkeel plc had not purchased the shares of Rostrevor plc. Additionally, Kilkeel plc wishes to set up a provision for future losses of £10 million which it feels will be incurred by rationalising the group.

(vi) The offer made to all of the shareholders of Rostrevor plc was 2.5 £1 ordinary shares of Kilkeel plc at the market price of £2.25 per share plus £1 cash, per Rostrevor plc ordinary share.

(vii) Goodwill is to be dealt with in accordance with FRS 10. The estimated useful economic life is deemed to be 10 years. The directors of Rostrevor plc informed Kilkeel plc that as at 31 May 2004, the brand names were worthless as the products to which they related had recently been withdrawn from sale because they were deemed to be a health hazard.

(viii) A full year's charge for amortisation of goodwill is included in the group profit and loss account of Kilkeel plc in the year of purchase.

Suggested solution – Kilkeel Plc

Calculation of amortisation of goodwill on the acquisition of Rostrevor plc by Kilkeel plc for the years ended 31 May 2005 and 2007

Fair values of net assets acquired at 31 May 2004 by Kilkeel plc

	£'000	£'000
Fixed assets		
Intangible (no readily ascertainable market values – note i)		Nil
Tangible		
Land and buildings (note ii)		20,000
Other (note ii)		18,000
		38,000
Current assets		
Stocks (note iii)	20,000	
Debtors (note iii)	23,200	
Cash (face value)	8,800	
	52,000	
Creditors: amounts falling due within one year (note iii)	24,000	
Net current assets		28,000
		66,000
Creditors: amounts falling due after more than one year (note iv)		
(£11m + 1 year's interest £1.1 = £12.1m × 10% for 4 years		(13,147)
= £16,105,100 / 1.07^3 = £13,146,559)		
Provisions for liabilities and charges (note v)		(886)
		51,967 × 80% 41,574
Purchase consideration		
Shares (note vi) 10m shares × 2.5/1 = 25m × £2.25 per share		56,250
Cash (note vi) 10m shares × £1 each		10,000
		66,250 × 80% 53,000
Goodwill		11,426

Amortisation year ended 31 May 2005 11,426 ÷ 10 years = £1,143 per annum
Amortisation year ended 31 May 2006

Net book value 2005 (11,426 − 1,143)	10,283
Fair value adjustment (3,000 × 80% × 9 years/10 years)	(2,160)
Revised goodwill	8,123
Amortisation (9 years)	914

FRS 7 *Fair Values in Acquisition Accounting* permits adjustments to fair values up to a full financial year following an acquisition. The valuation of land and buildings of

£23m should be taken into account in the fair value exercise for 2004, and not the original value of £20m.

Where an intangible asset cannot be measured reliably on acquisition, its value should be subsumed within purchased goodwill.

Stocks should be stated at current replacement cost but the fair value should not exceed the recoverable amount which is its net realisable value of £20m.

Provisions for future losses are expressly forbidden by FRS 7 but the reorganisation provision was set up prior to the acquisition so it can be included as part of the fair value exercise.

The deferred government grants should be ignored as the fair value of the assets to which they relate have already been included in the fair value exercise.

Financial Reporting Review Panel

Artisan Plc (February 2001)

The main matter at issue was the company's accounting treatment of purchased goodwill under FRS 10 that requires positive purchased goodwill to be capitalised and classified as an asset on the balance sheet. Where it is regarded as having a limited useful economic life, it should be amortised on a systematic basis over that life.

The company's stated accounting policy in respect of goodwill was in compliance with these requirements. However, of the £10.4 million goodwill arising on businesses acquired during the year, £7.4 million was written off to the company's merger reserve. This treatment was not consistent with the company's stated accounting policy and is contrary to the provisions of FRS 10.

Liberty International Plc (February 2002)

The single matter at issue was the company's accounting treatment of its acquisition, in November 2000, of the minority interest of shares in a 75% owned subsidiary, Capital Shopping Centres Plc ('CSC'), a property company specialising in the ownership, management and development of prime regional shopping centres. The Panel accepted the accounting treatment adopted by the company but only on the basis that there were 'special circumstances' attaching to the acquisition which justified the invocation of the 'true and fair' override (Section 227 (6) of the Companies Act 1985) on which it needed to rely.

In the December 2001 financial statements, the directors made certain restatements of the 31 December 2000 accounts and gave certain additional disclosures in response to the Panel's view. They (a) presented a revised fair value table, in which property assets were brought in at a fair value which was £193.2 million higher than previously reported; (b) as a consequence, recognised negative goodwill of £193.2 million which did not arise in the figures previously reported, and then credited it to reserves; and (c) restated certain notes to the accounts to include the disclosures required when the true and fair override is invoked.

The restatement involved no change to (a) the profit and loss account; (b) the balance sheet (save for the reclassification of group reserves); (c) distributable profits; (d) earnings or net assets per share; or (e) cash flows.

The question was raised whether the acquisition of a property investment company could give rise to any goodwill as it is common practice to treat such acquisitions as 'asset deals'. It was argued that the acquisition of CSC was, in substance, the purchase of a portfolio of property assets rather than a trading business to which goodwill could attach. The Panel held however that para. 51 was applicable to the transaction.

Secondly, application of FRS 2, para. 51, appeared to give rise to a substantial negative goodwill balance of £193.2 million, the directors having satisfied themselves that they had included all identifiable net assets in accordance with FRSs 7 and 10. FRS 10 attributes negative goodwill either to a bargain purchase or to future costs or losses that do not represent identifiable liabilities at the balance sheet date.

Thirdly, under FRS 10, negative goodwill is to be recognised in the profit and loss account in the periods in which the non-monetary assets are recovered, whether through depreciation or sale. As investment properties are exempt from the need to depreciate, and the directors had no intention of selling the underlying properties which are not easily replaceable, they envisaged negative goodwill being retained indefinitely on the balance sheet.

Under SSAP 19, investment properties are carried at their market value. Hence, the 'book value' of the portion of the investment property assets acquired by the company in September 2000, £807.1 million, approximately represented the market value of the properties at that date, an acceptable basis for the determination of fair value of tangible assets. The Panel queried the substance of the £192.3 million 'fair value' credit adjustment against the investment properties, which had the effect of bringing the fair value of the net assets acquired into equilibrium with the net value of the consideration. At 31 December 2000, the value of the investment properties was brought back up to market value through the usual annual revaluation process, required by SSAP 19, which included a reversal of the £193.2 million downwards adjustment.

The true and fair view override

Section 227(6) of the Companies Act 1985 requires directors to depart from the provisions of the Act, including applicable accounting standards, where compliance with any of those provisions would be inconsistent with the requirement to give a true and fair view. This is expected to happen only rarely and must be supported by 'special circumstances'.

The Panel agreed that the balance described as negative goodwill reflects a fundamental difference in the valuation bases of the consideration and the identifiable net assets acquired, including the fact that certain contingent liabilities are reflected in the share price but may not be recognised in the fair value process. It is not appropriate to carry this balance on the balance sheet indefinitely.

The Panel accepted that a true and fair view would be shown in the circumstances of this acquisition if the negative goodwill arising on consolidation were transferred to reserves. This treatment reflects the unrealised nature of the gain, is not inconsistent with the requirements of the Companies Act 1985 and was the accounting policy adopted by the company before FRS 10 introduced a different treatment.

Equator Group Plc (July 2002)

The Financial Reporting Review Panel has had under consideration the report and accounts of Equator Group plc for the year ended 31 December 1999. The matter at issue was the company's accounting for its purchase, in June 1999, of Equator Films Limited and the subsequent accounting for the principal assets acquired. Film libraries with a book value of £1,090,000 were revalued individually, at open market value at the date of acquisition to a total of £13,158,000. This gave rise to negative goodwill of £1,830,000.

Under the company's accounting policy, the film libraries were not to be amortised but impairment reviews were to be carried out at least annually and any permanent decreases in value were to be charged to the profit and loss account.

FRS 10 *Goodwill and Intangible Assets* requires intangible assets acquired as part of the acquisition of a business to be capitalised separately from goodwill if their value can be measured reliably on initial recognition. They should initially be recorded at fair value, subject to the constraint that, unless the assets have readily ascertainable market values, the fair values should be limited to amounts that do not create or increase negative goodwill arising on the acquisition.

In the Panel's view, although the rights attaching to each film were similar, the films themselves were unique and could not belong to a homogeneous population of assets that was equivalent in all respects. It was also of the view that the market in which film libraries are bought and sold is not an 'active market'. As the films acquired with the business of Equator Films Limited failed to meet either of the necessary tests the Panel concluded that they did not have a readily ascertainable market value, as defined in the standard. Hence, the revaluation of the films to fair value at the date of purchase of the business should have been limited to an amount that did not give rise to negative goodwill.

FRS 10 also includes a rebuttable presumption that the useful economic lives of purchased intangible assets are limited to periods of 20 years or less. An indefinite life can be assigned only where the assets are capable of continued measurement and their durability can be demonstrated and can justify a longer period. In its financial statements for the year ended 31 December 2000, the company changed its accounting policy and commenced amortisation of film libraries over a 20-year period to their residual values. Having regard to the factors on which durability depends the Panel welcomed the directors' decision to amortise the film libraries.

Under FRS 10, in amortising an intangible asset, a residual value can be assigned only if it can be measured reliably. This is likely only when there is a legal or contractual right to receive a certain sum at the end of the asset's period of use or where there is a readily ascertainable market. There is no legal right to receive an amount at the end of a film's useful life. Nor, for the reasons given above, was the Panel of the view that films have readily ascertainable market values. Therefore they should be amortised without regard to any estimate of residual value.

The directors accepted the Panel's views and in their preliminary announcement, they corrected both matters by way of prior year adjustment. The effect of this was a cumulative adjustment of £181,000.

Application in published accounts

When IFRS 3 is eventually incorporated as a national accounting standard there are likely to be a plethora of new intangible assets, rather than being included as part of goodwill.

These will include some wonderful new assets such as trade dress, secret recipes, production backlogs and customer lists! One company that has already started the process is British Airways plc, who have incorporated landing rights as an additional asset on the balance sheet this year. Details of its goodwill policy and intangible fixed assets schedule is also provided:

British Airways (31 March 2003)   Airline Operators

British Airways (BA) discloses that, in order to reflect an increase in purchases from other airlines, airport landing rights are classified now as intangible fixed assets under their own heading and amortised over a period not exceeding 20 years. This follows along the lines of FRS 10 *Goodwill and Intangible Assets*, which defines an intangible asset as a non-financial fixed asset which does not have physical substance but is identifiable and controlled by the entity through either custody or legal rights (para. 2). Previously, such costs were classified as tangible fixed assets and aggregated within property. Following this change, capitalised rights of £35 million have been reclassified as intangible fixed assets and are disclosed separately on the face of the balance sheet.

Accounting Policies (Extract)

Intangible fixed assets

a Goodwill
Prior to March 31, 1998, goodwill was set off against reserves on the acquisition of a business, including an equity interest in an associated undertaking. Goodwill will be released to the profit and loss account on disposal of the business to which it relates. From April 1, 1998, where the cost of acquisition exceeds the values attributed to such net assets, the resulting goodwill is capitalised and amortised over a period not exceeding 20 years.

b Landing rights
Landing rights acquired from other airlines are capitalised at cost and amortised over a period not exceeding 20 years.

The carrying values of goodwill and other intangible assets are reviewed for impairment at the end of the first full year following acquisition and in the other periods if events or changes in circumstances indicate the carrying value may not be recoverable.

Note 13 Intangible assets

£ million	Goodwill	Landing rights	Group total 2003	2002
Cost				
Balance at April 1	116	40	156	92
Additions		32	32	32
Other movements				(1)
Disposals	(2)		(2)	
Balance at March 31	114	72	186	156

Amortisation				
Balance at April 1	11	5	16	8
Charge for the year	6	2	8	8
Disposals	(2)		(2)	
Balance at March 31	15	7	22	16
Net book amounts				
March 31, 2003	99	65	164	
March 31, 2002	*105*	*35*	*140*	

Hampton Trust plc provide an example of a company which is continually reviewing the lives of its intangible assets and has decided to reduce goodwill from 20 to 10 years.

Hampton Trust Plc   Year Ended 31 March 2003   Property Investment

In its statement of accounting policies the company discloses that its previous policy was to amortise goodwill over a period of 20 years. Following a review of acquired development projects and the timing of likely profits, a decision has been made to amortise over a 10-year period, which results in the amortisation charge increasing by £400,000. This follows along the lines of FRS10 *Goodwill and Intangible Assets*, which states that the useful economic lives of goodwill should be reviewed at the end of each reporting period and revised if necessary. If the useful economic life is revised, the carrying value of the goodwill at the date of revision should be amortised over the revised remaining useful economic life (para. 33).

The final example covers the accounting treatment prior to the publication of FRS 10 and the ability to leave goodwill created before 1998 to be set off against opening reserves rather than being capitalised. It also covers the capitalisation of licences on the acquisition of a water supply contract in China and its amortisation over the life of the licence.

AWG Plc   Year Ended 31 March 2003   Water Supply and Sewerage

Accounting Policies (Extract)

c) Goodwill

On the acquisition of a subsidiary undertaking, fair values are attributed to the net identifiable assets or liabilities acquired. Goodwill represents the difference between the fair value of the purchase consideration and the fair value of the net assets acquired. Fair values are assessed in accordance with FRS 7 *Fair Values in Acquisition Accounting*. Goodwill arising on acquisitions prior to 31 March 1998 was set off directly against reserves and has not been reinstated on implementation of FRS 10 *Goodwill and Intangible Assets*. Positive goodwill arising on acquisitions since this date is capitalised in the financial statements as an intangible asset and amortised on a straight-line basis over its useful economic life. On disposal of a subsidiary any goodwill arising on acquisition that was previously written off to reserves, or that has not been amortised through the profit and loss account, is taken into account in determining the profit or loss on disposal.

Notes to the Financial Statements (Extract)

13 Intangible fixed assets

	Goodwill £m	Licences £m	Total £m
The group			
Cost			
At 1 April 2002	330.4	–	330.4
Exchange adjustments	(9.4)	–	(9.4)
Additions	–	14.1	14.1
Arising from acquisitions in the year (note 16)	15.1	–	15.1
Disposals	(0.2)	–	(0.2)
At 31 March 2003	335.9	14.1	350.0
Amortisation			
At 1 April 2002	73.3	–	73.3
Exchange adjustments	(0.7)	–	(0.7)
Charge for the year	13.8	0.5	14.3
Impairments (note 4)	4.4	–	4.4
At 31 March 2003	90.8	0.5	91.3
Net book value			
At 31 March 2003	245.1	13.6	258.7
At 31 March 2002	257.1	–	257.1

Intangible assets mainly comprise goodwill arising on acquisitions of subsidiaries and premiums paid to acquire unincorporated businesses. Goodwill is amortised over 20 years, being the directors' best estimate of its useful economic life.

A further £53.5 million of goodwill (2002: £57.0 million) arising on acquisitions prior to 31 March 1998 has been eliminated directly against reserves in prior years.

The intangible asset addition in the year of £14.1 million is a payment made to acquire the licence for the bulk supply of water to the Chinese city of Taizhou. The payment is being amortised over the 20-year period of the licence agreement.

There are no intangible assets in the company.

4

Asset valuation: accounting for stocks and work in progress

4.1 SSAP 9 *Stocks and Work in Progress* (May 1975, revised September 1988)

Background

Stocks and work in progress usually represent a material amount in most business's balance sheets. Any under- or over-valuations will have a considerable impact on the amount of profit reported in any one year.

The standard has been developed in such a way that it separates accounting for ordinary stocks from that of long-term work in progress.

Definitions

- *Stocks* comprise the following:
  - (i)   stocks purchased for resale;
  - (ii) consumable stores;
  - (iii) raw materials;
  - (iv) short-term work in progress; and
  - (v)   finished goods.
- *Long-term work in progress.* Represents a contract entered into for the design, manufacture or construction of a single substantial asset or the provision of a service where the time taken substantially to complete the contract is such that the contract activity falls into different accounting periods. It may well last longer than a year but this is not essential as long as a material amount is carried out during at least two accounting periods, e.g. a contract of 9 months' duration, 4 months in the first year and 5 months in the second year.

Accounting treatment – stocks

The underlying theory behind stocks is the accruals concept in that the cost of goods sold should be matched against the income derived from selling those goods. Stocks therefore should not be charged to profit and loss but held back on the balance sheet to be matched in the subsequent year against the revenue generated from selling those stocks.

Under SSAP 9, stocks should be recorded at the lower of their cost and net realisable value.

Essentially there are three key problems facing the accountant:

(i)   What is the cost of stock?
(ii) What happens if the stock becomes obsolete? and
(iii) What method of costing is permissible?

(i)   *What is the cost of stock?* The standard states that all expenditure which is necessary to bring the stocks to their present location and condition be incorporated as part of the cost of stocks. In practice this will incorporate the costs of purchase of raw materials consumed as well as the costs of conversion including payroll costs and related overheads in getting the stocks to that particular condition/location.

The costs of purchase comprise not just the purchase price of materials but indirect costs such as import duties, insurance and transport costs in getting the stocks to their present location less any trade discounts or subsidies received.

The costs of conversion should include any directly attributable labour costs and production overheads, and any other overheads which are necessary in bringing the product to its present location and condition. For example, in the long-term maturing of whisky, finance costs may be incorporated as being essential in ensuring that the product has matured to its final state.

Apart from the decision as to which overheads should be incorporated, a reporting entity must then decide on how much overhead to incorporate. This should be based on the firm's *normal level of activity*. Normal activity requires the accountant to examine the previous year's performance, current budgets and the maximum capacity of the plant and from that information decide on what is likely to be achieved in the forthcoming year.

Once the total overheads to be absorbed are known and the normal level of activity determined then an absorption rate can easily be computed and applied to the stock valuation process.

(ii) *What happens if the stock becomes obsolete?* If the stocks become obsolete or damaged then SSAP 9 insists that they be valued at the lower of cost and net realisable value. The latter is defined as the estimated proceeds from selling the stock less all further costs to completion and all marketing/selling costs which are directly related to the stocks.

(iii) *What method of costing is permissible?* SSAP 9 does not prescribe any particular method of costing to be adopted but it does insist that whatever method is adopted it should provide the fairest practicable approximation to cost. However, there are a number of methods that are expressly forbidden: last in first out (LIFO), base stock and replacement cost on the grounds either that they do not bear a reasonable relationship to actual costs or they are costs which have not yet occurred and therefore unacceptable under the historical cost model.

Methods such as 'standard cost' and 'selling price less estimated profit margin' are, however, perfectly acceptable, provided that they are reviewed frequently and are demonstrated to show a reasonable approximation to actual cost.

Accounting treatment – long-term work in progress

Long-term contracts by their nature cover more than one accounting period and they therefore should be assessed on a contract-by-contract basis by reflecting both turnover and related costs in the profit and loss account as the contract activity progresses. Turnover should be matched to its related costs under the accruals concept and should be recorded in the profit and loss account appropriately to the stage of completion the contract has reached, bearing in mind the industry in which the company operates.

Under the prudence concept, if the outcome of the contract is uncertain, then no profit should be recorded and it may be appropriate in the early stages to show turnover as equal to related costs. However, if a loss is expected then the full loss to the end of the contract must be provided and any loss in excess of work in progress recorded within the 'provisions for liabilities and charges' section of the balance sheet.

An example should help to clarify the appropriate accounting treatment:

Facts	£m	£m	£m
Total contract value	400	300	600
Progress payments received and receivable	180	220	500
Total costs to date	150	260	200
Total costs to complete	80	60	320
Value of work certified	200	280	250

Solution	£m	£m	£m
Profit and loss			
Turnover	200	280	200
Cost of sales	150	260	160
Provision for foreseeable loss		40	
Balance sheet			
Debtors (200 – 180)	20	60	
Provision for foreseeable losses		40	
Creditors (200 – 500)			300
Work in progress (200 – 160)			40

Disclosure

Stocks

- The accounting policy, if material.
- A subclassification into the main categories of stocks held, either on the face of the balance sheet or in the notes.

Long-term work in progress

- The accounting policy, if material.
- Amounts disclosed in the balance sheet:
  - –Turnover in excess of payments on account – debtors;
  - –Payments in excess of turnover and of the balance on long-term work in progress – creditors;

–Costs incurred less transfers to cost of sales – work in progress;

–Amount by which the provision for foreseeable losses exceeds any costs incurred – provisions for liabilities and charges.

FRED 28 *Inventories; Construction and Service Contracts* (May 2002)

In May 2002 the ASB published FRED 28 with the purpose of implementing two international standards in UK reporting in the spring of 2005. These are IAS 2 *Inventories* and IAS 11 *Construction and Service Contracts.*

The FRED is very similar to SSAP 9 except that it breaks it up into two separate accounting standards. It will bring in additional text to deal with contracts for services (included in IAS 11) and it will abolish LIFO as a legitimate method of stock valuation internationally. In addition, amounts received in advance from customers should be treated as a separate liability but no further analysis will be required and whatever balance remaining should be shown as a single asset or liability.

The introduction of these two IASs will therefore not materially change accounting for stocks/inventories or long-term construction contracts.

The following example provides an illustration of how ordinary stocks should be valued at the lower of their cost and net realisable value based on the normal level of activity generated by the company.

Example – Derg Ltd

The following information relates to Derg Ltd for its first year of trading to 31 December 2004:

COSTS	£'000	£'000
Wages and salaries		
Factory	90	
Administration	48	
Selling	28	
		166
Overheads		
Rent and rates	10	
Heat and power	6	
Depreciation		
Factory buildings and machinery	6	
Salesmen's motor vehicles	2	
Office building and furniture	2	
Sundry overheads		
Factory	12	
Administration	4	
Selling	6	
		48

Direct material cost of goods sold (80,000kg)   160
Closing stocks at cost – material value
Raw materials (20,000kg)   40
Work in progress (8,000kg, half completed)   16
Finished goods (16,000kg)   32

The factory occupies 75 per cent of the total area. Working a 40-hour week it was operational for 48 weeks of the year with a 4-week allowance for holidays. This will be the operating level. Turnover for the period was £331,000.

Suggested solution – Derg Ltd

Stock valuations

Raw materials stocks

20,000kg at £2 per kg   £40,000

Assume that this is lower than net realisable value (NRV). Even if NRV is lower, so long as the raw material can be incorporated into a finished product which will recover the £2 per kg, the cost is the correct value.

	£
Work in progress stocks	
Material 8,000 kg × £2 per kg	16,000
Conversion costs 8,000kg × 1/2	
= 4,000 kg × £1.21 per kg (W2)	4,840
	20,840

Assume that cost is lower than net realisable value.

Finished goods stocks	
Total cost of production (W2)	£3.21 per kg
Net realisable value (W3)	£3.69 per kg

This stock must be valued at the lower of cost and net realisable value, i.e. 16,000kg × £3.21 per kg = £51,360.

Notes to the balance sheet

Accounting policies (Extract)

Stocks and work in progress

Stocks have been valued in accordance with standard accounting practice at the lower of cost and net realisable value. Costs include all those factory and other overheads required to bring the stocks to their present condition and location.

Stocks

Stocks comprise the following:	£'000
Raw materials and consumables	40
Work in progress	21
Finished goods	51
	112

Trading and profit and loss account for the year ended 31 December 2004

	£'000	£'000	£'000
Sales			331
Cost of sales			
Material		160	
Labour (90 × 80%)		72	
Factory overhead (7.5 + 5.4 + 6 + 12) × 80%		24.7	
			256.7
Gross profit			74.3
Administration expenses			
Wages and salaries	48		
Rent and rates	2.5		
Heat and power	0.6		
Depreciation – office building & furniture	2		
Sundry overheads	4		
		57.1	
Selling expenses			
Wages and salaries	28		
Depreciation – salesmen's motor vehicles	2		
Sundry overheads	6		
		36	
			93.1
Net loss for the year			(18.8)

Workings

(1) Production

	kg
Sales	80,000
Closing stocks – finished goods	16,000
Closing stocks – work in progress	4,000
	100,000

(2) Factory cost of production

	£'000	£ per kg
Direct materials (£160,000 ÷ 80,000)		2.0
Wages and salaries – factory	90	
Rent and rates (75%)	7.5	
Heat and power (say 90%)	5.4	
Depreciation – factory	6	
Sundry overheads – factory	12	

	120.9	1.21
		3.21

(3) Determination of net realisable value

	£'000	£ per kg
Sales (80,000kg)	331	4.14
Less selling expenses (80,000kg)		
wages and salaries	28	(0.35)
depreciation – salesmen's motor vehicles	2	(0.03)
sundry overheads	6	(0.07)
	36	(0.45)
	295	3.69

The net realisable value of £3.69 per kg is greater than the cost of £3.21 per kg, therefore stocks of finished goods should be valued at the lower cost figure.

The second example covers the linkages between SSAP 13 and SSAP 9 and, in particular, covers the calculation of net realisable value.

Example – Donard Ltd

Donard Ltd is a chemical manufacturing company. The following items, in relation to the company's manufacturing processes, have been included in stocks and work in progress as on 31 July 2004:

(1) Stocks of Banoline have been valued at £426,000 based on the following amounts:

	£
Raw materials – cost	200,000
Other direct costs	144,000
Proportion of factory overheads	38,000
Proportion of selling office expenses	44,000
	426,000

Banoline is a steady selling product which shows reasonable profit margins.

(2) Laboratory costs to 31 July 2004 total £348,000 on research into a new tranquilliser called Calmdown. The research is being sponsored by a government agency on a one-year programme. The agency has agreed to reimburse the company on a cost plus 6 per cent basis at the end of the programme, up to a maximum contribution of £500,000.

(3)   Stocks of 1,300kg, held in bulk, of a chemical substance known as Apentone, are valued as follows:

	£
Raw materials – cost	340,000
Other direct costs	260,000
Proportion of factory overheads	47,000
Proportion of selling office expenses	59,000
	706,000

A competitor of Donard Ltd has recently introduced to the market a similar substance, which it is selling in handy 100g packs at £35 each. To meet the competition, Donard Ltd will also have to pack in 100g containers. The cost of packing the stock held will be £20,000, and additional advertising costs to clear the stock are estimated at £30,000.

(4)   Laboratory costs to 31 July 2004 of £365,000 on research into a new chemical substitute for Supositone, of which demand exceeds the world supply, include £100,000 for special items of plant required for the research programme.

Suggested solution – Donard Ltd

(1)   Banoline stocks

In accordance with the definition of cost described in SSAP 9 it would appear that the value of these stocks is overstated. It is incorrect to include a proportion of selling expenses as these have not been incurred in bringing the unsold stock to its present condition or location.

The inclusion of a proportion of factory overheads seems appropriate and therefore stocks would be valued fairly at £382,000.

Consideration of NRV is unlikely to change this value as the product is selling steadily and showing good profit margins.

The valuation of Banoline should be disclosed in the balance sheet under the heading of current assets. The accounting policy concerning the valuation of stocks should be included as part of the company's accounting policy section of the financial statements.

(2)   Research costs – Calmdown

Although £348,000 has been spent on research into a new tranquilliser, it is to be reimbursed by a government agency. Therefore it should be accounted for as work in progress and not as research and development expenditure.

As the work is performed over the course of the contract then a proportion could be recorded as turnover representing cost plus 6 per cent, and the cost up to that stage could be written off to cost of sales.

However, if any of the debt is likely to become irrecoverable then provision should be made for the probable loss in accordance with SSAP 9's concept of foreseeable losses.

(3)   Apentone stocks

As with the Banoline stocks, selling expenses should be excluded and thus the cost value of the stock is £706,000 − £59,000 = £647,000.

Under SSAP 9 it is a requirement to ensure that the NRV is not lower than cost. In the case of Apentone the NRV would be calculated as follows:

	£	£
Estimated sale proceeds		
(13,000 × 100g packs at £35 each)		455,000
Less further packing costs	20,000	
additional advertising costs	30,000	
proportion of selling office expenses	59,000	
		109,000
Net realisable value		346,000

Since the NRV of £346,000 is lower than the cost of £647,000, stocks should be valued at that reduced amount. The stocks should be recorded under current assets in the balance sheet and the accounting policy must be disclosed in the financial statements.

(4)   Laboratory costs

These are research costs which relate to the company's own products. As such they are not the subject matter of SSAP 9. This expenditure is governed by SSAP 13, and if the project is only in the embryo stages with no likelihood of future revenue then £265,000 should be written off immediately as an expense.

In addition any capital expenditure, albeit capitalised, should be depreciated and written off directly to the profit and loss account.

Under SSAP 13 research expenditure should be disclosed in the notes to the accounts unless the company comes under the small companies exemption from that standard. The net book value of the fixed assets should be included in the balance sheet under tangible fixed assets. The accounting policies for research expenditure should also be disclosed.

The third example covers the calculation of cost when there are two products being manufactured – one specialised and one for general stores.

Example – Par

A newly established electronics company, manufacturing components for a wide range of customers, has budgets for the first year indicating that approximately 60 per cent of turnover would be represented by one special component marketed under the name 'PAR'. The remainder would be represented by products manufactured specifically to customer specifications and design ('special orders').

Development expenditure relating to the 'PAR' product is £396,000. This amount is being amortised over 5 years on the straight-line basis. Technological changes now indicate that the product may be replaced in 3 years. The following information has been obtained about the company's first 3 months in business:

	£'000
(1) *Production costs*	
Purchases of raw materials	
Wiring	92
Other	348
Production labour costs	348
Fixed production overheads	128
Depreciation of equipment and factory buildings	102
(2) *Sales analysis*	
'PAR' brand sales	641
'Special order' sales	109

(3) Raw materials (other than wiring) purchased specifically for the 'special orders' amounted to £97,000. In addition, wiring material with an estimated cost of £10,000 was also used on these orders.

(4) 14,000 units of 'PAR' were manufactured in the 3-month period. The company expects to manufacture 100,000 units per annum, representing 70 per cent of full capacity.

(5) 50 per cent of the labour and overhead costs are estimated to be attributable to the 'PAR' product, and 50 per cent to the 'special orders'.

(6) At 31 March 2004, the following details of stocks were available:

Finished product – 'PAR'	3,000 units
Work in progress	nil
Raw materials – wiring (at cost)	£7,000
Raw materials – other (at cost)	
'PAR'	£42,000
'Special orders'	£5,000

(7) The managing director is concerned about the profitability of the first 3 months' trading and about the way in which closing stocks will be valued in preparing the financial statements for the 3-month period.

Possible solution – Par

The effect on reported profits of the valuation of stocks

	PAR		Other		Total	
	£'000	£'000	£'000	£'000	£'000	£'000
Sales (note 2)		641		109		750
Opening stocks:						
raw materials	Nil		Nil		Nil	
Purchases	333		107		440	
	333		107		440	
Less closing stocks:						
raw material (note 6)	49		5		54	
Cost of raw material						
Consumed	284		102		386	
Direct labour costs	174		174		348	
Production overheads:						
Fixed	64		64		128	
Depreciation	51		51		102	
Amortisation of development	33		–		33	
Cost of manufacture	606		391		997	
Closing stock:						
finished goods	(116)		–		(116)	
Cost of sales		490		391		881
Net profit/(loss)		151		(282)		(131)

Value of finished goods stock
At cost
3,000 units × £38.634 (working) = £115,902 (say £116,000)

Net realisable value
Average selling price of PAR = £641,000 ÷ 11,000 units sold = £58.27

Assuming that selling and distribution costs do not exceed £58.27 − £38.634 then production cost is lower than net realisable value.

Workings

Production costs relating to 14,000 units of PAR – 3 months ended 31 March 2004

	£'000	£'000	£'000
Wiring (purchases) (note 1)		92	
Less: special order transfer (note 3)	10		
closing stock (note 6)	7		
		17	
Cost of wiring consumed			75
Other raw material purchases (note 1)		348	
Less: special order transfer (note 3)	97		
closing stock (note 6)	42		
		139	
			209
Total raw materials consumed			284
Direct labour costs (£348,000 × 50%) (note 5)			174
			458

Production cost per unit of output £458,000 ÷ 14,000 = £32.714 per unit

Production overheads	£'000
Fixed production overheads £128,000 × 50% (note 5)	64
Depreciation of equipment and factory buildings	
£102,000 × 50% (note 5)	51
Amortisation of development expenditure	
£396,000 ÷ 3 years × 1/4 year	33
	148
Overhead recovery rate £148,000 ÷ 25,000 units	
(normal capacity 100,000 units per annum – note 4) =	£5.92 per unit
Total cost of production for stock valuation	
£32.714 + £5.92 per unit =	£38.634 per unit

The second half of SSAP 9 covers long-term contracts and the example below examines three separate contracts and outlines how revenues and costs are recorded as the contracts progress. In addition, where a loss is foreseen in the future before the contract is completed the accounting treatment of providing for all losses to the end of the contract is also included.

Example – Hilltown Ltd

Hilltown Ltd designs and builds luxury yachts to order. The company prepares its financial statements to 31 December each year and at 31 December 2004 had three contracts still to be completed. The following information is available:

	CONTRACTS		
	1	2	3
Start date	1 January 2004	1 November 2004	1 January 2004
Completion date	31 August 2005	31 December 2005	31 December 2005
	£'000	£'000	£'000
Contract price	10,800	8,400	18,200
Invoiced to date:			
Received	5,830	850	8,000
Outstanding	20	–	–
Costs incurred to date	5,350	980	8,960
Costs certified to date	5,290	800	7,750
Costs to compete	3,250	5,900	10,200

Additional information

(1)   Under the terms of each of the contracts, Hilltown Ltd is responsible for certain post-completion rectification work. This cost is not included in the 'costs

to complete' shown above, and is estimated by management at 2 per cent of the contract price.

(2) It is company policy to adjust cost of sales (which includes foreseeable losses, where appropriate) by the amount of attributable profit/loss to be recognised in the period (if appropriate) in order to arrive at turnover. This is done on a contract-by-contract basis.

Suggested solution – Hilltown Ltd

Profit and loss Account for the Year Ended 31 December 2004 (Extract)

	£'000
Turnover (£6,480 + £800 + £7,750)	15,030
Cost of sales (£5,290 + £800 + £7,750)	(13,840)
Provision for foreseeable loss	(1,324)
Gross loss	(134)

Balance Sheet as at 31 December 2004

	£'000
Stocks and work in progress (£60 + £180 – £50 + £1,210 – £250)	1,150
Debtors – amounts recoverable on long-term contracts	650
Provisions for liabilities and charges – foreseeable losses	(1,324)
	476 Dr

Workings

Estimate of total profit/(loss) on contracts

	Contract 1	Contract 2	Contract 3
	£'000	£'000	£'000
Contract price	10,800	8,400	18,200
Costs to date	5,350	980	8,960
Estimated costs to complete contracts	3,250	5,900	10,200
Rectification work to complete (2% price)	216	168	364
Estimated total contract costs	8,816	7,048	19,524
Estimated total contract profit/(loss)	1,984	1,352	(1,324)
Stage of completion	12/20 months = 60%	2/14 months = 14%	–
Costs certified/estimated total costs	£5,290/8,816 = 60%	£800/7,048 = 11%	–
Attributable profit/(loss)	1,190	149	(1,324)

Turnover

	£'000	£'000	£'000	£'000
Costs certified to date	5,290	800	7,750	13,840
Attributable profit	1,190	–		
	6,480	800	7,750	15,030

Stocks and work in progress

	£'000	£'000	£'000	£'000
Costs incurred to date	5,350	980	8,960	15,290
Cost of sales (certified to date)	5,290	800	7,750	13,840
	60	180	1,210	1,450
Deduct excess payments	–	(50)	(250)	(300)
	60	130	960	1,150

Debtors – amounts recoverable on contract

	£'000	£'000	£'000	£'000
Turnover	6,480	800	7,750	15,030
Payments on account	5,830	850	8,000	14,680
	650	(50)	(250)	350
Offset against work in progress	–	50	250	300
	650	Nil	Nil	650

The second example on long-term contracts is similar to the last example but also incorporates the distinction between the original version of SSAP 9 and the revised version whereby profit in the latter case is hidden in the revenues and costs reported in the profit and loss account. Under the original SSAP profits on uncompleted contracts were disclosed separately in the profit and loss and were added to the valuation of long-term work in progress reported on the balance sheet.

Example – Eagle Rock Ltd

Eagle Rock Ltd is a civil engineering company which at 31 July 2004 had three construction contracts in progress, information about which is as follows:

	Contract		
	A	B	C
Costs to date	£910,000	£1,500,000	£222,000
Future costs to complete	£545,000	£495,000	£666,000
Project started	1 February 2003	1 December 2002	1 October 2003
Likely completion	31 January 2005	15 April 2005	30 November 2004
Progress payments received	£757,000	£1,600,000	£200,000
Progress payments due but unpaid	–	£50,000	–
Tender value	£1,700,000	£2,100,000	£875,000

Suggested solution – Eagle Rock Ltd

(a) SSAP 9 (original)

Balance sheet

	£'000
Current assets (see workings)	
Stocks – long-term work in progress	315
Trade debtors (progress payments unpaid)	50
Creditors – amounts falling due within one year	71

(b) SSAP 9 (revised)

Balance sheet

	£'000
Stocks – long-term contract work in progress at cost	Nil
Trade debtors (306 + 19)	325
Creditors – amounts falling due within 1 year (excess payments on account)	21
Provisions for liabilities and charges	
Provision for future losses on long-term contracts	10

Note:

Costs to date as a proportion of estimated total costs are charged to profit and loss and turnover is matched by crediting the same proportion of total turnover.

Profit and loss account

	£'000
Turnover (1,063 + 1,579 + 219)	2,861
Cost of sales (910 + 1,500 + 222)	2,632
Expenses	
Provision for future losses on contract	10

Workings

Revised profit and loss account/balance sheet

(1) Calculation of overall profit/(loss)

	A		B		C	
		£'000		£'000		£'000
Tender price		1,700		2,100		875
Cost to date	(62.5%)	910	(75%)	1,500	(25%)	222
Future costs to complete	(37.5%)	545	(25%)	495	(75%)	666
		1,455		1,995		888
Profit/(loss) on contract		245		105		(13)

(2) Original balance sheet – SSAP 9 (original)

	A £'000	B £'000	C £'000	Total £'000
Cost to date	910	1,500	222	
Attributable profit to date	(62.5%) 153	(75%) 79	–	
	1,063	1,579	222	
Foreseeable losses	–	–	(13)	
	1,063	1,579	209	
Progress payments received and receivable	757	1,650	200	
Long-term work in progress	306		9	315
Creditors		(71)		(71)

(3) Contract accounts

	A £'000	B £'000	C £'000		A £'000	B £'000	C £'000
Cost to date	910	1,500	222	Cost of sales	910	1,500	222

(4) Contract profit and loss accounts

	A £'000	B £'000	C £'000		A £'000	B £'000	C £'000
Cost of sales	910	1,500	222	Sales	1,063	1,579	*219
Provision for foreseeable losses			10				*25% × 875

(5) Contract debtor

	A £'000	B £'000	C £'000		A £'000	B £'000	C £'000
Sales	1,063	1,579	219	Bank	757	1,600	200
Balance c/d		21		Balance c/d	306		19
	1,063	1,600	219		1,063	1,600	219
Balance b/d	306		19	Balance b/d		21	

Applications in published accounts

Most of the disclosure reported in published accounts concerns the reporting of long-term work in progress. In the example provided below accounting policies for both ordinary stocks and long-term contracts are provided by John Laing plc as well as details included within the balance sheet of stocks and debtors.

John Laing   Year Ended 31 December 2002   Construction

Accounting Policies (Extract)

(f) Long-term Contracts

Profits on long-term contracts are calculated in accordance with industry standard accounting practice and do not therefore relate directly to turnover. Profit on current contracts is only taken at a stage near enough to completion for that profit to be reasonably certain. Provision is made for all losses incurred to the accounting date together with any further losses that are foreseen in bringing contracts to completion.

Amounts receivable on contracts which are included in debtors are stated at cost, less attributable profit to the extent that this is reasonably certain after making provision for contingencies, less any losses incurred or foreseen in bringing contracts to completion, and less amounts received as progress payments. Costs for this purpose include valuation of all work done by subcontractors, whether certified or not, and all overheads other than those relating to the general administration of the relevant companies. For any contracts where receipts exceed the book value of work done, the excess is included in creditors as payments on account.

(g) Stocks and work in progress

Stocks and work in progress are stated at the lower of cost, including production overheads, and net realisable value.

Notes to the Accounts (Extracts)

17 Stocks and work in progress

	31 December 2002 £ million	31 December 2001 £ million
Work in progress	–	1.9
Raw materials and consumables	0.8	0.7
	0.8	2.6

The land and developments disclosed separately in the balance sheet represent land and related construction costs in respect of residential and commercial properties held for, or in the course of development.

18 Debtors

	31 December 2002		31 December 2001	
	Group £ million	Company £ million	Group £ million	Company £ million
Due within 1 year:				
Finance debtor	–	–	0.3	–
Amount recoverable on contracts	3.7	–	6.0	–
Amounts recoverable on PFI contracts	1.0	–	0.3	–
Trade debtors #	225.0	0.1	55.3	0.3
Amounts owed by subsidiaries	–	288.7	–	294.8

Amounts owed by joint ventures and associated undertakings	0.9	–	0.4	–
Prepayments	6.4	0.7	8.5	–
Taxation	3.0	0.2	2.6	–
Other taxation	7.9	–	4.4	–
SSAP 24 pension prepayment	18.8	–	–	
	266.7	289.7	77.8	295.1
Due after more than 1 year:				
Finance debtor	14.8	–	16.4	–
Amounts recoverable on contracts	1.6	–	0.8	–
Amounts recoverable on PFI contracts	119.1	–	42.8	–
Trade debtors	2.8	–	4.1	–
Prepayments and accrued income	1.6	1.6	–	–
SSAP 24 pension prepayment	0.6	–	27.5	–
	140.5	1.6	91.6	–

Included within the above were three outstanding loans to officers and managers of the company to a total value of £5,135 (2001 – £ nil).

On 1 November 2002 the Group sold its interest in Laing Homes Limited to George Wimpey plc for a consideration of £295.2 million, which was equivalent to net operating asset value plus £9.0 million. Proceeds of £330.0 million were received on completion with the balance to be settled against an agreed payments schedule. The deferred consideration has been discounted at the relevant rate of borrowing and an amount of £6.3 million is included as a credit item within trade debtors. The first scheduled payment of £50.0 million of the deferred consideration was received on 31 December 2002. Subsequent payments will be:

	£ million
31 March 2003	120.0
31 December 2003	95.2
	215.2

The second illustration (Balfour Beatty plc) covers long-term contracts as well but, in addition, provides a clear accounting policy on profit recognition on contracting activities as well as the normal notes on stocks:

Balfour Beatty Plc Year Ended 31 December 2003 Construction

Principal Accounting policies (Extract)

f)   Turnover

Turnover represents amounts invoiced to outside customers, net of trade discounts, value added and similar sales-based taxes, except in respect of contracting activities where turnover represents the value of work carried out during the year including amounts not invoiced. Turnover is recognised on property developments when they are subject to substantially unconditional contracts for sale.

g) Profit recognition on contracting activities

Profit on individual contracts is taken only when their outcome can be foreseen with reasonable certainty, based on the lower of the percentage margin earned to date and that prudently forecast at completion, taking account of agreed claims. Full provision is made for all known or expected losses on individual contracts, taking a prudent view of future claims income, immediately such losses are foreseen. Profit for the year includes the benefit of claims settled on contracts completed in prior years.

Pre-contract costs are expensed as incurred until it is virtually certain that a contract will be awarded, from which time further pre-contract costs are recognised as an asset and charged as an expense over the period of the contract. Amounts recovered in respect of costs that have been written off are deferred and amortised over the life of the contract.

j) Stocks

Stocks and unbilled contract work in progress are valued at the lower of cost and net realisable value. Cost, where appropriate, includes a proportion of manufacturing overheads. Applications for progress payments are deducted from cost, with any excess included in other creditors as advance progress applications.

Notes to the Accounts (Extract)

12 Stocks

	Group 2003 £m	Group 2002 £m	Company 2003 £m	Company 2002 £m
Contract work in progress	174	148	–	–
Progress applications	(96)	(80)	–	–
Net contract balances	78	68	–	–
Development land and work in progress	5	2	1	2
Manufacturing work in progress	2	3	–	–
Raw materials and consumables	19	20	–	–
Finished goods and goods for resale		5	–	–
	109	98	1	2

Profit and loss: accounting for taxation

5.1 SSAP 5 *Accounting for Value Added Tax* (April 1974)

Background

Value added tax (VAT) is a system of taxation whereby the tax is collected at each stage of the production and distribution chain. The trader acts as a collector of the tax on behalf of Customs and Excise and accounts for the difference between output and input tax to that body.

Accounting treatment

(1) Turnover should always be reported exclusive of VAT.
(2) Expenditure should be reported exclusive of VAT unless irrecoverable.
(3) Any non-deductible VAT (e.g. on motor cars and entertainment expenditure) must be included as part of the cost of the asset capitalised or written off as an expense to profit and loss.
(4) Any amount due to/from Customs and Excise should be included as a normal creditor/debtor and should not be separately disclosed.
(5) Capital commitments should be disclosed inclusive of irrecoverable VAT.

5.2 FRS 16 *Current Tax* (December 1999)

Background

The FRS replaces SSAP 8 *Accounting for the Imputation System of Taxation*, which covered the accounting treatment required under the imputation system of corporation tax whereby the whole of a company's taxable profits were taxable, irrespective of whether or not they were distributable.

However, if a dividend had been paid, an advance payment of corporation tax (ACT) had to be paid to the taxation authorities. ACT was normally offset against the total liability on its income for the same accounting period in which the ACT was paid, which may not have been the same year as it became payable. The net corporation tax due was called mainstream corporation tax (MCT). The ACT offset was restricted to the current income tax rate.

ACT became payable within 14 days after the end of the calendar quarter in which the dividends were paid and MCT 9 months after the end of the company's accounting period.

If ACT remained unrelieved against total corporation tax then any surplus ACT could have been set off against the total tax of the previous six years as well as being carried forward indefinitely without time limit.

EXAMPLE

Taxable profits	£1,800,000 year ended 31 January 1998
Dividend	£600,000 or £2,000,000 paid in November 1997

Assume corporation tax 31%, ACT 25% and income tax 23%

SOLUTION

Profits chargeable to corporation tax	£1,800,000
Corporation tax payable (31% × £1,800,000)	£558,000
ACT on dividend (25% × £600,000 or £2,000,000)	£150,000 or £500,000 payable 14. 1. 98
MCT	£408,000 or £414,000 (23% × £1,800,000)

Where dividend is £1,200,000, unrelieved ACT will arise of £500,000 − 144,000 (558,000 − 414,000) = £356,000, which can be carried back 6 years or carried forward indefinitely.

The imputation system was abolished by the budget of April 1999 and this led to a much simpler version of paying corporation tax, by instalments, with no need to pay ACT in advance. As such, the accounting treatment has become much simpler and there are only five basic principles in FRS 16.

Accounting treatment

(1)   *Current tax* (basically tax on this year's profits plus or minus adjustments to prior year estimates) should be recognised as an income or expense in the profit and loss account, except if the gain or loss has been recorded in the statement of total recognised gains and losses (STRGL). In that case the tax should also go to the STRGL.

Tax may need to be *allocated on a pro rata* basis or more appropriate method between the profit and loss and STRGL, if it is difficult to determine the specific link.

(2)   *Dividends paid and payable* should be recorded at the amount payable excluding any attributable tax credit (mainly United Kingdom), *but* inclusive of any withholding tax (mainly Republic of Ireland).

(3)   *Dividends receivable* should be recorded at the amount receivable without any attributable tax credit, *but* before deduction of withholding tax (i.e. gross and withholding tax part of tax charge).

(4)   Income and expenses subject to non-standard rates of tax should be included in pre-tax results on the basis of the amounts actually receivable or payable without adjusting for notional tax.
(5)   Current tax should be measured at the amounts expected to be paid using *tax rates enacted* or *substantially enacted* by the balance sheet date (i.e. Bill passed in the House of Commons or by the Dail or passed under the Provisional Collection of Taxes Act 1968).

Disclosure

The following major components of the current tax expense/income in the profit and loss account and STRGL should be disclosed separately:

(a)   UK/ROI tax for the current period but separately from adjustments to prior periods;
(b)   Foreign tax.

Both (a) and (b) should be analysed to distinguish tax for the current period and any prior year adjustments. Domestic tax should be disclosed before and after double taxation relief.

Illustration of Profit and Loss Account Disclosure

	£'000	£'000
UK corporation tax		
Of which:		
Current tax on income for the period	A	
Adjustments in respect of prior periods	B	
	C	
Double tax relief	(D)	
		E
Foreign tax		
Current tax on income for the period	F	
Adjustments in respect of prior periods	G	
		H
Tax on profit on ordinary activities		I

Date of effectance

Regarded as standard for all accounting periods ending on or after 23 March 2000.

Transitional arrangements for ACT (UK only)

A shadow ACT system has been set up to ensure that ACT carried forward after April 1999 is recovered only if it could have been recovered under the old ACT system. Recoverable ACT should only be recorded if recoverable and can be set off in the current period, or the past, properly set off against deferred tax or expected to be recoverable in the next accounting period.

Although ACT can be carried forward indefinitely, there is an overriding restriction on the use of ACT set off imposed by the shadow ACT system. In deciding whether recoverable or not, regard should only be paid to the immediate and foreseeable future, usually one year.

ACT should be deducted from the deferred tax account, if available, or recorded as a deferred asset.

If events occur that make ACT previously recoverable, now irrecoverable, it should be written off through the profit and loss account and separately disclosed. If it is written off but subsequently recovered it should be written back in the profit and loss account as a credit in the tax charge.

5.3   FRS 19 *Deferred Taxation* (December 2000)

Background

FRS 19 deals with the rules attached to accounting for deferred taxation. The problem emerges because the corporation tax payable by a company bears little resemblance to the potential tax which ought to be paid if based solely on the accounting profits achieved. There are two main reasons for this:

(i)   Permanent differences

Certain expenses charged in the profit and loss account are not allowable for tax, e.g. business entertainment, and therefore there will always be a permanent difference between the accounting and taxable profits.

These will never reverse, therefore there is no need to consider them any further.

(ii)   Timing differences

Certain income and expenses are included in the profit and loss account of one period but are treated in a different period for taxation purposes, e.g. capital allowances 25 per cent written down but depreciation at 10 per cent straight line. These eventually will reverse and therefore deferred tax should be provided on these timing differences. It is essentially an accruals-based approach – to match the tax charge in the profit and loss with the accounting profit earned.

Accounting treatment

FRS 19 requires the adoption of the full provision method, i.e. deferred tax should be provided on the full timing differences that have originated but not reversed by the balance sheet date. Originally, deferred tax had to be provided under the partial provision basis but this was amended due to pressure from the IASB to ensure international harmonisation and to comply with the Statement of Principles.

EXAMPLE

Assume an asset cost £100 with a first-year allowance of 100 per cent and an estimated useful life of 4 years. The accounting profit is assumed to be £120 per annum for each of the

4 years. The following would represent the 'correct' accounting treatment:

	Year 1	Year 2	Year 3	Year 4
	£	£	£	£
Profits as per financial statements	120	120	120	120
Add depreciation	25	25	25	25
	145	145	145	145
Less capital allowances	100	–	–	–
Taxable profit	45	145	145	145
Corporation tax (say 50%)	22.5	72.5	72.5	72.5
Deferred tax (at 50%)	37.5	(12.5)	(12.5)	(12.5)
Total taxed charged (full – per FRS 19)	60	(60)	(60)	(60)

However, if we assume that further capital expenditure of 120, 140 and 200 is likely to take place in years 2, 3 and 4 respectively, then the following results.

	Year 1	Year 2	Year 3	Year 4
	£	£	£	£
Profits	120	120	120	120
Add depreciation	25	55	90	140
	145	175	210	260
Less capital allowances	100	120	140	200
Taxable profit	45	55	70	60
Corporation tax (say 50%)	22.5	27.5	35	30
Deferred tax (at 50%)	37.5	32.5	25	30
Total tax charged (full)	60	60	60	60

Under the full provision basis, however, the total balance of deferred taxation outstanding in the balance sheet at the end of year 4 is £125 and, under current capital expenditure plans, appears never to have to be paid as it is rolled over by increasing investment in new equipment, etc. Under the previous SSAP 15, none of that deferred tax needed to be provided as it was argued that due to management's future intentions it would be unlikely to crystallise, i.e. be paid, in the foreseeable future. It merely had to be noted as a potential contingent liability in the notes to the accounts.

The ASB released FRS 19 in December 2000, which has moved deferred tax accounting back to full provision in line with international accounting standards. This had to be implemented for accounting periods ending on or after 23 January 2002. The new standard is not totally in line with international IAS 12 *Income Tax*, as it incorporates the possibility of discounting a deferred tax provision since there are, particularly in the utility companies, vast amounts of deferred tax not presently recorded on the balance sheet which would have a material impact on the gearing ratios of those companies. Discounting, however, is only recommended if it is material, it is justifiable on cost/benefit grounds and is normal industry practice. In addition FRS 19 prohibits the inclusion of tax on revaluation surpluses/deficits on the grounds that the assets may never be sold and thus no liability is incurred. Similarly, no tax is provided on rollover relief or on earnings not remitted by subsidiaries. That does leave a fairly wide gap between the ASB and the IASB, which may have to be resolved in future years.

More caution is required in the creation of a deferred tax asset on losses. This is only permitted if it is probable that the losses will be recovered by future profits but tax planning opportunities should be considered in assessing whether or not this will occur.

FRS 19 only permits the use of the liability method in computing the deferred tax charge and liability. In effect this means that, every time the corporation tax rate is changed, the liability must be adjusted accordingly to ensure that the 'correct' liability is recorded on the balance sheet. This also ties in with the Statement of Principles. The tax rates adopted should be those that have been substantially enacted by the tax authorities.

Disclosure

The deferred tax charge for the year should be included as part of the tax on profit or loss on ordinary activities, either on the face of the profit and loss account or in the notes, and analysed into its appropriate causes.

Any adjustments by way of changes in the corporation tax rate should be disclosed as part of the normal tax charge.

Any deferred tax liability should be disclosed on the face of the balance sheet under the heading 'provisions for liabilities and charges' but any deferred tax carried forward as an asset should be included under the heading 'prepayments and accrued income' and separately disclosed as it is not a 'true' current asset.

The first example looks at the three different possible methods of accounting for deferred tax – the flow through, and the partial provision and the full provision methods, and examines their advantages and disadvantages.

Example – Hilden Plc

Hilden plc is a plastic toy manufacturer. Its toy sales have been adversely affected by imports and it has been changing towards the supply of plastic office equipment. Profits are expected to continue to fall for the next 4 years when they are expected to stabilise at the 2004 level. There will be a regular programme of plant renewal.

The following information is available:

Year ended 30 April	Profit before depreciation	Capital allowances	Depreciation
	£	£	£
2001	1,250,000	400,000	80,000
2002	1,200,000	80,000	160,000
2003	1,100,000	80,000	240,000
2004	1,000,000	560,000	160,000

Assume a corporation tax rate of 33 per cent. On 1 March 2000 there was a nil balance on the deferred tax account. In addition Hilden plc had £1m 10 per cent debentures in issue at 30 April 2001 on which interest was payable half-yearly in arrears on 1 May and 1 November each year. The company proposes to repay £400,000 on 30 April 2003 with all interest due and a further £200,000 on 30 April 2004 with all interest due.

Suggested solution – Hilden Plc

Flow-through method (not acceptable under either SSAP 15 or FRS 19)

	Profit before dep'n and tax £	Capital allowances £	Taxable profit £	Corporation tax (33%) £	Deferred tax £	Total tax £
2001	1,250,000	400,000	850,000	280,500	Nil	280,500 (24.0%)
2002	1,200,000	80,000	1,120,000	369,600	Nil	369,600 (35.5%)
2003	1,100,000	80,000	1,020,000	336,600	Nil	336,600 (35.0%)
2004	1,000,000	560,000	440,000	145,200	Nil	145,200 (17.2%)

There will be no liability for deferred taxation on the balance sheet but the various corporation tax liabilities of £280,500, etc., will be classified as 'creditors: falling due within 1 year' as they will become payable within 9 months of the year end.

Full-provision method (FRS 19)

	Taxable profit	Corporation tax (33%)	Deferred tax	Timing diffs. CA + dep'n	Total tax
2001	850,000	280,500	105,600	(400,000 − 80,000 × 33%)	386,100 (33%)
2002	1,120,000	369,600	(26,400)	(80,000 − 160,000 × 33%)	343,200 (33%)
2003	1,020,000	336,600	(52,800)	(80,000 − 240,000 × 33%)	283,800 (33%)
2004	440,000	145,200	132,000	(560,000 − 160,000 × 33%)	277,200 (33%)
			158,400		

The liability for deferred tax on the balance sheet will vary from £105,600 in 2001, to £79,200 in 2002, £26,400 in 2003 and ending up with £158,400 at the end of 2004. This represents the net timing differences of excess capital allowances of £480,000 × 33%.

Partial-provision method (SSAP 15)

Net reversals in the foreseeable future at the end of 2001 are £26,400 + £52,800 = £79,200 and only this figure should be accrued. In 2002 only £52,800 should be accrued and zero at the end of both 2003 and 2004.

There will therefore be a need to provide a note to the accounts detailing all the potential deferred tax still outstanding, i.e.:

	Full potential − Provided = Unprovided
2001	105,600 − 79,200 = 26,400
2002	79,200 − 52,800 = 26,400
2003	26,400 − zero = 26,400
2004	158,400 − zero = 158,400

Debentures

	Profit and loss (accruals)	£	£	Paid
2002	£1m × 10%	100,000	100,000	(1/5/01, 1/11/01 = £1m × 10%)
2003	£1m × 10%	100,000	120,000	(1/5/02, 1/11/02 = £1m × 10% + £0.4 × 10% × 1/2, 30/4/03)
2004	£0.6m × 10%	60,000	70,000	(1/5/03, 1/11/03 £0.6m × 10% = £60,000 + £0.2 × 10% × 1/2, 30/4/03)
2005	£0.4m × 10%	40,000	40,000	(1/5/04, 30/11/04) £0.4m × 10%)
		300,000	330,000	

Deferred tax asset is £330,000 − £300,000 = £30,000 × 33% = £9,900. At 30 April 2001 the timing difference is £1m × 10% × 1/2= £50,000 accrued of which only £30,000 × 33% is provided. £20,000 × 33% = £6,600 is therefore not incorporated on the balance sheet. However, under FRS 19, that amount would need to be provided under the full-provision method.

The arguments for and against each of the methods are as follows:

The flow-through method

This method is based on the principle that only the corporation tax payable in respect of a period should be charged in the profit and loss account of that period. The effect on the balance sheet would be that it would only show the current liability relating to the tax payable.

On grounds of commercial reality, flow-through avoids the need to make assumptions about the future, which are uncertain as to outcome; on revenue grounds, recognising income tax when assessed is consistent with the Government's policy of assessing tax for the time period in accordance with the fiscal policy of the time. On accounting principle grounds, the flow-through method complies with the matching principle whereby the amount charged in the profit and loss account is based on tax payable in relation to the taxable profit of the accounting period.

If the reporting entity is able to plan its tax affairs so as to substantially reduce its liability then that fact should be reported to shareholders, i.e. the accounts should 'tell it as it is'.

The arguments against the method are that the commercial reality is that tax has been deferred, i.e. a temporary cash flow benefit, and not eliminated; the uncertainties surrounding deferred tax provisioning are similar to many other areas where management exercise judgement. Eventually the tax will have to be paid and therefore this liability should be recorded on the balance sheet. On the question of accounting principle and the matching concept, it is argued that the tax should be matched against the operating results of the accounting period and not the taxable profit. A particular problem is that the EPS is affected by any deferred tax charge. EPS can therefore be distorted by fiscal policy rather than give a fair reflection of operating performance, which it is supposed to measure.

Full-provision method

This method has strong support based on the accounting principles of matching and prudence. The tax charge is matched with the operating results and is prudent because the amount is the full potential tax liability based on the timing differences known at the date of the accounts.

The arguments against the method are largely based on commercial reality in that the result of full provisioning may be to accumulate provisions over time to the extent that they become a material item in the balance sheet without representing a genuine liability of the business. This occurs if the reporting entity has a policy of continual replacement and the originating timing differences always exceed any reversals thereby postponing the ultimate date of payment of tax almost indefinitely. There has been discussion about the advisability of discounting the provision, which would reduce its significance in the profit and loss account and balance sheet. However, it could be argued that discounting an accounting allocation is invalid and even if cash flows were identified they would be a subjective estimate of both the amounts and the years of reversals and a subjective choice of the most appropriate discount rate to use. However, this is the method that has been adopted by FRS 19 *Deferred Tax* and by the IASB. The provision may be discounted if the time value of money is material.

Partial-provision method

The approach (until January 2002) in the UK was to apply the partial-provision method calculating the charge using the liability method.

The arguments in favour of this method are largely based on realism. The tax charge reflects the amount of tax that will become payable based on current knowledge and intention; the provision in the balance sheet is a realistic estimate of the tax liability that will need to be discharged in the next 3 or 4 years.

The arguments against the method are mainly based on the need to consider the foreseeable future with a prediction of future events. This is subjective and can result in differing treatments of identical situations depending on the business's forecasts of future activity and profitability. It is too easy to manipulate and fails to comply with the definition of a liability under the Statement of Principles.

In conclusion, it is unclear whether a decision should be based on commercial reality or accounting principles. There is a conflict between the two, which SSAP 15 had attempted to resolve. Similar debates to that in the UK have occurred in other countries and within the IASB. The UK was out of step with international practice which overwhelmingly uses full provisioning and it is largely the reason why the ASB now require the implementation of the full-provision method.

Assuming that all of the shares in Hilden plc were acquired for cash by Lambeg plc on 1 May 2000, the following factors must be taken into account in determining the fair value of deferred tax as at the date of acquisition.

Determine on a group basis

Until the publication of FRS 19, FRS 7 provided that deferred tax assets and liabilities recognised in the fair value exercise be determined on a group basis by considering the enlarged group as a whole. At the end of the accounting period in which the acquisition occurred, the enlarged group's deferred tax provision was calculated as a single amount, on assumptions applicable to the group, and to determine the deferred tax of the acquired company as at the date of acquisition using different assumptions from those applying to the group as a whole would result in the post-acquisition profit and loss account reflecting the change from one set of assumptions to another, rather than any real change in the circumstances of the group. FRS 19 now insists that any fair value adjustments should not be recognised on non-monetary assets acquired at their fair value on acquisition.

The second example covers the calculation of deferred tax on a full provision basis.

Example – Portrush Plc

Portrush plc was a company that manufactured replacement keys. It had started with the manufacture of replacement metal keys for antique boxes where the original keys had been lost, and had become recognised as specialists within this field. Its expertise has since extended to the provision of electronic, as well as mechanical, entry devices. This has resulted in the need for an ongoing capital asset investment programme. The draft profit and loss account for the year ended 30 November 2003 showed a pre-tax profit of £375,000 and it was forecast that the profit for 2004 would increase by 20 per cent to £450,000.

The following information was available concerning the company's fixed assets as at 30 November 2003:

	£
Gross cost of fixed assets	1,000,000
Accumulated depreciation	400,000
Capital allowances	525,000

The following forecast information was available as at 30 November 2003 relating to depreciation charges and capital allowances for the next 5 years based on the assumption that the company goes ahead with the capital investment programme.

Year ending	Depreciation charge £	Capital allowances £
30. 11. 04	234,000	265,000
30. 11. 05	253,000	303,000
30. 11. 06	276,000	193,000
30. 11. 07	278,000	192,000
30. 11. 08	248,000	262,000

The forecast depreciation charge of £234,000 and capital allowance of £265,000 were amended in the accounts prepared for the year ended 30 November 2004 to £250,000 and £289,000 respectively.

The following forecast information was available as at 30 November 2004 relating to depreciation charges and capital allowances for the next 5 years:

Year ending	Depreciation charge £	Capital allowances £
30. 11. 05	250,000	289,000
30. 11. 06	278,000	197,000
30. 11. 07	275,000	193,000
30. 11. 08	253,000	265,000
30. 11. 09	254,000	278,000

Assume a corporation tax rate of 35 per cent.

Suggested solution – Portrush Plc

Calculating the deferred tax provision for inclusion in the balance sheet

Paragraphs 7–33 of FRS 19 explain how the deferred tax provision should be calculated for inclusion in the balance sheet:

(1)   The liability method should be adopted to compute the tax.
(2)   Provision for tax should be made in full for all timing differences with the exception of unremitted earnings of subsidiaries and revaluation surpluses and

revalued assets which have been sold and the gain rolled over against a replacement asset.

(3) The assumptions should take into account all relevant information available to the board of directors up to the date on which the financial statements are approved. In particular the tax rate should be based on tax rates that have passed the House of Commons bill stage.

(4) A deferred tax asset should not be carried forward as an asset unless it is likely to be recovered.

(5) The full provision may be discounted if the time value of money is material using a Government bond rate with similar maturity dates to the deferred tax liability/asset.

Balance sheet extract as at 30 November 2003
Taxation, including deferred taxation (extract)   £43,750

Notes to the balance sheet

Note 18: Deferred taxation	*Total*
Excess capital allowances	£43,750

Workings

Year	Depreciation	Capital allowances		Timing differences Cumulative	Partial provision (SSAP 15)
	£'000	£'000	£'000	£'000	£'000
2004	234	265	31	31	
2005	253	303	50	81	
2006	276	193	(83)	(2)	
2007	278	192	(86)	(88) × 35% = 30.8	
2008	248	262	14	(74)	

Full provision 2003	£525,000 C. Allowances	or	£475,000 WDV
(FRS 19)	£400,000 Depreciation		£600,000 NBV
	£125,000		£125,000
	× 35% = £43,750		

Profit and loss account and balance sheet extracts as at 30 November 2004

Profit and loss account (extract)
Taxation (extract for deferred tax only £57,400 − £43,750)   £13,650

Balance sheet (extract)
Taxation, including deferred taxation (extract)   £57,400

Notes to the balance sheet
Note 18: Deferred taxation

	Total
	£57,400

Workings

Year	Depreciation	Capital allowances	Timing differences	Cumulative	Partial provision (SSAP 15)
	£'000	£'000	£'000	£'000	£'000
2005	250	289	39	39	
2006	278	197	(81)	(42)	
2007	275	193	(82)	(124) × 35% = 43.4	
2008	253	265	12	(112)	
2009	254	278	24	(88)	

Full provision 2004 (FRS 19)	£289,000 Cap. allowances	or	WDV XX
	£250,000 Depreciation		NBV XX
	£39,000		XX
	+ £125,000 = £164,000		
	× 35% = £57,400		

The third example covers the effects on deferred taxation of a fair value adjustment on an acquisition as well as the deferred tax liability on a revaluation.

Example – Dervock Plc

Dervock plc has the following net assets at 30 November 2004:

Fixed assets	£'000	£'000	Tax value (£'000)
Buildings		33,500	7,500
Plant and equipment		52,000	13,000
Investments		66,000	66,000
		151,500	86,500
Current assets		15,000	15,000
Creditors: amounts falling due within 1 year			
Creditors	13,500		(13,500)
Liability for health care benefits	300		–
	(13,800)		–
Net current assets		1,200	1,500
Provision for deferred tax		(9,010)	(9,010)
		143,690	78,990

Dervock plc acquired 100 per cent of the shares of Dunluce Ltd on 30 November 2004. The following statement of net assets relates to Dunluce Ltd on 30 November 2004:

	£'000 Fair value	£'000 Carrying value	£'000 Tax value
Buildings	500	300	100
Plant and equipment	40	30	15
Stock	124	114	114
Debtors	110	110	110
Retirement benefit liability	(60)	(60)	–
Creditors	(105)	(105)	(105)
	609	389	234

There is currently no deferred tax provision in the accounts of Dunluce Ltd. In order to achieve a measure of consistency Dervock plc decided that it would revalue its land and buildings to £50 million and the plant and equipment to £60 million. The company did not feel it necessary to revalue the investments. The liabilities for retirement benefits and healthcare costs are anticipated to remain at their current amounts for the foreseeable future.

The land and buildings of Dervock plc had originally cost £45 million and the plant and equipment £70 million. The company has no intention of selling any of its fixed assets other than the land and buildings which it may sell and lease back. Dervock plc currently utilises the full-provision method to account for deferred taxation. The projected depreciation charges and tax allowances of Dervock plc and BZ Ltd are as follows for the years ending 30 November:

	£'000 2003	£'000 2004	£'000 2005
Depreciation			
(Buildings, plant and equipment)			
Dervock plc	7,010	8,400	7,560
Dunluce Ltd	30	32	34
Tax allowances			
Dervock plc	8,000	4,500	3,000
Dunluce Ltd	40	36	30

The corporation tax rate had changed from 35 per cent to 30 per cent in the current year. Ignore any indexation allowance or rollover relief and assume that Dervock plc and Dunluce Ltd are in the same tax jurisdiction.

Suggested solution – Dervock Plc

Fair-value adjustment

The issue is whether fair-value adjustments in acquisition accounting give rise to deferred tax if the full-provision method is used. At present, fair-value adjustments are not timing differences in SSAP 15, but permanent differences. It is felt that deferred tax should not be provided on fair-value adjustments because these adjustments are made as a consolidation entry only. They are not taxable or tax-deductible and do not affect the overall tax burden of the company. An acquisition does not, by itself, increase the tax.

It is argued that providing for deferred tax on fair-value adjustments is not an allocation of an expense but a smoothing device. Finally, the difference between the carrying value of the net assets acquired and their fair value is goodwill, and therefore no deferred tax is required.

The arguments in favour of deferred tax are conceptual by nature. If the net assets of the acquired company are shown in the group accounts at fair value, then this will affect the post-acquisition earnings of the group. For example, an increase in the stock value by £10,000 will result in profit being reduced by £10,000 in the post-acquisition period. It seems consistent, therefore, to exclude the tax on these profits from the post-acquisition period also. That stock is inherently less valuable than similar purchased stock as the baseline for tax will be the original and not the revalued figures.

Additionally, since an acquisition gives rise to no tax effect, the effective tax rate in the profit and loss account should not be distorted as a result of the acquisition. Providing for deferred tax ensures that distortion does not occur.

Some commentators feel that deferred tax should be provided on assets purchased in an acquisition as a 'valuation' adjustment. If the asset had been purchased in an arm's-length transaction – for example, stocks – then this cost would have been totally tax-deductible. As this is not the case, the asset is worth less to the company because it is not tax-deductible. Therefore, deferred tax should be provided as an adjustment to reflect the reduction in the true value of the asset. FRS 19 has expressly come down on the side of not making provisions for deferred tax in these instances.

Revaluations of fixed assets

The revaluation of a fixed asset can be seen as creating a further timing difference because it reflects an adjustment of depreciation, which is itself a timing difference. An alternative view is that it is a permanent difference as it has no equivalent within the tax computation. The revaluation is not seen as a reversal of previous depreciation, simply that the remaining life of the asset will be measured to reflect a different amount. The additional depreciation charge has no tax equivalent and it would be incorrect to make any tax adjustments in respect of this amount. If, however, the revaluation takes the asset value above its original cost, then a chargeable gain may arise and a provision for tax should be considered if disposal is likely.

As with fair-value adjustments, it can be argued that deferred tax is a valuation adjustment and, while a revaluation does not directly give rise to a tax liability, the tax status of the asset is inferior to an equivalent asset at historical cost; therefore, provision for deferred tax should be made in order to reflect the true after-tax cost of the asset. The revalued asset would not attract the same tax allowances as an asset purchased for the same amount and, therefore, if deferred tax was not provided it would distort the post-revaluation effective tax rate. (This would only be the case if the asset is the type which is deductible for tax purposes. Rollover relief postpones rather than extinguishes any tax liability and therefore should not affect the recognition of deferred tax.) FRS 19 again does not require provision for deferred tax on revaluations.

Full-provision

	NBV	Valuation	Tax value	FRS 19 Full difference (NBV)	SSAP 15 Temporary difference
Dervock plc		£'000	£'000	£'000	£'000
Buildings (revalued)	33,500	50,000	7,500	26,000	42,500
Plant and equipment (revalued)	52,000	60,000	13,000	39,000	47,000
Healthcare benefits	(300)	(300)	–	(300)	(300)
	85,200	109,700	20,500	64,700	89,200
Dunluce Ltd					
Buildings	300	500	100	200	400
Plant and equipment	30	40	15	15	25
Stock	114	124	114	–	10
Retirement benefit	(60)	(60)	–	(60)	(60)
	384	604	229	155	375
	85,584	110,304	20,729	64,855	89,575

	£'000	SSAP 15 £'000	FRS 19 £'000	
Deferred tax liability	89,935 @ 30%	26,980	19,565	65,215 × 30%
Deferred tax asset	(360) @ 30%	(108)	(108)	(360) × 30%
(1)	89,575 @ 30%	26,872	19,457	64,855 × 30%
Less: opening deferred tax liability		(9,010)	(9,010)	
Adjustment due to change in tax rate: 9,010 × 100/35 × 5%		1,287	1,287	
Deferred tax expense for year		19,149	11,734	

The deferred tax expense relating to the revaluation of assets would not be shown in the group profit and loss account as it relates to items credited to equity.

Partial-provision – only permitted by SSAP 15 not FRS 19
Group position based on carrying values before any fair-value adjustment or revaluation

£'000

Balance at 30. 11. 04

Buildings
   Dervock plc   33,500
   Dunluce Ltd   300

Plant and equipment
   Dervock plc   52,000
   Dunluce Ltd   30
                   85,830

Tax values at 30. 11. 04

Building
   Dervock plc   7,500
   Dunluce Ltd   100

Plant and equipment
   Dervock plc   13,000
   Dunluce Ltd   15
                   20,615
Timing differences   65,215

Timing differences	30.11.04 £'000	30.11.05 £'000	30.11.06 £'000	30.11.07 £'000
Depreciation		(7,040)	(8,432)	(7,594)
Tax allowances		8,040	4,536	3,030
	65,215	1,000	(3,896)	(4,564)
Cumulative	65,215	66,215	62,319	57,755

Maximum reversal: 65,215,000 − 57,755,000 = £7,460,000
Provision required: £7,460,000 @ 30% = £2,238,000

Therefore there will be a release of the existing provision if deferred tax were calculated using the partial-provision method. However, because the land and buildings had originally cost £45m and the revaluation takes the value above this amount, an additional provision of (£50m − £45m × 30% =) £1.5m must be provided.

Thus, the deferred tax provision will be reduced to:

£'000
2,238 timing differences
1,500 tax on revaluation – chargeable gain
3,738

The deferred tax released to the profit and loss account will be (9,010,000 − 3,738,000) = £5,252,000.

There will be no deferred tax consequences of the retirement benefit liability or healthcare costs under the partial-provision method as it is anticipated that there will be no movement in the balance sheet amount.

Application in published accounts

One of the most detailed accounting policies in relation to deferred tax is that provided by BP plc. It describes how deferred tax is treated on disposals of previously revalued fixed assets on unremitted earnings of overseas subsidiaries – two major differences between international accounting standards and national standards.

BP Plc   Year Ended 31 December 2003   Oil and Gas Exploration and Distribution

Deferred Taxation

Deferred tax is recognised in respect of all timing differences that have originated but not reversed at the balance sheet where transactions or events have occurred at that date that will result in an obligation to pay more, or a right to pay less, tax in the future. In particular:

* Provision is made for tax on gains arising from the disposal of fixed assets that have been rolled over into replacement assets, only to the extent that, at the balance sheet, there is a binding agreement to dispose of the replacement assets concerned. However, no provision is made where, on the basis of all available evidence at the balance sheet date, it is more likely than not that the taxable gain will be rolled over into replacement assets and charged to tax only where the replacement assets are sold.
* Provision is made for deferred tax that would arise on remittance of the retained earnings of overseas subsidiaries, joint ventures and associated undertakings only to the extent that, at the balance sheet date, dividends have been accrued as receivable.

Deferred tax assets are recognised only to the extent that it is considered more likely than not that there will be suitable taxable profits from which the underlying timing differences can be deducted.

Deferred tax is measured on an undiscounted basis at the tax rates that are expected to apply in the periods in which timing differences reverse, based on tax rates and laws enacted or substantially enacted at the balance sheet date.

Notes to the Accounts (Extract)

11 Taxation

	$ million	
Tax on profit on ordinary activities	*2003*	*2002*
Current tax:		
UK corporation tax	11,435	1,304
Overseas tax relief	(10,293)	(301)
Overseas	1,142	1,003
Overseas	3,525	1,883
Group	4,667	2,886
Joint ventures	158	75
Associated undertakings	94	187
	4,919	3,148
Deferred tax:		
UK	426	433
Overseas	655	761
Group	1,081	1,194
Joint ventures	(14)	–
Associated undertakings	(14)	–
	1,053	1,194
Tax on profit on ordinary activities	5,972	4,342

Included in the charge for the year is a charge of $123 million ($125 million) relating to extraordinary items.

Tax included in statement of total recognised gains and losses	*2003*	*2002*
Current tax		
UK	–	57
Overseas	(11)	(54)
	(11)	3
Deferred tax		
UK	48	138
Overseas	–	1
	48	139
Tax included in statement of total gains and losses	37	142

Factors affecting current tax charge

The following table provides a reconciliation of the UK statutory corporation tax rate to the effective current tax rate of the group on profit before taxation.

	$million	
	2003	2002
Analysis of profit before taxation:		
UK	5,513	2,822
Overseas	10,896	8,442
	16,409	11,264
Taxation	5,972	4,342
Effective tax rate	36%	39%

	% of profit before tax	
UK statutory corporation tax rate	30	30
Increase (decrease) resulting from:		
UK supplementary and overseas taxes at higher rates	10	9
Tax credits	–	(3)
Restructuring benefits	(2)	–
Current year losses unrelieved (prior year losses utilised)	(3)	1
No relief for inventory holding losses (inventory holding gains not taxed)	(1)	(2)
Acquisition amortisation	4	7
Other	(2)	(3)
Effective tax rate	36	39
Current year timing differences	(6)	(11)
Effective current tax rate	30	28

Current year timing differences arise mainly from the excess of tax depreciation over book depreciation.

Factors that may affect future tax charges

The group earns income in many countries and, on average, pays taxes at rates higher than the UK statutory rate. The overall impact of these higher taxes, which include the supplementary charge of 10% on UK North Sea profits, is subject to changes in enacted tax rates and the country mix of the group's income. However, it is not expected to increase or decrease substantially in the near term.

The tax charge in 2002 reflected a benefit from US 'non-conventional fuel credits' which were no longer available after 31 December 2002. The effect of the loss of these credits on the overall tax charge was offset in 2003 by benefits from restructuring and planning initiatives. The group has around $5.4 billion ($5.3 billion) of carry-forward tax losses in the UK, which would be available to offset against future taxable income.

To date, tax assets have been recognised on $285 million ($840 million) of those losses (i.e. to the extent that it is recognised as more likely than not that suitable taxable income will arise). During 2003 the group disclaimed tax depreciation allowances, which will be available in future periods, in order to optimise the utilisation of tax losses. This is reflected in the movement in tax losses carried forward between the end of 2002 and 2003. Carry-forward losses in other taxing jurisdictions have not been recognised as deferred tax assets, and are unlikely to have a significant effect on the group's tax rate in future years.

The group's profit before taxation includes stock holding gains or losses. These gains (or losses) are not taxed (or deductible) in certain juisdictions in which the group operates, and therefore give rise to decreases or increases in the effective tax rate. However, over the longer term, significant changes in the tax rate would arise only in the event of a substantial and sustained change in oil prices.

The impact on the tax rate of acquisition amortisation (non-deductible depreciation and amortisation relating to the fixed asset revaluation adjustments and goodwill consequent upon the ARCO and Burmah Castrol acquisitions) is unlikely to change in the near term.

The main component of timing differences in the current year is accelerated tax depreciation. Based on current capital investment plans, the group expects to continue to be able to claim tax allowances in excess of depreciation in future years at a level similar to the current year.

Deferred tax

	$ million	
	2003	2002
Analysis of provision:		
Depreciation	15,613	14,990
Other taxable timing differences	1,957	1,837
Petroleum revenue tax	(601)	(567)
Decommissioning and other provisions	(1,429)	(2,192)
Tax credit and loss carry forward	(105)	(273)
Other deductible timing differences	(162)	(281)
Deferred tax provision	15,273	13,514
Of which – UK	3,741	2,906
– Overseas	11,532	10,608

Analysis of movements during the year

	$ million	
	2003	2002
At 1 January	13,514	11,702
Exchange adjustments	630	477
Acquisitions	–	6
Charge for the year on ordinary activities	1,081	1,194
Charge for the year in the statement of total recognised gains and losses	48	139
Deletions/transfers	–	(4)
At 31 December	15,273	13,514

	$ million	
	2003	*2002*
The charge for deferred tax on ordinary activities:		
Origination and reversal of timing differences	1,081	839
Effect of the introduction of supplementary UK corporation tax of 10% on opening liability	–	355
	1,081	1,194
The charge for deferred tax in the statement of total recognised gains and losses:		
Origination and reversal of timing differences	46	139

Profit and loss: earnings per share and reporting financial performance

6.1 FRS 14 *Earnings per Share* (October 1998)

Background

One of the key financial ratios adopted by financial analysts has been the price/earnings ratio (P/E ratio). It is a widely used performance indicator and is published in the *Financial Times* on a daily basis. If the P/E ratio starts to veer away from the 'norm' for the industrial sector concerned, analysts may well advise their fund managers to sell shares in the company, resulting in a fall in the share price of that company and its overall value to shareholders.

The P/E ratio is defined as:

$$\frac{\text{Current market share price}}{\text{Earnings per share}}, \quad \text{e.g.} \frac{580\text{p}}{72.5\text{p}} = 8$$

In the example above it would take an investor eight years of current earnings of 72.5p to recover the initial investment of 580p.

FRS 14 (originally SSAP 3) was published in order to clarify and standardise the calculation of the bottom line of that ratio, earnings per share (EPS), which is published at the foot of the profit and loss account for every listed company in their annual report. This should serve to enhance comparability across listed companies. It only applies to listed companies, although if published by unlisted companies, the calculations must be the same.

Definition

Basic earnings per share should be calculated by dividing the net profit or loss for the period attributable to ordinary shareholders by the weighted average number of ordinary shares outstanding during the period.

FRS 14 also permits the adoption of alternative EPS figures based on other versions of profits. If adopted, a listed company must reconcile the alternative EPS back to the official EPS by itemising and quantifying the adjustments. The additional version must not be made more prominent, however, than the official version.

A further alternative EPS may be calculated based on the first *Statement of Investment Practice* published by the Institute of Investment Management and Research (IIMR), which excludes non-trading items such as the profits/losses on termination of a discontinued operation, profits/losses on the sale of fixed assets and any permanent diminutions in the value of fixed assets from the calculation of earnings. It is therefore now possible to calculate three different basic versions of EPS – the official, alternative and IIMR.

Basic earnings per share – problems

Preference dividends unpaid

Deduct if cumulative or if participating (fixed proportion).

Losses

Losses per share should still be calculated in the same manner as earnings.

Changes in share capital

 (i)   Issue at full market price;
 (ii) Capitalisation or bonus issue;
(iii) Share-for-share exchange;
(iv) Rights issue at less than market price.

 (i)   *Issue at full market price*

     Where new equity shares are issued for cash at full market price the new shares should be included on a weighted average time basis on the grounds that the cash received will generate earnings only for the period after the cash is received.

     EXAMPLE

Earnings year 2	£10m	1:5 Full market price issue @ £2/share on 30. 6. 04
Number of shares prior to issue	5m	
Earnings per share	£2	1m × 1/2yr – 0.5m + 5m – 5.5m

     Assume earnings of £10m incorporates additional earnings boosted by the cash received for the second half of the year.
     Earnings £10m ÷ 5.5m = £1.81 per share

 (ii) *Capitalisation or bonus issue*

     Where new equity shares are issued by way of conversion of reserves into equity capital, no increase in earnings has occurred but the bottom line has increased. To ensure comparability with prior years both the current and prior year are boosted *in full* by the issue of shares regardless of the date of issue.

     EXAMPLE

Earnings year 2	£10m	1:5 bonus issue on 30. 6. 04
Number of shares prior to issue	5m	
Earnings per share	£2	1m × full year = 1m + 5m = 6m

Assume earnings of £10m are unaffected by the issue of shares as no cash has been received.

Earnings £10m ÷ 6m = £1.67 per share

Assume prior year EPS was £1.8, then prior year EPS is restated to £1.8 × 5/6 = £1.5.

(iii) *Share-for-share exchange*

Where shares are exchanged in an acquisition for shares in the acquiree the shares are assumed to be included on a weighted average basis from the period from which the profits of the acquiree are included in the consolidated accounts.

EXAMPLE

Earnings year 2	£10m	Original shares	5m
Earnings of acquiree		Shares in exchange	
(1. 4 to 31.12 only)	4m	(4m × 3/4)	3m
	£14m		8m

Earnings per share £14m ÷ 8m shares = £1.75 per share

(iv) *Rights issue*

Where shares are issued at a discount from their normal market price, the issue of shares is in reality a mixture of a full market price issue and a free bonus issue, i.e. a mixture of (i) and (ii) above.

EXAMPLE

Earnings year 2	£10m	1:5 rights issue on 31. 03. 04	
		@ £4 per share	
Number of shares pre-rights issue	5m	(i.e. discount of 20% from market price of	
		£5 per share)	
Earnings per share	£2		

Number of shares pre-rights	5m @	£5 cum	£25m
Rights issue (1:5)	1m @	£4	£4m
Total shares	6m	£4.83	£29m
Adjustment factor £5/£4.83 = £1.035			

Pre-rights	5m × 1.035 × 1/4 year =	1.294m
Post-rights	6m × 3/4 year =	4.500m
		5.794m

Earnings per share £10m ÷ 5.794m = £1.73 per share

Prior year (say £9m ÷ 5m) adjusted £9m ÷ (5m × 1.035) = £1.74 per share

Diluted earnings per share – problems

If a company has issued a separate class of equity shares which do not rank immediately for dividends in the current period (but will do so in the future), or if it has certain types of convertible loans or warrants which have the right to convert into ordinary shares at some future date, then these may well dilute earnings per share in the future. Users of financial statements should therefore be made aware of their likely impact.

As a result a second version of EPS is required to be disclosed on the face of the profit and loss account, if the diluted EPS is either equal to or below the basic EPS. It is not disclosed above basic EPS as it is argued that this will not happen because it would not be in the interests of the holders of those securities to exercise their rights.

There are three main types of diluting instrument:

(i)   Convertible preference shares;
(ii) Convertible loan stock;
(iii) Share options or warrants.

(i)   *Convertible preference shares*

There will be a saving in preference dividends and holders are assumed to transfer at the best conversion rate.

EXAMPLE

Basic earnings per share (assume)	£1.50	10% convertible preference shares	1m
Basic share structure (assume)	2m	(convertible 0.5 ordinary for every	
		£1 ordinary)	
Basic earnings	£3m		

Diluted earnings per share £3m + £0.1m = £3.1m ÷ (2m + 0.5m) = £1.24 per share, which is dilutive and therefore must be disclosed.

(ii) *Convertible loan stock*

There will be a saving in interest payments but because these are tax allowable the company will also lose the tax relief that it is currently saving. The net interest to be saved is therefore added back to basic earnings.

The bottom line will be increased by the maximum shares which the loan holders can earn if they convert into equity.

EXAMPLE

Basic earnings (as above)	£3.00m	£4m 8% convertible loan stocks convertible as	
Add net interest saved	£2.24m	follows (assume tax at 30%):	
	£5.24m	1.0m	year 5
		1.2m	year 6
		1.5m	year 7
		2.0m	year 8
Basic shares (assume)	2m		
Add convertible loans	2m		
(£4m × year 8 = 2m)	4m		

Basic earnings per share	£3m ÷ 2m = £1.50 per share
Diluted earnings per share	£5.24m ÷ 4m = £1.31 per share, a dilution and therefore disclosable.

(iii) *Share options*

The company is assumed to have to pay out shares to their employees/directors at an exercise price which is lower than current market, thus resulting in a dilution in earnings for existing shareholders. No dividends or interest are currently being paid to option holders so no adjustment is made to the top line of the ratio.

The bottom line is assumed to be increased by the discounted element of the number of shares to be issued.

EXAMPLE

Assume there are 5m share options. Option holders can exercise their rights at a price of £2 per share. Currently the shares have a market value of £3 each.

Basic and adjusted earnings		£3m
Basic shares (assume)	2m	
Share options 5m × 1/3rd	1.67m	
Total shares		3.67m
Basic earnings per share	£3m ÷ 2m = £1.50 per share	
Diluted earnings per share	£3m ÷ 3.67m = £0.82 per share, a dilution and therefore disclosable.	

FRS 14 also provides guidance on the order in which to include dilutive securities in the calculation of weighted average number of shares.

FRED 26 *Earnings per Share* (May 2002)

Although FRS 14 is fairly close to the existing IAS 33 *Earnings per Share*, the IASB republished a revised version in December 2003. The ASB have thus issued FRED 29 to ensure that IAS 33 will be implemented in late 2004 into UK reporting. There are a number of minor changes being proposed:

1. FRED 26 will require both basic and diluted EPS to be disclosed for both net profit/loss and also for continuing operations, on the face of the profit and loss account.
2. FRED 26 provides more guidance on the adjustments required to calculate basic EPS when there are preference shares. Any loss on settlement or excess fair value on early conversion of preference shares must be deducted in arriving at ordinary earnings.
3. FRED 26 includes an example of a situation where there are increasing rate preference dividends and an example where convertible bonds may be settled in shares or cash at an issuer's option.

The example below illustrates how to calculate a basic earnings per share as well as introducing a simple calculation of diluted earnings per share where share options exist:

Example – Killinchy Plc

Killinchy plc is a listed company. The issued share capital of the company at 1 April 2003 was as follows:

* 500 million equity shares of 50p each.
* 100 million £1 non-equity shares, redeemable at a premium on 31 March 2008. The effective finance cost of these shares for Killinchy plc is 10 per cent

per annum. The carrying value of the non-equity shares in the financial statements at 31 March 2003 was £110 million.

Extracts from the consolidated profit and loss account of Killinchy plc for the year ended 31 March 2004 showed:

	£m
Turnover	250
Cost of sales	(130)
Gross profit	120
Other operating expenses	(40)
Operating profit	80
Exceptional gain	10
Interest payable	(25)
Profit before taxation	65
Taxation	(20)
Profit after taxation	45
Appropriations of profit	(26)
Retained profit	19

Note – appropriations of profit:
- To non-equity shareholders   11
- To equity shareholders   15
       26

The company has a share option scheme in operation. The terms of the option are that option holders are permitted to purchase one equity share for every option held at a price of £1.50 per share. At 1 April 2003, 100 million share options were in issue. On 1 October 2003, the holders of 50 million options exercised their option to purchase, and 70 million new options were issued on the same terms as the existing options. During the year ended 31 March 2004, the average market price of an equity share in Killinchy plc was £2.00.

There were no changes in the number of shares or share options outstanding during the year ended 31 March 2004 other than as noted in the previous paragraph.

Suggested solution – Killinchy Plc

Computation of basic earnings per share

Profits after taxation	£45m
Appropriations to non-equity shareholders	11m
Basic earnings	£34m

Share structure

1. 4. 2003 Equity shares	500m
1. 10. 2003 Exercise of share options 50m × 1/2	25m
Basic share structure	525m

Basic EPS

Computation of diluted earnings per share

As per basic earnings		£34m
As per basic share structure	525m	
Options 100m × 1/2 year = 50m		
Options 120m × 1/2 year = 60m		
110m × 50 p/£2	27.5m	
		552.5m

$$\frac{\text{Dilutive earnings}}{\text{Diluted share structure}} = \frac{£34m}{552.5m} \times 100 = 6.15p$$

The second example brings in an added complication of having two potentially dilutable securities for a reporting entity within the one accounting period and the need to rank these from the most to the least dilutive first before calculating diluted earnings per share on a piecemeal basis:

Example – Dundrum Plc

The directors of Dundrum plc have supplied you with summarised profit and loss account information for the years ended 30 September 2003 and 2004 as follows:

	30 September 2004	30 September 2003
	£'000	£'000
Profit before tax	1,747	1,492
Taxation	(523)	(395)
Profit after tax	1,224	1,097
Minority interests	(87)	(57)
Dividends – ordinary	(100)	(100)
– preference	(35)	–
	1,002	940

The figure of profit after taxation for the year ended 30 September 2004 supplied to you is arrived at after charging extraordinary items of £279,000 net of taxation.

The earnings per share for the year ended 30 September 2003 was disclosed as 10.40p, there having been no changes in the number of shares in issue during that year.

On 1 January 2004 the company had a one-for-four rights issue at 60p per share which was fully subscribed. The price at the close of trading on 31 December 2003 was 84p and 10,000,000 50p ordinary shares were in issue at that date.

On 1 July 2004, in order to raise funds for additional working capital, the company issued a package of units, each comprising one £1 7 per cent convertible preference share plus one warrant for one ordinary share. The issue realised a total of £2.4 million with the preference shares being issued at a premium of 20p. The conversion terms were as follows:

£100 nominal preference shares in June 2014	110 ordinary 50p shares
or in June 2015	120 ordinary 50p shares
or in June 2016	130 ordinary 50p shares

and one warrant for one ordinary share with the consideration being 60p at the date on which the holder exercises his conversion rights.

The dividend on the preference shares is declared annually on 30 June. The price of 2.5 per cent consolidated stock at 30 June 2004 was 27 xd.

Assume a corporation tax rate of 35 per cent.

Suggested solution – Dundrum Plc

Calculation of basic earnings per share

2000	£'000	£'000
Earnings		
Profits after taxation		1,224
Less minority interests	87	
Preference dividends	35	
		122
		1,102

FRS 14: computation of adjustment factor

$$\frac{(10m \times 84p) + (2.5m \times 60p)}{10m + 2.5m} = 79.2p \text{ OR } (4 \times 84p = 336) + (1 \times 60p = 60)$$

$$\frac{\text{Cum } 84.0p}{\text{Ex } 79.2p} = 1.06 \qquad\qquad 5 \times (79.2) = 396$$

$$\frac{£1,102,000}{(10m \times 1.06 \times 3/12) + (12.5m \times 9/12)} = 9.2p$$

Calculation of diluted earnings per share   FRS 14

2000	£'000
Earnings	
Basic earnings (as above)	1,102
Add saving on preference dividend	35
	1,137

Number of shares

Basic number of shares	12,027
Add preference shares 1. 7. 00	
£2.4m ÷ £1.20 = 2,000,000 × 1.3 (highest conversion)	
= 2,600,000 × 1/4 year issued	650
Warrants 2,000,000 (as above) × 1/4 year × $\frac{24p}{84p}$ discount	
	142.847
	12,819.847

FRS 14: calculation of diluted earnings per share

Increase in earnings attributable to ordinary shareholders on conversion of potential ordinary shares

	Increase in earnings	Increase in number of ordinary shares	Earnings per incremental share
	£'000	£'000	£'000
Warrants			
Increase in earnings	Nil		
Incremental shares issued for			
no consideration			
2,000,000 × [(84p − 60p) ÷			
84p] × 1/4		142.847	Nil[1]
Preferences shares			
Increase in net profit	35		
Incremental shares		650 (1/4 × 2,600)	5.38[2]

Computation of diluted earnings per share

	Net profit attributable £	Ordinary shares	Earnings per incremental share
As reported	1,102,000	12,027,000	9.2p
Warrants	–	142,857	
	1,102,000	12,169,857	9.06p
Convertible preference shares	35,000	650,000	
	1,137,000	12,819,857	8.87p

The diluted earnings per share is 8.87p and *must* be disclosed under FRS 14.

The third example is the most complicated as it includes the issue of both bonus and full market issues of ordinary shares during the year as well as the requirement to use the ranking process in dermining the order in which dilutable securities should be brought into the calculation of diluted earnings per share. The example includes profits both from continuing and from discontinued operations, the latter of which must initially be excluded in the calculation of diluted earnings per share. Under the revised IAS 33 *Earnings Per Share*, which the ASB have promised to implement shortly, the diluted earnings per share will have to be calculated twice, one inclusive and one exclusive of discontinued operations. The example, therefore, covers most of the situations likely to be encountered in practice.

Example – Mourne Plc

The following financial statement extracts for the year ending 31 May 2003 relate to Mourne, a public limited company.

	£'000	£'000
Operating profit		
Continuing operations	26,700	
Discontinued operations	(1,120)	25,580
Continuing operations		
Profit on disposal of tangible fixed assets		2,500
Discontinued operations		
(Loss) on sale of operations		(5,080)
		23,000
Interest payable		(2,100)
Profit on ordinary activities before taxation		20,900
Tax on ordinary activities		(7,500)
Profit on ordinary activities after tax		13,400
Minority interests – equity		(540)
Profit attributable to members of parent company		12,860
Dividends:		
Preference dividend on non-equity shares	210	
Ordinary dividend on equity shares	300	
		(510)
Other appropriations – non-equity shares (note iii)		(80)
Retained profit for year		12,270

Capital as at 31 May 2003	£'000
Allotted, called-up and fully paid ordinary shares of £1 each	12,500
7% convertible redeemable preference shares of £1	3,000
	15,500

Additional information

(i)   On 1 January 2003, 3.6 million ordinary shares were issued at £2.50 in consideration of the acquisition of June Ltd for £9 million. These shares do not rank for dividend in the current period. Additionally the company purchased and cancelled £2.4 million of its own £1 ordinary shares on 1 April 2003. On

1 July 2003, the company made a bonus issue of one for five ordinary shares before the financial statements were issued for the year ended 31 May 2003.

(ii)   The company has a share option scheme under which certain directors can subscribe for the company's shares. The following details relate to the scheme:

Options outstanding 31 May 2002:

(a)   1.2 million ordinary shares at £2 each
(b)   Two million ordinary shares at £3 each;

both sets of options are exercisable before 31 May 2004.

Options granted during year 31 May 2003:
One million ordinary shares at £4 each exercisable before 31 May 2006, granted 1 June 2002.
During the year to 31 May 2003, the options relating to the 1.2 million ordinary shares (at a price of £2) were exercised on 1 March 2003. The average fair value of one ordinary share during the year was £5.

(iii) The 7 per cent convertible cumulative redeemable preference shares are convertible at the option of the shareholder or the company on 1 July 2004, 2005 and 2006 on the basis of two ordinary shares for every three preference shares. The preference share dividends are not in arrears. The shares are redeemable at the option of the shareholder on 1 July 2004, 2005 and 2006 at £1.50 per share. The 'other appropriations – non equity shares' item charged against the profits relates to the amortisation of the redemption premium and issue costs on the preference shares.

(iv)   Mourne issued £6 million 6 per cent convertible bonds on 1 June 2002 to finance the acquisition of Saintfield Ltd. Each bond is convertible into two ordinary shares of £1. Assume a corporation tax rate of 35 per cent.

(vi)   The interest payable relates entirely to continuing operations and the taxation charge relating to discontinued operations is assessed at £100,000 despite the accounting losses. The loss on discontinued operations relating to the minority interest is £600,000.

Suggested solution – Mourne Plc

Earnings per share – basic

		£'000
Profit attributable to members of parent company		12,860
Less: Preference dividend	(210)	
Other appropriations – non-equity shares	(80)	
		(290)
Basic earnings		12,570

Weighted average number of shares ('000)

	Shares	Weight	No.
1 June 2002	10,100	1.0	10,100
1 January 2003 (Note i – non-ranking)	3,600	5/12	1,500
1 March 2003	1,200	3/12	300
1 April 2003	(2,400)	2/12	(400)
	12,500		11,500
Bonus issue (post y/end but prior to issue) (1:5)			2,300
			13,800

Basic earnings $\dfrac{12,570}{13,800} \times 100 = 91.08\text{p}$

Weighted average shares

Diluted earnings per share

	£'000
Basic earnings	12,570
Add: Interest saved on 6% convertible bonds	234
Non-equity costs on preference shares	290
	13,094
Number of shares	29,340

Diluted earnings per share $\dfrac{13,094}{29,340} \times 100 =$ 44.6p

Ranking of dilutive securities

	£'000 Increase in earnings	'000 Increase in shares	£ Increase in earnings/share
Options	Nil	$1,200 \times \dfrac{9}{12} \times \dfrac{5-12}{5} = 540$	Nil
		$2,000 \times \dfrac{5-3}{5} = 800$	
		$1,000 \times \dfrac{5-4}{5} = 200$	
Convertible preference shares	290	$3,000 \times 2/3 = 2,000$	£0.145
Convertible bonds	234		
(6% × 6,000 × 65%)		$6,000 \times 2 = 12,000$	£0.0112
		15,540	
Basic shares		13,800	
		29,340	

Ranking – 1 options, 2 convertible bonds and 3 convertible preference shares

Computation of dilutive/anti-dilutive EPS

	£'000	Ordinary shares	Per share
Net profit from continuing operations	18,270	13,800	132p
Options	Nil	1,540	
	18,270	15,340	119p dilutive
6% bonds	234	12,000	
	18,504	27,340	67.7p dilutive
Convertible preference shares	290	2,000	
	18,794	29,340	64.1p dilutive

Net profit from continuing operations	£'000
Profit as per basic	12,860
Add discontinued loss (1,120 + 100)	1,220
Loss on sale of operations (5,080 − 600)	4,480
Non-equity shares appropriations	(290)
Net profit from continuing operations	18,270

Applications in published accounts

Kingfisher plc provides a good example where a company must prepare the official basic and diluted earnings per shares in accordance with FRS 14 but the group has the opportunity to publish further supplementary EPSs if they feel they would provide a better representation of the performance for the year. Kingfisher have decided to exclude a number of exceptional items from the figures revealing a 50% increase in earnings performance from the official figures. Generally most companies that provide supplementary EPSs only do so if it enhances their performance. However, companies are not allowed to provide special prominence for those supplementaries and they must provide a reconciliation between the official and adjusted EPS.

Kingfisher Plc   2 February 2002

Extract from Notes to the Accounts

12 Earnings per share
Basic earnings per share is calculated by dividing the earnings attributable to ordinary shareholders by the weighted average number of ordinary shares in issue during the year, excluding those held in the ESOP (see note 36) which are treated as cancelled. The weighted average number of shares has been adjusted for the share consolidation on 28 August 2001 as approved by the shareholders at an extraordinary general meeting on 24 August 2001, when the ordinary shares of 12.5p were consolidated on a 10 for 11 basis into ordinary shares of 13.75p. Figures for the prior year have been restated accordingly.

For diluted earnings per share, the weighted average number of ordinary shares in issue is adjusted to assume conversion of all dilutive potential ordinary shares. These represent share options granted to employees where the exercise price is less than the average market price of the company's shares during the year.

Supplementary earnings per share figures are presented. These exclude the effects of operating and non-operating exceptional items, acquisition goodwill amortisation and, for the year ended 3 February 2001, Liberty Surf losses as the directors do not believe it is meaningful to aggregate these with the profits from the established Group businesses.

Earnings per share for continuing operations are presented in order to provide a more meaningful comparison.

Continuing operations

	2002			As restated 2001		
	Earnings	Weighted average number of shares	Per share amount	Earnings	Weighted average number of shares	Per share amount
	£millions	millions	pence	£millions	millions	pence
Basic earnings per share						
Earnings attributable to ordinary shareholders	181.4	1,258.3	14.4	246.3	1,245.0	19.8
Effect of dilutive securities						
Options		13.1	(0.1)		13.8	(0.2)
Convertible loan stock in subsidiary undertaking	(3.6)		(0.3)	(6.0)		(0.5)
Diluted earnings per share	177.8	1,271.4	14.0	240.3	1,258.8	19.1
Supplementary earnings per share						
Basic earnings per share	181.4	1,258.3	14.4	246.3	1,245.0	19.8
Effect of exceptionals						
Operating exceptional items	97.9		7.8	(5.8)		(0.5)
(Profit)/loss on the sale of operations	(57.7)		(4.6)	13.3		1.1
Loss/(profit) on the disposal of fixed assets	34.7		2.7	(0.2)		–
Tax impact arising on exceptional items	(1.8)		(0.1)	2.1		0.1
Minority share of exceptional items	(1.8)		(0.1)	1.6		0.1
Acquisition goodwill amortisation (net of tax)	14.1		1.1	14.6		1.2
Basic – adjusted earnings per share	266.8	1,258.3	21.2	271.9	1,245.0	21.8
Diluted earnings per share	177.8	1,271.4	14.0	240.3	1,258.8	19.1
Effect of exceptionals						
Operating exceptional items	97.9		7.7	(5.8)		(0.5)
loss on the sale of operations	(57.7)		(4.6)	13.3		1.1
Loss/(profit) on the disposal of fixed assets	34.7		2.7	(0.2)		–
Tax impact arising on exceptional items	(1.8)		(0.1)	2.1		0.1
Minority share of exceptional items	(1.9)		(0.1)	1.7		0.1
Acquisition goodwill amortisation (net of tax)	14.1		1.1	14.6		1.2
Diluted – adjusted earnings per share	263.1	1,271.4	20.7	266.0	1,258.8	21.1

The second example shows that reporting entities must disclose both basic and diluted losses per share as well as earnings per share:

Securicor Plc   30 September 2001

Extract from Notes to the Accounts

7 (Loss)/earnings per share

	2001 £m	2000 £m
Basic		
(Loss)/profit after taxation	(24.0)	34.4
Minority Interests	(2.1)	(0.6)
(Loss)/profit attributable to shareholders	(26.1)	33.8
Weighted average number of share outstanding	620.4m	614.8m
Basic (loss)/earnings per share	(4.2)p	5.5p
Fully diluted		
Adjusted (loss)/earnings:		
(Loss)/profit attributable to shareholders	(26.1)	33.8
Interest on future issues net of tax	0.3	0.3
Adjusted attributable (loss)/profit	(25.8)	34.1
Weighted average number of shares in issue	631.5m	620.2m
Since on this basis the diluted loss per share is reduced, the incremental effect is ignored		
Fully diluted (loss)/earnings per share	(4.2)p	5.5p

The final example, PNC Telecom, provides another illustration of a company providing alternative EPS calculations. However, the disclosure also provides an example of two adjustments to calculating basic earnings, i.e. deferred consideration payable and a share options/warrants adjustment in the calculation of diluted earnings per share.

PNC Telecom Plc 31 March 2001

Extract from Notes to the Accounts

13. Earnings Per Share

The weighted average number of shares used was:

	2001 No. '000	2000 No.'000
Basic	42,215	28,440
Deferred consideration adjustment	829	656
Share options and warrants adjustment	1,065	617
Diluted	44,109	29,713

The profits/(losses) used were:

	2001 £'000	2001 p	2000 £'000	2000 p
Basic				
Loss for the year	(5,940)	(14.07)	(478)	(1.68)
Amortisation of goodwill and intangibles and exceptional items	7,895	18.70	1,106	3.89
Profit/(losses) excluding amortisation of goodwill and intangibles and exceptional items	1,955	4.63	628	2.21
Discontinuing activities – other costs	574	1.36	(35)	(0.12)
Continuing activities excluding amortisation of goodwill and intangibles and exceptional items	2,529	5.99	593	2.09
Diluted				
Loss for the year	(5,940)	(14.07)	(478)	(1.68)
Amortisation of goodwill and intangibles and exceptional items	7,895	18.50	1,106	3.79
Profit/(losses) excluding amortisation of goodwill and intangibles and exceptional items	1,955	4.43	628	2.11
Discontinued activities – other costs	574	1.30	(28)	0.09
Continuing activities excluding amortisation of goodwill and intangibles and exceptional items	2,529	5.73	600	2.02

The presentation of alternative earnings per share figures is given to enable shareholders to make comparisons with other companies in the industry and to demonstrate the underlying performance of the company before exceptional and non-recurring items.

6.2 FRS 3 *Reporting Financial Performance* (October 1992, amended June 1993)

Background

One of the major creative accounting techniques of the 1980s was the deliberate manipulation of earnings per share by the inclusion of large 'exceptional' profits above the line and the exclusion of 'extraordinary' losses below the line. The main reason for this manipulation was the tendency for financial analysts to overconcentrate on earnings as the 'be all and end all' to an analysis of company performance. They failed to investigate more fully the various components of performance or the financial position of the company at the year end. The ASB therefore set out with a number of objectives to try to improve financial reporting:

(i) to move users' attention away from their fixation on earnings per share;

(ii) to introduce a number of different performance measures apart from earnings per share; and

(iii) to provide more detailed information within the profit and loss account of operating performance.

Key issues

Profit and loss account

A number of specific adjustments have been introduced to improve the relevance of the profit and loss account. These can be summarised as follows:

(i) *The demise of extraordinary items*

Due to legal reasons these cannot be abolished totally as they are contained within the schedules to the Companies Acts. However, the ASB has extended the definition of ordinary activities so as to encompass almost any activity that the reporting entity can get up to. It is almost impossible to imagine any items that could now be classified as extraordinary. As Sir David Tweedie said at the time of its introduction, 'unless Martians were to land on earth nothing could be said to be extraordinary'.

(ii) *The new definition of earnings per share*

Earnings per share is now defined as profits after taxation, minority interests, preference dividends but also after deducting all exceptional and extraordinary items divided by the number of shares issued and ranking for dividend. Thus the incentive to include material losses as extraordinary items is no longer in existence as it does not matter whether they are classified as exceptional or extraordinary since both must be incorporated within earnings.

(iii) *The profit and loss account should be split between continuing operations, discontinued activities and acquisitions*

It is now compulsory to split both turnover and operating profit on the face of the profit and loss account between its three subcomponents of continuing operations, discontinued operations and acquisitions. The detailed breakdown, however, of cost of sales, administration and distribution costs need not be recorded on the face of that document but instead may be incorporated in the notes to the financial statements.

The most difficult part of the analysis is the requirement to report discontinued operations as a separate section of turnover and operating profit. Discontinued operations must satisfy all four of the following conditions:

- The sale/termination must be completed during the accounting period or a maximum of 3 months into the next accounting period. However, if the accounts are approved earlier than 3 months, then that date becomes the deadline.
- If terminated, the activities must have ceased permanently.
- The sale/termination must have a material effect on the nature and focus of the entity's operations, e.g. a material reduction in operations arising from a withdrawal from a particular market. It must be a major strategic decision, not merely the closure of a loss-making facility.

- The assets, liabilities and results of the entity must be clearly distinguished for both financial accounting and operational purposes.

(iv) *The advent of 'super-exceptional' items*

Because of the demise of extraordinary items the former extraordinary items will now become classified as exceptional and should be recorded within their own headings in the profit and loss account and detailed in the notes to the accounts. However, there are three 'super-exceptional' items that must be classified on the face of the profit and loss account itself, between operating profits and interest payable. These are:

- profits/losses on the disposal of fixed assets;
- profits/losses on the sale or termination of an operation; and
- costs of a fundamental reorganisation.

Other performance measures

Statement of total recognised gains and losses (STRGL)

A new primary performance statement which should incorporate both operating profits/losses and also any other gains/losses which are not realised but represent increases/decreases in wealth creation. This is to be treated with equal respect to the other three primary statements, i.e. the profit and loss account, balance sheet and the cash flow statement.

Apart from the earned operating profits/losses it should also include any prior year adjustments, revaluation gains/losses and any foreign exchange gains/losses arising from the adoption of the closing rate method of translation.

Note of historical cost profits and losses

This is a new note to be attached to the back of the financial statements and will only be applicable to those entities that have adopted a modified form of historical cost accounting rather than the strict historical cost approach. It is designed to make those companies which have adopted the modified approach comparable to companies which have remained with historical cost. The statement starts with the modified profit/loss and is then adjusted for two items to reconcile it back to historical profit/loss:

(i) the excess depreciation charged; and
(ii) the difference in the profit/loss on disposal as calculated under historical cost accounting and that under modified historical cost accounting.

Reconciliation of movements in shareholders' funds

This third new statement may either be recognised as a fifth primary statement or treated merely as a note to the financial statements. It reconciles the opening and closing totals of shareholders' funds and will incorporate all the changes in wealth included within the STRGL but also the introduction of new capital, the payment of dividends and the write-off of goodwill and its subsequent reinstatement on disposal of a subsidiary.

Prior period adjustments

Prior year adjustments were included in the former SSAP 6 *Extraordinary Items and Prior Year Adjustments* and they have been retained under the new FRS. They still incorporate both fundamental errors and changes in accounting policies. However, they do not include the normal changes in accounting estimate which are still to be recorded under normal operating activities. Prior period adjustments must be charged/credited directly to opening reserves and any comparatives should also be amended for previous years. Prior period adjustments must also be amended against opening reserves in the *Reconciliation of Movements in Shareholders' Funds* and as a reduction/increase in wealth creation in the *Statement of Total Recognised Gains and Losses.*

Comparatives

Unfortunately, reporting entities will not be able to adopt the last period's figures as their comparatives. These will need to be restated, particularly where there are discontinued operations during the current year which would previously be recorded under the heading of continuing operations.

Future changes

In December 2003 the IASB issued a revised version of IAS 8 *Accounting Policies, Changes in Accounting Estimates and Errors*, which will be implemented in January 2005. There are a number of controversial recommendations but, in particular, a proposal to change the term 'fundamental error' to 'material error' as one of the two permissible prior year adjustments. Once implemented there is a fear that there will be numerous 'bad news' material errors of previous years which would then bypass the profit and loss and in reality reintroduce the problem of extraordinary items back into financial reporting that was solved by FRS 3. The ASB would have liked to see the present definition of a fundamental error retained so that there are very few opportunities for reserve accounting.

In addition, the ASB published FRED 22 *Revision of FRS 3: Reporting Financial Performance* in December 2000, which essentially is a proposal to replace the existing profit and loss account and statement of total recognised gains and losses with a brand new single Statement of Financial Performance. That statement will be split into three sections – an operating, financing and treasury, and an 'other gains and losses' section. There are also other important proposals that include:

(1) The removal of dividends from the profit and loss account to a reserve movement with a possible footnote at the bottom of the profit and loss.
(2) The requirement to prepare EPS only on the sum of the first two headings and therefore to exclude other gains and losses from the calculation.
(3) The proposal to make the Reconciliation of the Movement in Ownership Interest a major primary statement (currently a Reconciliation of the Movement in Shareholders' Funds).
(4) The retention of disclosure of turnover and operating profit into three sections. However, the term discontinued operations will be replaced by IAS 35's *Discontinuing Operations*, which means that a major part of the business need not

necessarily be closed down or sold off, but merely that a public announcement must take place that the operation is to be discontinued. (Since abandoned by IFRS 5).

(5)   The *removal* of exceptional items from the face of the profit and loss (commonly called 'super-exceptionals') and the need to record these within their appropriate heading in the new performance statement.

Since that document was published concentration has moved from a national to an international solution to the problem. The IASB are intending to issue a draft standard by the end of 2005, which is likely to introduce a new Statement of Comprehensive Income that will combine the profit and loss account with the statement of total recognised gains and losses.

The first example illustrates how to prepare the profit and loss account when there are acquisitions and discontinued operations during an accounting period. In addition it provides examples of when an operation may be classified as discontinued in the first place:

Example – Blacklion Ltd

Blacklion Ltd is a divisionalised company engaged in a range of activities. Its core business is the wholesaling of mechanical equipment and heavy machinery for the construction industry.

Over the years, it has become involved in various retail and manufacturing operations associated with its core business. The company commenced a rationalisation programme during 2004 and decided to run down some of its non-core activities while also strengthening its wholesaling business.

Set out below is a summary of the company's results for the years ended 31 December 2004 and 2003 as well as additional information on the activities during the year.

	2004	2003
	£m	£m
Turnover	500	484
Cost of sales	388	360
Gross profit	112	124
Distribution costs	28	20
Administration expenses	50	42
Operating profit	34	62
Interest payable	12	8
Profit before taxation	22	54

Additional information

(1)   To assist with expansion into new geographical markets, the company acquired another wholesaling business which contributed £22 million to turnover and £4 million to operating profits during 2004.

(2)   In line with the policy of concentrating upon the core wholesaling business, management decided to withdraw from the retail market and sold the company's retail division at a profit of £14 million (credited to cost of sales) on 30 June 2004. Up to the point of sale, this division had contributed turnover of £40 million (£50 million in 12 months to 31 December 2003) and an operating loss of £10 million (£10 million profit in 12 months to 31 December 2003). While the sale of the assets and liabilities of this business will have a

material effect on the nature and focus of Blacklion Ltd's operations, management believes that the company will benefit in the longer term.

(3) A manufacturing division, which only produced specialised lifting equipment to order, was run down and discontinued in October 2004. Its turnover had been £30 million in 2004 (£48 million in the 12 months to 31 December 2003) and it had made operating losses of £16 million (£12 million in the 12 months to 31 December 2003). Implementing the decision to curtail the company's presence in this market was straightforward as the division's activities were clearly distinguishable from the other operations. Costs associated with the closure, which are included in cost of sales, were as follows:

	£m
Redundancy	1
Loss on sale of fixed assets	3
Stock write-offs	2
	6

(4) During 2004, the company closed one of its plant hire depots and incurred costs of approximately £60,000 relating to the reorganisation of activities. This has been charged to distribution costs. Staff were either transferred to other duties within the company or accepted early retirement. The assets were transferred to other depots and no decline in customer base is anticipated.

(5) During 2004, the company sold an office building for £12 million. As it had originally cost £12 million, no profit or loss on disposal has been reported in the 2004 profit and loss account. The balance sheet carrying value of the building at the date of the disposal was £13 million.

Suggested solution – Blacklion Ltd

Blacklion Ltd – profit and loss account for the year ended 31 December 2004

	2004		2003	
	£m	£m	£m	£m
Turnover				
Continuing (W1)	408		386	
Acquisitions	22		–	
	430		386	
Discontinued operations	70		98	
Total turnover		500		484
Cost of sales (W2)		(396)		(360)
Gross profit		104		124
Distribution costs	(28)		(20)	
Administration expenses	(50)		(42)	
		(78)		(62)

Operating profit

Continuing (W3)	48		64	
Acquisitions (note 1)	4		–	
	52		64	
Discontinued operations (notes 2, 3)	(26)		(2)	
		26		62

Exceptional items

Loss on sale of property in continuing operations (W4, note 5)	(1)		–	
Profit on sale of operations (W5, note 2)	14		–	
Costs of discontinuance (W6, note 3)	(6)		–	
		7		–
		33		62
Interest payable		(12)		(8)
Profit on ordinary activities before taxation		21		54

Workings

(1)

	2004	2003
	£m	£m
Turnover	500	484
Acquisitions (note 1)	(22)	–
Discontinued operations		
retail (note 2)	(40)	(50)
manufacturing (note 3)	(30)	(48)
Continuing operations	408	386

(2)

	2004
	£m
Original cost of sales	388
Error in credit to cost of sales on disposal of retail division (note 2)	14
Error in debit to cost of sales of continuance (note 3)	(6)
	396

(3)

	2004	2003
	£m	£m
Operating profit	34	62
Exceptional items (excl. property sale)	(8)	–
Discontinued operations		
retail (note 2)	10	(10)
manufacturing (note 3)	16	12
Acquisitions (note 1)	(4)	–
Continuing operations	48	64

(4) Loss on disposal calculated in accordance with FRS 3:

	2004
	£m

Net sale proceeds	12
Balance sheet carrying value	13
Loss on sale of fixed assets	(1)

(5) The profit on sale of operations should always be shown on the face of the profit and loss account.

(6) The exceptional item relating to the costs of discontinuance should be interpreted in two ways:

   (i) as one of three specific non-operating 'super-exceptional' items to be disclosed on the face of the profit and loss account (as per solution given);

   (ii) the loss on disposal of fixed assets could be included on the face of the profit and loss account and the other items relating to the discontinuance charged to cost of sales, etc., with relevant disclosure in the accounts.

(7) The closure of the hire depot is not expected to lead to a material reduction in turnover in the continuing market and therefore does not meet the conditions in para. 4 c of FRS 3. The operations of the closed depot are not therefore discontinued. If the costs are thought to be material they may have to be disclosed in the notes. They do not appear to fall into one of the categories listed in para. 20 of FRS 3, as there is no material effect on the nature and focus of operations. The costs are therefore charged in arriving at operating profit.

The second example concentrates on the second half of FRS 3 and the need to publish three additional statements in the published accounts, i.e. Statement of Total Recognised Gains and Losses, the Note of Historic Profits and Losses and the Reconciliation of Movements in Shareholder's Funds:

Example – Coleraine Group Plc

Coleraine Group plc has prepared its financial statements for the year ended 31 January 2004. However, the financial accountant of Coleraine Group plc had difficulty in preparing the statements required by FRS 3 *Reporting Financial Performance* and approached you for help in preparing those statements. The financial accountant furnished you with the following information:

(i) *Profit and loss account extract for year ended 31 January 2004*
   Coleraine Group plc

	£m
Operating profit - continuing operations	290
Profit on sale of property in continuing operations	10
Profit on ordinary activities before taxation	300
Tax on ordinary activities	(90)
Profit after taxation	210
Dividends	(15)
Retained profit for year	195

The financial accountant did not provide for the loss on any discontinued operations in the profit and loss account. (However, you may assume that the taxation provision incorporated the effects of any provision for discontinued operations.)

(ii)   The shareholders' funds at the beginning of the financial year were as follows:

	£m
Share capital – £1 ordinary shares	350
Merger reserve	55
Revaluation reserve	215
Profit and loss reserve	775
	1,395

(iii)   Coleraine Group plc regularly revalues its fixed assets and at 31 January 2004, a revaluation surplus of £375 million had been credited to revaluation reserve. During the financial year, a property had been sold on which a revaluation surplus of £54 million had been credited to reserves. Further, if the company had charged depreciation on a historical cost basis rather than the revalued amounts, the depreciation charge in the profit and loss account for fixed assets would have been £7 million. The current year's charge for depreciation was £16 million.

(iv)   The group has a policy of writing off goodwill on the acquisition of subsidiaries directly against a merger reserve. The goodwill for the period amounted to £250 million. In order to facilitate the purchase of subsidiaries, the company had issued £1 ordinary shares of nominal value £150 million and share premium of £450 million. The premium had been taken to the merger reserve. All subsidiaries are currently 100 per cent owned by the group.

(v)   During the financial year to 31 January 2004, the company had made a decision to close a 100 per cent owned subsidiary, Articlave plc. However, the closure did not take place until May 2004. Coleraine Group plc estimated that as at 31 January 2004 the operating loss for the period 1 February 2004 to 31 May 2004 would be £30 million and that in addition redundancy costs, stock and plant write-downs would amount to £15 million. In the event, the operating loss for the period 1 February 2004 to 31 May 2004 was £65 million, but the redundancy costs, stock and plant write-downs only amounted to £12 million.

(vi)   The following information relates to Articlave plc for the period 1 February 2004 to 31 May 2004.

	£m
Turnover	175
Cost of sales	(195)
Gross loss	(20)
Administrative expenses	(15)
Selling expenses	(30)
Operating loss before taxation	(65)

Suggested solution – Coleraine Group Plc

Statement of total recognised gains and losses

	£m
Profit for the financial year	165
Other recognised gains and losses for the year	
Unrealised surpluses on revaluation of fixed assets	375
Total recognised gains and losses for the year	540

Reconciliation of movements in shareholders' funds

	£m	
Profit for the financial year	165	
Dividends	(15)	
	150	
Other recognised gains and losses		
for the year after dividends	375	
New share capital issued	600	
Goodwill written off on acquisitions	(250)	(Note: no longer permitted by FRS 10)
Net additions to shareholders' funds	875	
Opening shareholders' funds	1,395	
Closing shareholders' funds	2,270	

Analysis of movements on reserves

	Merger reserve £m	Revaluation reserve £m	Profit and loss £m	Total £m
Opening balance	55	215	775	1,045
Profit for financial year			165	165
Property revaluation		375		375
Total recognised gains and losses for year	–	375	165	540
Transfer of previous revaluation reserve				
surplus realised in year		(54)	54	–
Depreciation on revalued assets less				
historical cost depreciation		(9)	9	–
Adjustments to reported profit to give profit				
on historical cost basis	–	(63)	63	–
Issue of shares	450			450
Goodwill written off	(250)			(250)
Dividend for year			(15)	(15)
Closing balance	255	527	988	1,770

Note of historical cost profits and losses

	£m
Reported profit on ordinary activities before taxation	255
Realisation of property revaluation gains of previous year	54
Difference between historical cost depreciation	
and depreciation calculated on revalued amount	9

Historical cost profit on ordinary activities before tax	318
Historical cost profit for the period retained after taxation, extraordinary items and dividends	213

Workings

Extract from profit and loss account – 31 January 2004

	£m
Profit on ordinary activities before taxation – continuing operations	300
Provision for loss on operations to be discontinued	(45)
Profit on ordinary activities before taxation	255
Taxation	(90)
Profit for the financial year	165
Dividends	(15)
	150

As the decision to close the subsidiary was made before the year-end, but the closure will not occur until the following year, a provision for loss on operations to be discontinued would be required in the financial statements for the year ending 31 January 2004. The provision would comprise any direct costs of closure and any operating losses up to the date of closure. In this case the provision will contain the estimated operating loss from 1 February 2004 to 31 May 2004 of £30 million and the redundancy costs, stock and plant write-downs of £15 million: a total of £45 million.

As the closure does not qualify as a discontinued operation for the year ending 31 January 2004, the results of the subsidiary should be included in continuing operations, with the provision being shown as an exceptional item. In the notes to the financial statements it may be appropriate to disclose separately the results of operations which, although not discontinued, are in the process of being discontinued. Thus, the results of Articlave plc for the year ending 31 January 2004 will be given and classified as 'discontinuing', not 'discontinued'. It should not be disclosed on the face of the profit and loss account as a 'super-exceptional' item.

In the year to 31 January 2005, the closure of Articlave plc will qualify as a discontinued operation. The following figures will appear in the financial statements of Coleraine Group plc in respect of the subsidiary, Articlave plc.

Articlave plc – 31 January 2005

	£m	£m
Turnover – discontinued operations		175
Cost of sales		(195)
Gross loss		(20)
Administrative expenses	(15)	
Selling expenses	(30)	
Less provision released	30	
		(15)
Operating loss – discontinued operations		(35)

Loss on disposal of discontinued operations	(12)
Less release of provision	15
	3
Loss on ordinary activities before tax	(32)

The provision of £45 million was provided for in the 2004 financial statements and it has to be allocated between the operating loss and the loss on disposal. The actual loss in the period to 31 May 2004 was £65 million and the provision made against this in the previous period's financial statements of £30 million would be offset against this loss. The turnover and operating profit for the period to 31 May 2005 would be classified as discontinued in the financial statements to 31 January 2005.

In the financial statements to 31 January 2005, the provision of £15 million would be released against the loss on the disposal of discontinued operations.

The third example examines a subsidiary as a distinct operation as well as shutting down one of its main manufacturing units so the example incorporates the issue of discontinued operations within the context of preparing group financial statements.

Example – Greencastle Plc

Greencastle plc is engaged in the paper-making industry and has one subsidiary Moville plc and several autonomous manufacturing units. Greencastle plc owns 60 per cent of the voting shares of Moville plc, which were acquired on 1 September 2002, when the profit and loss account balance of Moville was £1.4 million. The draft profit and loss accounts for the year ended 31 August 2004 including discontinued activities were:

	Greencastle plc		Moville plc	
	£'000	£'000	£'000	£'000
Turnover		15,050		12,340
Cost of sales		(12,679)		(10,622)
Gross profit		2,371		1,718
Dividend income (net)		280		64
		2,651		1,782
Loss on disposal of unit	180			
(net of all provisions for losses)				
Distribution costs	1,042		824	
Administrative expenses	766		307	
		(1,988)		(1,131)
Net profit before tax		663		651
Corporation tax		(268)		(96)
Net profit after tax before dividends		395		555

Additional information

(a)   During the year Greencastle plc had closed down one of its largest manufacturing units. The following details relate to the closure of this unit up to the date of its discontinuance in July 2004, and are included in the profit and loss account of Greencastle plc.

	£'000	£'000
Turnover		1,300
Cost of sales		(1,225)
Gross profit		75
Distribution costs		(100)
Administrative expenses		(285)
Operating loss		(310)
Provision for losses at 1. 9. 2001		
operational loss	50	
loss on disposal	70	
	120	
Loss on disposal of unit	(300)	
		(180)
		(490)
Taxation relief		82
Loss on discontinued activities		(408)

Greencastle plc is currently developing a new paper-making machine, which will become operational in 2006. The auditors have agreed that the project has commercial viability and are happy that the outcome of the project will be successful and be beneficial to the company. The current year's expenditure of £36,000 has been included in administrative expenses.

Moville plc has been attempting to create a chemical product which will neutralise the caustic effects of the waste paper it produces. This would enable it to reduce the costs of disposal of the waste paper. Currently this research has proved to be unsuccessful. The costs of this research amounting to £72,000 have been charged to cost of sales.

It is the group policy to defer research and development expenditure to future periods wherever this is possible within the terms of SSAP 13 *Accounting for Research and Development.*

Greencastle plc proposes to declare a final dividend of 5p per ordinary share. Moville plc has already paid an interim dividend of 10p per ordinary share (on 1 May 2004) and does not propose to pay a final dividend. The issued share capital of Greencastle plc is 600,000 ordinary shares of 50p each and of Moville plc is 200,000 ordinary shares of £1 each. Greencastle plc accounts for dividends received on a cash basis.

The profit and loss account balances at 1 September 2003 were £1.75 million for Greencastle plc and £1.6 million for Moville plc.

Moville plc occasionally trades with its parent company. During the year Greencastle plc had purchased goods amounting to £275,000 from Moville plc, and Moville plc had purchased goods from Greencastle plc amounting to £450,000. These transactions had occurred early in the financial year and none of these goods remained in stock at the financial year end. Inter-company sales are charged at cost plus 25 per cent profit.

Suggested solution – Greencastle Plc

Greencastle plc – Consolidated profit and loss account for the year ended 31 August 2004

	£'000	£'000
Turnover (W1)		
Continuing operations	25,365	
Discontinued operations	1,300	
		26,665
Cost of sales (W1)		(22,576)
Gross profit		4,089
Net operating expenses (W1)		(2,521)
Operating profit		1,568
Continuing operations (W1)	1,828	
Discontinued operations	(310)	
Less 2001 provision	50	
	1,568	
Loss on disposal of discontinued operations	(300)	
Less 2001 provision	70	
		(230)
Profit on ordinary activities before taxation		1,338
Tax on profit on ordinary activities (W3)		(364)
Profit on ordinary activities after taxation		974
Minority interests (W4)		(222)
Profit for financial year		752
Dividends (600,000 × 5p)		(30)
Retained profit for the financial year		722
Earnings per share (W5)		125.3p

Group structure

```
          G
                60%
          A
                40%     Minority interests
```

Workings

(W1) *Consolidated profit and loss schedule*

	Greencastle £'000	Moville £'000	Inter Co £'000	Total £'000	Discontinued £'000	Continuing £'000
Sales	15,050	12,340	(725)	26,665	1,300	25,365
Cost of sales	12,679	10,622	(725)	22,576	1,225	21,351
Gross profit	2,371	1,718	–	4,089	75	4,014
Net operating expenses						
Distribution costs	1,042	824	–	1,866	100	1,766
Administrative expenses	730[1]	307	–	1,037	285	752

Other operating income

Investment income (net)	(280)	(64)	(12)[2]	(332)		(332)
Net operating expenses	1,492	1,067	(12)	2,571	385	2,186
Net profit	879	651	(12)	1,518	(310)	1,828
Provision for discontinuance				50	50	
				1,568	260	1,828

Net operating expenses = 2,571 above − provision for discontinuance 50 = 2,521

1   Admin 766 − R&D36 = 730
2   See working 2

(W2) *Inter-company dividend*

60% of 20 (200,000 × 10p) = 12 (net)

(W3) *Tax on profit on ordinary activities*

	£'000
Greencastle	268
Moville plc	96
	364

(W4) *Minority interest*

Moville plc net profit after tax	555
Minority interest 40% thereof	222

(W5) *Earnings per share*

£'000

$$\frac{\text{Profits for financial year}}{\text{No. of ordinary shares}} = \frac{752}{600} \times 100 = 125.3p$$

Group profit/loss account as at 31 August 2004

	£'000	£'000
Greencastle plc profit/loss account at 1. 9. 03		1,750
Moville plc profit/loss account at 1. 9. 03	1,600	
Less profit/loss account at acquisition	(1,400)	
	200	
Group share thereof 60%		120
Profit and loss for year		722
Group resources at 31 August 2004		2,592

The final example embraces both the need to prepare a profit and loss account with its attendant problems of discontinued operations as well as the preparation of the new performance statements required by FRS 3. The example also recognises that in the preparation of final published accounts a number of SSAPs/FRSs need to be investigated and adhered to in order to provide a true and fair view and as such incorporates SSAP 9 and 19 and FRS 12:

Example – Buncrana Plc

Buncrana plc is a very successful company involved in the business of manufacturing and selling various components and accessories to the motor trade. The trial balance of Buncrana plc as at 31 December 2003 is set out below:

Trial balance as at 31 December 2003

	Dr. £m	Cr. £m
Sales		300
Cost of sales	210	
Selling and distribution costs	12	
Administration expenses	8.5	
Debenture interest	1.2	
Finance charges	0.5	
Dividends proposed	8	
Tax on profits	10	
Exceptional item	15	
Corporation tax payable		10
Fixed assets at cost:		
Land	5	
Investment property	5	
Buildings	100	
Plant and machinery	120	
Fixtures and fittings	30	
Accumulated depreciation		
Buildings		16
Plant and machinery		36
Fixtures and fittings		12
Stocks	30	
Debtors and creditors	80	70
Cash at bank	40	
12% debenture loan		10
Deferred taxation		5
£1 ordinary share capital		100
Profit and loss account		116.2
	675.2	675.2

Additional information

(1) Depreciation is to be provided on a straight-line basis and charged to cost of sales as follows:
    Buildings   50 years
    Plant and machinery 10 years
    Fixtures and fittings 5 years

(2)   Investment property, which is currently stated at cost in the trial balance, should be revalued at 31 December 2003 to £7.5 million.

(3)   Stocks at 31 December 2003 included headlights valued at original cost of £3 million. However, the market value, as evidenced by subsequent sales in January 2004, was £2.2 million, ignoring selling and distribution costs of £200,000. The replacement cost of the stock is £1.75 million.

(4)   The company has received a claim for unfair dismissal from a former director for £1 million and the directors believe that the courts will uphold the claim.

(5)   Turnover includes £45 million relating to a company acquired during the year. It contributed £10 million to operating profits.

(6)   Buncrana plc manufactures and supplies exhausts and mounting brackets to both car manufacturers and a number of well-known chains of car repair outlets. During 2003, the company carried out a review of its manufacturing processes in relation to the mounting brackets and decided it would be cost effective in the long term to subcontract the manufacture of these brackets. The company ceased manufacture of the mounting brackets prior to the year end, but continued to sell to the same customer base using supplies from subcontractors. It is estimated that mounting brackets contributed £8.5 million in turnover and £1.2 million in operating profits during the year.

(7)   The company closed down one of its manufacturing divisions during the year. This division had manufactured low-cost plastic grilles and fittings, but had been unable to compete against cheaper foreign imports. All buildings and equipment were sold. The directors acknowledge that the closure will have a material effect on the nature and focus of operations. However, withdrawal from this market is consistent with the company's long-term plans.

This division had contributed £30 million in turnover and £8 million in operating profits during the year. The exceptional item shown on the trial balance relates to the costs incurred in closing down this division. (Ignore tax implications.)

(8)   The Board of Buncrana plc took the decision on 23 December 2003 to close an operation that is loss making. At the year end it was estimated that it will take 1 year to close down the operation and that the operation will lose a further £2.5 million over that period. Land, with a book value of £1.8 million, is expected to have a recoverable value not exceeding £1 million as a result of the closure decision. Implementation of the closure had not commenced at the balance sheet date and no public announcement had been made.

(9)   Capital commitments at 31 December 2003 comprised contracts for new plant and machinery amounting to £1.9 million. The directors have also authorised a further £900,000 of capital expenditure on buildings. These have not yet been provided for.

Suggested solution – Buncrana Plc

Profit and loss account for the year ended 31 December 2003

		£m	£m
Turnover			
Continuing operations		225	
Acquisitions	(W5)	45	
		270	
Discontinued operations		30	300
Cost of sales	(W1)		(231)
Gross profit			69
Selling and distribution costs	(W1)		(12)
Administration expenses	(W1)		(9.5)
Operating profit			
Continuing operations		29.5	
Acquisitions		10	
		39.5	
Discontinued operations		8	47.5
Impairment of fixed assets	(W8)		(0.8)
Exceptional closure costs – plastic operations	(W7)		(15)
			31.7
Interest payable (1.2 + 0.5)			(1.7)
Profit on ordinary activities before taxation			30
Tax on ordinary activities			(10)
Profit on ordinary activities after taxation			20
Dividends proposed			(8)
Retained profits for the year			12
Retained profits brought forward at 1. 1. 2003			116.2
Retained profits carried forward at 31. 12. 2003			128.2

Balance sheet as at 31 December 2003

		£m	£m
Fixed assets			
Tangible assets	(W10)		177.7
Current assets			
Stocks	(30 − 1 (W3))	29	
Debtors		80	
Cash at bank		40	
		149	
Creditors: amounts falling due within one year	(70 + 1 (W4) + 10)	81	
Net current assets			68
			245.7
Creditors: amounts falling due after more than 1 year			
12% debenture loans			(10)
			235.7
Provisions for liabilities and charges			
Deferred taxation			(5)
			230.7

Capital and reserves
Called-up share capital   100
Investment property revaluation reserve   (W2)   2.5
Profit and loss account   128.2
    230.7

Statement of total recognised gains and losses

	£m
Profit for the financial year	20
Unrealised surplus on revaluation of investment properties	2.5
Total recognised gains and losses	22.5

Reconciliation of movements in shareholders' funds

	£m
Profit attributable to the members of Buncrana plc	20
Dividends proposed	(8)
	12
Other recognised gains and losses for the year	2.5
	14.5
Opening shareholders' funds	216.2
Closing shareholders' funds	230.7

Workings

W1 Allocation of costs

	Cost of sales £m	Distribution costs £m	Administrative expenses £m	
Per the T/B	210	12	8.5	
Depreciation – buildings				
£100m/50 years	2			Note 1
Depreciation – plant				
£120m/10 years	12			
Depreciation – fixtures				
£30m/5 years	6			
Stock obsolescence	1(W3)			
Unfair dismissal claim			1	
	231	12	9.5	

W2 Investment property – SSAP 19

	£m	
Cost	5	
Surplus on revaluation	2.5 IP reserve	Note 2
Value on balance sheet	7.5	

W3 Stock valuation – SSAP 9

Headlights	NRV £2.2m – £0.2m selling costs =	£2m	
	Cost	3m	Note 3
	Loss to profit and loss	(1m)	

W4 Unfair dismissal claim – FRS 12

This is an obligation – legal – and it is probable and can be reliably measured at £1m; therefore it should be provided under FRS 12   Note 4

W5 Turnover and operating profits – acquisitions – FRS 3

Should disclose £45m as a separate sub-column for turnover and operating profit, as well as £10m in operating profit   Note 5

W6 Cessation of manufacturing – FRS 3

Under FRS 3, the entity is in the process of discontinuing this activity but it is not actually discontinued yet. It is also not really a change in the nature and focus of operations – it is still subcontracting the operations. No adjustment should take place under FRS 3   Note 6

W7 Closure of manufacturing division – FRS 3

This is a major change in the nature and focus of operations; therefore under FRS 3, it should be separately disclosed as a discontinued activity – turnover £30m, operating profit £8m   Note 7

W8 Provision for the closure of loss-making operation – FRS 12

The implementation of the closure decision has not yet commenced and no public announcement has been made to that effect. It is not permitted to be provided in the financial statements, under FRS 12   Note 8

W9 Capital commitments

Purely a legal disclosure in the notes to the accounts.

W10 Tangible fixed assets

	Land & buildings £m	Investment property £m	Plant & machinery £m	Fixtures & fittings £m	Total £m
Cost					
Balance at 1. 1. 2003 and 31. 12. 2003	105	5	120	30	260
Surplus on revaluation	–	2.5	–	–	2.5
Balance at 31. 12. 2003	105	7.5	120	30	262.5

Accumulated depreciation					
Balance at 1. 1. 2003	16	–	36	12	64
Charge for the year	2	–	12	6	20
Impairment	0.8	–	–	–	0.8
Balance at 31. 12. 2003	18.8	–	48	18	84.8
Net book value 31. 12. 03	86.2	7.5	72	12	177.7

Financial Reporting Review Panel

Eurotherm Plc (March 1993)

In 1990 Eurotherm set aside £2.8m as a provision for the closure costs of a manufacturing facility in Guernsey. This was treated as EXTRAORDINARY. In 1991, however, it wrote back £513,000 of over-provision as an EXCEPTIONAL credit. The company believed it was correctly applying UITF Abstract 2. The Panel was more concerned with consistency and the company has now agreed to restate the prior years results in accordance with the abstract.

Strategem Plc (June 1998)

There were two matters at issue for year ended 31 August 1997:

(i)   A settlement of a law suit was disclosed as an exceptional item but positioned after profit on ordinary activities. This would not be classified as a 'super' exceptional item under FRS 3. However, the directors were able to convince the panel that the costs were part of a fundamental restructuring and thus were 'super' items but they agreed that this should have been made clearer in the description of the item.

(ii) FRS 3 requires 'super' exceptionals to be shown after operating profit and before interest. However, they were in fact shown after operating profit but after interest.

PWS Holdings Plc (January 2000)

Similarly to Reuters the company had included goodwill amortisation as a separate line between operating profit and interest payable, i.e. as a 'super' exceptional item. The directors have agreed to change their presentation and include the amortisation within normal trading expenses, as a non-exceptional item.

Ensor Holdings Plc (July 2000)

This case was a breach of FRS 3 in that the company included transfers between reserves as a movement in the Statement of Total Recognised Gains and Losses. Only real increases/decreases in wealth are permitted to go through this statement, not mere transfers. The company was also asked to amplify its disclosure in relation to its accounting policy for goodwill and certain details required under FRS 13.

Princedale Group Plc (August 2001)

In the company's 2000 profit and loss account, £3.7 million loss arising from the sale of a subsidiary, and including 1.9 million write-back of goodwill (1998, £1.5 million profit and £1.2 million loss respectively), was disclosed on the face of the profit and loss account after profit after tax rather than operating profit. The effect was that the company reported a profit before tax of £694,000 rather than a loss before tax of £3.1 million (1998: profit before tax of £1.4 million instead of profit before tax of £1.7 million).

The Panel did not accept that, because the disposal related to a non-core activity, the presentation adopted highlighted the real profitability and underlying value of the ongoing business. In the Panel's view, the effect of the non-compliance with paragraph 20 of FRS 3 was compounded by certain of the comments in the Chairman's Report and Operating and Financial Review which interpreted the trend of results. The Company has agreed to amend the comparatives for the 2001 accounts.

Application in published accounts

Because of the dearth of extraordinary items on the publication of FRS 3 many reporting entities find themselves with a deluge of exceptional items which must be included in arriving at the operating profit for the year. Only three 'super' exceptionals are allowed to be disclosed separately on the face of the profit and loss account. To get around this problem reporting entities have started to use multi-column reporting in which usually there are three columns – pre-exceptional, exceptional items and total. Invariably the exceptionals will be 'bad news' and thus the reader's attention is being drawn to normal performance by concentrating on the pre-exceptional figures on the left of the document rather than on the overall total itself.

On the face of its profit and loss account, Chrysalis makes use of a multi-column format to highlight the results of its new media business. Chrysalis discloses that during the year it has disposed of the majority of its new media activities, writing down all new media investments to zero, to concentrate on a single new media subsidiary. Chrysalis discloses a loss before interest and tax for new media activities amounting to some £22 million and a profit before interest and tax for core businesses of £8.2 million.

On the face of its profit and loss account, Chrysalis does not, however, disclose a breakdown of turnover and operating profit split into continuing and discontinued operations and acquisitions and hence does not follow along the lines of FRS 3 *Reporting Financial Performance* (para. 14). In a note to the accounts, Chrysalis discloses that an acquired entity recorded turnover of £8.2 million, an operating profit of £153,000 and a loss after interest and before tax of £32,000.

Chryalis Plc (Year Ended 31 August 2001)

Profit and Loss Account (Extract)

Music and Visual Entertainments

	Note	Core Business £'000	New Media £'000	31st August 2001 £'000	Core Business As restated £'000	New Media As restated £'000	31st August 2000 As restated £'000
Turnover (including acquisitions)							
Group and share of joint ventures and associates	2	191,736	309	192,045	168,215	4	169,219
Less: share of joint ventures and associates	3	(4,231)	(67)	(4,298)	(5,560)	(4)	(5,564)
Group turnover	2	187,505	242	187,747	162,655	–	162,655
Operating costs before depreciation and amortisation		(175,923)	(10,458)	(186,381)	(153,207)	(1,754)	(154,961)
Depreciation of tangible fixed assets	15	(3,158)	(811)	(3,969)	(3,130)	–	(3,130)
Net amortisation of intangible assets and acquired goodwill	14	(982)	(220)	(1,202)	(415)	(86)	(501)
Exceptional accelerated amortisation of New Media goodwill	5	–	(1,464)	(1,464)	–	–	–
Group operating costs		(180,063)	(12,953)	(193,016)	(156,752)	1,840	(158,592)
Other operating income		786	–	786	–	–	–
EBITDA	2	12,368	(10,216)	2,152	9,448	(1,754)	7,694
Group operating (loss)/profit (including acquisition)	4	8,228	(12,711)	(4,483)	5,903	(1,840)	4,063
Share of results of joint ventures	3	36	–	36	(120)	–	(120)
Share of results of associates	3	(110)	(1,775)	(1,885)	(183)	(1,164)	(1,347)
Total operating (loss)/profit		8,154	(14,486)	(6,332)	5,600	(3,004)	2,596

	Note						
Non operating items:							
Exceptional losses on disposal and termination of New Media operations	6	—	(7,940)	(7,940)	—	(296)	(296)
(Loss)/profit before interest and tax		8,154	(22,426)	(14,272)	5,304	(3,004)	2,300
Interest receivable and similar income	7			920			637
Interest payable and similar charges	8			(3,491)			(2,006)
(Loss)/profit on ordinary activities before taxation	2,9			(16,843)			931
Taxation	11			(520)			(161)
(Loss)/profit on ordinary activities after taxation				(17,363)			770
Minority interests (equity interests)				642			(25)
(Loss)/profit for the financial year				(16,721)			745
Dividends	12			(916)			(961)
Retained loss for the financial year				(17,637)			(216)
Basic and diluted (loss)/earnings per share	13			(10.02)p			0.45p

Core Business relates to all the Group's ongoing Radio, Music, Television and Media Products business activities other than New Media and including central corporation overhead.

Turnover includes Core Business turnover of £8,371,000 and New Media turnover of £241,000 derived from acquisitions. Group operating (loss)/profit includes Core Business operating profit of £298,000 and New Media operating loss of £7,212,000 derived from acquisitions (see note 4).

EBITDA comprises earnings before interest, tax, depreciation and amortisation.

The results are derived from continuing operations. The historical cost (loss)/profit is the same as that shown above.

A good example of compliance with FRS 3 in relation to the need to publish three additional statements is the disclosure provided by Courts plc. Note that the Statement of Total Recognised Gains and Losses incorporates a prior year adjustment and the group must publish a Note of Historic Cost Profits and Losses as it has a policy of revaluing its properties and thus needs to restate what its profits would have been had they stayed with historical cost accounting:

Courts Plc   Year Ended   Home Furnishing and
**   31 March 2002   Retail Electrical Products**

Group Statement of Total Recognised Gains and Losses for the year ended 31 March 2002

	2002	2001 as restated
	£'000	£'000
(Loss)/profit for the financial year after tax and minorities and including discontinued operations	(9,685)	25,930
Currency translation on foreign currency net investment	(2,736)	10,393
Total recognised (losses) and gains relating to the financial year	**(12,421)**	36,323
Prior year adjustment (see Accounting Policies)	(5,613)	
Total recognised losses since last annual report	**(18,034)**	

Note of Group Historical Cost Profits and Losses for the year ended 31 March 2002

	2002	2001 as restated
	£'000	£'000
Profit on ordinary activities before taxation	9,865	54,557
Realisation of revaluation surplus/(deficit) of previous years	300	(189)
Difference between historical cost depreciation charge and actual depreciation charge for the year calculated on the revalued basis	486	548
Historical cost profit on ordinary activities before taxation	**10,651**	54,916
Historical cost (loss)/profit for the year ended after taxation, minority interest and dividends	**(12,209)**	22,882

Reconciliation of Movements in Shareholders' Funds for the year ended 31 March 2002

	2002	2001 as restated
(Loss)/profit for the financial year after tax and minorities and including discontinued operations	(9,685)	25,930
Dividends	(3,310)	(3,407)
	(12,995)	22,523
Other recognised (losses)/gains relating to the financial year	(2,736)	10,393
Net movement in shareholders' funds	(15,731)	32,916
Opening shareholders' funds (originally £212,346,000 before deducting prior year adjustment of £5,613,000)	206,733	173,817
Closing shareholders' funds	**191,002**	206,733

The final example in the chapter looks at the Scottish brewing company, Belhaven Group plc, which has no recognised gains and losses other than those arising from its operating performance and revaluation surpluses. A note, however, to the effect that profits equate to historic cost must be disclosed in the accounts and Belhaven have incorporated this at the bottom of their profit and loss account:

Belhaven Group Plc   Year Ended 30 March 2003   Brewing

Consolidated Statement of Total Recognised Gains and Losses for the year ended 30 March 2003

	Note	52 weeks ended 30 March 2003 £'000	52 weeks ended 31 March 2002 £'000
Profit for the financial year		7,501	6,545
Revaluation surplus	11	1,598	–
Total recognised gains and losses relating to the year		9,099	6,545

A statement of reserves is given in Note 19.

Consolidated Profit and Loss Account (Footnote)

The profit for the financial year equates to the historic cost profits for the financial year in all material respects.

Reconciliation of Movements in Equity Shareholders' Funds

	GROUP		COMPANY	
	52 weeks ended 30 March 2003 £'000	52 weeks ended 31 March 2002 £'000	52 weeks ended 30 March 2003 £'000	52 weeks ended 31 March 2002 £'000
Profit for the financial year	7,501	6,545	2,621	2,273
Dividends paid and proposed	(2,210)	(1,981)	(2,210)	(1,981)
Surplus on revaluation	1,598	–	–	–
Called up share capital	32	7	32	7
Share premium account	589	111	589	111
Funds set aside for new shares to be issued Under LTIP scheme	84	–	–	–
Opening equity shareholders' funds	40,860	36,178	24,353	23,943
Closing equity shareholders' funds	48,454	40,860	25,385	24,353

Cash flow statements

7.1 FRS 1 *Cash Flow Statements* (1991, revised 1996 and 1997)

Background

FRS 1 superseded SSAP 10 *Statement of Source and Application of Funds*, which had tried to explain how changes in working capital had occurred during the year. FRS 1 switched attention to an explanation of how different types of cash flows affect the business and was argued to be more relevant to explaining the liquidity of the reporting entity and its ability to remain solvent. The funds flow statement was too easy to manipulate as a decrease in cash could be obscured by an increase in stocks or debtors. Cash flow is more widely understood than working capital and is also more widely adopted in forecasting.

FRS 1 was introduced on a 3-year trial basis, at the end of which it was to be reviewed. As a result of this process FRS 1 was amended in 1996 to extend the number of headings in the document and also to provide a link between all three primary statements, i.e. to ensure that all three statements actually 'speak to each other'. This was achieved by the introduction of a requirement to reconcile operating profit as per the profit and loss account to operating cash flows (the indirect method) and the reconciliation of net cash flow to the movement in net debt.

Key issues

Objectives

- To ensure that a reporting entity explains how it generates cash and how that cash is absorbed by highlighting significant components of cash flow.
- To provide information that helps to assess the liquidity, solvency and financial adaptability of the reporting entity.

Scope

Applies to all reporting entities with the exception of small companies, pension funds and 90 per cent or more subsidiaries.

Format

There are nine main headings in the standard format:

(1)   Operating activities;
(2)   Dividends received from associated companies;
(3)   Returns on investments and servicing of finance;
(4)   Taxation;
(5)   Capital expenditure and financial investment;
(6)   Acquisitions and disposals;
(7)   Equity dividends paid;
(8)   Management of liquid resources;
(9)   Financing.

(1)   *Operating activities*
      Generally represents cash flows from operations and relates to operating or trading activities normally disclosed in the profit and loss account in arriving at operating profit.
          The indirect method is compulsory and adjusts operating profit for non-cash items as well as the movements in working capital. It links the profit and loss account to the cash flow statement. The indirect method may be presented on the face of the cash flow statement but only as a preamble, not as part of it. As an alternative the reconciliation may still be presented as a note to the cash flow statement as per the original FRS 1.
          The direct method is only a voluntary extra and should reveal the actual cash received from customers, the actual cash payments to suppliers, cash payments to employees and any other cash payments.

(2)   *Dividends received from associated companies*
      In November 1997 the ASB decided to amend FRS 1 to include a separate heading in the cash flow statement to incorporate dividends received from associated companies rather than including them in the operating profit section of the statement.

(3)   *Returns on investments and servicing of finance*
      Included in this section of the cash flow statement are all interest receipts and payments inclusive of the interest element of any finance lease repayments. Dividends received are also included apart from those from associates. Dividends paid to shareholders are, however, excluded apart from those paid to preference shareholders or to minority interests.
          Dividends paid to equity shareholders are included later in the statement as a discretionary flow.

(4)   *Taxation*
      Basically includes corporation tax only.

(5)   *Capital expenditure and financial investment*
      This section includes cash outflows to acquire new fixed assets and the inflows emerging from their subsequent scrapping or resale. However, it also includes the cash movements associated with the purchase and sale of investments that are neither associates/subsidiaries nor short-term investments, i.e. all investments not covered elsewhere.
          At the end of the fifth section there is a requirement to provide a subtotal which some entities have described as 'free cash flow', indicating the choice now left to companies on

how to spend surplus funds, i.e. to pay out dividends or to acquire new acquisitions or perhaps, in a deficit situation, to sell off subsidiaries/associates.

(6) *Acquisitions and disposals*

These represent the cash outflows and inflows from acquiring or disposing of subsidiaries/associates. This is largely regarded as a discretionary cash flow.

(7) *Equity dividends paid*

This section comprises dividends paid out to equity shareholders only and is separately recorded as it is also argued to be a discretionary flow.

There is a second subtitle at this stage which can sometimes be recorded by companies as 'cash flows before financing and management of liquid resources'.

(8) *Management of liquid resources*

Included within this section are the cash flows pertaining to short-term finance, i.e. those investments that may be sold in the short term in an active market such as treasury bonds and gilt-edged stocks.

(9) *Financing*

The final section of the cash flow statement has remained unchanged from the original FRS and incorporates all those flows relating to the raising and repayment of long-term finance for the business, i.e. shares and debentures.

At the end of the statement there should be a final figure representing the increase or decrease in cash for the period concerned. Cash is basically defined as cash in hand, cash at the bank plus any bank overdrafts.

Analysis of net debt

Apart from the need for a standard format to the cash flow statement there is also a new requirement to reconcile the movement in net cash for the period as shown in the statement, with the movement in net debt on the balance sheet. Net debt is defined as loans and borrowings (as defined per FRS 4 *Financial Instruments*) plus finance leases but less cash and liquid resources.

The movement should be analysed in detail in an *Analysis of Net Debt* statement in the notes to the financial statements. It should reconcile the opening and closing balances of net debt and explain the movement for the year. Inevitably this will not only include cash movements but should incorporate foreign exchange differences, non-cash movements such as the creation of new finance leases and net debt acquired on the acquisition of subsidiaries.

A summary of the *Analysis of Net Debt* should be included in the *Reconciliation of the Movement in Cash to the Movement in Net Debt* incorporated either in the notes to the financial statements or at the foot of the cash flow statement. In the latter case it would reconcile all three primary statements together on the one page for the first time and the reader would be able to see clearly how they articulate with each other.

Other problems

Groups

A group cash flow statement should be prepared excluding internal flows but 90 per cent or more controlled subsidiaries need not prepare their own statement so long as a group cash flow statement is publicly available.

Non-cash flow transactions

The cash flow statement should not include any non-cash movements at all but if these are material then users should be made aware of them in their notes, e.g. acquisitions/disposals, creation of new finance leases, etc.

Additional disclosure – acquisitions and disposals

In the year of acquisition/disposal the cash flow statement should provide a detailed note providing a summary of the effect of acquisitions/disposals including any cash element of acquisitions consideration. Only the actual cash consideration received/paid, however, may be included on the cash flow statement itself. This should be disclosed separately from any net cash balances acquired/disposed of at the same time.

The first example requires the production of a cash flow statement for a single entity. Most of the headings in the statement are covered with the exceptions of group cash items such as dividends received from associated undertakings and dividends paid to minority interests. As in all cash flow statements three documents are required as well as the detailed notes to the accounts, i.e. opening and closing balance sheets and a profit and loss account. In this particular case there are some movements in reserves that need to be carefully watched as they may not involve the movement of cash and thus must be excluded from the statement. Another problem to look out for is how to treat finance leases. The interest element is always classified as part of interest paid but the principal element is classified as part of financing cash flows:

Example – Garrison PLc

The following financial statements relate to Garrison plc for the year ended 31 May 2004:

Profit and loss account for the year ended 31 May 2004

	£m	£m
Turnover		335
Cost of sales		(177)
Gross profit		158
Distribution costs	(31)	
Administrative expenses	(27)	
		(58)
Operating profit		100
Interest payable	(7)	
Interest receivable	(3)	
		(4)
Profit before tax		96
Taxation		(22)
Profit for the financial year		74
Dividends		(12)
Retained profit for financial year		62

Balance sheets at 31 May

	2004		2003	
	£m	£m	£m	£m
Tangible fixed assets		272		196
Intangible fixed assets (development expenditure)		3		4
		275		200
Current assets				
Stock	140		155	
Debtors	130		110	
Cash and cash equivalents	102		23	
	372		288	
Creditors: amounts falling due within 1 year	(249)		(172)	
Net current assets		123		116
Total assets less current liabilities		398		316
Creditors: amounts falling due after more than 1 year		(80)		(90)
		318		226
Capital and reserves				
Ordinary share capital		120		100
Share premium account		45		35
Capital redemption reserve		12		–
Profit and loss account		141		91
		318		226

Additional information

(1) *Ordinary share capital*

	£m
£1 Shares fully paid at 1. 6. 03	100
Issued during year	10
Purchase of own shares	(12)
Shares converted	22
	120

(2) *Reserves*

	Share premium account	Capital redemption reserve	Profit and loss account
	£m	£m	£m
At 1. 6. 03	35		91
Premium on issue (net of issue costs of £1m)	3		
Premium on conversion of debentures	7		
Transfer to CRR		12	(12)
Profit for period			62
	45	12	141

(3) *Creditors: Amounts falling due after more than 1 year*

	2004	2003
	£m	£m
Obligations under finance leases	49	30
6% Debentures 2004–2010	31	60
	80	90

£29m of 6% debentures 2004–2010 were converted into £22m of ordinary shares during the year and interest paid in the year amounted to £2m.

(4)   *Creditors: Amounts falling due within 1 year*

	2004	2003
	£m	£m
Bank overdraft	8	20
Obligations under finance leases	5	3
Trade creditors	220	131
Taxation	16	10
Dividends	–	8
	249	172

(5)   *Tangible fixed assets*

	£m
Carrying value at 1. 6. 03	196
Additions: finance leases	28
purchases at cost	104
Disposals at carrying value	(19)
Depreciation for the year	(37)
Carrying value at 31. 5. 04	272

The fixed assets disposed of realised £21m.

(6)   *Cash and cash equivalents*

	2004	2003
	£m	£m
Treasury Stock 8.5% 2116	60	–
Treasury Stock 12.75% 2004 (June)	20	20
Loan notes repayable on demand	15	–
Cash at bank and in hand	7	3
	102	23

(Note that all of the interest due on the Treasury Stock for the year ending 31. 5. 04 had been received and there was no interest due on 31. 5. 03)

(7)   *Interest payable*

	2004
	£m
Bank overdraft	2
Finance charges payable under finance leases	3
Debentures not wholly repayable within 5 years	2
	7

(8)   *Obligations under finance leases*

	2004	2003
	£m	£m
Amounts payable:		
within 1 year	6	4
within 2 to 5 years	55	33
	61	37
Less finance charges allocated to		
future periods	(7)	(4)
	54	33

Interest paid on finance leases in the year to 31 May 2004 amounted to £3m.

Suggested solution – Garrison Plc

Garrison Plc – cash flow statement for year ended 31 May 2004

	£m	£m
Net cash inflow from operating activities (note 1)		220
Returns on financing and servicing of finance		
Interest received	3	
Interest paid (7 − 3)	(4)	
Interest element of finance lease rental payment	(3)	
Net cash outflow from servicing of finance		(4)
Taxation		
Corporation tax paid (10 + 22 − 16)		(16)
Capital expenditure and financial investment		
Payments to acquire tangible fixed assets	(104)	
Receipts from sales of tangible fixed assets	21	
		(83)
		117
Equity dividends paid (12 + 8)		(20)
Net cash inflow before financing		97
Movement in net liquid resources		
Payments to acquire 8.5% Treasury Stock 2117	(60)	
Payments to acquire loan notes repayable on demand	(15)	
		(75)
Financing		
Issue of ordinary share capital	14	
Share issue costs	(1)	
Purchase of own shares	(12)	
Capital repayments under finance leases	(7)	
Net cash outflow from financing		(6)
Increase in cash		16

Reconciliation of movement in net cash flow to movement in net debt (Note 2)

	£m
Increase in cash for the period	16
Cash paid to increase liquid resources	75
Cash repaid on finance leases	7
	98
New finance leases	(28)
Conversion of 6% debentures into shares	29
Movement in net debt in the period	99
Net debt at 1. 6. 03	(90)
Net funds at 30. 5. 04	9

Notes

(1) Reconciliation of operating profit to net cash inflow from operating activities

	£m
Operating profit	100
Depreciation	37
Amortisation of development expenditure	1
Profit on sales of fixed assets	(2)
Decrease in stocks	15
Increase in debtors	(20)
Increase in creditors	89
Net cash inflow from operating activities	220

(2) Analysis of changes in net debt

	1 June 2003 £m	Cash flow £m	Non-cash changes £m	Reclassification £m	31 May 2004 £m
Treasury Stock 8.5% 2117	–	60			60
Treasury Stock 12.75% 2004	20	–			20
Loan notes	–	15			15
		75			
Cash at bank	3	4			7
Bank overdraft	(20)	12			(8)
		16			
Obligations under finance lease (ST)	(3)	4		(6)	(5)
6% Debentures 2004–2010	(60)	–	29		(31)
Obligations under finance lease (LT)	(30)	3	(28)	6	(49)
		7			
	(90)	98	1	Nil	9

The second example requires the publication of a consolidated cash flow statement. It is slightly complicated by the introduction of an acquisition of a subsidiary during the year and the need to exclude those net assets from the movements in cash for the year. The only cash movement would be a combination of the cash part of the consideration plus any cash/bank balances taken over at the time of the acquisition. The example also incorporates an associated company and shows that only the dividends received from the associate is included in the statement.

Example – Moneyglass Plc

Moneyglass plc is a listed company incorporated in 1958 to produce models carved from wood. In 1975 it acquired a 100 per cent interest in a wood-importing company, Kilrea Ltd; in 1989 it acquired a 40 per cent interest in a competitor, Garvagh

Ltd; and on 1 October 2003 it acquired a 75 per cent interest in Tobermore Ltd. It is planning to make a number of additional acquisitions during the next 3 years.

The draft consolidated accounts for the Moneyglass Group are as follows:

Draft consolidated profit and loss account for the year ended 30 September 2004

	£'000	£'000
Operating profit		1,485
Share of profits of associated undertakings		495
Income from fixed asset investment		200
Interest payable		(150)
Profit on ordinary activities before taxation		2,030
Tax on profit on ordinary activities		
Corporation tax	391	
Deferred taxation	104	
Tax attributable to income of associated undertakings	145	
Tax attributable to franked investment income	45	
		(685)
Profit on ordinary activities after taxation		1,345
Minority interests		(100)
Profit for the financial year		1,245
Dividends paid and proposed		(400)
Retained profit for the year		845

Draft consolidated balance sheet as at 30 September

	2003		2004	
	£'000	£'000	£'000	£'000
Fixed assets				
Tangible assets				
Buildings at net book value		2,200		2,075
Machinery: Cost	1,400		3,000	
Aggregate depreciation	(1,100)		(1,200)	
Net book value		300		1,800
		2,500		3,875
Investments in associated undertaking		1,000		1,100
Fixed asset investments		410		410
Current assets				
Stocks	1,000		1,975	
Trade debtors	1,275		1,850	
Cash	1,820		4,515	
	4,095		8,340	
Creditors: Amounts falling due within 1 year				
Trade creditors	280		500	
Obligations under finance leases	200		240	
Corporation tax	217		462	
Dividends	200		300	
Accrued interest and finance charges	30		40	
	927		1,542	
Net current assets		3,168		6,798
Total assets less current liabilities		7,078		12,183

Creditors: Amounts falling due after more than 1 year		
Obligations under finance leases	170	710
Loans	500	1,460
Provisions for liabilities		
Deferred taxation	13	30
Net assets	6,395	9,983
Capital and reserves		
Called-up share capital in 25p shares	2,000	3,940
Share premium account	2,095	2,883
Profit and loss account	2,300	3,045
Total shareholders' equity	6,395	9,868
Minority interest	–	115
	6,395	9,983

Note 1

There had been no acquisitions or disposals of buildings during the year.

Machinery costing £500,000 was sold for £500,000 resulting in a profit of £100,000. New machinery was acquired in 2004 including additions of £850,000 acquired under finance leases.

Note 2

Information relating to the acquisition of Tobermore Ltd:

	£'000
Machinery	165
Stocks	32
Trade debtors	28
Cash	112
Less:	
Trade creditors	(68)
Corporation tax	(17)
	252
Less:	
Minority interest	(63)
	189
Goodwill	100
	289

	£'000
880,000 shares issued as part consideration	275
Balance of consideration paid in cash	14
	289

It is group policy to write off goodwill to reserves despite not being in accordance with FRS 10 *Goodwill and Intangible Assets.*

Note 3

Loans were issued at a discount in 2004 and the carrying amount of the loans at 30 September 2004 included £40,000, representing the finance cost attributable to the discount and allocated in respect of the current reporting period.

Suggested solution – Moneyglass Plc

Consolidated cash flow statement for the year ended 30 September 2004

	£'000	£'000
Net cash inflow from operating activities (note 1)		372
Dividend received from associates		
(1,000 + 495 − 145 tax − 1,100)		250
Returns on investments and servicing of finance		
Interest paid (150 + 30 − 40 − 40 discount)	(100)	
Dividend paid to minority interest		
(0 + 100 P&L + 63 − 115)	(48)	
Dividend received from fixed asset		
Investments (200 − 45)	155	
		7
Corporation tax paid		
(217 + 13 + 495 P&L − 462 − 30 + 17 acq)		(250)
Capital expenditure and financial investment		
Payments to acquire tangible fixed assets		
(3,000 − 1,400 + 500 − 165 − 850)	(1,085)	
Proceeds on disposal of machine	500	
		(585)
		(206)
Acquisitions and disposals		
Cash consideration on purchase of Tobermore Ltd	(14)	
Cash balances acquired on acquisition	112	98
Equity dividends paid (200 + 400 P&L − 300)		(300)
Net cash outflow before use of liquid resources and finance		(408)
Management of liquid resource		–
Financing		
Issue of shares (3,940 + 2,883 − 2,000 − 2,095 − 275 acq)	2,453	
Issue of loan stock (1,460 − 500 − 40 discount)	920	
Capital loan repayments (200 + 170 + 850 adds − 240 − 710)	(270)	
		3,103
Increase in cash		2,695

Reconciliation of net cash flow to movement in net debt

	£'000
Increase in cash	2,695
Cash Inflow from issue of loans	(920)
Cash outflow from lease repayments	270
	2,045
New finance leasing	(850)
Notional interest	(40)
	1,155
Net funds at 1. 1. 04	950
Net funds at 31. 12. 04	2,105

Notes

(1)   Reconciliation of operating profit to net cash flow from operating activities

	£'000	
Operating profit	1,485	
Depreciation charges	325	W1
Profit on sale of machinery	(100)	
Increase in stocks	(943)	W2
Increase in trade debtors	(547)	W3
Increase in trade creditors	(152	W4
Net cash inflow from operating activities	(372	

(2)   Analysis of changes in net funds

	At 1. 1. 2004 £'000	Cash flow £'000	Acquisition (excl. cash & overdrafts) £'000	Other non-cash changes £'000	At 31.12. 2004 £'000
Cash	1,820	2,695			4,515
Obligations under finance lease	(370)	270		(850)	(950)
Loans	(500)	(920)		(40)	(1,460)
	950	2,045		(890)	2,105

Workings

(W1) Depreciation charges	£'000	£'000
Buildings		125
Machinery:		
Closing aggregate amount	1,200	
Less opening aggregate amount	(1,100)	
	100	
Add depreciation on disposal	100	
		200
		325

(W2) Stock	£'000	£'000
Closing balance		1,975
Less:		
Opening balance	1,000	
Arising from the acquisition	32	
		(1,032)
Cash outflow		943

(W3) Trade debtors	£'000	£'000
Closing balance		1,850
Less:		
Opening balance	1,275	
Arising from the acquisition	28	
		(1,303)
Cash outflow		547

(W4) Trade creditors	£'000	£'000
Closing balance		500
Less:		
Opening balance	280	
Arising from the acquisition	68	
		(348)
Cash inflow		152

Assume the following information is provided in addition

(i) Moneyglass plc had constructed a laser cutter which is included in the machinery cost figure of £73,000. The cost comprises:

	£'000
Materials	50
Labour	12
Overheads	6
Interest capitalised	5
	73

(ii) The cash figures comprised the following:

	1. 10. 03	30. 9. 04
	£'000	£'000
Cash in hand	10	15
Bank overdrafts	(770)	(65)
Bank	1,080	1,890
10% Treasury Stock 2003	1,500	–
Bank deposits	–	1,125
Gas 3% 2000–2005	–	1,550
	1,820	4,515

The 10% Treasury Stock 2003 was acquired on 1 September 2003 and redeemed on 31 October 2003. The bank deposits were made on 1 January 2004 for a 12-month term.

The Gas 3% was acquired on 1 June 2004 and the company proposes to realise this investment on 30 November 2004.

The treatment of capitalised interest and liquid resources
FRS 1 requires capitalised interest to be shown within the interest paid heading in the *Returns on Investments and Servicing of Finance* section of the cash flow statement.

The effect of this will be to increase the interest paid from £100,000 to £105,000. The purchase of tangible fixed assets will be reduced by the same amount from £1,085,000 to £1,080,000.

The treatment of cash and liquid resources
We have noted that the cash figures comprised the following:

	1. 10. 03 £'000	30. 9. 04 £'000
Cash in hand	10	15
Bank overdrafts	(770)	(65)
Bank	1,080	1,890
10% Treasury Stock 2003	1,500	–
Bank deposits	–	1,125
Gas 3% 2000–2005	–	1,550
	1,820	4,515

Applying the FRS 1 definition of liquid resources as current asset investments held as readily disposable stocks of value:

- The 10% Treasury Stock 2003 was acquired on 1 September 2003 and redeemed on 31 October 2003 and falls within the FRS definition of a liquid resource.
- The bank deposits were made on 1 January 2004 and the amount deposited will become available on 31 December 2004. However, they will not be treated as a liquid resource: they are cash.
- The Gas 3% was acquired on 1 June 2004 and matures on 30 September 2006. It should be recorded as a liquid resource.

The effect on the consolidated cash flow statement is:

- The management of liquid resources section will include the 10% Treasury Stock and Gas 3% as a purchase of liquid resources at a figure of £50,000.
- The revised cash flow statement totals will be:

	£'000
Operating activities	372
Dividends received from associates	250
Returns on investments	2
Taxation	(250)
Capital expenditure and financial investment	(580)
	(206)
Acquisition and disposals	98
Equity dividends	(300)
	(408)
Movement in liquid resources	(50)
Financing	3,103
Increase in cash	2,645

Application in published accounts

One of the best examples of a published group cash flow statement is provided by CRH plc. In addition to the statement itself, it provides a Reconciliation of Movement of net cash inflow to the movement in debt, an Analysis of Net Debt and a Reconciliation of Operating Profit to Net Cash Flow from Operating activities:

CRH Plc   Year Ended 31 December 2003   Aggregates, Building Supplies

Group cash flow statement

For the year ended 31 December 2003

Notes		2003 €m	2002 €m
28	Net cash inflow from operating activities	1,396.2	1,553.5
	Dividends received from joint ventures and associates	19.4	23.5
	Returns on investments and servicing of finance		
	Interest received	36.1	57.7
	Interest paid	(140.5)	(183.2)
	Finance lease interest paid	(0.7)	(0.7)
8	Preference dividends paid	(0.1)	(0.1)
		(105.2)	(126.3)
	Taxation		
	Irish corporation tax paid	(19.6)	(17.2)
	Overseas tax paid	(83.3)	(145.1)
		(102.9)	(162.3)
	Capital expenditure		
11	Purchase of tangible assets	(402.0)	(367.4)
22	Less capital grants received	0.1	0.1
		(401.9)	(367.3)
13	Disposal of fixed assets	77.9	104.4
		(324.0)	(262.9)
	Investments in subsidiary, joint venture and associated undertakings		
29	Acquisition of subsidiary undertakings	(1,439.0)	(793.7)
	Deferred acquisition consideration	(56.8)	(80.3)
12	Investments in and advances to joint ventures and associates	(79.5)	(22.0)
		(1,575.3)	(896.0)
8	Equity dividends paid	(122.8)	(111.6)
	Cash inflow/(outflow) before use of liquid investments and financing	(814.6)	17.9
	Cash inflow/(outflow) from management of liquid investments	110.4	(169.7)

	Financing		
26	Issue of shares	**13.7**	13.8
26	Expenses paid in respect of share issues	**(0.1)**	(0.4)
	Increases in term debt	**688.4**	192.5
	Capital element of finance leases repaid	**(3.1)**	(5.1)
		698.9	200.8
	(Decrease)/increase in cash and demand	**(5.3)**	49.0
	debt in the year		

Reconciliation of net cash inflow to movement in net debt

Notes		*2003*	*2002*
		€m	*€m*
	(Decrease)/increase in cash and demand		
	debt in the year	**(5.3)**	49.0
	Increase in term debt including finance leases	**(685.3)**	(187.4)
	Cash (inflow)/outflow from management of		
	liquid investments	**(110.4)**	169.7
		(801.0)	31.3
19	Change in net debt resulting from cash flows		
19, 29	Loans and finance leases, net of liquid investments,		
	acquired with subsidiary undertakings	**(40.0)**	(95.8)
		(841.0)	(64.5)
19	Translation adjustment	**242.8**	248.3
	Movement in net debt in the year	**(598.2)**	183.8
	Net debt at 1 January	**(1,709.9)**	(1,893.7)
	Net debt at 31 December	**(2,308.1)**	(1,709.9)

19   Analysis of net debt

	At 1 January 2003	*Cash flow*	*Acqui-sitions*	*Non-cash changes*	*Transla-tion adjust-ment*	*At 31 Dec-ember 2003*
	€m	*€m*	*€m*	*€m*	*€m*	*€m*
Cash	**239.2**	**20.3**	–	–	**(35.8)**	**223.7**
Bank overdrafts and demand loans	**(79.9)**	**(25.6)**	–	–	**8.1**	**(97.4)**
Total cash and demand debt	**159.3**	**(5.3)**	–	–	**(27.7)**	**126.3**
Liquid investments	**1,294.0**	**(110.4)**	**1.9**	–	**(111.2)**	**1,074.3**
Loans repayable within one year	**(151.5)**	**227.9**	**(20.4)**	**(460.5)**	**(3.5)**	**(408.0)**
Loans repayable after more than 1 year	**(2,996.9)**	**(916.3)**	**(9.1)**	**460.5**	**383.3**	**(3,078.5)**
Finance leases	**(14.8)**	**3.1**	**(12.4)**	–	**1.9**	**(22.2)**
Total term finance	**(3,163.2)**	**(685.3)**	**(41.9)**	–	**381.7**	**(3,508.7)**
Net debt	**(1,709.9)**	**(801.0)**	**(40.0)**	–	**242.8**	**(2,308.1)**

28   Reconciliation of operating profit to net cash inflow from operating activities

	2003 €m	2002 €m
Group operating profit (before goodwill amortisation)	**1,004.5**	1,014.6
Depreciation charges	**458.2**	456.3
Capital grants released	**(2.0)**	(1.9)
Net movement on provisions during the year	**(2.5)**	18.0
(Increase)/decrease in working capital (note 17)	**(62.0)**	66.5
Net cash inflow from operating activities	**1,396.2**	1,553.5

CHAPTER

8

Accounting disclosure standards: post balance sheet events, provisions and contingencies, pensions and segmental reporting

8.1 SSAP 17 *Accounting for Post Balance Sheet Events* (August 1980)

Background

Events occurring after the year end must be considered when preparing the financial statements. They should only be incorporated in the financial statements if they are material and able to provide additional evidence of conditions existing at the balance sheet date. However, they may also have to be noted in the financial statements if, by their non-inclusion, the financial statements would fail to provide a true and fair view.

The objective of SSAP 17 is to ensure that the balance sheet at a particular point in time reveals a true and fair view and that certain post balance sheet events may have to be adjusted in the financial statements and others in the notes to the accounts in order to achieve that objective.

Definitions

- *Post balance sheet events.* These are events, both favourable and unfavourable, which occur between the balance sheet date and the date on which the financial statements are approved by the board of directors.
- *Adjusting events.* These are events that provide new or additional evidence of conditions existing at the balance sheet date and must therefore be incorporated in the financial statements.

    Examples might include the net realisable value of stocks, the discovery of errors, the insolvency of a debtor or the declaration of a dividend.
- *Non-adjusting events.* These are events that do not affect conditions existing at the balance sheet date and should therefore only be noted in the financial statements if they are material and would also affect a user's opinion on whether or not the financial statements show a true and fair view. Examples might include mergers and acquisitions; reconstructions; the issue of shares and debentures; nationalisation; and a loss due to a major fire or flood.

Accounting treatment

Adjusting events

Should be adjusted in the financial statements, e.g. stocks reduced to a lower net realisable value.

Non-adjusting events

Should be recorded in the notes to the financial statements and the following disclosed:

(i) the nature of the event; and
(ii) an estimate of the financial effect or a statement that it is not practicable to make such a statement.

Window dressing

Basically represents an attempt to design certain transactions so as to rearrange the balance sheet, which would provide a misleading or unrepresentative impression of the financial statements, e.g. the deliberate withholding of payments to creditors to make the bank balance more attractive to a bank manager.

Going concern

If a non-adjusting event has the impact of destroying the going concern concept then the transaction should be incorporated into the financial statements as these perhaps should now be prepared on a break-up basis.

FRED 27 *Events After the Balance Sheet Date* (May 2002) (Now FRS 21 April 2004)

This FRED is part of the convergence project to bring UK accounting standards closer to those published by the IASB. FRED 27 effectively will implement IAS 10 *Events After the Balance Sheet Date*. There are relatively few changes to SSAP 17 but the main one is the removal of proposed dividends as an adjusting event in line with international practice and because they do not meet the definition of a liability at the balance sheet date. It also provides more guidance on the date of authorisation of the financial statements. If an entity submits its accounts to shareholders prior to approval then the authorisation date is the date of original issuance – not the date of approval itself. Included in FRED 27 is a requirement to disclose both the date of authorisation and the names of those who gave the authorisation. The FRED was published as a full standard in April 2004.

A mini case study example is provided below which attempts to distinguish between those events that are adjusted in the financial statements and those which are merely disclosed in the notes as non-adjusting. The linkages with other FRSs/SSAPs are also covered, particularly with FRS 12 *Provisions, Contingent Liabilities and Contingent Assets*.

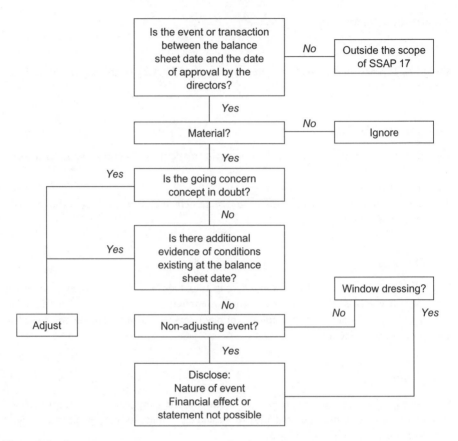

Figure 8.1   Summary.

Example – Cashel Plc

You are the accountant of Cashel plc, a small but diverse group. You are in the process of drafting the financial statements for the year to 30 June 2004, and the following issues have been referred to you for resolution or comment:

(1)   Subsequent to 30 June 2004, a subsidiary, Caher Ltd, suffered a flood at a warehouse which destroyed stock with a book value of £350,000. The insurance company has agreed a claim for £250,000 in respect of the stock.

In addition, a major customer of Caher Ltd has just been placed in receivership. The amount owed to Caher Ltd at 30 June 2004 was £34,000 but a further delivery at an invoiced value of £40,000 was made on 2 July 2004. Caher Ltd has no reservation of title clauses in its trading terms and no provision has so far been made in respect of these balances, which remain outstanding.

The draft accounts of Caher Ltd for the year disclose a profit before tax of £180,000 and net assets of £1,260,000.

(2)   The group acquired the freehold interest in a listed building for £850,000 during the year through a wholly owned subsidiary, Bandon Ltd, which was incorporated specifically for that purpose. Bandon Ltd currently leases the property to a third party at arm's length but your managing director is considering moving the group head office personnel into this building when the lease expires. The building is recorded in the books at cost, but has been valued at £1 million.

(3)   On 1 September 2003 a major design fault was found in a new product and it was withdrawn from the market. Stocks of the product have been returned to Cashel plc's supplier for a full refund. The company had committed itself to an advertising schedule for this new product involving total expenditure of £300,000, to be written off evenly over 3 years. £150,000 had been spent in the first year to 31 July 2004.

(4)   On 15 September 2003 torrential rain caused flooding at the company's riverside warehouse, resulting in an uninsured stock loss totalling £200,000.

(5)   Bills receivable of £120,000 had been discounted at the bank on 15 July 2003. The bills were dishonoured on presentation at the maturity date on 16 September 2003.

Suggested solution – Cashel Plc

(1) – Stock destroyed

The event (i.e. the flood) occurred after the year end and is therefore non-adjusting. The net loss after insurance is expected to be £100,000. This should be disclosed if its non-disclosure would affect the user's ability to reach a proper understanding of the financial statements. As this represents over 55 per cent of the profits before tax, it is certainly material and should be disclosed. In next year's accounts it should be written off as an exceptional item within the figure for profit before tax.

– Debtor in receivership

The event (i.e. the debtor of £34,000) existed at the year end and the subsequent evidence indicates that the debt may not be recovered due to the receivership of the company. The provision for bad debts should be based on the likely non-recovery at the time of the accounts being approved but prudence may dictate 100 per cent provision if no evidence exists at that time.

The additional sale of £40,000 occurred after the year end and should be matched against a bad debt provision in the next year. No provision should be made at this stage as the event did not exist at the year end. However, this represents over 20 per cent of profits and therefore could be considered to be sufficiently material to be disclosed as a non-adjusting event.

Note 19. Post balance sheet events

(1) Subsequent to the year end, a severe flood at our warehouse in Romcard destroyed stock to the value of £350,000. Insurance proceeds have recovered £250,000 of this loss but a net loss of £100,000 has been incurred.

(2) One of Caher's major customers, Brickbat Ltd, went into receivership after the year end. Full provision has been made in the accounts for amounts owing at the year end but £40,000 sales since then have not been provided as they relate to next year.

(2) Listed building

Under SSAP 19 *Accounting for Investment Properties*, if an asset is held by the group purely for investment potential with a rental income at arm's length, then it need not be depreciated. It should be recorded in the books at its open market value of £1m. This is an uplift of £150,000 from its original cost, which must be credited to a separate investment property revaluation reserve.

Bandon Ltd was set up this year to acquire the listed building and it is 100 per cent owned by the group. The company should be consolidated as it is no longer permissible, under the Companies Act 1989 and FRS 2 on subsidiary undertakings, to argue that Bandon's activities are so dissimilar that consolidation would be misleading. It is now necessary to prove that, if the subsidiary is included, the group accounts would no longer show a true and fair view. If that were the case, then the company would be equity accounted and neither the asset nor its related revaluation reserve would appear in the group accounts.

The proposal to move group head office would mean that the building no longer meets the criteria as an investment property because property let to another group company is specifically excluded. The building would then need to be depreciated unless maintenance expenditure renders the charge immaterial or residual values are considered to be as high as cost. The building need no longer be revalued, but if it is, then the revaluation should follow the rules set out in FRS 15 and revaluation should take place on a regular basis, i.e. once every 5 years.

(3) Withdrawal of faulty design products

The major design fault was discovered on 1 September 2003, one month after the year end. Therefore, although the event did not exist at (i.e. was not discovered before) the year end, it could be argued that the stocks did exist in a faulty state at that time. It would therefore be treated as an adjusting post balance sheet event under SSAP 17.

The committed advertising expenditure of £300,000 should be written off and fully accrued by the year end as it is unlikely to be recovered. However, if the unspent £150,000 could be avoided or switched to other products then only the £150,000 expenditure incurred to date would need to be expensed. The write-off may be so material that it is abnormal in relation to usual expenditure and it should therefore be disclosed as an exceptional item in the annual accounts, as per FRS 3. However, under FRS 12 the committed but unspent expenditure of £150,000 would be treated as a mere intention and not an obligation. Therefore it may not be provided as a liability in 2004.

The stocks returned will be refunded in full to the customer but hopefully this will be countered by a refund to Brickbat from its own suppliers. This is a counter-claim contingency. If it is probable that a refund will be received and thus no loss crystallises, then the financial statements should record the liability and, separately, a probable asset. If, however, it is only possible that a refund will be received, then the liability should be accrued and any possible gain ignored, following the prudence concept. These recommendations are in accordance with FRS 12 *Provisions, Contingent Liabilities and Contingent Assets*. Under FRS 12 a counter-claim should be treated completely separately from the accounting treatment for the claim, as it is argued to be illegally offsetting an asset against a liability.

It is important to understand that the likelihood of success and the probable amounts of the claim/counter-claim must be separately assessed and disclosed, if appropriate. Only if the possibility of the loss is remote should no disclosure be made. If a possible material contingency is disclosed, the following are required:

(a)   Details of the nature of the contingency.
(b)   Any uncertainties expected to affect its ultimate outcome.
(c)   A prudent estimate of its financial effect or a statement to the effect that it is not practicable to make such an estimate.

In addition, under the *Statement of Principles* and FRS 5 it is unlikely that the advertising expenditure would result in future economic benefits. Therefore it must not be capitalised and should be written off to the profit and loss account.

(4) Flood at warehouse destroying stock

The uninsured stock loss of £200,000 was caused by a torrential downpour of rain resulting in a flood at the company's new riverside warehouse. This event occurred after the year end, therefore the condition did not exist at the year end. The loss would be considered as non-adjusting under SSAP 17 unless it could affect the going concern of the business. If the latter were the case then the accounts would need to be prepared on a break-up basis.

However, assuming that the company is a going concern, the non-adjusting event would require the following disclosures if non-disclosure would affect the user's ability to reach a proper understanding of the financial statements:

(a)   Details of the nature of the event.
(b)   An estimate of the financial effect before accounting for taxation, and any tax implications, to effect a proper understanding of the financial position.

(5) Bills dishonoured

The bills were discounted by the bank 2 weeks before the year end. They subsequently became dishonoured on maturity after the year end. This is a post balance sheet event and gives additional evidence of a condition existing at the year end. It should be treated as an adjusting event under SSAP 17 and the loss of £120,000 should be accrued in the financial statements.

The company would obviously take action to make a counter-claim. If success is probable then, under SSAP 18, the probable gain would have been offset against the liability to the bank. However, if success is no more than possible then, under the prudence concept, no disclosure can be made. FRS 12, however, has effectively banned the offsetting procedure and the claim liability must be kept separate from the probable counter-claim asset.

Applications in published accounts

Very little information is disclosed in financial statements about adjusting events as these are automatically included within normal assets/liabilities or incomes/expenses and unless they are of an exceptional nature would not be disclosed. On the other hand SSAP 17 (and now FRS 21) does require a reasonable amount of disclosure for non-adjusting events and the first example below (Corus plc) provides an illustration of major changes to the board of directors and its bank facilities, and the announcement of the sale of a major part of their business. The second example provides an announcement of a major merger between Granada plc and the Carlton Group:

| **Corus Group Plc** | **Year Ended 31 December 2002** | **Manufacture of Steel** |

Notes to the Accounts (Extract)

36. Post Balance Sheet Events

(i)   As discussed in Note 20, on 30 Dec 2002 the company reduced its main available bank facility by voluntary cancellation of €460m, of which €260m would have matured in Jan 2003 and €100m in Mar 2003. The facility nows stands at €1,400m of which €455m was utilised as at 31 Dec 2002.

(ii) On 23 Oct 2002, Corus announced that it had agreed in principle to the sale of its Aluminum Rolled Products and Extrusions businesses to Pechiney SA for €861m (approximately £543m). It was intended that a definitive sale and purchase agreement would be entered into following completion of internal consultation, advice and approval processes. However, the Supervisory Board of Corus Nederland BV decided on 10 Mar 2003 to reject the recommendation to proceed with the sale. On 11 Mar 2003 Corus Group plc announced it would commence proceedings before the Enterprise Chamber of the Amsterdam Court of Appeal to seek redress in respect of this decision. However, this request was unsuccessful and, as no appeal procedure is available to resolve the issue in time for the sale to proceed, Corus accepts the Court's decision as final. Pechiney has been informed that Corus will not now proceed with the sale and as a result, a break fee of €20m is payable to Pechiney.

(iii) In the light of the Company's performance, the Board including Mr Tony Pedder, Chief Executive, concluded that a change of leadership was required. Mr Pedder tendered his resignation on 13 Mar 2003 and this was accepted with immediate effect. The procedure for the recruitment of a new Chief Executive is underway. Mr Stuart Pettifor, a main Board executive director, was appointed Chief Operating Officer, taking responsibility for all operational matters. Sir Brian Moffat agreed to defer his planned retirement to become full-time Chairman until his successor is appointed.

Granada Plc   Year Ended 30 September 2002   Television Broadcasting

Notes to the Accounts (Extract)

36. Post Balance Sheet Events

On 16 October 2002 Carlton and Granada plc announced agreed terms for a proposed merger to pave the way for a fully consolidated ITV. The merger is conditional on regulatory clearances, including from the competition authorities. A joint submission by Carlton and Granada was filed with the Office of Fair Trading on 25 November 2002.

One of the most obvious of non-adjusting events was the effects of the aftermath of the 9/11 tragedy in New York, and WH Smith plc have provided an example thereof for their accounts to 31 August 2001, and in particular, of the effects on their US retail business:

WH Smith Plc   12 Months Ended   Book and Publication
31 August 2001   Sellers

Notes to the Accounts (Extract)

The tragic events in the USA on 11 September 2001 and their aftermath had a material adverse effect on the trading of WH Smith USA Travel Retail. The majority of WH Smith USA Travel Retail's stores are based in airports and city centre hotels. Like-for-like sales in WH Smith USA Travel Retail have fallen 24 per cent in the 6 weeks to 13 October 2001.

The Group has initiated a restructuring of the WH Smith USA Travel Retail operations to align the business with the current market conditions but it is too early to estimate the full continuing financial effect of 11 September 2001.

In accordance with SSAP 17 *Accounting for Post Balance Sheet Events*, the events of 11 September 2001 and their aftermath constitute a 'non-adjusting event', as they do not relate to conditions that existed at the balance sheet date. Accordingly it is not appropriate to reflect any financial effect of these events in the balance sheet at 31 August 2001.

The costs of restructuring, together with any adjustments to asset carrying values and additional liabilities which may arise as a result of the events of 11 September 2001 and any subsequent developments, will therefore be included in the accounts for the year ending 31 August 2002.

8.2   FRS 12 *Provisions, Contingent Liabilities and Contingent Assets* (September 1998)

Background

This standard partially replaces the former SSAP 18 *Accounting for Contingencies* as well as incorporating new rules on how to account for provisions. Provisions are liabilities of uncertain timing or amount, whereas contingent liabilities represent potential liabilities that exist at the balance sheet date but whose existence will only be confirmed by the occurrence/non-occurrence of an uncertain future event not wholly within the control of the reporting entity. Both topics therefore concentrate on uncertainty – effectively a provision is a probable uncertain liability but a contingent liability is merely possible. A practical example of each would be the public announcement of a decision to reorganise the entity's activities in such a way that the employees will take action and look for alternative employment (provision) and a court case where either party to the action could win (contingent liability).

Not all provisions are covered by FRS 12. For example, provisions governed by a more specific accounting standard (e.g. pensions under FRS 17 and deferred tax under FRS 19), are exempt. In addition provisions which represent reductions in asset values, such as doubtful debts and stock obsolescence, are not covered in FRS 12.

FRS 12 applies the principles of recognition and measurement of liabilities contained in the Statement of Principles to the subject of provisions and contingencies.

Definitions

*   *Provision*. A liability of uncertain timing or amount.
*   *Contingent liability*. Represents a possible liability that arises from past events and whose existence will be confirmed only by the occurrence of one or more uncertain future

events not wholly within the entity's control or a present obligation which is not probable or of an amount that cannot be measured sufficiently reliably.

- *Contingent asset*. A possible asset that arises from past events and whose existence will be confirmed only on the occurrence of one or more uncertain future events not wholly within the entity's control.

Accounting treatment

Provisions

Should be recognised, provided that:

(1)   There is a present obligation (legal or constructive) as a result of a past event;
(2)   A transfer of economic benefits will probably be required to settle the obligation;
(3)   The amount of the obligation can be reliably measured.

These provisions should be reviewed at each balance sheet date and adjusted to reflect the best estimate. Provisions should be reversed if a transfer of economic benefits is no longer probable but also increased if not sufficient. No virement is allowed across the provisions; each must exist completely separately from each other.

Only three specific provisions are discussed in the body of the standard: provisions for future operating losses are banned; those for restructuring are permitted so long as there is clearly a constructive obligation; and, finally, provisions should be made for losses on onerous contracts. The latter have become very popular and represent the unavoidable costs of meeting the contract's obligations where these exceed the economic benefits expected to be received.

If there are any counter-claims resulting in reimbursements by other parties, the reimbursement must be treated as a separate asset and not netted off against the related provision. However, prudence dictates that an asset should only be created if it is virtually certain that it will be received.

The disclosure required for provisions includes a reconciliation of the opening and closing provisions under their material headings. This numerical analysis will incorporate the creation of new and additional provisions, their reversal if not required, the amount used in the period and any discounting. Discounting is required in measuring both the provision and, where applicable, any related asset where the time value of money is material. Also, reporting entities must use their best estimate of the amount likely to be transferred to the other party but may adopt the expected value technique to measure the liability. The disclosure in FRS 12 also requires reporting entities to explain in narrative terms the purpose of the provisions and their likely timing.

In some cases, especially landfill sites or oil and gas fields, the provision for abandonment should be estimated in full initially, discounted and then recorded as an addition to the fixed asset as well as a provision. Any unwinding of the discount should subsequently be treated as an interest cost in the profit and loss account.

Contingent liabilities should merely be disclosed in the notes unless a transfer of benefits is likely to be remote. A contingent asset is disclosed where an inflow is probable but it is not recorded in the profit and loss on the grounds of prudence. However, the following should be disclosed in the notes to the financial statements:

(i)   the nature of the contingency;
(ii) the uncertainty which is expected to affect the ultimate outcome of the condition;
(iii) a prudent estimate of the potential financial effect (before tax) of the contingency or a statement that this is not possible.

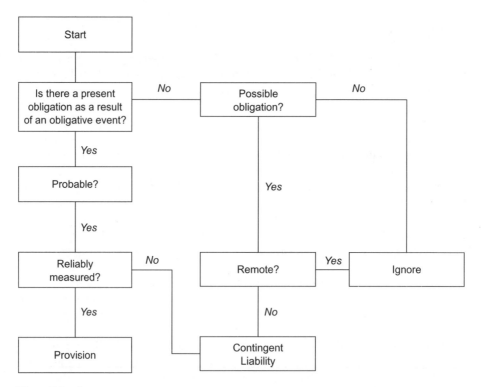

Figure 8.2   Summary.

The example below provides a mini case study as to how FRS 12 should be applied. It also illustrates that often a provision will trigger off an impairment review of an entity's assets and the standard needs to be considered in conjunction with FRS 11 *Impairment of Goodwill and Fixed Assets*.

Example – Killyleagh Plc

Killyleagh plc, a company which prepares its accounts to 31 December each year, has two independent income streams: power generation, and the recycling and disposal of nuclear waste.

The company has no subsidiary or associate undertakings and no goodwill is carried on the company's balance sheet. All fixed assets are stated at depreciated historical cost. The net assets directly involved in the power generation and nuclear waste income streams are being carried at £160 million and £180 million respectively at 31 December 2003. In addition, there are head office net assets with a carrying value of £15 million at the same date. Head office resources are used by the power generation and nuclear waste income streams in the proportion 40:60.

Before the financial statements for the year ended 31 December 2003 can be finalised, a number of issues need to be resolved. These are set out below.

Outstanding issues

(1) During 2003 there was a significant adverse change in the power generation regulatory environment, suggesting that the net assets of this income stream might not be fully recoverable. The company's power generation licensing agreement expires on 31 December 2013, and management estimate that the useful life of the existing assets is approximately 10 years. Company-approved budgets for the power generation income stream indicate that future net cash inflows for the next 10 years are estimated at £20 million per annum, before taking account of cash outflows of £4 million per annum relating to tax and financing costs. The net realisable value of the power generation net assets at 31 December 2003 is estimated at £100 million, after selling costs of £10 million. The current weighted average cost of capital of a listed company, whose cash flows have similar risk profiles to those of the power generation income generating unit, is 7 per cent. This weighted average cost of capital has been calculated on a pre-tax basis.

(2) Increased competition and stricter safety regulations have put pressure on profit margins with respect to the recycling and disposal of nuclear waste. Accordingly, management has prepared a formal plan to reorganise this part of the company's business and they wish to include a provision of £15 million in the financial statements for the year ended 31 December 2003 to cover redundancies and relocation costs associated with the proposed reorganisation. Management has decided that, given the competitive nature of the business, a public announcement regarding the reorganisation would not be appropriate at this time.

(3) On 1 January 2003, legislation dealing with emission levels came into effect. As a result, Killyleagh was required to fit special filters by 30 June 2003. Due to management changes and cash flow problems, the company was unable to install the new filters during 2003. The company hopes to start and complete this work during the first half of 2004, at an estimated cost of £5 million. No provision has yet been made in the 2003 financial statements for this, nor for

the fines of £1 million payable at 31 December 2003 under the legislation. It is estimated that additional fines of £750,000 will become payable before the filters are fitted and operational.

(4)   On 1 January 2003, Killyleagh entered into a 5-year contract with the Government to dispose of nuclear waste in the North Sea. Under the terms of the contract, Killyleagh is responsible for restoring the sea bed at the end of the contract. It is estimated that this will cost £6 million. No provision has been made in the 2003 financial statements for this future expenditure, but management intend to disclose in the notes to the financial statements their obligation to restore the sea bed. The current weighted average cost of capital of a listed company, whose cash flows have similar risk profiles to those of the recycling and disposal of nuclear waste income generating unit, is 7 per cent. The risk-free rate is 4 per cent.

Suggested solution – Killyleagh Plc

Issue 1 Impairment of power generation income stream - FRS 11

	Power generation unit £m
Direct net assets attributable to power generation	160
Share of head office net assets (£15m × 40% given)	6
Net book value (NBV)	166
Recoverable amount is the higher of NRV and NPV	
Net realisable value (NRV) (£110m − £10 selling costs)	100

Higher figure is £140.468m

Net present value (NPV)	
£20m per annum × 10 years × 7% WACC	
£20m × 7.0234	140.468

(Cash flows relating to tax and financing should not be considered)

Under FRS 11 *Impairment of Fixed Assets and Goodwill*, the fixed assets should not be carried at more than their recoverable amount, which is the higher of NRV and NPV. The impairment at 31 December 2003 is £166m − £140.468m = £25.532m.

This write-down should be reflected within operating costs, and, if material, it should be recorded as an exceptional item in the notes to the financial statements. The impairment should be recorded within cumulative depreciation since the fixed assets have been carried on a historical cost basis.

The company should disclose the discount rate adopted. Impairment losses recognised when FRS 11 was first implemented should be recorded as changes in accounting estimate and should not be treated as changes in accounting policy. The ASB believes that the FRS is simply codifying existing practice and thus any adjustments should be treated as adjustments to current estimated lives and therefore treated as additional depreciation.

Issue 2 Provision for reorganisation of nuclear waste plant – FRS 12

FRS 12 *Provisions, Contingent Liabilities and Contingent Assets* states that a provision should only be created when an entity has a present obligation (i.e. either legal or constructive) as a result of a past transaction or event. It should also be probable (i.e. more than 50 per cent chance of occurring) and be capable of being reliably measured.

In the case of a reorganisation, a provision should only be created if a constructive obligation exists. This is deemed to have arisen when an entity not only has a detailed formal plan but has actually started to implement the plan or at least has announced the main features of the plan to those people affected by the decision. It must raise a valid expectation in those affected that it will carry out the restructuring.

FRS 12 notes that, by actually starting to implement the plan, it makes those people affected realise that the plan will be carried out. Examples of such events that trigger constructive obligations include the decommissioning of plant, the selling off of assets or the making of a public announcement. The announcement, however, must be outlined in sufficient detail, setting out main features of the plan so that it gives rise to a valid expectation in other parties, e.g. customers, suppliers, employees, trade unions, etc., that the entity will actually carry out the restructuring.

It is not acceptable, post-implementation of FRS 12, simply to include the £15m provision because, at the year end, Killyleagh plc has not started to implement the plan or announced its main features to those affected by it. The company, therefore, does not have a constructive obligation.

FRS 12 does not permit the inclusion of certain costs in restructuring provisions. These include retraining or relocation costs. These relate to the future operation of the business.

The standard expects that there will not be a long delay between creating the provision and commencing the reorganisation. If there were a significant delay, it is unlikely that the plan would raise an expectation on the part of others that the entity was committed to the restructuring. Under the disclosure requirements of FRS 12, reporting entities must now disclose when the provision is likely to crystallise.

Issue 3 Fitting of special filters – FRS 12

At 31 December 2003, there is no obligation for the costs of fitting the filters because no obligating event has occurred (i.e. the fitting of filters). However, the appendix to FRS 12 suggests that an obligation to pay fines does exist due to non-compliance with the regulations. The company should therefore provide for £1m in fines but should not provide for the additional £750,000 as there is not a present obligation at the balance sheet date.

However, an opposing opinion would suggest that the entity must ultimately comply with the new legislation and therefore £5m should be provided at once.

This may be discounted to its present value if it is unlikely to be paid in the near future.

The disclosures required under FRS 12 include a brief description of the obligation, the expected timing of any resulting transfer of economic benefits and an indication of the uncertainties about the amount or timing of those transfers.

Details are also required of the carrying amount at the start and end of the accounting period, any additional provisions created or reversed in the period and the discount rate applied.

Issue 4 Provision for decommissioning costs – FRS 12

Under FRS 12, Killyleagh plc has a legal obligation to restore the sea bed at the end of the contract. This should be provided at once. However, it may be discounted to its present value. It could be argued that the correct double entry would be to create a fixed asset which is then depreciated over the period of the contract. It is regarded as a 'negative' residual value because when the entity enters the contract it has to put the sea bed back to its original state and it is therefore part of the cost of purchasing the contract in the first place.

The measurement of the liability at present value means that interest has to be accounted for to unwind the discount. The finance cost is purely notional as no interest is paid. However, it must be regarded as part of interest payable and it should not be treated as an operating expense.

The details of the costs to be charged to profit and loss and the balance sheet assets and liabilities are computed as follows:

Year	Operating costs £	Finance costs £	Fixed assets (NBV) £	Fixed assets (provision) £
31. 12. 2003	986,280	197,256	3,945,120	5,128,656
31. 12. 2004	986,280	205,146	2,958,840	5,333,802
31. 12. 2005	986,280	213,352	1,972,560	5,547,154
31. 12. 2006	986,280	221,886	986,280	5,579,040
31. 12. 2007	986,280	230,960	Nil	6,000,000
	4,931,400	1,068,600		

Depreciation £6m × 0.8219 (annuity for 4 years at 4% risk-free rate) = £4,931,400/5 years = £986,280

Finance costs	£4,931,400 × 4% = £197,256	2003
	£5,128,656 × 4% = £205,146	2004
	£5,333,802 × 4% = £213,352	2005
	£5,547,154 × 4% = £221,886	2006
	£5,579,040 × 4% = £230,960	2007 (bal. fig.)

The second example is similar to the first in that it incorporates decommissioning costs but, in addition, it examines the case as to whether or not provisions for operating losses may be permitted:

Example – Beragh Plc

Assume the following provisions have been accounted for by Beragh plc. Consider whether they are acceptable under FRS 12 *Provisions, Contingent Liabilities and Contingent Assets*:

Provisions and long-term commitments
(i) Provision for decommissioning the group's radioactive facilities is made over their useful life and covers complete demolition of the facility within 50 years of it being taken out of service together with any associated waste disposal. The provision is based on future prices and is discounted using a current market rate of interest.

Provision for decommissioning costs

	£m
Balance at 1. 12. 02	675
Adjustment arising from change in price levels charged to reserves	33
Charged in the year to profit and loss account	125
Adjustment due to change in knowledge (charged to reserves)	27
Balance at 30. 11. 03	860

There are still decommissioning costs of £1,231m (undiscounted) to be provided for in respect of the group's radioactive facilities as the company's policy is to build up the required provision over the life of the facility.

Assume that adjustments to the provision due to change in knowledge about the accuracy of the provision do not give rise to future economic benefits.

(ii) The company purchased an oil company during the year. As part of the sale agreement, oil has to be supplied for a 5-year period to the company's former holding company at an uneconomic rate. As a result a provision for future operating losses has been set up of £135m, which relates solely to the uneconomic supply of oil. Additionally, the oil company is exposed to environmental liabilities arising out of its past obligations, principally in respect of remedial work to soil and ground water systems, although currently there is no legal obligation to carry out the work. Liabilities for environmental costs are provided for when the group determines a formal plan of action on the closure of an inactive site and when expenditure on remedial work is probable and the cost can be measured with reasonable certainty. However, in this case, it has been decided to provide for £120m in respect of the environmental liability on the acquisition of the oil company. Beragh has a reputation of ensuring that the environment is preserved and protected from the effects of its business activities.

Suggested solution – Beragh Plc

(i) *Provision for decommissioning costs*

FRS 12 *Provisions, Contingent Liabilities and Contingent Assets* has had a major impact on accounting for decommissioning costs. In the past most extractive/oil companies gradually built up a provision over the life of the associated mine/oilfield. The provision was often created on a unit-of-production basis to match the cost of decommissioning with the associated revenue being created from the sale of associated oil, etc. This was a profit and loss or accruals based approach. This is the accounting treatment adopted by Beragh plc.

Since the publication of FRS 12 these provisions must now comply with the balance sheet approach and it is argued that a nuclear energy company has an immediate obligation on the day that the damage occurs, i.e. on the opening up of the radioactive facilities, etc. A provision must be created in full immediately and, if not payable for several years, then it should be discounted to its present value. In the case of the group, the discount rate adopted is market rate. Under FRS 12 companies should adopt a real interest rate or future prices should be discounted by a nominal rate. A risk-free rate should be adopted where a prudent estimate of future cash flows already reflects risk (e.g. Government Bond rate).

The unwinding of the discount should be charged to the profit and loss account, not as part of decommissioning costs but as part of interest payable.

(ii) *Provision for future operating losses*

Under FRS 12 no provision for future operating losses may be created. However, if the company has entered into an onerous contract then a provision should be created. An onerous contract is one in which the entity cannot avoid the excess costs over revenues of fulfilling a contract. Clearly the company has entered into such a contract and the provision of £135m should be set up for the uneconomical supply of oil.

FRS 12 does not spell out specifically any rules on environment liabilities. However, in the appendix, it is recommended that where legislation has been broken or if the entity has a dark green policy then provisions should be made for such costs on the grounds that they are clearly legal or constructive obligations. If the company has created a valid expectation that the environmental liabilities will be paid out then a provision should be set up. It will depend on the subjective judgment of both auditor and preparer.

The company only sets up a provision when a formal plan of action on the closure of an inactive site has been set up and when the expenditure on remedial work is probable and the cost can be measured with reasonable certainty. This would appear to be a satisfactory basis on which to set up a provision. The provision of £120m should therefore be permitted.

Application in published accounts

Rentokil Initial plc have a number of provisions on their balance sheet but the most interesting is the retention of a self-insurance provision which was specifically examined in the appendices to FRS 12 and was thought not to comply with the definition of a provision in FRS 12. However, the group has taken actuarial advice to work out the likely future cost of accidents etc. based on that advice and on past experience. The group also provides a very good example of the back-up movement note for the provisions during the year and also the narrative back-up explaining the rationale for the provision as well as a broad outline of when it is likely to be settled.

Rentokil Initial Plc	Year Ended 31 December 2002	Environmental Protection

Accounting Policies (Extract)

Provisions

Provision is made in accordance with FRS 12 for:

Vacant property	– in respect of vacant and partly sub-let leasehold properties to the extent that future rental payments are expected to exceed future rental income.
Environmental	– for all known liabilities to remediate contaminated land on the basis of management's best estimate of the costs of these liabilities.
Self-insurance	– for all claims incurred as at the balance sheet date based on actuarial assessments of these liabilities.
Other provisions	– for all other constructive or legal obligations which exist at the year end based on management's best estimate as to the cost of settling these liabilities.

Note 19 Provisions For Liabilities and Charges

	Vacant Properties £m	Environmental £m	Self-Insurance £m	Other £m	Deferred tax £m	Total £m
Consolidated						
At 1 January 2002	46.3	43.1	50.4	7.9	88.3	236.0
Exchange adjustments	–	(1.4)	(2.4)	0.1	(0.7)	(4.4)
Additions during the year	–	–	16.1	0.3	–	16.4
Utilised in year	(4.7)	(6.2)	(19.2)	(0.4)	–	(30.5)
Transfer to current taxation	–	–	–	–	(9.7)	(9.7)
Acquired with acquisitions	–	–	–	–	0.1	0.1
Transfer (to)/from profit and loss account	(0.1)	–	(1.0)	–	2.9	1.8
At 31 December 2002	41.5	35.5	43.9	7.9	80.9	209.7

Parent

At 1 January 2002	–	–	1.2	–	1.1	2.3
Utilised in year	–	–	(0.2)	–	–	(0.2)
Transfer (to)/from profit and loss account	–	–	(0.3)	–	–	(0.3)
At 31 December 2002	–	–	0.7	–	1.1	1.8

Vacant properties

The group has a number of vacant and partly sub-let leasehold properties, with the majority of the head leases expiring before 2020. Provision has been made for the residual lease commitments together with other outgoings, after taking into account existing subtenant arrangements and assumptions relating to later periods of vacancy.

Environmental

The group owns a number of properties in the UK, Europe and the USA where there is land contamination and provisions are held for the remediation of such contamination.

Self-insurance

The company purchases external insurance from a portfolio of international insurers for its key insurable risks in order to limit the maximum potential loss that the company could suffer in any one year. Individual claims are met in full by the company up to agreed self-insured limits in order to limit volatility in claims.

The calculated cost of self-insurance claims, based on an actuarial assessment of claims incurred at the balance sheet date, is accumulated as claims provision. The annual review of these provisions by external actuaries resulted in a reduction in the reserves and in the insurance charge to the profit and loss account in the year of £1.0m (2001: £1.2m).

Other provisions

Other provisions principally comprise amounts required to cover obligations arising, warranties given and costs relating to disposed businesses.

	Consolidated		Parent	
	2002	2001	2002	2001
	£m	£m	£m	£m
Deferred tax				
Provision for deferred tax comprises:				
Accelerated capital allowances	52.7	47.6	0.3	0.3
Other	28.2	40.7	0.8	0.8
	80.9	88.3	1.1	1.1

Unprovided deferred tax assets in respect of unutilised tax losses amount to £11.5m (2001: £12.6m). Deferred tax assets have not been recognised due to the uncertainty regarding their utilisation.

One of the main attempts to circumvent the principles of the standard has been the creation of a growing number of onerous contract provisions. These are specifically included as permittable provisions in the body of the FRS. A good example of this is provided by the Canary Wharf Group, who have nearly £200m in their 2003 balance sheet. They have also provided, as per FRS 12, a detailed narrative explanation for the creation of a large provision on one of their properties:

Canary Wharf Group Plc   Year Ended   Property
30 June 2003   Development

Accounting Policies (Extract)

Vacant Leasehold Property
Provision is made for the present value of the anticipated net commitments in relation to leasehold properties where there is a shortfall in rental income receivable against the rent and other costs payable.

Notes to the Financial Statements
18 Provision for Liabilities and Charges

	At 30 June 2003 £m	At 30 June 2002 £m
Vacant leasehold properties	123.5	–
Other lease commitments	27.3	–
Deferred taxation	47.9	51.6
	198.7	51.6

Vacant leasehold property:
On 6 November 2000, the group entered into an Agreement for Lease with Clifford Chance for the lease of 10 Upper Bank Street, which reached practical completion on 31 July 2003. The group also acquired the sub-leasehold interest (with approximately 14 years now unexpired) in 200/202 Aldersgate Street, a 440,000 sq ft office building in the City of London, and let the premises to Clifford Chance for a term of approximately 5 years at the same rent as that under the sub-lease. Clifford Chance has given notice to terminate the lease on 29 September 2003. The group will now seek to sublet the premises or dispose of its interest on the open market.

In accordance with UK GAAP the group has recognised a provision for the estimated net liability under the lease of 200/202 Aldersgate Street. In arriving at the quantum of the provision the directors have consulted with FPDSavills, the group's valuers, to determine the assumptions on which the provision should be computed, including such matters as the void period, the rent achievable on re-letting and the incentive package payable. Based on the valuers' assessment of the market at 30 June 2003 a provision of £123.5 million has been recognised which includes an allowance for refurbishment of the building prior to re-letting. This provision is based on the following key assumptions, which will be reviewed at each subsequent balance sheet date:

Passing rent	–	£16.7 million (£38 per sq ft)
Average void period	–	2 years
Rent-free period on reletting	–	2 years
Headline rent on reletting	–	£35 per sq ft
Refurbishment cost	–	£55 per sq ft

This provision is stated at present value calculated on the basis of a discount rate of 6.0%, being the group's weighted average cost of debt, and will be amortised to the profit and loss account, after allowing for the unwind of the discount, on a straight-line basis over the period to the first open market rent review on 10 Upper Bank Street in 2013.

There is a very strong link between FRS 12 and FRS 15 *Tangible Fixed Assets* in that provisions for the future maintenance or overhaul of fixed assets are no longer permitted under FRS 15. They do not meet the definition of liabilities under either FRS 12 or the Statement of Principles but are mere intentions of the reporting entity which could be reversed in the future. As a result, many entities have had to replace these provisions by investigating FRS 15 and breaking their rather large assets into smaller components, and then accelerating the depreciaion on these components so any replacements are treated as capital and not revenue expenditure. This enables the reporting entity to continue on with its income smoothing policy. One example of this is Ryanair Plc who, in 1999, on the publication of FRS 12 changed their policy from provisions for major overhaul to a component fixed asset policy and the note they published at that time is disclosed below:

Ryanair Plc   Year Ended 31 March 1999   Airline Operator

Accounting Policies (Extract)

1. **Prior year adjustment**
    Provision for maintenance of aircraft
    In previous years, provision for the cost of major maintenance checks was made by providing for the estimated future costs of maintenance over the period from the date of acquisition to the date of the next check on the basis of hours flown.
    Under the revised policy, which is in accordance with the povisions of Financial Reporting Standard (FRS 12 *Provisions, Contingent Liabilities and Contingent Assets*, major maintenance checks are capitalised as incurred and written off over the shorter of the period to the next check or the estimated useful life of the aircraft.

Depreciation

Previously, the entire cost of an aircraft was depreciated over its estimated useful life. During the year the group changed its accounting policy for the depreciation of its aircraft to comply with the provisions of FRS 15 *Tangible Fixed Assets*. Under the revised policy, the cost of an aircraft is split into its separable components which are depreciated over their estimated useful lives. As a result, that element of the cost attributed to the service potential of its separable components reflecting their maintenance condition is amortised over the shorter of the period to the next check or the remaining life of the aircraft. In order to present prior period results on a comparable basis, the profit and loss account for the year ended 31 March 1998 and the balance sheet as at 31 March 1998 have been restated.

FRS 12 covers contingent liabilities as well as provisions and one industry which has a number of legal cases being filed against it in recent years has been tobacco. The industry has fought off every major case, usually successfully, but it must recognise the possibility that some cases may result in large payments being made to its customers for damage to health. As a result, all industry companies publish a fairly lengthy contingent note outlining the nature of the problem, the uncertainties surrounding future court cases and sometimes the possible financial effect. The latter is not a popular disclosure as it could seriously harm their case in court and is normally not disclosed. British American Tobacco is the example provided below:

British American   Year Ended 31 December 2003   Tobacco Tobacco Plc

Notes on the Accounts (Extract)

23 Contingent liabilities and financial commitments (Extract)

There are contingent liabilities in respect of litigation, overseas taxes and guarantees in various countries.

Product liability litigation

Group companies, notably Brown & Williamson Tobacco Corporation (B&W), as well as other leading cigarette manufacturers, are defendants, principally in the United States, in a number of product liability cases. In a number of these cases, the amounts of compensatory and punitive damages sought are significant.

US litigation

The total number of US product liability cases pending at year end involving the Group companies was 4,302 (2002: 4,219 cases). UK-based Group companies have been named as co-defendants in some 1,128 of those cases (2002: 1,272 cases). Only perhaps a couple of dozen cases or fewer are likely to come to trial in 2004. Since many of the pending cases seek unspecified damages, it is not possible to quantify the total amounts being claimed, but the aggregate amounts involved in such litigation are significant. External legal fees and other external product liability defence cost £66 million in 2003 (2002: £66 million). The cases fall into four broad categories.

(1) Medical reimbursement cases

These civil actions seek to recover amounts spent by Government entities and other third party providers on healthcare welfare costs claimed to result from illnesses associated with smoking.

Despite the almost uniform success of the industry's defence to these actions to date, the United States Department of Justice has filed suit against the leading US cigarette manufacturers, certain affiliated companies (including parent companies) and others, seeking reimbursement for Medicare and other health expenses incurred by the US Federal Government as various equitable remedies, including paying over of proceeds from alleged unlawful acts.

The court has dismissed reimbursement claims (and has dismissed B.A.T. industries plc on jurisdictional grounds) but is allowing the Government to proceed with its claims for equitable relief, which includes a claim for disgorgement of profit up to US $289 billion from the industry. The court has scheduled trial for September 2004.

As at 31 December 2003, similar reimbursement suits were pending against B&W, among others, by two Indian tribes by one county or other political subdivisions of the states. The Master Settlement Agreement with the 46 states included credit for any amounts paid in suits brought by the states' political subdivisions; nevertheless, B&W intends to defend the cases vigorously.

Based on somewhat different theories of claim are some five non-Governmental medical reimbursement cases and legal insurers claims. To date, eight federal appelate courts have issued decisions dismissing this type of case entirely and some but not all state courts have issued similar decisions. In 2001, B&W tried one health insurer case in New York Federal Court (Empire Blue Cross), where the jury returned a defence verdict on three of the five claims. The two BAT UK-based company cases were dismissed, that of B.A.T. industries plc by agreement with the plaintiff and a full defence verdict was obtained for the remaining BAT UK company. On the two claims where the jury found for the plaintiff, the jury awarded US $2.8 million. The trial judge has US $37.8 million in fees in respect of the plaintiffs' lawyers; that that amount has not been allocated among individual defendants is now under appeal before the 2nd Circuit Court of Appeals, one of the eight federal appelate courts that has already given a decision dismissing this type of case entirely. No third party reimbursement cases are currently scheduled for trial.

(2) Class actions

As at 31 December 2003, B&W was named as a defendant in some 36 (2002: 47) separate actions attempting to assist claims on behalf of classes of persons allegedly injured or financially impacted by smoking. While most courts refused to do so, thirteen have certified classes of tobacco claimants in cases involving B&W but six of these classes have subsequently been decertified. Even if the classes remain certified and the possibility of class-based liability is eventually established it is likely that individual trials will still be necessary to resolve any actual claims. If this happens, it is possible that many of the defences that have contibuted to more than 600 individual cases being successfully disposed of over the year by B&W will be available.

8.3 SSAP 24 *Accounting for Pension Costs* (May 1988) FRS 17 *Retirement Benefits* (November 2000)

Background

There are two major types of pension schemes in the United Kingdom – *defined contribution* and *defined benefit*.

A defined contribution scheme is one in which the benefits are determined by the amount of contributions paid into the pension fund plus the investment return thereon. The risk of a poor pension is therefore taken on by the employee, not the employer.

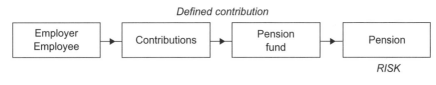

Defined contribution

Figure 8.3

On the other hand a defined benefit scheme is one in which the benefits (e.g. two thirds final salary, 1.5 lump sum commutation, etc.) are determined in advance for the employee and the employer has therefore an obligation to make good any shortfall in the scheme.

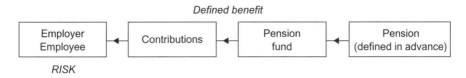

Defined benefit

Figure 8.4

The funding and the accounting treatment is therefore more complicated for the latter type of scheme.

Funding

It is the role of the actuary to determine the best method of funding a pension scheme. There are a wide variety of methods available, e.g. accrued benefits, prospective benefits, etc., but SSAP 24 only required the actuaries to build up the funds in the scheme in a prudent and controlled manner and did not attempt to precisely dictate the method of funding. FRS 17, however, now results in only one method being permitted in the future to ensure as much comparability as possible across reporting entities, i.e. the projected unit method.

In a defined benefit scheme, if a reporting entity, through its actuaries, discovers a shortfall then the actuary will recommend that the rate of contribution be increased or else a lump sum invested to make good that shortfall. If it were to be charged immediately to profit and loss then it would have an extremely volatile effect on earnings per share. This could be argued to fail to provide a true and fair view of current performance since it is really a long-term and not a short-term problem for the entity. There are no such problems in defined contribution schemes because whatever is contributed to the scheme in any year should be a fair charge as there are no hidden surpluses/shortfalls.

Accounting treatment

Defined contribution schemes

The cost is known to the employer. There are no hidden open-ended liabilities, therefore the amount paid in contributions should represent a fair charge to the profit and loss account (both SSAP 24 and FRS 17).

The disclosure required is therefore also fairly limited:

* Nature of the scheme;
* The accounting policy adopted;
* The pension cost for the period;
* Any accruals/prepayments.

Defined benefit schemes

The uncertainty surrounding the final benefits payable to an employee makes this a very difficult scheme to account for. Shortfalls/surpluses will be bound to occur at the triennial valuation of the scheme as it is highly unlikely that the actuary's original assumptions will hold on such items as life expectancy, labour turnover, age of retirement, rate of return on investments, rate of increase in salaries and wages, etc.

Under FRS 17 there is now a requirement to update some of the actuarial assumptions at each balance date, especially the discount rate adopted and the market value of the assets in the scheme.

The accountant's role under SSAP 24 was not to take the actuary's funding as the basis for a fair charge to profit but instead to spread any surplus/deficit over the average remaining service lives of the employees in the scheme, i.e. a matching or accruals-based system. That will change with FRS 17, which will require normal service and past costs to be charged to profit and loss but the actuarial deficit/surplus will have to be charged directly to reserves and therefore also recorded in the statement of total recognised gains and losses (STRGL).

SSAP 24 resulted in a prepayment arising on the balance sheet when a company was in a deficit position and a provision when a company was in surplus. Effectively it introduced a number of very dubious assets and liabilities on the balance sheet.

Under the Statement of Principles, now applied in FRS 17, this 'spreading' or accruals-based approach is abandoned and instead the proper recording of the balance sheet assets and liabilities has become the focus of the revised accounting standard. An example is provided below.

EXAMPLE

A company has discovered a £2m deficit which will be spread over the five remaining average service lives of employees in the scheme under SSAP 24. The deficit will be funded by equal additional lump sums of £1m each in years 1 and 2. Under the FRS 17 balance sheet approach the full liability is recorded immediately.

SOLUTION

		SSAP 24				FRS 17		
		Profit and loss			Asset	Provision	Profit	Reserves
	Funding	Normal charge	Deficit	Total charge			& loss	(STRGL)
Year	£m	£m	£m	£m	£m	£m	£m	£m
1	1.4	0.4	0.4	0.8	0.6	1.0	0.4	(2.0)
2	1.4	0.4	0.4	0.8	1.2	–	0.4	–
3	0.4	0.4	0.4	0.8	0.8	–	0.4	–
4	0.4	0.4	0.4	0.8	0.4	–	0.4	–
5	0.4	0.4	0.4	0.8	–	–	0.4	–
	4.0	2.0	2.0	4.0		1.0	2.0	2.0

Surpluses in defined benefit schemes, at present, may be treated in one of three different ways by reporting entities:

(i)   Contribution holiday until surplus winds down;
(ii)   Improvement of final benefit schemes payable to employees up to the maximum permitted by the revenue authorities; and
(iii) Refund to the employer but this is subject to tax at 40 per cent.

In the example below, a contribution holiday is taken for 2 years prior to recommencement of the normal funding arrangements.

EXAMPLE

		SSAP 24				FRS 17		
Year	Funding	Normal charge	Surplus	Total charge	Liability	Asset	Profit & loss	Reserves (STRGL)
	£m	£m	£m	£m	£m	£m	£m	£m
1	–	0.4	(0.16)	0.24	0.24	0.4	0.4	0.8
2	–	0.4	(0.16)	0.24	0.48	–	0.4	–
3	0.4	0.4	(0.16)	0.24	0.32	–	0.4	–
4	0.4	0.4	(0.16)	0.24	0.16	–	0.4	–
5	0.4	0.4	(0.16)	0.24	–	–	0.4	–
	1.2	2.0	(0.80)	1.20		0.4	2.0	0.8

The following disclosures have to be made for defined benefit schemes. These are extensive due to the open-ended liability nature of the schemes and have been considerably extended by FRS 17. The main requirements include:

(i)   The nature of the scheme, e.g. defined benefit final pay scheme;

(ii) The date of the most recent full actuarial valuation;

(iii) The contributions made in respect of the accounting period and any agreed contribution rates for future years;

(iv) For closed schemes the fact that the current service cost will increase as members approach retirement;

(v)   The following main assumptions at the start and end of the year:

> the inflation assumption,
> the rate of increase in salaries,
> the rate of increase for pensions in payment and deferred pensions,
> the discount rate used to discount scheme liabilities,

(vi) A fair value table breaking up the market value of the scheme assets into their main categories, the actuarial value of the liability and the actuarial deficit/surplus. In addition the long-term rate of return on each of the main asset categories should be disclosed;

(vii) Details of the charges to profit and loss split between those included within operating profit and those included in interest payable. A 5-year history of experience of gains/losses charged/credited to reserves and the STRGL should also be provided to ensure that entities do not deliberately bypass the profit and loss account.

The disclosure requirements of FRS 17 were implemented in two transitional phases into UK reporting – at 23 June 2001 and 23 June 2002 but the ultimate recording of deficits/surpluses on the balance sheet has been postponed until such time as the IASB finalise their own proposals to amend the international accounting standard IAS 19 *Employee Benefits* (now determined as 1 January 2005).

Currently many reporting entities are deciding to close down their defined benefit schemes for new employees on the grounds that the liabilities have become too open-ended and, with the increased rate of labour turnover, defined contribution schemes are more portable. The case of *Barbour v Guardian Royal Exchange plc* highlighted the problem by forcing UK companies to ensure that all aspects of remuneration between men and women are treated equally, including pension schemes. Defined contribution schemes are more certain from the employer's point of view but they are probably not as attractive from the employee's viewpoint compared to the benefits promised in defined benefit schemes. However, the main reason for the switch is the fall in equity markets over the last few years, the increasing longevity of employees (estimated two additional years of life over the last decade) and the fact that many employees are retiring at a younger age. FRS 17 is not the cause of the demise of defined benefits schemes but it is the 'final nail in the coffin'.

The following example provides a mini case study of two straightforward defined benefit schemes, one in deficit and one in surplus, and how FRS 17 differs from the 'old' SSAP 24 in placing the emphasis on the balance sheet asset/liability rather than trying to adopt a profit and loss approach and smooth over deficits/surpluses over the average remaining services lives of employees in the schemes:

Example – Richill Plc

The directors of Richill plc have received a report from their actuaries dealing with each of the company's two non-contributory pension schemes, based upon data at 1 January 2004.

Extracts from the report are as follows:

Works scheme

The closure of the Loughgall division (a material segment) in June 2004 will require an immediate contribution of £2 million to ensure that the assets of the scheme are sufficient to cover the liabilities in respect of the accrued benefits of the former employees at that location.

Other assets of the scheme were insufficient to cover the liabilities in respect of the prospective benefits for continuing employees. The extent of the deficiency was some £5.5 million. It is recommended that one lump-sum payment of £3 million be made on 31 December 2004 followed by a payment of £2.7 million on 31 December 2005, and that the contributions thereafter be at the rate of £1 million per annum until 31 December 2010 and £800,000 per annum thereafter.

The average age of the continuing employees is 50 years, their average retirement age is 61 years and benefits are determined by pensionable salary at date of retirement.

Staff scheme

A surplus in respect of the prospective benefits of £2.2 million has been disclosed by the valuation, partly due to changes in the actuarial assumptions. It is recommended that a contribution holiday be taken in 2004 and 2005 and thereafter that contributions be £400,000 per annum to 31 December 2007 and £750,000 per annum thereafter. The age profile of this scheme is similar to that of the works scheme. Benefits are determined by pensionable salary at date of retirement.

Suggested solution – Richill Plc

Profit and loss account for the year ended 31 December 2004

	SSAP 24 £	FRS 17 £
Regular pension cost (£800,000 + £750,000 – see workings)	1,550,000	1,550,000
Variations from regular cost (£500,000 – £200,000)	300,000	–
	1,850,000	1,550,000
Exceptional charge	2,000,000	2,000,000

Note: Under FRS 3 this would be separately noted as an exceptional item on the face of the profit and loss account, between operating profit and interest payable.

Balance sheet as at 31 December 2004

	£	£
Prepayment	1,700,000	1,450,000
Provisions for liabilities and charges	550,000	3,300,000

Notes to the accounts

The company operates two main pension schemes, works and staff, providing benefits based on final pay. The assets in both schemes are held separately from those of the company.

The company's accounting policy is to charge the cost of the pensions against profits on a systematic basis over the average expected service lives of the employees in the schemes.

The pension cost is assessed in accordance with the advice of professionally qualified actuaries, and in respect of the principal schemes the pension cost for the year ended 31 December 2004 was:

	£'000
Regular pension cost (constant percentage of earnings over the employees' service lives)	1,550
Variations from regular cost based on a constant percentage of current and estimated future earnings over the average remaining service lives of current employees	300
Net pension cost to operating profits	1,850

The closure of the Loughgall division entailed an immediate contribution of £2,000,000 to ensure that the assets of the works scheme were sufficient to cover the liabilities in respect of the accrued benefits of the former employees at that location. This has been treated as an exceptional item.

Details of the most recent valuation of the pension scheme:

Date of most recent valuation	1 January 2004
Methods used	Projected Unit Method
Main assumptions	
Rate of price inflation	X %
Return on investments	X %
Increase in projected salaries	X %
Increase in pension costs	£X

Workings

(1) Works scheme (excluding Loughgall division)

	Funding	Accounting charge Regular		Variation	Total	Balance sheet prepayment
	£'000	£'000		£'000	£'000	£'000
2004	3,000	800	+	500	1,300	1,700
2005	2,700	800	+	500	1,300	3,100
2006	1,000	800	+	500	1,300	2,800
2007	1,000	800	+	500	1,300	2,500
2008	1,000	800	+	500	1,300	2,200
2009	1,000	800	+	500	1,300	1,900
2010	1,000	800	+	500	1,300	1,600
2011	1,000	800	+	500	1,300	1,300
2012	1,000	800	+	500	1,300	1,000
2013	800	800	+	500	1,300	500
2014	800	800	+	500	1,300	Nil

Variation from regular cost £5,500,000 ÷ 11 years = £500,000 p.a.

Under FRS 17, the full deficit of £5.5m would be charged directly to reserves (and reported as a recognised loss in the statement of total recognised gains and losses). The profit and loss would still be charged with £800,000 as a normal service cost. The difference between the funding of £3m and charge of £6.3m, i.e. £3.3m, will be recorded as a provision on the balance sheet.

(2) Staff scheme

	Funding	Accounting charge Regular		Variation	Total	Balance sheet provision
	£'000	£'000		£'000	£'000	£'000
2004	–	750	–	200	550	550
2005	–	750	–	200	550	1,100
2006	400	750	–	200	550	1,250
2007	400	750	–	200	550	1,400
2008	750	750	–	200	550	1,200
2009	750	750	–	200	550	1,000
2010	750	750	–	200	550	800
2011	750	750	–	200	550	600
2012	750	750	–	200	550	400
2013	750	750	–	200	550	200
2014	750	750	–	200	550	Nil

Variation from regular cost £2,200,000 ÷ 11 years = £200,000 p.a.

Under FRS 17, the full surplus would be recorded as an asset (provided recovery probable). Thus, although the normal service cost of £750,000 would go to the profit and loss, an asset of £1.45m would be recorded and separately disclosed under current assets. That surplus would be a recognised gain in the statement of total recognised gains and losses.

Application in published accounts

Although companies are not required to fully implement FRS 17 until the deadline of 1 January 2005, a large number of UK plcs have decided to implement early. That is largely for two reasons:

i)   There is confidence that the IASB will follow the ASB's standard fairly closely; and
ii) Most companies are currently in deficit and they would prefer to charge that to reserves rather than seeing it being spread as an additional expense through their future profit and loss accounts.

One example of this approach has been that taken up by WH Smith for their August 2003 financial statements, which is illustrated below.

**WH Smith Plc   For the 12 Months Ended   Book Retailers
31 August 2003**

Accounting Policies (Extract)

h) Pension costs
The Group's two UK pension funds are both defined benefit schemes which are self-administered. In accordance with FRS 17 *Retirement Benefits*, the service cost of the pension provision relating to the period, together with the cost of any benefits relating to past service, is charged to the profit and loss account. A charge equal to the increase in the present value of the scheme liabilities (because the benefits are closer to settlement) and a credit equivalent to the group's long-term expected returns on assets (based on the market value of the scheme assets at the start of the period), are included in the profit and loss account under 'interest'.

The difference between the market value of the assets of the scheme and the present value of the accrued pension liabilities is shown as an asset or liability on the balance sheet net of deferred tax. Any difference between the expected return on assets and that actually achieved is recognised in the Statement of Total Recognised Gains and Losses along with differences arising from experience or assumption changes.

Further information on pension arrangements is set out in Note 3 to the accounts.

Notes to the Accounts (Extract)

3 Pension arrangements
i) Restatement of comparatives
Financial Reporting Standard 17 *Retirement Benefits* (FRS 17) has been adopted with effect from 1 September 2002. The adoption of FRS 17 has required a change to the

accounting treatment of pensions and the prior year results have been restated accordingly as follows:

Consolidated balance sheet		Other creditors	Provisions		
	Debtors	Due after more than	for liabilities and	Net pension	Profit and loss
£m		one year	charges	liabilities	account
At 31 August 2002	196	(3)	(28)	–	215
Adoption of FRS 17	(4)	1	3	(104)	(104)
31 August 2002 restated	192	(2)	(25)	(104)	111

Under FRS 17, the difference between the market value of the assets of the group's principal defined benefit pension funds and the present value of accrued pension liabilities is shown as an asset or liability on the balance sheet, net of deferred tax. Previously the only balance sheet items were a prepayment representing the cumulative difference between pension charges included in the profit and loss account, and actual payments made to the scheme and a provision for un-funded pension obligations and other post retirement benefits.

ii) Consolidated profit and loss account

	Operating Profit	Interest	Profit attributable to
£m			shareholders
At 31 August 2002	89	–	52
Adoption of FRS 17	(13)	8	(5)
31 August 2002 restated	76	8	47

The profit and loss charge, under Statement of Standard Accounting Practice *Accounting for Pension Costs* (SSAP 24), comprised a regular pension cost net of spreading of the surplus over the average remaining service lives of the relevant employees and a notional interest credit. Under FRS 17, the following items are included in the profit and loss account:

Charged to operating profit

- the full service cost of pension provision relating to the period, together with the costs of any benefits relating to past service.

Included in interest

- a charge equal to the expected increase in the present value of the scheme liabilities (because the benefits are closer to settlement) and netted against this;
- a credit equivalent to the group's long-term expected return on assets based on market value of the scheme assets at the start of the period.

Included in the statement of total recognised gains and losses is the difference between the expected return on pension assets at the start of the period and the actual return achieved along with the differences, which arise from experience or assumption changes, in pension liabilities.

If FRS 17 had not been adopted for the year ended 31 August 2003, profit on ordinary activities before taxation would have been £30m and profit on ordinary activities after taxation would have been £1m. The corresponding net assets would have been £583m.

Pension plans

The group operates pension plans in a number of countries around the world. Pension arrangements for UK employees are operated through two defined benefit schemes (WHSmith Pension Trust and Holder Headline Staff Retirement Benefits Plan) and a defined contribution scheme, WHSmith Pension Builder. The most significant is the defined benefit WHSmith Pension Trust for the Group's UK employees. In other countries, benefits are determined in accordance with local practice and regulations and funding is provided accordingly. There are defined benefit arrangements in the UK and the United States of America with the remainder being either defined contribution or state sponsored schemes. The assets of the pension plans are held in separate funds administered by Trustees, which are independent of the group's finances.

WHSmith Pension Trust

The latest full actuarial valuation of the scheme was carried out as at 31 March 2003 by independent actuaries, Mercer Human Resource Consulting, using the market value basis. A full actuarial valuation of the scheme is carried out every 3 years with interim reviews in the intervening years. This scheme was closed in September 1995 and under the projected unit method the current service cost would be expected to increase as members approach retirement and the age profile of members increases. The group has reached agreement with the pension trustees to substantially increase the contributions to fund the deficit. Annual cash contributions of £42m have been approved for the year ended 31 August 2004. This will be subject to an annual review.

Holder Headline Staff Retirement Benefits Plan

The latest full actuarial valuation of the scheme was carried out as at 1 July 2001 by independent actuaries, Mercer Human Resource Consulting, using the projected unit method. A full actuarial valuation of the scheme is carried out every 3 years with interim reviews in the intervening years. Annual cash contributions of £2m have been approved for the year ended 31 August 2004. This will be subject to an annual review.

Pension valuations

The valuation of the group's defined benefit pension schemes used for the FRS 17 disclosures are based upon the most recent actuarial valuations. These have been updated by professionally qualified actuaries (Mercer Human Resource Consulting) to take into account the requirements of FRS 17 and to assess the liabilities of the schemes at 31 August 2003. Scheme assets are stated at their market value at 31 August 2003.

The weighted average principal long-term assumptions used in the actuarial valuation were:

%	2003	2002	2001
Rate of increase in salaries	4.4%	4.2%	4.3%
Rate of increase in pensions payments and deferred pensions	2.7%	2.4%	2.5%
Discount rate	5.5%	5.6%	5.8%
Inflation assumptions	2.7%	2.4%	2.5%

The aggregate fair values of the assets in the group's defined benefit schemes, the aggregate net pension liabilities and their expected weighted average long-term rates of return at 31 August 2003 were:

	2003		2002 As restated		2001 As restated	
	£m		£m		£m	
Equities	408	7.6%	372	7.4%	475	8.0%
Bonds	219	4.6%	219	4.5%	213	4.8%
Cash	4	4.6%	5	4.2%	5	5.7%
Total fair value of assets	631		596		693	
Present value of liabilities	(846)		(740)		(694)	
Deficit in the schemes	(215)		(144)		(1)	
Related deferred tax asset	64		43		–	
Net defined benefit schemes liabilities	(151)		(101)		(1)	
Net retirement medical benefits	(5)		(3)		(3)	
Net pension liabilities	(156)		(104)		(4)	

i) Defined benefit pension schemes
Analysis of the amount charged to operating profit

£m	2003	2002
Current service cost	(13)	(13)

Analysis of the amount (charged)/credited to interest

£m	2003	2002
Expected return on pension scheme assets	38	47
Interest on pension scheme liabilities	(41)	(39)
	(3)	8

Analysis of the actuarial loss in the statement of total recognised gains and losses

£m	2003	2002
Actual return less expected return on pension scheme assets	6	(117)
Experience gains and losses arising on the scheme liabilities	3	(19)
Changes in assumptions underlying the present value of the scheme liabilities	(86)	(6)
	(79)	(142)

£2m (2002: £1m) of actuarial loss relates to the US pension scheme.

Movement in scheme deficit during the period

£m	2003	2002 As restated
At beginning of period	(144)	(1)
Current service cost	(13)	(13)
Contributions	22	4
Interest (cost)/income	(3)	8
Actuarial loss	(77)	(142)
Deficit in scheme at end of period	(215)	(144)

History of the weighted average experience gains and losses

	2003	2002 As restated	2001
Difference between actual and expected return on assets:			
Amount (£m)	6	(117)	(180)
% of scheme assets	1%	(20%)	(26%)
Experience gains and losses on scheme liabilities:			
Amount(£m)	3	(19)	–
% of present value of the scheme liabilities	1%	(3%)	–
Total amount recognised in statement of total recognised gains and losses:			
Amount (£m)	(77)	(142)	(215)
% of present value of the scheme liabilities	9%	(20%)	(31%)

Post retirement medical benefits

WH Smith PLC provides retirement medical benefits to certain pensioners. Total premiums paid during the year in respect of those benefits were £0.4m (2002: £0.3m). The present value of the future liabilities under this arrangement have been assessed by our actuary (Mellon Human Resources & Investor Solutions (Actuaries & Consultants) Limited) and this amount is included on the balance sheet, net of deferred taxation under pension and other post retirement liabilities as follows:

£m	2003	2002
Post retirement medical benefits	(5)	(3)

ii) Defined contribution pension scheme

The group's pension cost charge to its defined contribution scheme, WHSmith Pension Builder, for the period amounted to £2m (2002: £2m).

8.4   SSAP 25 *Segmental Reporting* (June 1990)

Background

This was the last accounting standard to be published by the former ASC. It does not affect the content of the primary statements but it does expand on some of the information disclosed in the notes to the financial statements.

The main rationale for the standard is the need to disaggregate consolidated data into more detailed segment information to provide sufficient information to the reader as to how significant components of the overall business have performed. The need for the standard has emerged from the diversification which many large entities have decided to embark on strategically to avoid having 'all of their eggs in one basket', e.g. BAT plc originally tobacco but diversifying into financial services. Also, most large plcs are now multinational entities and it is important for the investor to understand the actual and potential risks and rewards from investing in different parts of the world.

Scope

The standard is only applicable to plc's, banking and insurance companies and large companies (i.e. those which are ten times the size of a medium-sized company for filing purposes). Similarly, a subsidiary (not of a banking or insurance company) can avoid disclosure, provided that the parent provides segmental information in compliance with the standard.

A further exemption occurs when the reporting entity believes that such disclosure would be 'seriously prejudicial' to the interests of the reporting entity. This is not acceptable internationally and therefore it is likely that an amendment to SSAP 25 will eventually be made to remove this exemption in due course.

Accounting treatment – class of business segment

SSAP 25 leaves it up to the directors to decide how many classes of business segment there should be and how to define them. However, guidance is provided by SSAP 25, which recommends that such classes should be largely split where segments earn different returns or are subject to different degrees of risk. Normally a segment should not be under 10 per cent of third-party turnover, of total net assets or of the combined profit or loss result, whichever is the greater. Business segments can be divided between different products, markets, distribution channels, or their organisational framework or even, if required, for legislative purposes, e.g. a bank or insurance company.

In practice most companies do not exceed four to five segments in total as comparative information must also be provided for each of the segments chosen.

Accounting treatment – geographical

The geographical segments can be on an individual or group of countries basis. They should be divided up on the same risks/rewards basis as the class of business segmentation but this should take into account such factors as unstable political regimes, exchange rate or control problems and expansionist/restrictive economic climates. Ultimately the choice of segment is left up to the directors.

Other issues

Common costs

In reporting segmental information there is a problem of how to apportion certain common costs among the chosen segments. There are several possible approaches that are totally acceptable but no SSAP 25 requirement is involved and it is therefore perfectly appropriate to deduct common costs in total from the combined result without any apportionment being necessary.

Associated companies

If an associate represents 20 per cent or more of the total results or net assets of a segment then the group's share of its results and net assets should be incorporated into the overall breakdown of a segment's results/net assets.

Disclosure

The key part of the standard is the disclosure requirements:

Class of business

  (i)   Definition of segments;
 (ii)   Turnover split between external and inter-segment sales;
(iii)   Profit/loss before taxation and minority interests or profit before interest and taxation;
(iv)   Net assets.

Geographical

(i) Definition of segments;
(ii) Turnover by origin and destination, unless not materially different as well as split between external and inter-segment turnover;
(iii) Profit/loss before tax and minority interest or profit before interest and tax;
(iv) Net assets.

Comparatives are also required and a reconciliation is made to the information in the consolidated financial statements if automatic reconciliation has not already been effected.

Directors can redefine the segments, if appropriate, but they will need to adjust the comparatives accordingly. This would not represent a change in accounting policy as it does not affect the primary statements themselves.

Future direction of SSAP 25

A discussion paper on the topic was published in May 1996. Essentially it looks at the possibility of changing the definition of segments from a risks/returns approach to a managerial one (as per the FASB in the USA). It concludes by favouring the retention of the existing approach as this is in line with IASC thinking but it also proposes a considerable expansion in the amount of disclosure. For example, details of gross assets, gross liabilities, capital commitments, contingent liabilities, depreciation charges, exceptional items, etc., are proposed. Nothing of any substance has occurred in UK reporting since 1996 and the discussion paper is effectively 'on ice' at present.

As SSAP 25 is purely a disclosure standard it is fairly easy to put into practice but does involve a considerable amount of space in the annual report. A good example of how to compute the data to be included is provided in the illustration below.

Example – Kesh Plc

Kesh plc is preparing a segmental report to include with its financial accounts prepared for the year ended 30 June 2004.

The relevant information given below is based on the consolidated figures of Kesh plc and its subsidiaries. Associate information is not shown.

	2004 £'000	2003 £'000
Sales to customers outside the group by the Fruit Growing Division	12,150	13,500
Sales to customers outside the group by the UK companies	27,000	24,300
Sales not derived from Fruit Growing, Canning or Bureau activities	2,700	1,350
Sales made to customers outside the group by the Canning Division	17,550	13,095
Assets used by the US companies	32,400	24,300
Assets not able to be allocated to Fruit Growing, Canning or Bureau activities	13,500	11,003
Assets used by the Fruit Growing Division	33,750	32,400

	2004	2003
Sales by the Canning Division to other group members	2,970	3,105
Assets used by the Bureau service	18,765	17,563
Assets used by the UK companies	43,200	40,500
Sales by the Fruit Growing Division to other group members	1,485	1,688
Sales not allocated to the UK, USA or other areas	2,700	1,350
Sales made by group to other areas of the world	1,350	1,215
Expenses not allocated to UK, USA or other areas	4,590	3,834
Sales to customers outside the group by US companies	6,750	5,130
Expenses not allocated to the Fruit Growing, Canning or Bureau service	5,130	4,104
Sales by US companies to group members	2,160	1,215
Sales to customers outside the group for Bureau service	5,400	4,050
Sales made by UK companies to other group members	2,700	1,890
Assets used by the Canning Division	40,500	33,750
Assets used by the group in other areas	18,360	19,683
Assets not allocated to UK, USA or other areas	12,555	10,233
Segmental net operating profit by industry		
Fruit Growing	2,565	3,375
Canning	4,725	3,600
Bureau	412	540
Consolidated segmental net operating profit	7,695	6,750
Segmental net operating profit by geographical area		
UK	5,130	4,590
USA	2,430	1,890
Other areas	270	405
Consolidated segmental net operating profit by geographical area	7,155	6,480

Suggested solution – Kesh Plc

Published segment report for inclusion in the annual report

Classes of business

	Fruit		Canning		Bureau		Other		Group	
	2004	2003	2004	2003	2004	2003	2004	2003	2004	2003
	£'000	£'000	£'000	£'000	£'000	£'000	£'000	£'000	£'000	£'000
Turnover	13,635	15,188	20,520	16,200	5,400	4,050	2,700	1,350	42,255	36,788
Inter-segment	1,485	1,688	2,970	3,105	–	–	–	–	4,455	4,793
Third party	12,150	13,500	17,550	13,095	5,400	4,050	2,700	1,350	37,800	31,995
Profit before taxation	2,565	3,375	4,725	3,600	412	540	–	–	7,702	7,515
Inter-segment profits	–	–	–	–	–	–	–	–	(7)	(765)
	2,565	3,375	4,725	3,600	412	540	–	–	7,695	6,750
Common costs									5,130	4,104
Group profit before taxation									2,565	2,646

Net assets										
Segment net assets	33,750	32,400	40,500	33,750	18,765	17,563			93,015	83,713
Unallocated assets									13,500	11,003
									106,515	94,716

Geographical

	UK		USA		Other		Unallocated		Group	
	2004	2003	2004	2003	2004	2003	2004	2003	2004	2003
	£'000	£'000	£'000	£'000	£'000	£'000	£'000	£'00	£'000	£'000
Turnover by destination										
Sales to third parties	XX	XX	XX	XX	XX	XX	XX	XX	XX	XX
Turnover by origin										
Total sales	29,700	26,190	8,910	6,345	1,350	1,215	2,700	1,350	42,660	35,100
Inter-segment	2,700	1,890	2,160	1,215	–	–	–	–	4,860	3,105
Third party	27,000	24,300	6,750	5,130	1,350	1,215	2,700	1,350	37,800	31,995
Profit before taxation	5,130	4,590	2,430	1,890	270	405			7,830	6,885
Inter-segment profits									(675)	(405)
									7,155	6,480
Common costs									4,590	3,834
Group profit before taxation									2,565	2,646
Net assets										
Segment	43,200	40,500	32,400	24,300	18,360	19,683			93,960	84,483
Unallocated									12,555	10,233
Total net assets									106,515	94,716

Application in published accounts

There are many excellent examples of good practice in the disclosure of segment informa-tion. However, one of the best and certainly one of the most detailed is provided by CRH plc. They have decided to break down the overall business into four geographical and three class of business sections:

CRH Plc   Year Ended 31 December 2003   Aggregates and Building Supplies

Notes on financial statements

1 Segmental Information (Extract)
Geographical analysis
The geographical analysis of turnover and profits is based on market/destination. There is no material difference between this analysis and the split of sales and profits by origin.

Turnover	2003		2002	
	€m	%	€m	%
Republic of Ireland	731.6	6.6	713.9	6.6
Britain & Northern Ireland	691.5	6.3	698.4	6.5
Mainland Europe	3,635.3	32.8	3,020.6	28.0
The Americas	6,021.4	54.3	6,361.2	58.9
Total including share of joint ventures	11,079.8	100	10,794.1	100
Less share of joint ventures	(305.5)		(276.9)	
Total excluding share of joint ventures	10,774.3		10,517.2	

Profit on ordinary activities before interest

	2003				
		Operating profit	Goodwill amortisation	Profit on disposal	Trading profit
	%	€m	€m	€m	€m
Republic of Ireland	12.4	129.6	(0.3)	3.4	133.0
Britain & Northern Ireland	5.5	57.4	(5.1)	3.5	55.8
Mainland Europe	28.5	297.8	(34.0)	3.1	266.9
The Americas	53.6	559.6	(36.1)	3.0	526.5
Total including share of joint ventures	100	1,044.7	(75.5)	13.0	982.2
Less share of joint ventures		(40.2)	1.5	(1.1)	(39.8)
Total excluding share of joint ventures		1,004.5	(74.0)	11.9	942.4

	2002				
		Profit	Goodwill amortisation	Profit on disposal	Trading Operating profit
	%	€m	€m	€m	€m
Republic of Ireland	12.5	131.3	(0.3)	7.8	138.8
Britain & Northern Ireland	5.3	55.8	(5.4)	2.8	53.2
Mainland Europe	22.3	233.5	(28.6)	3.3	208.2
The Americas	59.9	627.5	(35.3)	1.8	594.0
Total including share of joint ventures	100	1,048.1	(69.6)	15.7	994.2
Less share of joint ventures		(33.5)	2.0	(1.2)	(32.7)
Total excluding share of joint ventures		1,014.6	(67.6)	14.5	961.5

Net assets	2003		2002	
	€m	%	€m	%
Republic of Ireland	327.0	4.2	303.3	4.2
Britain & Northern Ireland	483.5	6.2	542.8	7.6
Mainland Europe	3,068.5	39.6	2,168.0	30.4
The Americas	3,869.8	50.0	4,126.3	57.8
Total including share of joint ventures	7,748.8	100	7,140.4	100
Trade and other investments	12.1		22.1	
Unallocated liabilities – dividends proposed	(105.0)		(94.2)	
	7,655.9		7,068.3	

Reconciliation of total net assets

Total assets less current liabilities	8,872.5	8,812.1
Less cash and liquid investments	(1,298.0)	(1,533.2)
Add bank loans and overdrafts	510.3	232.8
Less deferred acquisition consideration due after more than one year	(96.5)	(142.5)
Less provisions for liabilities and charges (excluding deferred taxation)	(332.4)	(300.9)
	7,655.9	7,068.3

The impact of acquisitions completed during 2003 (see note 29 for detailed list) is summarised below:

	Turnover €m	Operating profit €m	Net assets at year end €m
Cementbouw	212.5	20.9	692.3
Europe – other acquisitions	215.3	21.4	318.0
Total Europe	427.8	42.3	1,010.3
The Americas	404.2	46.5	487.8
Total acquisitions including share of joint ventures	832.0	88.8	1,498.1
Materials	237.1	26.1	319.0
Products	379.8	46.0	682.1
Distribution	215.1	16.7	497.0
Total acquisitions including share of joint ventures	832.0	88.8	1,498.1

Analysis by division/class of business
The group is organised into four divisions, two in Europe and two in the Americas:

Materials businesses are primarily involved in the production of cement, aggregates, asphalt and readymix concrete.

Products businesses are involved in the production of concrete products and a range of construction-related products and services.

Distribution businesses are engaged in the marketing and sale of builders' supplies to the construction industry and of materials and products to the DIY market.

			2003		
	Materials	Products	Distribution	Total Products & Distribution	Total Group
Turnover	€m	€m	€m	€m	€m
Europe	1,983.8	1,720.6	1,361.8	3,082.4	5,066.2
Americas	2,831.3	2,196.3	986.0	3,182.3	6,013.6
	4,815.1	3,916.9	2,347.8	6,264.7	11,079.8
Less share of joint ventures	(190.8)	(66.0)	(48.7)	(114.7)	(305.5)
	4,624.3	3,850.9	2,299.1	6,150.0	10,774.3

Operating profit

Europe	273.3	142.6	70.1	212.7	486.0
Americas	290.7	215.6	52.4	268.0	558.7
	564.0	358.2	122.5	480.7	1.044.7
Less share of joint ventures and associates	(27.7)	(5.8)	(6.7)	(12.5)	(40.2)
	536.3	352.4	115.8	468.2	1,004.5

Goodwill amortisation

Europe	(20.3)	(16.1)	(3.0)	(19.1)	(39.4)
Americas	(17.9)	(14.0)	(4.2)	(18.2)	(36.1)
	(38.2)	(30.1)	(7.2)	(37.3)	(75.5)
Less share of joint ventures and associates	1.4	1.6	(1.5)	0.1	1.5
	(36.8)	(28.5)	(8.7)	(37.2)	(74.0)

Profit/(loss) on disposal of fixed assets

Europe	6.3	2.6	1.1	3.7	10.0
Americas	2.8	(0.7)	0.9	0.2	3.0
	9.1	1.9	2.0	3.9	13.0
Less share of joint ventures and associates	(0.9)	(0.1)	(0.1)	(0.2)	(1.1)
	8.2	1.8	1.9	3.7	11.9

Profit on ordinary activities before interest

Europe	259.3	129.1	68.2	197.3	456.6
Americas	275.6	200.9	49.1	250.0	525.6
	534.9	330.0	117.3	447.3	982.2
Less share of joint ventures and associates	(27.2)	(4.3)	(8.3)	(12.6)	(39.8)
	507.7	325.7	109.0	434.7	942.4

	2003		2002	
	€m	%	€m	%
Net assets				
Europe Materials	1,482.9	19.1	1,519.3	21.3
Europe Products	1,567.4	20.2	1,171.6	16.4
Europe Distribution	828.6	10.7	322.5	4.5
Americas Materials	2,522.2	32.6	2,691.9	37.7
Americas Products	1,163.3	15.0	1,218.3	17.1
Americas Distribution	184.4	2.4	216.8	103.0
	7,748.8	100	7,140.4	100.0
Trade and other investments	12.1		22.1	
Unallocated liabilities – dividends proposed	(105.0)		(94.2)	
	7,655.9		7,068.3	

Group accounting

9.1 FRS 2 *Accounting for Subsidiary Undertakings* (July 1992)

Background

Prior to the Companies Act 1989 the definition of a subsidiary was largely governed by two rules. If a 'parent' held more than 50 per cent of the shares in the other investment or if it could appoint more than 50 per cent of the directors to the board, then a subsidiary relationship existed. This led to deliberate manipulation by investing companies to avoid consolidation of investments over which the 'parent' clearly had control.

This could be achieved by allocating more votes to the directors of the investor than other parties or to the parent's shareholding, thus getting round the apparent deadlock of a 50:50 equal number of shares/directors. Two examples should suffice to show the effect:

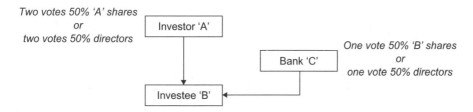

Figure 9.1

An alternative would be for a 'parent' to set up a company in which it owned 0 per cent of the shares and therefore could not appoint any directors, but over which it still had control. This would be achieved by way of a separate written control contract whereby all major decisions would have to get the permission of the so-called parent before being undertaken. Most of the day-to-day working capital, however, would be provided by the parent in exchange for convertible loan stock which could be converted into shares at the option of the parent, i.e. when the other entity started to make profits! Consolidation had therefore now become effectively optional in practice:

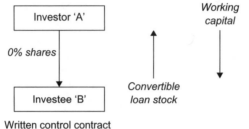

Figure 9.2

FRS 2 has largely been drafted to enlarge the definition of a subsidiary to incorporate not only both of the above examples as subsidiaries but also to ensure that any entity set up by another and controlled by that other either be incorporated as a subsidiary under the Companies Act and FRS 2 or be caught as a quasi-subsidiary under FRS 5.

FRS 2 also 'puts the flesh around the bare bones' of the legislation introduced by the Companies Act 1989 which discusses such diverse subjects as exemptions from consolidation, method of preparing group accounts and how to account for changes in stake.

Key issues

Parent/subsidiary undertaking

A parent/subsidiary relationship is now defined as one which meets one of the following five criteria:

(i)   Parent holds a majority of the *voting rights* at the annual general meeting;
(ii) Parent can appoint a director holding a majority of the *voting rights* at the board meetings;
(iii) Parent can exercise a *dominant influence* over a subsidiary via its memorandum or articles of association.
(iv) Parent has a *participating interest* (i.e. a long-term interest to secure future contributions to profits) and actively exercises a dominant influence or manages both entities on a *unified basis* (i.e. total operations of both entities intertwined).
(v)   Parent holds a subsubsidiary relationship, i.e. A controls B and B controls C, therefore C is controlled indirectly by A.

Preparation of group accounts

The only acceptable method of preparing group accounts is *consolidation.*

Exemptions

Consolidated financial statements are not required if:

(i)   the group is medium or small as per the Companies Act;
(ii) it is a 100 per cent owned subsidiary and its immediate parent is in the EU;
(iii) all of its subsidiaries are excluded (see below).

Exclusion of subsidiaries

(i)   Immateriality in relation to group but not simply on the grounds of disproportionate expense or undue delay.
(ii) Severe long-term restrictions preventing the exercise of control, e.g. UN sanctions over the use of Iraqi subsidiaries.
(iii) Subsidiary is only held temporarily with a view to its subsequent resale and it has never previously been consolidated.
(iv) Subsidiary is so different from others that its inclusion would not permit a true and fair view. However, simply being dissimilar would not be sufficient grounds for exclusion and therefore most finance subsidiaries are now consolidated with their associated retail or manufacturing groups.

Minority interests

Must be separately recorded on the balance sheet and profit and loss account and the minority charged/credited for their share of any inter-company profits/losses.

Consolidation adjustments

(i)   All inter-company profits/losses should be eliminated together with all inter-company debtors/creditors.
(ii) Uniform accounting policies should be adopted.
(iii) The same accounting periods should be adopted but, if this is not possible, then interim accounts for the subsidiaries should be adopted to ensure that they have the same accounting periods as the parent. If this is not possible then the actual financial statements may be used so long as the periods relating thereto are not more than 3 months earlier.

Changes in group composition

(i)   A subsidiary is created when *control* passes to the parent and it ceases when *control* ceases, i.e. when a parent no longer has the ability to direct the operating and financial policies of the subsidiary.
(ii) On the date of cessation – all profits/losses of subsidiaries should be included in the group accounts to that date and any profits/losses on disposal should be calculated as the difference between the value of net assets and the purchase consideration received.

Changes in stake

(i)   Piecemeal acquisition – fair values should be computed at each stage of the acquisition and goodwill calculated at those times.

(ii) Disposal of interest – any profits/losses on disposal should be the difference between their net book value and any proceeds received. The minority interest should also be adjusted.

Consultation Paper (May 2002)

The Consultation Paper sets out a revised IAS 27 which itself outlines the requirements to be applied in the preparation and presentation of consolidated financial statements for a group. It also deals with the treatment of accounting for investments in subsidiaries, jointly controlled entities and associates. FRS 2 covers the same ground but the ASB does not propose to issue IAS 27 at this time as the standard is likely to be changed again as a result of further IASB projects that address the requirements for consolidation.

The first example looks at an unusual share structure in making a decision to whether or not an entity should be classified as a legal subsidiary under FRS 2. It also brings in the link between FRS 2 and FRS 5 *Reporting the Substance of Transactions* and discusses situations where a quasi-subsidiary is created:

Example – Aughnacloy Plc

The directors of Aughnacloy plc are proposing to set up a new company, Bearnagh plc, to which it would transfer patent rights that had been developed by Augnacloy Group companies with a view to Bearnagh plc entering into licensing agreements which would provide a long-term source of finance for the group.

Bearnagh plc was to be formed with a share capital that would comprise 1,000,000 ordinary shares of 25p each to be held by Aughnacloy plc and 1,000,000 10 per cent voting convertible preference shares of 25p each to be held by a third party that was friendly to Aughnacloy plc.

The preference shares would be convertible in 15 years and Aughnacloy plc would have a call option to acquire the shares after 10 years and the holders of the shares would have a put option to sell the shares to Aughnacloy plc after 12 years.

Should Bearnagh plc fail to be treated as a subsidiary under the provisions of the Companies Act 1985 as revised by the Companies Act 1989 in any consolidated accounts that Aughnacloy Group prepares, what additional information would be required in order to be able to provide proper advice?

If it were the case that the directors of Aughnacloy plc have been successful in establishing a structure which ensures that the legal effect is that Bearnagh plc is a controlled non-subsidiary whereas the commercial effect is that it is a subsidiary undertaking, then explain the measures being taken by the accounting profession, such as the proposals in FRS 5 *Reporting the Substance of Transactions in Assets and Liabilities* to ensure that consolidated accounts provide the holding company shareholders with information that is relevant, understandable, reliable and comparable.

Suggested solution – Aughnacloy Plc

Is Bearnagh plc to be treated as a subsidiary under the Companies Act 1985?

The definition of a subsidiary has been changed with the implementation of the EC 7th Directive on group accounting. Underlying the philosophy behind the directive is the concept of reflecting economic substance/control within group accounting. The revised definition is more widely drawn to try to 'bring back into the net' certain 'subsidiaries' which previously were not legally defined as subsidiaries but which were very largely dependent upon a 'parent undertaking'.

The new definition is contained in Section 258, Paras 2 and 4, which state that an undertaking is a parent of another if any of the following statements apply:

(1) It holds a majority of the *voting rights* in that undertaking. Aughnacloy owns 50 per cent but not a majority.
(2) It is a member of the other undertaking and can appoint or remove a *majority* of its *board of directors*. No information is provided for Aughnacloy.
(3) It has a right to exercise a *dominant influence* over the other undertaking either via provisions in the entity's articles/memorandum or via a *control contract*. No information is provided for Aughnacloy.
(4) It is a member and controls, in agreement with others, a *majority* of the *voting rights* in the other undertaking. No information is provided for Aughnacloy.

An undertaking is also a parent if it has a *participating interest* and:

(1) it actually exercises a *dominant influence*. Aughnacloy appears to be in that situation as the friendly third party holds the rest of the shares in Bearnagh plc, or
(2) both are managed on a *unified basis*. There is not sufficient information on Aughnacloy to indicate fully unified operations rather than just unified management.

On balance the information appears to indicate that a subsidiary undertaking has been created, but confirmation would be required to ensure that the parent has in fact dominant influence over Bearnagh plc.

The effect of FRS 5

FRS 5 *Reporting the Substance of Transactions* requires companies to disclose all assets and liabilities which currently fail the legal definition. This is achieved by requiring a company to record transactions so that their commercial effect is fairly reflected.

For example, an asset is 'a resource controlled by an enterprise as a result of past events and from which future economic benefits are expected to flow to the enterprise'.

In terms of quasi-subsidiaries, control is defined as control via the medium of another enterprise, whereby effective control exists over and risks arise from the assets of another enterprise as if it were a subsidiary.

Quasi-subsidiaries should also be consolidated in the group accounts. Under company legislation they fail to meet the statutory definition of a subsidiary. Therefore the 'true and fair' override must be applied to make the financial statements as relevant and reliable as possible, and ensuring that they are consolidated.

Application in published accounts

Under FRS 2, entities must calculate goodwill at each stage of a piecemeal acquisition but this is in conflict with the Companies Act 1985. Companies therefore have to invoke the 'true and fair view' override in order to comply with accounting standards. An example of the required disclosure is provided by Dixons plc and this is illustrated below:

Dixons Group Plc   Year Ended 3 May 2003   Retail

Notes to the Financial Statements (Extract)

1.1 Accounting convention and basis of consolidation

The consolidated financial statements are prepared under the historical cost convention. The consolidated financial statements incorporate the financial statements of the company and all of its subsidiaries and associated undertakings. These subsidiaries are included from the date on which control passes. The net assets of subsidiaries acquired are recorded at values reflecting their condition at that date. The results of subsidiaries disposed of are included up to the effective date of disposal. Associated undertakings are accounted for using the equity method of accounting.

1.5 Goodwill (Extract)

On a change from an investment in associated undertaking to a subsidiary, goodwill is calculated in accordance with FRS 2 *Accounting for Subsidiary Undertakings*. This represents a departure, for the purpose of showing a true and fair view, from the requirements of para. 9, Schedule 4A to the Companies Act 1985. Under the Companies Act 1985, goodwill in a subsidiary is determined as a one-stage calculation by considering the difference between the fair value of assets and liabilities and the aggregate consideration payable by the date that control passes and the entity is consolidated in the group's balance sheet. Under FRS 2, separate calculations of goodwill are made at each stage of acquisition.

FRS 2 does provide a list of legitimate exclusions of subsidiaries from being incorporated within the group financial statements. One of these is the existence of 'severe long-term restriction' over the control over a subsidiary. Reckitt Benckiser plc provides an illustration:

Reckitt Benckiser Plc   Year Ended   Household Goods
December 2003

Basis of Consolidation

The accounts of the group represent the consolidation of Reckitt Benckiser plc and its subsidiary undertakings. The accounts of subsidiary undertakings which do not conform with group policies are adjusted on consolidation in order that the group accounts may be presented on a consistent basis. In the case of acquisitions and disposals of businesses, the results of trading are consolidated from or to the date upon which control passes.

The results and net assets of the group's subsidiary in Zimbabwe have been excluded from the consolidated group results with effect from 1 July 2002, on the basis that severe long-term restrictions exist that hinder the exercise of the group's rights over the assets employed, in particular the remittance of funds. The results for the first half of 2002 are included within discontinued and deconsolidated operations (half-year to 30 June 2002: net revenues £13m; operating profit £1m). Results for the second half of 2002 and 2003, and the balance sheets as at 31 December 2002 and 31 December 2003, were insignificant.

The results of an agency agreement under which the group sold Bayer Pest Control Products in Italy are shown as discontinued in 2002 following the termination of the agreement with effect from 31 December 2002. This has no impact on net revenues, but reclassifies operating profit by £2m into discontinued business for the year ended 31 December 2002. No income was recorded in 2003.

9.2   FRS 6 *Acquisitions and Mergers* (September 1994)

Background

The field of accounting for business combinations has been fertile ground over the last decade for the creative accountant. In particular there has been considerable flexibility in the choice of combination technique adopted, and the method that provided the most favourable result for both the company and its directors was often employed. FRS 6 was published specifically to counter the manipulation of the technique of merger accounting. In fact it could be subtitled 'when can I adopt merger accounting?'.

The problem initially arose due to the considerable advantages of adopting merger as opposed to acquisition accounting. These can be summarised as follows:

(i)   The investment in the 'subsidiary' is recorded at nominal value; thus any differences between the nominal value of the purchase consideration and the nominal value of the net assets would be quite small and are regarded as consolidation differences to be written off to reserves. No goodwill is created.

(ii)   Both sets of retained profits may be added together and are available for distribution, i.e. there is no freezing of pre-acquisition profits.

(iii) No quasi capital account, i.e. share premium, is set up as the investment is recorded at nominal value.

(iv)   Because there are no revaluations at the date of acquisition, there is no additional charge for depreciation in future years and therefore no decrease in earnings per share.

Under the former SSAP 23 the only material rule that prevented all combinations from being treated as mergers was the requirement that 90 per cent or more of the fair value of the purchase consideration needed to be in the form of a share-for-share exchange. This rule was easily circumvented by techniques such as vendor placing and vendor rights.

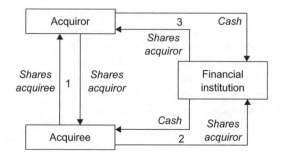

Figure 9.3

These were so popular that by the end of the 1980s all business combinations were being treated as mergers, even though in reality they were acquisitions! The vendor placing/rights techniques, however, were eventually eclipsed by an even more inventive use of acquisition accounting by way of s.131 Companies Act and Merger Relief (see FRS 7 *Fair Values in Acquisition Accounting*). However, there is always a danger that if acquisition accounting were to be tightened up then companies would switch back to merger accounting in droves. That is the basic reason why both FRS 6 and FRS 7 had to be published and be effective from the same day.

The new standard, however, does not take a rule-based approach to solving the problem as it realised that any rules devised could be bent by the good creative accountant. Thus the new standard has been built up on principles. The main principle is that if a business combination does not meet the definition of a merger then it must be treated as an acquisition.

Definitions

- *Merger.* A business combination that results in the creation of a new reporting entity formed from the combining parties, in which the shareholders of the combining parties come together in a partnership for the mutual sharing of the risks and benefits of the combined entity, and in which no party to the combination in substance obtains control over any other, or is seen to be dominant, whether by virtue of the proportion of its shareholders' rights in the combined entity, the influence of its directors or otherwise.
- *Acquisition.* A business combination that is not a merger.

The emphasis in FRS 6 lies in ensuring that only genuine mergers are reported under merger accounting and therefore the definition is fairly narrow. However, the definition, by itself, would not be sufficiently strong and thus FRS 6 also puts forward five criteria that should be investigated, in an overall context, to see whether or not a combination actually complies with the definition. This is not meant to be a checklist and the reporting accountant must look at all five together and make a subjective opinion on whether or not the combination is a merger:

Key issues

Criteria for merger

(i)   Neither party to the combination is portrayed as either an acquiror or acquiree.
(ii) All parties participate in the formation of the new management team.
(iii) No one party is large enough to dominate the other and a rebuttable size test of no more than 50 per cent the size of the other is suggested.
(iv) The bulk of the purchase consideration should be in the form of equity shares.
(v)   There should be no earn out clauses, i.e. there must be mutuality of risks and rewards.

Group reconstructions

Essentially a group reconstruction does permit the use of merger accounting since the ultimate shareholders remain the same, their rights are unchanged and there is no alteration of the minority interest's share in the net assets of the group.

Disclosures

There are extensive disclosures required under FRS 6 for both methods of combination but there are fourteen as opposed to seven requirements for the acquisition approach. This is because of the fair value exercise required and thus the acquiror must provide full details of the composition of the purchase consideration and of the net assets acquired in the form of a fair value table. This must be broken down into its component parts, e.g. uniformity of accounting policies, revaluation of certain assets, provisions for certain liabilities, etc.

Merger accounting is under considerable threat from developments in the USA and, the IASB has followed (IFRS 3) the US approach of banning mergers. Canada, Australia and New Zealand have already gone down that road.

9.3   FRS 7 *Fair Values in Acquisition Accounting* (September 1994)

Background

This standard was released on the same day as FRS 7, largely to clean up the creative accounting and manipulation that had emerged in the late 1980s and early 1990s in the field of acquisition accounting. One of the clearest examples of this was exemplified by the Burton plc takeover of Debenhams.

Burtons paid £627m to acquire a 100 per cent holding in Debenhams and this consideration was broken down as follows:

	£
Cash	180m
Loan stock	31m
Ordinary shares (50p nominal value, market price £4.55 each)	416m

The company could not have adopted merger accounting as over 10 per cent of the consideration was in the form of non-shares but, of course, it could have arranged a vendor placing/rights with a friendly financial institution and adopted merger accounting by the back door (see FRS 6 *Acquisitions and Mergers*). However, Burtons decided to persist with acquisition accounting.

Under s.131 Companies Act 1985, provided that 90 per cent or more of each class of equity share is acquired then the acquiror could offset any goodwill on acquisition against the share premium being created on the share-for-share exchange. When Burtons valued the net assets of Debenhams originally, at fair value, they amounted to £300m and thus goodwill of £627 − £300 = £327m arose. However, the share premium part of the share exchange amounted to £371m and the offsetting resulted in a net balance of £44m still remaining as share premium (now renamed merger reserve). Burtons decided that this was a fairly useless quasi capital account that would never be distributed so it decided to get rid of it immediately on acquisition. This was achieved by reducing the net assets acquired by a further £44m by providing for future reorganisation costs of that amount and therefore increasing goodwill up to £371m for exact offset with the share premium. This was particularly beneficial to the directors as, in the following year, expenses which would normally be charged to the profit and loss suddenly found themselves bypassing that document and instead being offset against the provision. This had the effect of boosting post-acquisition profits and coincidently the directors' bonus payments in the following accounting year!

The merger reserve technique spread so very fast across the country that by the end of 1992 nearly all business combinations were adopting s.131 and even if they could not pass the 90 per cent rule they were able to go to court to obtain permission to reduce their share premium accounts.

Clearly this approach was within the law but not the spirit of the 'old' standard and the ASB therefore felt obliged to act to stop companies from providing spurious liabilities at the time of acquisition of another entity. FRS 7 was therefore published. It could be subtitled 'How to value goodwill' as it essentially provides the accountant with a clear guideline on how to value both the purchase consideration and the net assets acquired at their fair value.

Key issues

Objective

The objective of FRS 7 is to ensure that all assets and liabilities are recorded at their fair value on acquisition reflecting their condition as at that date. Any subsequent changes post-acquisition must be reflected in post-acquisition performance.

Effectively the following provisions are now banned:

   (i)   provisions for future impairments;
  (ii)   provisions for future losses; and
 (iii)   provisions for reorganisations.

Fair value exercise

The identifiable assets and liabilities to be recognised should only be those of the acquired entity at the date of acquisition and they should be measured at fair values that reflect the conditions as at that date. Fair value basically means the amount that an asset/liability could be exchanged for in an arm's-length transaction between a willing seller and a willing buyer.

- *Tangible fixed assets.* Fair value should be market value, if possible, or at depreciated replacement cost but it should not exceed the recoverable amount of the assets.
- *Intangible fixed assets.* Fair value should be its replacement cost – normally its estimated market value.
- *Stocks and work in progress.* Value at the lower of replacement cost and net realisable value but specialised stocks (e.g. commodity) can be valued at market value.
- *Quoted investments.* Normally value at market price unless unusual price fluctuations arise.
- *Monetary assets and liabilities.* Fair value is the amount expected to be received/paid but also taking the timing into account. Discounting is permitted.
- *Businesses acquired for subsequent resale.* Treat as a single asset and value at either net proceeds to be received or receivable.
- *Contingencies.* Should adopt a reasonable estimate of the amounts to be paid.
- *Pensions.* The fair value of a deficiency or surplus should be recognised as a liability or asset.
- *Deferred taxation.* Should be recognised by considering the enlarged group as a whole.

The exercise can be completed in provisional format at the time of acquisition and for the year end in which the acquisition has occurred. However, it must be finalised in the following year, with any adjustments to the provisional figures clearly explained in detail in an adjusted fair value table.

Cost of acquisition

Most of the problems in practice have been in relation to the calculation of the fair value of assets acquired. However, there are one or two issues also affecting the cost of acquisition:

(i) *Contingent consideration.* Need to incorporate a reasonable estimate of the amounts expected to be paid in the future and goodwill adjusted accordingly.
(ii) *Direct costs.* Any costs which are incremental and directly involved in the acquisition can be added to the cost of acquisition. However, these must not be related to the creation of a new capital instrument or be internal or only indirectly related.

Essentially the standard now insists that the residual in the fair value exercise be goodwill and FRS 7 has now tidied up the calculation of both the fair value of net assets acquired and the fair value of the consideration paid to achieve that objective.

FRS 7 is mainly computational in nature and does require fair values to be calculated for both the consideration paid and the net assets acquired in an acquisition. The example below provides an illustration of how to go about that process. It does include a number of 'red herrings' which preparers need to ensure are not included in the calculation of fair values, e.g. redundancy costs and future investment in plant and machinery.

Example – Rostrevor Plc

You are the group accountant at Rostrevor plc and need to make adjustments to the draft accounts for the year ended 30 June 2004 to reflect the acquisition of a subsidiary and to calculate the earnings per share.

Information in respect of the new subsidiary is as follows:

(1) On 1 October 2003, Rostrevor plc acquired a 90 per cent interest in Warrenpoint Inc., a US corporation. The consideration of £2,450,000 comprised £1,500,000 satisfied by the issue of 5,000,000 25p ordinary shares in Rostrevor plc to the vendors and £950,000 cash payable as to £750,000 at completion and £200,000 on 1 October 2004.

(2) The financial statements of Warrenpoint Inc. at 30 September 2003 showed net assets of $4,370,000, before deducting costs totalling $380,000 in respect of redundancies which were identified at acquisition and subsequently paid.

(3) At a board meeting to approve the acquisition, the directors of Rostrevor plc were informed that an investment in plant and machinery would be required in Warrenpoint Inc. of $300,000 in the period to 30 June 2004.

(4) Professional fees for advice in respect of the acquisition amounted to £30,000 and your finance director has estimated that the time and expenses incurred by the directors of Rostrevor plc in negotiating and completing the deal amounted to £20,000.

(5) Warrenpoint Inc. valued stocks on the LIFO (last in first out) method in its financial statements. On 30 September 2000, the value of stocks held by Warrenpoint Inc. would have been $150,000 greater if valued on the FIFO method consistent with that used by Rostrevor plc.

(6) The share capital of Rostrevor plc at 1 July 2003 comprised 47,500,000 ordinary shares of 25 pence each. Except for the transaction described above, there were no other movements in share capital during the ensuing year.

(7) The exchange rate at 1 October 2003 was £1 = $1.8.

(8) Rostrevor plc amortises goodwill arising on consolidation over a 3-year period.

Suggested solution – Rostrevor Plc

Calculation of fair value of Warrenpoint Inc. as at 1 October 2003

	$'000		£'000
Net assets per Warrenpoint Inc. 30. 9. 03 (note 2)	4,370		
Adjustments to reflect fair value			
Redundancy costs (note 2)	–		
Uniformity of accounting policies (note 5)	150		
Fair value of Warrenpoint Inc.	4,520	$1.8/£1	2,511

Redundancy costs (note 2)
The costs are clearly defined and identified at acquisition and are confirmed by subsequent payments. Undoubtedly these would have been considered by Rostrevor plc in calculating the purchase price for Warrenpoint Inc. However, FRS 7 *Fair Values in Acquisition Accounting* would appear to preclude such a provision as it represents the acquiror's future intentions in controlling the new subsidiary. Therefore it should be recorded as a post-acquisition expense.

Investment in plant and machinery (note 3)
These are prospective acquisitions. If Warrenpoint Inc. had invested in plant prior to the takeover, either cash/bank or creditors would also have been affected, thereby leaving net assets unaffected. It is merely a switch within the individual components of the same total net assets. No adjustment is therefore needed to fair value as at 1 October 2003.

Professional fees and directors' time and expenses (note 4)
These are costs incurred by Rostrevor plc in order to help the directors decide whether or not to purchase Warrenpoint Inc. As such they relate to the cost of the investment, not to the fair value of the net assets of Warrenpoint Inc.

Only the professional fees have been included in the fair value of consideration as the directors' time and expenses are not evidenced by a market transaction and should be disregarded.

Stocks (note 5)
Part of the fair value exercise should be to ensure uniformity of accounting policies, and under SSAP 9 the LIFO method for stock valuation is not permitted. An adjustment has therefore been made to increase the net assets of Warrenpoint Inc. at acquisition by $150,000.

Calculation of goodwill in the consolidated balance sheet at 30 June 2004

	£'000	£'000
Fair value of consideration 1. 10. 03		
Ordinary shares (5m × 25p) at		1,500
30p market value		
Cash – paid	750	
– deferred	200	
		950
		2,450
Acquisition costs: professional fees		30
Fair value of consideration		2,480
Fair value of net assets acquired 1. 10. 03		
£2,511,000 (from a) × 90% interest		2,260
Goodwill arising on consolidation 1. 10. 03		200

	£'000
Amortisation to 30. 6. 04 9/12 × 1/3 × 220 =	55
Net book value 30. 6. 04 (220 − 55) =	165

Note: Prior to FRS 10 *Goodwill and Intangible Assets* the company could adopt 'merger relief' under S131 Companies Act 1985/A141 CO 86. The excess of the fair value, i.e. the goodwill of £220,000, would have been offset against the share premium of 5m × 5p, i.e. £250,000. Now it must be capitalised.

The second example examines the differences between the two major methods of business combination – merger and acquisition accounting. Although merger accounting is under threat it is still likely to survive for a few more years for domestic accounting:

Example – Port Plc and Noo Plc

The balance sheets of Port plc and Noo plc at 31 December 2003, the accounting date for both companies, were as follows.

	Port plc £'000	Noo plc £'000
Tangible fixed assets	60,000	40,000
Stocks	10,000	9,000
Other current assets	12,000	10,000
Current liabilities	(9,000)	(8,000)
Quoted debentures	(15,000)	(12,000)
	58,000	39,000
Equity share capital (£1 shares)	30,000	20,000
Share premium account	10,000	5,000
Profit and loss account	18,000	14,000
	58,000	39,000

On 31 December 2003, Port plc purchased all the equity shares of Noo plc. The purchase consideration was satisfied by the issue of six new equity shares in Port plc for every five equity shares purchased in Noo plc. At 31 December 2003 the market value of a Port plc share was £2.25 and the market value of a Noo plc share was £2.40. Relevant details concerning the values of the net assets of Noo plc at 31 December 2003 were as follows:

- The fixed assets had a fair value of £43.5 million;
- The stocks had a fair value of £9.5 million;
- The debentures had a market value of £11 million;
- Other net assets had a fair value that was the same as their book value.

The effect of the purchase of shares in Noo plc is *not* reflected in the balance sheet of Port plc, which appears above.

Suggested solution – Port Plc and Noo Plc

Consolidated balance sheet as at 31 December 2003

Acquisition accounting

	£	£
Fair value of purchase consideration		54m
(6 shares for 5 for 20m × £2.25 per share)		
Fair value of net assets acquired		
Fixed assets	43.5m	
Stocks	9.5m	
Other current assets	10.0m	
Current liabilities	(8.0m)	
Quoted debentures	(11.0m)	
		44m
Goodwill		10m

Cost of control

	£		£
Purchase	54m	Share capital	20m
consideration		Share premium	5m
		Profit and loss account	14m
		Revaluation reserve (3.5 + 0.5 + 1.0)	5m
		Goodwill	10m
	54m		54m

Merger accounting Cost of control

	£		£
Purchase	24m	Share capital	20m
consideration			
		Profit and loss account	4m
	24m		24m

Consolidated balance sheet

	Acquisition £	Merger £	
Intangible fixed assets	10.0m	Nil	
Tangible fixed assets (60 + 40) (+ 3.5)	103.5m	100.0m	
Stocks (10 + 9) (+ 0.5)	19.5m	19.0m	
Other current assets (12 + 10)	22.0m	22.0m	
Current liabilities (9 + 8)	(17.0m)	(17.0m)	
Quoted debentures (15 + 12) (− 1.0)	(26.0m)	(27.0m)	
	112.0m	97.0m	
Equity share capital (30 + 24 new capital)	54.0m	54.0m	
Share premium (10 + 0) + (24m × £1.25)	40.0m	15.0m	(10 + 5)
Profit and loss account (18 + 0)	18.0m	28.0m	(18 + 14 − 4 adj.)
	112.0m	97.0m	

Requirements of FRS 6 – Merger accounting

FRS 6 defines a merger as:

> A business combination that results in the creation of a new reporting entity formed from the combining parties, in which the shareholders of the combining entities come together in a partnership for the mutual sharing of risks and benefits of the combined entity, and in which no party to the combination in substance obtains control over any other, or is otherwise seen to be dominant, whether by virtue of the proportion of its shareholders' rights in the combined entity, the influence of its directors or otherwise.

The definition has been drawn narrowly to reduce the number of reporting entities that could fall under its mantle. They should be rare combinations. On the other hand, the definition of an acquisition has been drawn to cover every 'business combination that is not a merger'.

The rationale behind the standard is that mergers should only result if, in substance, there is a genuine pooling of interests of the two parties. In effect, neither an acquirer nor an acquiree can be identified.

The definitions by themselves would not be sufficient and that is why FRS 6 introduces a number of additional criteria that need to be investigated before making a final decision in relation to the combination of Port and Noo. The following should be considered:

(*i*)   *The way the roles of each party to the combination are portrayed.*
   Does either party appear to be an acquirer or acquiree and is a new logo to be introduced containing both parties' former names? There is nothing in the facts provided that can give an opinion either way. More information is required in this regard.

(*ii*) *The involvement of both parties in selecting the new management team.*
   No information is available on this and therefore more information is required.

(*iii*) *The relative sizes of the parties to the combination.*
   Port holds 58,000/97,000 or 59.8 per cent and Noo holds 39,000/97,000 or 40.2 per cent. This is fairly close as no one party is 50 per cent larger than the other. Thus merger accounting would be a possibility.

(*iv*) *Whether the shareholders of the combining entities receive any material consideration other than equity shares as part of the deal.*
   In this case the entire exchange was in the form of equity and thus again merger accounting is a possibility.

(*v*)   *Are there any earn-out clauses or material minority interests?*
   In neither of these situations is this the case so, again, merger accounting is a possibility.

Overall, there is not enough information yet to make a final decision as to whether or not a combination is a merger or an acquisition. However, there are a number of favourable points in favour of merger accounting. The decision can only be taken after all five criteria have been investigated and the decision must be taken on the overall commercial reality or substance of the combination transaction.

There are major advantages in adopting merger accounting, which are:

(i)   There is no goodwill created and thus no charge to profit and loss for the amortisation of that goodwill;

(ii)   There is no share premium account created, which is generally regarded as a quasi capital balance, not available for distribution;

(iii) There is no revaluation of the acquiree's net assets, resulting in future increased charges for depreciation;

(iv) None of the reserves of the merged entities need be frozen and those of both are still available for future distribution.

The next examples bring together both FRS 6 and FRS 7 which, in reality are inseparable. In the first instance the reader is taken through the decision as to whether a particular business combination meets the definition of a merger or not. Once the decision has been made to treat it as an acquisition then FRS 7 comes into play in trying to calculate goodwill properly by applying the fair value exercise to both the calculation of purchase consideration and the net assets acquired.

Example – Whitehead Plc

Whitehead plc has carried on business as a food retailer since 1900. It had traded profitably until the late 1980s when it suffered from fierce competition from larger retailers. Its turnover and margins were under severe pressure and its share price fell to an all-time low. The directors formulated a strategic plan to grow by acquisition and merger. It has an agreement to be able to borrow funds to finance acquisition at an interest rate of 10 per cent per annum. It is Whitehead plc's policy to amortise goodwill over 10 years.

(1) *Investment in Islandmagee plc*

On 15 June 2003 Whitehead plc had an issued share capital of 1,625,000 ordinary shares of £1 each. On that date it acquired 240,000 of the 1,500,000 issued £1 ordinary shares of Islandmagee plc for a cash payment of £164,000.

Whitehead plc makes up its accounts to 31 July. In early 2004 the directors of Whitehead plc and Islandmagee plc were having discussions with a view to a combination of the two companies.

The proposal was that:

(i)   On 1 May 2004 Whitehead plc should acquire 1,200,000 of the issued ordinary shares of Islandmagee plc which had a market price of £1.30 per share, in exchange for 1,500,000 newly issued ordinary shares in Whitehead plc which had a market price of £1.20p per share. There has been no change in Whitehead plc's share capital since 15 June 2003. The market price of the Islandmagee plc shares had ranged from £1.20 to £1.50 during the year ended 30 April 2004.

(ii) It was agreed that the consideration would be increased by 200,000 shares if a contingent Liability in Islandmagee plc in respect of a claim for wrongful dismissal by a former director did not crystallise.

(iii) After the exchange the new board would consist of six directors from Whitehead plc and six directors from Islandmagee plc, with the managing director of Whitehead plc becoming managing director of Islandmagee plc.

(iv) Whitehead plc head office should be closed and the staff made redundant and the Islandmagee plc head office should become the head office of the new combination.

(v)   Senior managers of both companies were to reapply for their posts and be interviewed by an interview panel comprising a director and the personnel managers from each company. The age profile of the two companies differed, with the average age of the Whitehead plc managers being 40 and that of Islandmagee plc 54, and there was an expectation among the directors of both boards that most of the posts would be filled by Whitehead plc managers.

(2) *Investment in Ballynure Ltd*

Whitehead plc is planning to acquire all of the 800,000 £1 ordinary shares in Ballynure Ltd on 30 June 2004 for a deferred consideration of £500,000 and a contingent consideration payable on 30 June 2008 of 10 per cent of the amount by which profits for the year ended 30 June 2008 exceeded £100,000. Ballynure Ltd has suffered trading losses and its directors, who are the major shareholders, support a takeover by Whitehead plc. The fair value of net assets of Ballynure Ltd was £685,000 and Whitehead plc expected that reorganisation costs would be £85,000 and future trading losses would be £100,000. Whitehead plc agreed to offer 4-year service contracts to the directors of Ballynure Ltd.

The directors had expected to be able to create a provision for the reorganisation costs and future trading losses but were advised by their finance director that FRS 7 required these two items to be treated as post-acquisition items.

Suggested solution – Whitehead Plc

Acquisition/merger of Islandmagee Plc

FRS 6 requires that to determine whether a business combination meets the definition of a merger, it should also be assessed against certain specified criteria:

> *A business combination that results in the creation of a new reporting entity formed from the combining parties, in which the shareholders of the combining entities come together in a partnership for the mutual sharing of the risks and benefits of the combined entity, and in which no party to the combination in substance obtains control over any other, or is otherwise seen to be dominant, whether by virtue of the proportion of its shareholders' rights in the combined entity, the influence of its directors or otherwise.*

Failure to broadly meet these criteria indicates that the definition was probably not met and thus that merger accounting is not to be used for the combination, as in substance the combination is an acquisition. This entails considering the following five criteria:

Criterion 1

No party to the combination is portrayed as either acquirer or acquiree, either by its own board or management or by that of another party in the combination.

Para. 61 of FRS 6 elaborates on this, stating that where the terms of a share-for-share exchange indicate that one party has paid a premium over the market value of the shares acquired, this is evidence that that party has taken the role of acquirer unless there is a clear explanation for this apparent premium other than its being a premium paid to acquire control.

This is relevant in the present situation where the value of the Whitehead plc shares issued as consideration was (1,500,000 × £1.20p = £1,800,000) to acquire Islandmagee plc shares valued at £1,560,000, resulting in a premium of £240,000.

This indicates *prima facie* that it was an acquisition. However, the exchange price was within the range (£1.20–£1.50) of market prices for Islandmagee plc during the previous year. There could well be a clear explanation for this apparent premium other than its being a premium paid to acquire control.

The circumstances surrounding the transaction also support the view that this is a merger. For example, the closure and redundancy programme applied to Whitehead plc and not to Islandmagee plc.

Criterion 2

All parties to the combination, as represented by the boards of directors or their appointees, participate in establishing the management structure for the combined entity and in selecting the management personnel, and such decisions are made on the basis of a consensus between the parties.

The need for reapplication for posts and appearance before an interview panel indicates that there will be a consensus decision on appropriate personnel which would satisfy Criterion 2 even though the final result might be that the posts are largely filled by Whitehead plc managers.

Criterion 3

The relative sizes of the combining entities are not so disparate that one party dominates the combined entity by virtue of its relative size.

This requires a consideration of the proportion of the equity of the combined entity attributable to the shareholders of each of the combining parties to test if one is more than 50 per cent larger than the other. This 50 per cent is a rebuttable presumption. In this case, Whitehead plc shareholders hold 1,625,000 shares and Islandmagee plc 1,500,000 shares. This indicates that the criterion is satisfied even though the 1,500,000 shares are in consideration of only 80 per cent of Islandmagee plc's capital.

Criterion 4

Under the terms of the combination or related arrangements, the consideration received by equity shareholders in relation to their shareholding comprises primarily equity shares in the combined entity; and any non-equity consideration, or equity shares carrying substantially reduced voting or distribution rights, represents an immaterial proportion of the fair value of the consideration received by the equity shareholders. Where one of the combining entities has, within the period of 2 years before the combination, acquired equity shares in another of the combining entities, the consideration for this acquisition should be taken into account in determining whether this criterion has been met.

This indicates that the cash payment made on 15 June 2003 should be taken into account, being less than 2 years before the combination on 1 May 2004. Appendix 1 of FRS 6 refers to the Companies Act requirements for a transaction to be treated as a merger. This includes the provision that the fair value of any consideration other than the issue of equity shares given pursuant to the arrangement by the parent company did not exceed 10 per cent of the nominal value of the equity shares issued.

The transaction does not comply with this requirement and would be required to be treated as an acquisition.

Criterion 5

No equity shareholders of any of the combining entities retain any material interest in the future performance of only part of the combined entity.

This criterion is concerned with situations where the allocation depended to any material extent on the post-combination performance of the business. In the present case, the allocation is dependent on the determination of the eventual value of a specified liability as opposed to the future operating performance and the criterion is satisfied, i.e. there are no earn-out clauses in the agreement. On balance it would appear that the combination should be treated as an acquisition.

Change of terms
The Companies Act requirement is not met because the cash payment of £164,000 in 2003 is more than 10 per cent of the nominal value of the shares issued, which was £1,500,000.

The company acquired 16 per cent of the shares of Islandmagee plc in 2003 and 80 per cent in 2001. The company could require the holders of the remaining 4 per cent to sell their shares on the same terms as those offered to the holders of the 80 per cent but, even if it did this, the new shares issued as consideration would be 1,575,000 and the Companies Act requirement would still not be satisfied with the cash payment of £164,000 being 10.4 per cent.

A further, and more common, possibility is that Whitehead plc could make a small bonus issue, say 1 for 10, prior to the exchange, thus increasing the nominal value of the equity given from £1,500,000 to £1,650,000. The cash payment of £164,000 is then reduced to less than 10 per cent of the nominal value.

Treatment in the balance sheet of Whitehead plc as at 31 July 2004 on Acquisition of Ballynure Ltd
The discounted deferred consideration payable is a form of debt instrument. It is this amount that will appear as the investment's cost in the acquiring company's balance sheet, i.e. £402,685. The same amount would appear as a creditor for the deferred consideration (100,000 × 0.9090 + 150,000 × 0.8264 + 250,000 × 0.7513). The liability would be split into £90,900 payable within 1 year and £311,785 payable in more than 1 year.

Treatment in the profit and loss account of Whitehead plc for the year ended 31 July 2004
Because the deferred consideration is a form of debt instrument, the difference of £97,315 between the discounted amount of the payments and the total cash amount (500,000 − 402,685) is treated as a finance cost to be charged as an interest expense in Whitehead plc's profit and loss account over the period the liability is outstanding so that the annual cost gives a constant rate on the liability's carrying amount. The finance cost charged in the accounts to 31 July 2004 is £3,335, representing 1 month's charge on £402,685 at 10 per cent finance charge.

Goodwill calculation
Goodwill is calculated as at the date of acquisition based on the discounted amount of the cash payments. This results in a negative goodwill figure of £282,315 (402,685 − 685,000).

Effect of deferred consideration
There is no adjustment to this figure on the stage payments of the consideration. Whitehead plc has obtained the benefit of deferring the payment of the consideration and the cost of the benefit is charged in the profit and loss account over the period of the deferral.

Effect of contingent consideration

The terms of the agreement are such that it is impossible to say whether and how much additional consideration will be paid and the appropriate treatment is to deal with the matter by disclosure rather than provision.

Enquiries would be needed to establish whether the service agreement with the directors of Ballynure Ltd constitutes a payment for the business acquired or an expense for services. If the substance of the agreement is payment for the business acquired the payments would be accounted for as a part of the purchase consideration and, as they are quantified, they would be included within the goodwill calculation.

Treatment of negative goodwill

SSAP 22 required in para. 40 that any excess of the aggregate of fair values of the separable assets acquired over the fair value of the consideration given (negative goodwill) should be credited directly to reserves.

There have been a number of possible approaches which could be applied when accounting for negative goodwill.

One is the approach followed in the USA, which is to say that although the separable net assets are worth more than the value of the business as a whole they did not cost the acquirer that much and that accordingly the negative goodwill should be applied to reduce the separable assets to their cost to the acquiring company by proportionately writing down the value of the fixed assets of the acquired company, other than any marketable securities. However, this approach was considered in FRED 7, para. 53, and rejected on the grounds that a requirement to eliminate the negative consolidation difference by making an arbitrary allocation to reduce the otherwise determined fair values of non-monetary assets does not provide balance sheet information that is useful to those who wish to make assessments of the values of assets acquired in a business combination.

Another approach is to identify why the negative goodwill arose and to account for it based on that analysis. For example, in its Discussion Paper *Accounting for Goodwill* issued by the ASC in 1980, paras 11.2–11.4 state: 'negative goodwill may arise as a consequence of the expectations of future losses or reduced profits or alternatively may just represent a bargain purchase by the acquiror. The logical treatment of negative goodwill which is related to future losses would be to amortise the capital reserve over the expected period of such losses by crediting it to the profit and loss account as the provision is progressively realised over this period.'

In the present example the negative goodwill has arisen partly because there is an expectation of poor trading results with a loss of £100,000, which means that the business as a whole is at present worth less than is indicated by the values of the separable net assets.

Following on from FRED 7, FRS 10 *Goodwill and Intangible Assets* requires negative goodwill to be initially recorded as a negative asset (dangling credit) on the face of the balance sheet immediately below positive goodwill. It must then be transferred to the profit and loss account as the non-monetary assets acquired are sold or used up in subsequent years.

Financial Reporting Review Panel

Reckitt & Colman Plc (May 1997)

The panel reviewed the company's disclosure under FRS 6 for its fair value adjustments. Reckitt & Colman bought the L&F household products business for c. £1bn in 1994 and were only able to make a provisional adjustment for fair value for their December 1994 financial statements. This resulted in an increase of £750.46m to the net assets acquired.

FRS 7 permits provisional figures for the first post-acquisition accounts only. Consequently the 1995 accounts included additional and final fair value adjustments of £81.2m in respect of the acquisition, with a corresponding adjustment to goodwill. No further information, however, was provided.

Para. 27 of FRS 6 requires that any material adjustments to fair value be explained and therefore this should include an analysis of the adjustments and an explanation of the reasons for them. The directors included a note in the 1996 accounts in respect of the 1995 adjustment giving the necessary additional information required by FRS 6.

Stratagem Group Plc (December 1997)

The Stratagem Group plc failed to adequately disclose the information and explanations necessary under FRS 6 in respect of their acquisition of NRC Refrigeration Ltd in January 1996. The accounts included a fair value table showing both the book and the fair values at the date of acquisition but it failed to show the fair value adjustments of £4.9m analysed into revaluations, adjustments to achieve consistency of accounting policies, and other significant adjustments as required under FRS 6. These have now been provided in the group's 1997 accounts.

H & C Furnishings Plc (now Harveys Furnishing Plc) (October 1998)

The directors have been forced to revise the 1997 accounts by way of supplementary note. The consideration paid for Harvey Holdings plc was shares in Cantor plc (former name of H & C Furnishings plc). It was viewed as a reverse takeover but it should have had FRS 7 applied, which requires a fair value to be placed on the consideration. In this case it should be the market price of Cantor's shares at the date of acquisition, i.e. £1.65.

The directors felt that the price was unreliable and instead adopted a value of £1 ruling at a date 4 months earlier when the transaction had been negotiated.

The FRRP did not agree as there had been a substantial rise in Cantor's share price between March and July 1996 and also post-acquisition; therefore there appeared to be no grounds for adopting an alternative value. The directors accepted the FRRP's rule.

Concentric Plc (November 1998)

The matter of concern to the Panel was the extent of the company's disclosures relating to its acquisition of Weed Instrument Inc. in July 1997 for £4.4 million. The acquisition was referred to in the chairman's statement and the group profile but the cost was not disclosed in the financial statements. The profit and loss account recorded the contribution made to turnover and profit before tax and a note referred to the goodwill write-off arising on the transaction of £2.3 million.

The company's disclosures did not satisfy the relevant requirements of FRS 6 in so far as they refer to acquisitions made during the year. In particular, no fair value table was produced as required by FRS 6 in support of the calculation for goodwill. The fair value of the consideration is also required to be disclosed under SSAP 22 (now FRS 10).

Photobition Group Plc (November 1999)

The information given in the accounts for the year ended 30 June 1998 did not comply with FRS 6 re the additional disclosures required on a 'substantial' acquisition. Neither had the company provided the geographical analysis of operating profit/net assets required under SSAP 25.

In particular, in the 'substantial' takeover of Novo Group plc, the post-acquisition results of the acquired entity were not shown as part of continuing operations nor was a summarised profit and loss account or statement of total recognised gains and losses disclosed for the period from the beginning of the financial year to the effective date of acquisition.

These were all incorporated in the 1999 financial statements.

QA Services (No. 2) Limited (Formerly Pontis Consulting Plc) (November 2001)

The information in the accounts did not comply with Financial Reporting Standard (FRS) 6 *Acquisitions and Mergers* in two respects. The accounts did not include a fair value table in respect of the assets and liabilities transferred to the company by Pontis Consulting (a partnership) on 1 June 1998. Nor was any explanation given of the £180,000 fair value adjustment disclosed in the fair value table that was presented in respect of the acquisition of Pontis Research BV, a company also acquired on 1 June 1998.

Application in published accounts

A very good recent example of a merger was that between the Halifax Building Society and the Bank of Scotland in forming a new group, HBOS plc. The detailed disclosures required by FRS 6 are provided in the first published accounts of the new group and these are illustrated below:

HBOS Plc   Year Ended 31 December 2003   Banking

Accounting Policies (Extract)

Basis of Consolidation
1.   Basis of Preparation
The merger of Bank of Scotland Group and Halifax Group has been accounted for using the merger accounting principles set out in Financial Reporting Standard (FRS) 6 *Acquisitions and Mergers* and the results have been presented as if the new group had been established throughout the current and comparative accounting periods.

The directors are satisfied that the substantially equal proportion of equity in HBOS plc held by former institutional shareholders of the Bank of Scotland and Halifax Group plc at the date of merger, rebuts the presumption of dominant influence contained in FRS 6 resulting from the 63 per cent interest in ordinary share capital of HBOS plc held by the former Halifax Group plc shareholders at that date.

Prior to the merger, Bank of Scotland Group prepared accounts to 28/29 February. Upon the merger becoming effective, Bank of Scotland changed its year end of 31 December. In preparing the merged financial statements of HBOS plc for the year ended 31 December 2000, the financial statements of Bank of Scotland have been prepared to cover the year to that date.

The Group's accounting policies, detailed below, represent the development of a consistent set of accounting policies derived from those followed by Bank of Scotland Group and Halifax Group prior to the merger of the two groups. The effect on the results of the group of adopting these accounting policies is not material.

Prior to the merger, Bank of Scotland Group adopted the transitional rules of FRS 15 *Tangible Fixed Assets* whereby the gross value relating to previously revalued fixed assets was retained. Halifax Group's accounting policy was to state property at cost with no revaluation. In adopting a standard set of accounting policies for HBOS plc, the fixed assets of Bank of Scotland Group, previously revalued, have been restated at 1 January 2000 to show property at cost. The impact of this merger-related adjustment is set out in note 59.

58. Business Merger

The merger of the Bank of Scotland Group and Halifax Group was completed on 10 September 2001. The book value of net assets at the time of the merger together with adjustments arising from the alignment of accounting policies were:

Bank of Scotland Group	£ million
Book value of net assets at time of merger	3,925
Accounting adjustments relating to merger alignment (note 59)	(53)
Restated net assets at time of merger	3,872
Hallfax Group	
Book value of net assets at time of merger	7,587
Accounting adjustments relating to merger alignment (note 59)	(7)
Restated net assets al lime of merger	7,580

Analysis of contribution to the profit and loss attributable to shareholders made by the combining groups in the period prior to the merger date of 10 September 2001, together with the contribution from the combined group in the period subsequent to the merger, is as follows:

Profit & Loss Account	Bank of Scotland Group Pre merger £ million	Halifax Group Pre merger £ million	Combined Post merger £ million	Total £ million
Net interest income	1,426	1,491	1,256	4,173
Non-interest income	623	964	1,122	2,699
Net operating income	2,049	2,455	2,368	6,872
Administrative expenses	(872)	(1,038)	(1,057)	(2,967)
Depreciation and goodwill amortisation	(59)	(146)	(333)	(538)
Provisions for bad and doubtful debts	(328)	(87)	(193)	(608)
General insurance claims	(12)	(34)	(22)	(68)
Amounts written off fixed asset investments	(4)	–	(17)	(21)
Operating profit	774	1,150	746	2,670
Before exceptional items and Intelligent Finance	774	1,269	928	2,971
Exceptional items		(9)	(138)	(147)
Intelligent Finance		(110)	(44)	(154)
Share of operating profits/(losses) of joint ventures and Associated undertakings	30	(2)	8	36
Merger costs – exceptional	(40)	(36)	–	(76)
Profit on ordinary activities before taxation	764	1,112	754	2,630
Before exceptional items and intelligent Finance	804	1,267	936	3,007
Exceptional items	(40)	(45)	(138)	(223)
Intelligent Finance	–	(110)	(44)	(154)
Taxation	(272)	(331)	(162)	(765)
Profit on ordinary activities after taxation	492	781	592	1,865
Before exceptional items and Intelligent Finance	532	901	722	2,155
Exceptional items	(40)	(43)	(99)	(182)
Intelligent Finance	–	(77)	(31)	(108)
Minority interests	(59)	(76)	(54)	(189)
Profit for the period attributable to shareholders	433	705	538	1,676

Pre-merger results are adjusted for the effect of alignments of accounting policies and practices, which are not material.

The same information is also provided for the previous year to 31 December 2001.

59. Accounting Policy Alignment

The Group's accounting policies are set out on pages 65 and 66. These harmonise the policies used within Bank of Scotland Group and Halifax Group prior to the merger of the two groups on 10 September 2001.

The Group has adopted a consistent approach to the transitional implementation arrangements of FRS 15 *Tangible Fixed Assets*. This has resulted in Bank of Scotland Group restating the carrying value of its tangible fixed assets to a historical cost basis. The effect of this merger adjustment at 31 December 2000 was to decrease the group tangible fixed assets by £47 million, with a corresponding decrease of the Group's profit and loss account reserves.

The impact of this merger adjustment on profit on ordinary activities before taxation in 2001 and 2000 is not material to the group.

General provision policy has been standardised based on an expected loss methodology. The loan estimate makes use of, *inter alia*, historical loan loss experience and economic and other business climate conditions. Specific loan loss provision methodology has also been standardised within all divisions of HBOS. The impact on 2001 results of aligning general and specific provisioning policy methodologies is not significant.

While a number of accounting policies and practices have now been aligned across the group, none of these is material to the group.

The next example shows the adoption of merger accounting in a group reconstruction and demerger scenario. One of the concerns over future developments in international accounting is the possibility that merger accounting could be banned in these situations despite the fact that in a reconstruction there is no real change in substance to the group:

BT Group Plc   Year Ended 31 March 2002   Telecommunications

Notes to the Financial Statements (Extract)

1. Accounting for the reorganisation and demerger, changes in accounting policy and presentation and discontinued activities

(a) Reorganisation and demerger

On 19 November 2001, the legal separation of the mmO_2 business from the rest of the former British Telecommunications plc group was completed and BT Group plc (BT Group) became the ultimate parent company of British Telecommunications plc (BT). The legal structure of the transaction was such that BT transferred the mmO_2 business to mmO_2 plc and BT Group Investments Limited (BTGI) became the immediate parent company of BT on 16 November 2001. On 19 November 2001, mmO_2 plc transferred the shares in BTGI to BT Group, as consideration for the issue to former BT shareholders of one ordinary share of 115p in the company, credited as fully paid, for each ordinary share in BT held on 16 November 2001.

On 21 November 2001, following the approval of the Court, the nominal value of BT Group shares was reduced from 115p per ordinary share to 5p per ordinary share by way of a reduction of capital under s. 135 of the Companies Act 1985. The surplus of £9,537 million arising from this reduction has been credited to the group profit and loss reserve.

The transfer of BTGI to the company has been accounted for as a group reconstruction in accordance with the principles of merger accounting set out in Financial Reporting Standard 6 (FRS 6) and Schedule 4A to the Companies Act 1985. The consolidated financial statements are therefore presented as if the company had been the parent company of the group throughout the years ended 31 March 2000 and 2001 and up to the date of the demerger. The results of mmO$_2$ have been included in discontinued activities in all three years.

The transfer of BT to BTGI on 16 November 2001 was a group reorganisation effected for non-equity consideration. This transaction has been accounted for in these financial statements using the principles of merger accounting as if BT had been owned and controlled by BTGI throughout the years ended 31 March 2000 and 2001 and up to 16 November 2001. This is not in accordance with the Companies Act 1985 since the group reorganisation does not meet all the conditions for merger accounting. If acquisition accounting had been applied to account for the reorganisation whereby BTGI became the parent company of BT, this would have resulted in all the separable assets and liabilities of the BT Group as at 16 November 2001 being recorded at their fair values, substantial goodwill and goodwill amortisation charges arising and only the post demerger results being reflected within the BT Group consolidated financial statements. The directors consider that to have applied acquisition accounting in preparing these financial statements would have failed to give a true and fair view of the group's state of affairs and results. This is because, in substance, BT Group is the successor to BT and its shareholders have had a continuing interest in the BT business both before and after the demerger. The directors consider that it is not practicable to quantify the effects of this departure from the requirements of the Companies Act 1985.

In the company's financial statements, its investment in BTGI is stated at the nominal value of shares issued. In accordance with sections 131 and 133 of the Companies Act 1985, no premium was recorded on the ordinary shares issued (see note 37). On consolidation, the difference between the nominal value of the shares issued and the aggregate share capital, share premium and capital redemption reserve of BT at the date of the demerger (the merger difference), has been debited to the other reserves (see note 28).

The third example in the series provides details of the acquisition of Go by easyJet plc and it incorporates the linkages between FRS 7 and FRS *Goodwill and Intangible Assets*. Details of the intangible fixed schedule are also provided in the notes to the accounts:

easyJet Plc   Year Ended 30 September 2002   Airline Operator

Notes (Extract)

8. Intangible Fixed Assets

	Goodwill £000
Cost	
At 1 October 2001	3,398
Additions – purchase of Newgo 1 Limited	349,781
At 30 September 2002	353,179
Amortisation	
At 1 October 2001	403
Charge for the year	3,091
At 30 September 2002	3,494
Net book value	
At 30 September 2002	349,685
At 30 September 2001	2,995

Goodwill, which arose on the initial investment in easyJet Switzerland SA and the subsequent acquisition of that undertaking, is amortised to the consolidated profit and loss account over its estimated useful life of 20 years.

On 31 July 2002, the group acquired Newgo 1 Limited, the ultimate holding company of Go Fly Limited, an operator of low cost airline services between London Stansted, Bristol and East Midlands airports and Western Europe and the Czech Republic. The total consideration payable, including the costs of acquisition, was £387.1 million, which was satisfied by cash. The cash was partly funded by the issue of 104.4 million ordinary shares of 25p at £2.65 each, generating net proceeds of £271.9 million, plus cash of £115.2 million. Acquisition accounting has been used as the basis for consolidating the results of Newgo 1 Limited within those of the easyJet group. Goodwill arising from the acquisition has been included as an intangible fixed asset on the group's balance sheet, and will be depreciated over a period of 20 years in accordance with the directors' opinion as to the estimated useful economic life of the goodwill purchased. The investment in Newgo 1 Limited has been included in the company's balance sheet at cost, which is not less than its fair value, at the date of acquisition.

Analysis of the acquisition of Newgo 1 Limited

	Book Value	Adjustments – revaluation	Notes	Fair value to the group
	£000	£000		£000
Tangible and intangible fixed assets	118,821	(113,241)	(1)	5,580
Debtors	34,456	1,618	(2)	36,074
Cash	126,531	–		126,531
Creditors due within 1 year	(250,782)	145,499	(3)	(111,629)
		(6,346)	(4)	
Provisions for liabilities and charges	(19,197)	–		(19,197)
Net assets	9,829	27,530		37,359
Goodwill arising on acquisition				349,781
Consideration				387,140

Satisfied by:	£000
Cash	373,492
Costs associated with the acquisition	13,648
	387,140

Fair value adjustments, which are provisional, are as follows:

(1)   write-off of previously capitalised goodwill
(2)   recording of Go's fuel hedging instruments at market value
(3)   repayment of payables as part of the acquisition agreement
(4)   recording of Go's dollar hedging instruments at market value

During the period from 1 August 2002 to 30 September 2002, Newgo 1 Limited used £24.3 million of the group's net operating cash flows, received £0.6 million in respect of net returns on investments and servicing of finance, paid £nil in respect of taxation and utilised £0.2 million for capital expenditure and financial investment.

9.4   FRS 9 *Associates and Joint Ventures* (November 1997)

Background

The development of investments in associated companies first emerged in the 1960s as a method of avoiding the inclusion of the net worth in an investment on the consolidated balance sheet. Initially the investments were recorded at cost only and the consolidated profit and loss account only included dividend income received from associates.

SSAP 1 was introduced in 1971 to ensure that instead of the dividend income being recorded as part of profits, the investor's share of its results in an associate should be incorporated in the consolidated profit and loss as well as disclosing the investment at cost plus share of post-acquisition retained profits in the consolidated balance sheet.

An associate was largely defined as one in which an investor had both a participating interest and could exercise a significant influence over the investee's affairs but a 20 per cent or more shareholding was presumed to result in an associate relationship being created.

In 1982 SSAP 1 was revised cosmetically to ensure that the investment in the balance sheet was no longer recorded at cost plus share of post-acquisition retained profit but instead at the investor's share of net assets plus goodwill in the investee, thereby avoiding the inclusion of an unrealised profit in the valuation of the investment.

Unfortunately there were still three major weaknesses in the standard:

(i)   SSAP 1 was too rule based and companies were able to manipulate the 20 per cent rule so that all profit makers (i.e. 20.0001 per cent or more) were incorporated in the profit and loss and all loss makers (i.e. 19.999 per cent) were excluded. This was achieved by simply buying and selling a few shares in the investee to achieve the required result;
(ii) SSAP 1 failed to incorporate any accounting rules in the growing area of joint venture accounting;
(iii) SSAP 1 had inadequate disclosures about the impact of major associates on business.

Definitions

- *Associate*. An entity in which another entity has a *participating interest* and over whose operating and financial policies the investor exercises a *significant influence*. Essentially it must represent a long-term interest and the entity must exercise control over that investment which is linked by the exercise of significant influence. Significant influence essentially means that the investor must be actively involved and influential in the investee's strategic issues such as dividend policy, changes in products/markets and expansion/contraction.
- *Joint venture*. An entity in which the reporting entity holds a long-term interest and is jointly controlled by the reporting entity. All major decisions require each co-venturer's consent.
- *Joint arrangement*. A contractual arrangement under which participants engage in joint activities that do not create an entity because it is not carrying out a trade of its own.

Accounting treatment

Associate

Should adopt the *equity* method of accounting in the consolidated accounts, i.e.:

- include share of operating profit/loss separately after share of joint ventures operating profits/losses;
- include share of exceptional items separately;

- include share of taxation separately in a note;
- ensure all post-tax items are included within the group total;
- can include, in a memorandum, share of turnover but this must be clearly distinguished from the group;
- include share of total recognised gains/losses separately, if material;
- include share of net assets separately, together with any goodwill reported;
- dividends from associates – separately recorded within the cash flow statement between 'operating activities' and 'returns on investments, etc.'.

Joint venture

Should adopt the *gross equity* method of accounting in the consolidated accounts, i.e. the same as equity but will also incorporate the separate disclosure of the share of turnover in the joint venture and the share of both gross assets and gross liabilities as an amplification of the net investment in the joint venture.

Can adopt additional supplementary information in a cohesive format showing share of individual assets/liabilities on the consolidated balance sheet and share of all pre-profit before tax items on the consolidated profit and loss. However, these are disclosed in a memorandum columnar format and are not part of the overall group totals.

Joint arrangements

Should be accounted for according to the investor's own share of the assets, liabilities and cash flows as per the agreement.

Disclosure

All associates and joint ventures

Names of principal associates/joint ventures disclosing:

- percentage of shares held in each class;
- the accounting period adopted;
- the nature of business.

Major notes re contingent liabilities, capital commitments, exchange rate/control restrictions, FRS 8 related party disclosures.

Fifteen per cent of business represented by associates or joint ventures (of gross assets, liabilities, turnover or 3-year profit record)

Share of total associates or joint ventures split:

- share of fixed assets;
- share of current assets;
- share of creditors falling due under 1 year;
- share of creditors falling due after more than 1 year;
- share of turnover (only for associates).

Twenty-five per cent of business represented by one associate or joint venture (of gross assets, liabilities, turnover or 3-year profit record)

Share of individual associate or joint venture split:

- share of fixed assets;
- share of current assets;
- share of creditors falling due under 1 year;
- share of creditors falling due after more than 1 year;
- share of turnover;
- share of profits before taxation;
- share of profits after taxation.

Consultation Paper (May 2002)

This paper sets out the revised IAS 28 but is very similar to FRS 9. The international standard is likely to change as a result of further IASB projects that are expected to address the requirements for consolidation, including accounting for associates and thus IAS 28 will not be implemented immediately in the UK and Ireland.

The example below shows integration of the results of an associated undertaking into the consolidated financial statements of a group using equity accounting. It also examines situations where a decision must be made as to whether a reporting entity is an associate or not in cases of complicated shareholdings.

Example – Cushendall Ltd

Cushendall Ltd has acquired interests in subsidiary and associated companies as follows:

Glendun Ltd	80% holding
Glenwhirry Ltd	70% holding
Glenshesk Ltd	25% holding (associated company).

Glenshesk Ltd is a holding company with a 90 per cent holding in Glencorp Ltd. Cushendall Ltd, Glendun Ltd and Glenshesk Ltd have each acquired holdings in Glentaisie Ltd as follows:

Cushendall Ltd – 12%   Glendun Ltd – 5%   Glenshesk Ltd – 24%

55 per cent of the shares in Glentaisie Ltd are held by a major shareholder.

The directors of Cushendall Ltd are of the opinion that the results of Glenshesk Ltd are not material but those of Glentaisie Ltd are material, within the context of the financial statements of Cushendall Ltd. Cushendall Ltd prepared draft group financial statements for the year ended 31 May 2004. The following notes were appended thereto:

Notes to the profit and loss account

(1)   Analysis of turnover

	£
Cushendall Ltd	500,000
Glendun Ltd	100,000
Glenwhirry Ltd	80,000
Glenshesk Ltd	40,000
Glentaisie Ltd	300,000
As per profit and loss account	1,020,000

(2)   This note gave an analysis, similar to note (1), of depreciation; total as per the profit and loss account – £56,000.

(3)

	Profit before tax	Tax	Profit after tax
	£	£	£
Cushendall Ltd (actual for year)	126,000	31,000	95,000
Glendun Ltd (actual for year)	24,000	10,000	14,000
Glenwhirry Ltd (actual for year)	(14,000)	–	(14,000)
Glenshesk Ltd (25% of actual for year)	3,000	1,000	2,000
Glentaisie Ltd (22% of actual for year)	22,000	5,000	17,000
As per profit and loss account	161,000	47,000	114,000

(4) Minority interests in current year's profits:

	£
Glendun Ltd 20% £14,000	2,800
Glenwhirry Ltd 30% (£14,000)	(4,200)
As per profit and loss account	(1,400)

(5)   Retained current year profits were £112,600 (i.e. £114,000 − £1,400).
(6)   This note gave detailed information as to how the profit brought forward was apportioned between pre-acquisition profits, minority interests and the group's share of post-acquisition profits.
(7)   This showed the figure for retained profits carried forward.

(8) Shares in associated companies are stated in the balance sheet at £120,000. This total is made up as follows:

	£	£
25% net assets (excluding goodwill) – Glenshesk Ltd		20,000
22% net assets (excluding goodwill) – Glentaisie Ltd		60,000
		80,000
25% goodwill – Glenshesk Ltd		30,000
Premium on purchase – Glenshesk Ltd	15,000	
Discount on purchase – Glentaisie Ltd	(5,000)	
		10,000
		120,000

(9) Loans amounted to £150,000. They comprised the following:

	£
Loan from Laharna Ltd	120,000
Loan from Glenshesk Ltd	60,000
Loan to Glentaisie Ltd	(30,000)
	150,000

Suggested solution – Cushendall Ltd

(1) Turnover

Both subsidiaries and the holding company should be included (Glendun, Glenwhirry and Cushendall – see Appendix) but neither Glenshesk nor Glentaisie should have been in turnover.

Glentaisie is not an associated undertaking (see Appendix) as control of 17 per cent would be below the normal 20 per cent presumption in FRS 9 for significant influence. There could be evidence to rebut this but a major shareholder controls 55 per cent of the company, so it would seem unlikely that the company could exercise sufficient influence. Turnover from Glentaisie should therefore be excluded.

(2) Depreciation

For the same reasons as (1) above, the depreciation of both Glenshesk Ltd and Glentaisie Ltd should be excluded.

(3) Profit before tax/tax

Once again Glentaisie Ltd should be excluded because it is not an associated undertaking. However, 25 per cent of Glenshesk's profit before tax and tax charges should be included. The information for the associates should be disclosed separately from the group companies.

(4) Minority interests

The calculations are correct. If a minority holds shares in an associate then that share should be reflected in the minority interest account.

(5) to (7) Retained profits

The retained profits for the year should be analysed between holding company, subsidiaries and associated undertakings, i.e. Cushendall £95,000, subsidiaries (£1,400) (2,800 – 4,200) and associated undertakings £2,000.

If Glentaisie is not considered to be an associate, the dividend received/receivable should be included.

(8) Balance sheet – associated undertakings

The only associated undertaking is Glenshesk Ltd, which should be valued as follows:

	£
Share of net tangible assets	20,000
Share of goodwill	30,000
Goodwill on acquisition	15,000
	65,000

(can be combined: Share of goodwill 30,000 and Goodwill on acquisition 15,000)

Glentaisie Ltd should be included as an investment at cost.

(9) Loans

The loan from Glenshesk Ltd (associate) should be separately disclosed. That to Glentaisie Ltd should be included with other loans to companies outside the group.

Appendix

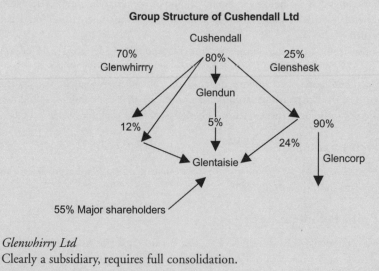

Group Structure of Cushendall Ltd

Glenwhirry Ltd
Clearly a subsidiary, requires full consolidation.

Glendun Ltd
Clearly a subsidiary, requires full consolidation.

Glenshesk Ltd

Presumed to be an 'associated undertaking' because more than 20 per cent of the shares are controlled. Evidence is required of significant influence by way of, perhaps, board representation and active involvement in strategic decision-making in the company.

It could be a subsidiary if there is evidence of 'dominant influence' by Cushendall Ltd, i.e. control over the operating and financial policies of Glenshesk Ltd.

Glencorp Ltd

This is a subsidiary of Glenshesk Ltd and therefore should be included with the group accounts of Glenshesk Ltd. 25 per cent of that combined result will be included as an 'associated undertaking' of Cushendall Ltd.

Glentaisie Ltd

For associated company status it is permissible to add the 12 per cent directly held by Cushendall plus 5 per cent via its subsidiary Glendun. The 24 per cent held by an associate must be excluded. 17 per cent would not be classified as an associated undertaking under normal circumstances. Again, this can be rebutted if Cushendall is able to exercise significant influence over the affairs of Glentaisie Ltd.

The following example examines situations where an entity has to distinguish between an associate, joint venture, joint arrangement and simple trade investment. In addition it provides an example of the calculation of goodwill and how to account for associates and joint ventures in both the consolidated profit and loss and balance sheets.

Example – Castlerock Plc

The following financial statements relate to Castlerock, a public limited company.

Profit and Loss Account for year ended 31 December 2003

	£m	£m
Turnover		212
Cost of sales		(170)
Gross profit		42
Distribution costs	17	
Administration expenses	8	
		(25)
		17
Other operating income		12
		29
Exceptional item		(10)
Interest payable		(4)
Profit on ordinary activities before tax		15
Taxation on ordinary activities		(3)
		12
Ordinary dividend – paid		(4)
Retained profit for year		8

Balance Sheet at 31 December 2003

	£m	£m
Fixed assets – tangible	30	
– goodwill	7	
		37
Current assets	31	
Creditors: amounts falling due within 1 year	(12)	
Net current assets		19
Total assets less current liabilities		56
Creditors: amounts falling due after more than 1 year		(10)
		46
Capital and reserves		
Called-up share capital		
Ordinary share capital		10
Share premium account		4
Profit and loss account		32
		46

(i)   Castlederg, a public limited company, acquired 30 per cent of the ordinary share capital of Castlerock plc at a cost of £14 million on 1 January 2002. The share capital of Castlerock has not changed since acquisition, when the profit and loss reserve of Castlerock was £9 million.

(ii) At 1 January 2002 the following fair values were attributed to the net assets of Castlerock plc but not incorporated in its accounting records.

	£m
Tangible fixed assets	30 (carrying value £20m)
Goodwill (estimate)	10
Current assets	31
Creditors: amounts falling due within 1 year	20
Creditors: amounts falling due after more than 1 year	8

(iii) Aghadowey, an associated company of Castlederg, also holds a 25 per cent interest in the ordinary share capital of Castlerock. This was acquired on 1 January 2003.

(iv) During the year to 31 December 2003, Castlerock sold goods to Castlederg to the value of £35 million. The inventory of Castlederg plc at 31 December 1998 included goods purchased from Castlerock plc on which the company made a profit of £10 million.

(v) The policy of all companies in the Castlederg group is to amortise goodwill over 4 years and to depreciate tangible fixed assets at 20 per cent per annum on the straight-line basis.

(vi) Castlerock does not represent a material part of the group and is significantly less than the 15 per cent additional disclosure threshold required under FRS 9 *Associates and Joint Ventures*.

Suggested solution – Castlerock Plc

Distinguish between trade investment and associate

The main difference between an associate and an ordinary trade investment is that, in the latter case, the investor takes a passive role in the running of the business but in the former the shareholders do exercise considerable influence over the operating and financial policies of the investee. The associate normally implements accounting policies that are consistent with those of the investor. Under FRS 9 *Associates and Joint Ventures* the investor must actually both exercise a significant influence and have a participating interest so as to ensure that the investor secures a contribution to its activities by the exercise of control or influence.

FRS 9 states that a holding of 20 per cent or more of the voting rights suggests, but does not ensure, that the investor exercises significant influence. There is a presumption that the investor is involved in the strategic decisions made by the company. The FRS also suggests that the attitude towards the investee's dividend policy may indicate the status of the investment. In order to have associate status it would appear that the investor should have board representation in order for it to be able to participate in the decision-making process. The investor must be able not only to exercise influence but be able to exercise it actively.

Distinguish between a joint arrangement and a joint venture

A joint venture is an entity whereas a joint arrangement is not. An entity is normally a limited company, partnership or incorporation association which has been set up to carry on a business or trade of its own. A number of oil companies setting up a pipeline in the Alaskan tundra constitutes a joint arrangement. This would be set up as it is too expensive and also environmentally unfriendly for a number of pipelines to be set up separately by each of the companies. All significant decisions are taken by all the participants.

However, a joint venture is where a separate entity has been set up and all parties require the consent of each other for any decision to be taken. Joint ventures are set up, however, for the purpose of making profits.

The accounting treatment of a joint arrangement is that the investor should record its own share of the joint venture's assets and liabilities and its incomes/expenses. However, in joint ventures, because they are legal entities they can only record the entity's share of profits/losses and gross assets/gross liabilities on the profit and loss account and balance sheet. It is illegal to record individual assets/liabilities on balance sheet as the entity has no control over the usage of such assets. Joint arrangements are, in effect, recorded as proportional consolidations.

How should the investment in Castlerock plc be treated in the consolidated balance sheet and profit and loss account?

The investment should be disclosed as a single line under FRS 9 as follows:

Calculation of goodwill

	At 1 January 2003 – fair value of assets
	£m
Tangible fixed assets	30
Current assets	31
Creditors – within 1 year	(20)
Creditors – more than 1 year	(8)
	33
Shareholding 30% × £33m	9.9
Fair value of investment (note i)	14
Goodwill (bal. fig.)	4.1

Disclosure in balance sheet

	£m
Cost of investment	14
Post-acquisition profits 30%	3.9
× (32 − 10 [share capital]	
plus 9 [profit and loss reserve])	
Goodwill written off (2 years × £1m per annum)	(2)
Additional depreciation charge (2 years × 20%	(1.2)
× (30 [fair value] − [20 cost]) × 30%	
Investment in associate	14.7

Alternative disclosure	
Share of net assets	36
(46 − [share of stock profits] 10)	
Revaluation of tangible fixed assets	10
Additional depreciation	(4)
(£10m × 20% = £2m × 2 years)	42
Shareholding 30% × £42m	12.6
Share of goodwill (£4.1m *less*	
2 years' amortisation £2m)	2.1
Investment in associate	14.7

The alternative disclosure is more correct since it does not disclose any element of profit as part of the investment.

Disclosure in the profit and loss account

	£m
Share of operating profit in associate	
(30% × £29m = £8.7m − [goodwill] 1	4.1
− [inter-co. profit] 3 − [depreciation] 0.6.m)	
Exceptional item − associate (30% × £10m)	(3.0)
Interest payable − associate (30% × £4m)	(1.2)
Tax on profit on ordinary activities	
Associate (30% × £3m)	(0.9)

The treatment of Castlerock plc changes if Castlerock were classified as an investment in joint venture

Joint venture − gross equity method

	Consolidated profit and loss £m
Turnover: Group and share of joint ventures	X + 53.1
(£212m gross less inter-company turnover £35m × 30%)	
Less share of joint venture turnover	(53.1)
Group turnover	X
Consolidated balance sheet	
Share of gross assets	*21.3
Share of gross liabilities (30% × 12 + 10)	(6.6)
	14.7

*Computation of share of gross assets

Fixed assets	£37m + £10m revaluation		
	− 4 additional depreciation	= 43 × 30% =	12.9
Stocks £31m − 10 [inter-company profit on stocks]		= 21 × 30% =	6.3
			19.2
Goodwill	£4.1m − amortised £2m		2.1
			21.3

Applications in published accounts

FRS 9 permits companies to adopt an alternative gross equity method, which requires companies to replace their net investment in the joint ventures with their share of individual assets and liabilities. This must be disclosed in the form of multi columns as it is illegal under UK law to apply proportional consolidation to entities which are not under the control of the reporting entity. The official column is the total column with effectively additional disclosure for the joint ventures and group on the right hand side. A good example of this is provided by Arena Leisure plc:

Arena Leisure Plc   Year Ended 31 December 2001   Leisure Industry

Consolidated Profit and Loss Account (Year Ended 31 December 2001)

	Note	Year ended 31 December 2001 Group £000	Interest in Joint venture £000	Total £000	9 months ended 31 December 2000 Group £000
Turnover	2	26,604	3,265	29,869	15,700
Cost of sales		(19,852)	(5,233)	(25,085)	(11,486)
Gross profit/(loss)		**6,752**	**(1,968)**	4,784	4,214
Administrative expenses	3	(8,531)	(1,976)	(10,507)	(9,250)
EBITDA		6	(3,941)	(3,935)	(3,801)
Depreciation		(1,478)	(3)	(1,481)	(1,004)
Amortisation		(307)	–	(307)	(231)
Operating loss	5	(1,779)	(3,944)	(5,723)	(5,036)
Share of operating loss in					
Joint venture	6	(3,944)			–
Associate	7	(308)			–
Goodwill amortisation in respect of joint venture	8	(14)			–
Total operating loss:					
Group and share of joint ventures and associates		(6,045)			(5,036)
Interest receivable	9	1,295			82
Interest payable	9	(1,421)			(1,253)
Loss on ordinary activities before and after taxation and retained	2,10,11,23	(6,171)			(6,207)
		Pence			Pence
Basic and diluted loss per share	12	(1.95)			(2.29)

The notes on pages 23 to 32 form part of these financial statements.
All recognised gains and losses are included above.
All amounts relate to continuing activities.

Balance Sheet at 31 December 2001 (Group only)

	Note	2001 Group £000	Interest in joint venture £000	Total £000	2000 Group £000
Fixed assets					
Intangible assets	13	5,494	–	5,494	5,801
Tangible assets	14	54,531	120	54,651	52,608
Investments – in associate	15	325	–	325	–
– other	15	345	–	345	345
		670	–	670	345
		60,695	120	60,815	58,754
Current assets					
Stock	16	146	–	146	167
Debtors – due within 1 year	17	2,490	2,291	4,781	2,911
Debtors – due in more than 1 year	17	20,950	3,436	24,386	–
		23,440	5,727	29,167	2,911
Blocked bank deposit	21	39,050	–	39,050	–
Cash in bank and in hand		4,535	1,214	5,749	1,478
		43,585	1,214	44,799	1,478
		67,171	6,941	74,112	4,556
Creditors: amounts falling due within 1 year	18	(11,836)	(2,540)	(14,376)	(17,013)
Net current assets/(liabilities)		55,335	4,401	59,736	(12,457)
Total assets less current liabilities		116,030	4,521	120,551	46,297
Creditors: amounts falling due after 1 year					
Share of net liabilities of joint venture	15	(3,929)	3.929	–	–
Goodwill in respect of joint venture	15	2,245	–	2,245	–
		(1,684)	3,929	2,245	–
Other		(13,485)	(8,450)	(21,935)	(19,863)
	19	(15,169)	(4,521)	(19,690)	(19,863)
Provisions for liabilities and charges	20	–	–	–	–
Net assets		100,861	–	100,861	(289)
Capital & Reserves					
Called-up share capital	22	18,036		18,036	13,527
Share premium account	23	87,564		87,564	11,186
Merger reserve	23	5,417		5,417	5,417
Revaluation reserve	23	15		15	15
Special reserve	23	4,564		4,564	4,564
Profit & loss account	23	(14,735)		(14,735)	(8,564)
Shareholders' Funds	24	100,861		100,861	26,145

The final practical application (Jarvis plc) covers the additional disclosure that is required under FRS 9 if a material associate/joint venture exceeds 25% of one of three key figures, i.e. turnover, operating results over a 3-year period or net assets. In addition, it provides details of the movement in fixed assets investments for the year.

Jarvis Plc   Year Ended 31 March 2003

Notes to the Financial Statements

14 (i) Fixed asset investments in joint venture undertakings

	Joint venture undertakings		
	Investments	Loans	Total
	£m	£m	£m
Group			
At 1 April 2002	14.0	3.2	17.2
Additions	56.3	–	56.3
Disposals	(1.0)	–	(1.0)
Loans advanced less repaid	–	0.3	0.3
Reclassification	(1.6)	1.6	–
Revaluation of properties	0.1	–	0.1
Share of retained profit	1.4	–	1.4
At 31 March 2003	69.2	5.1	74.3

Additions to investments of £56.3 million include £45.0 million in respect of deferred consideration for Tube Lines (Holdings) Limited.

The additional disclosure under FRS 9 as the joint venture undertakings exceed the 15% aggregate threshold and Tube Lines (Holdings) Limited exceeds the 25% individual threshold is as follows:

	31 March 2003 Tube Lines (Holdings) Ltd	31 March 2003 Other	31 March 2003 Total	31 March 2002 Tube Lines (Holdings) Ltd	31 March 2002 Other	31 March 2002 Total
	£m	£m	£m	£m	£m	£m
Profit and loss account						
Group's share of:						
Turnover	**41.4**	**70.3**	**111.7**	–	44.7	44.7
Profit before taxation	3.2	(0.2)	3.0	–	0.4	0.4
Taxation	1.2	–	1.2	–	–	–
Profit after taxation	**2.0**	**(0.2)**	**1.8**	–	0.4	0.4
Balance sheet						
Share of assets						
Fixed assets	8.6	84.5	93.1	–	55.6	55.6
Current assets due within 1 year	93.5	45.8	139.3	–	35.5	35.5

Assets due after more than 1 year	164.4	320.5	484.9	–	185.4	185.4
Deferred consideration	45.0	–	45.0	–	–	–
	311.5	450.8	762.3	–	276.5	276.5
Share of goodwill less amortisation	–	10.8	10.8	–	3.2	3.2
	311.5	**461.6**	**773.1**	–	**279.7**	**279.7**
Share of liabilities						
Liabilities due within 1 year	50.8	38.7	89.5	–	31.5	31.5
Liabilities due after more than 1 year	214.1	400.3	614.4	–	234.2	234.2
	264.9	**439.0**	**703.9**	–	**265.7**	**265.7**
Share of net assets	**46.6**	**22.6**	**69.2**	–	**14.0**	**14.0**

Amortisation of goodwill charged to the profit and loss account for the year, in respect of joint venture undertakings, was £0.4m (2002: £0.1m).

Foreign currency translation

10.1 SSAP 20 *Foreign Currency Translation* (April 1983)

Background

This standard was developed to deal with major accounting issues in connection with foreign trading. These are:

(i) How to account for foreign transactions, i.e. imports/exports of goods and services.
(ii) How to translate a foreign branch/subsidiary from a foreign currency into sterling prior to the process of consolidation.

Accounting treatment – transactions

The following are the normal rules of accounting for transactions:

(i) The exchange rate at the date of the transaction should be adopted but if exchange rates remain stable then an average rate should be adopted for all transactions in the same period.
(ii) Non-monetary assets, i.e. stocks and tangible fixed assets, should not be retranslated.
(iii) Monetary assets and liabilities should be retranslated at the exchange rates ruling at both the balance sheet and settlement dates.
(iv) Any exchange gain/loss must be included in arriving at the profits/losses on ordinary activities.

There are a number of exceptions to the normal rules. For example, if a forward foreign exchange contract is taken out then the forward rate may be adopted instead, so avoiding any exchange gain/loss being created.

Also, where companies enter into currency hedging operations by borrowing foreign currency to cushion against exchange rate movements in foreign currency assets, then the non-monetary assets (i.e. the investment) can be floated and any exchange gain/loss on that investment matched against the exchange rate gain/loss on the associated borrowings. However, there are a number of conditions attached to this:

(a) The exchange gains/losses on borrowings may only be offset to the extent of exchange gains/losses on the equity investments.
(b) Foreign currency borrowings should not exceed the total cash that the investments are expected to generate.
(c) The accounting treatment must be applied consistently from period to period.
(d) It can only apply if the closing rate method is adopted for consolidation purposes.

Accounting treatment – translation

There are two recognised methods in SSAP 20 for translating a foreign trading entity into sterling prior to consolidation. These are the closing rate and temporal methods.

Normally the closing rate method should be adopted but the decision as to which is most appropriate will largely depend on the financial and operating relationships that exist between the investor and its foreign enterprise.

Closing rate method

The investor, in this technique, is not interested in the value of the individual assets and liabilities in the foreign enterprise but instead in the overall net worth in the investment. Any exchange differences are argued to be unrealised as there is no intention to dispose of the subsidiary. They should therefore be adjusted directly within reserves and not charged through the profit and loss account.

The profit and loss account should be retranslated at either the closing rate or at an average rate. Present practice tends to favour the average (which must be a weighted average) due to the volatility of exchange rates. Whether average or closing rates are adopted, they must be used consistently.

Temporal method

Most foreign operations are autonomous and semi-independent bodies but if this is not the case and the foreign enterprise is a 'direct extension' of the parent company, then the temporal method should be adopted instead. The results of the foreign enterprise are really regarded as being more dependent on the economic environment of the investing company's local currency than on its own reporting currency.

The transactions of the foreign enterprise are treated as if they had been carried out by the company itself in its own currency. It is in reality a method identical to that adopted for transactions accounting.

The following list of factors should be taken into account when deciding on whether or not the temporal method is appropriate:

(a) The extent to which the cash flows of the enterprise have a direct impact upon those of the investor;

(b)   The extent to which the enterprise is dependent directly upon the investor;

(c)   The currency in which the majority of trading transactions are denominated;

(d)   The major currency to which the operation is exposed in its financing structure.

Hyper-inflation

Under UITF Abstract 9, if an investor has an investment in a country with a 100 per cent or more inflation rate over a 3-year period, then the foreign enterprise must be first restated in terms of current money before being translated. This can be achieved by either adopting a form of current purchasing power accounting or by the use of a relatively stable currency, e.g. US dollar.

Disclosure

The following information should be disclosed re foreign currency translation:

(1)   The translation methods adopted;

(2)   The treatment of exchange differences, i.e. in the profit and loss account or direct to reserves;

(3)   The net amount of exchange gains/losses on foreign currency borrowings;

(4)   The net movement on reserves re exchange differences.

FRED 24   *The Effects of Changes in Foreign Exchange Rates* (May 2002) *Financial Reporting in Hyper-inflationary Economies* (May 2002)

Both SSAP 20 and UITF 9 will be replaced in early 2003 by two new separate accounting standards – IAS 21 and IAS 29 respectively, with the above titles. Most of the changes are merely matters of emphasis but there are a number of significant differences. These can be summarised as follows:

(1)   FRED 24 introduces the notion of presentation currency as well as functional currency. It requires entities to measure its results in its functional currency but report in any currency it chooses. There are a number of factors that need to be considered before identifying a functional currency.

(2)   FRED 24 will abolish the closing rate method for translating the profit and loss account. Only the average rate may be adopted.

(3)   FRED 24 will require exchange differences on monetary items to go to the profit and loss account in a single entity's statements but, in consolidated accounts, they should go direct to reserves and the STRGL.

The example below illustrates how to deal with foreign currency transactions, particularly the export and import of goods and services and how exchange differences are dealt with in the profit and loss account. It also covers hedging techniques as well as accounting for an overseas branch.

Example – Neagh Plc

Neagh plc, whose registered office is in London, conducts operations and transactions both in the United Kingdom and overseas.

During the year ended 31 December 2003 the company was involved in various transactions in foreign currencies. Relevant exchange rates, except where given separately in the individual circumstances, were as scheduled below:

At	Rolads (R) R = £1	Nidars (N) N = £1	Krams (K) K = £1	Sarils (S) S = £1
31 December 2002	1.6	0.52	6.9	2,210.0
27 February 2003			7.0	
4 March 2003		0.65		
25 May 2003	1.5		6.7	
25 August 2003		0.50		
2 September 2003				2,224.0
11 November 2003	1.8			
31 December 2003	2.0	0.54	7.5	2,250.0
Average for 2003	1.7			

The transactions concerned are identified by the letters (A) to (F) and are detailed thus:

(A) Neagh plc bought equipment (as a fixed asset) for 130,000 nidars on 4 March 2003 and paid for it on 25 August 2003 in sterling.

(B) On 27 February 2003 Neagh plc sold goods which had cost £46,000 for £68,000 to a company whose currency was krams. The proceeds were received in krams on 25 May 2003.

(C) On 2 September 2003 Neagh plc sold goods which had cost £17,000 for £24,000 to a company whose currency was sarils. The amount was outstanding at 31 December 2003 but the proceeds were received in sarils on 7 February 2004 when the exchange rate was S2,306.0 = £1. The directors of Neagh plc approved the final accounts on 28 March 2004.

(D) Neagh plc borrowed 426,000 rolads on 25 May 2003 and repaid it in sterling on 11 November 2003.

(E) On 9 November 2002 Neagh plc had acquired an equity investment at a cost of 196,000 krams when the rate of exchange was K7.3 = £1. This investment was hedged by a loan of 15,000 nidars, at an exchange rate of N0.56 = £1, obtained on the same day.

(F) Neagh plc has an overseas wholesale warehouse which is financed locally in rolads and is treated as an independent branch for accounting purposes. The net investment in the branch was R638,600 on 1 January 2003 and R854,700 on 31 December 2003. During the year 2003 the branch had made a net profit of R423,400, of which R207,300 had been remitted to the UK parent company; these had realised £116,727.

In accounting for the branch, Neagh plc uses the average annual rate in translating profit and loss account items.

Suggested solution – Neagh Plc

Transaction A

		£	£
4. 3. 03	Dr Fixed assets (130,000 nidars ÷ 0.65)	200,000	
	Cr Creditors		200,000
25. 8. 03	Dr Creditors	200,000	
	Exchange loss – profit & loss	60,000	
	Cr Bank (130,000 nidars ÷ 0.50)		260,000

This is a normal trading transaction and should be written off as 'other operating expenses' in the profit and loss account.

Transaction B

		£	£
27. 2. 03	Dr Debtors (476,000 krams ÷ 7/£1)	68,000	
	Cr Sales		68,000
27. 2. 03	Dr Cost of sales	46,000	
	Cr Stock		46,000
25. 5. 03	Dr Bank (476,000 krams ÷ 6.7/£1)	71,045	
	Cr Debtors		68,000
	Exchange gain – profit & loss		3,045

This is a normal trading transaction and should be disclosed under the appropriate headings of sales, cost of sales, and gross profit. The exchange gain should be included under the heading 'other operating income' in the profit and loss account.

Transaction C

		£	£
2. 9. 03	Dr Debtors (53.376m sarils ÷ 2,224/£1)	24,000	
	Cr Sales		24,000
2. 9. 03	Dr Cost of sales	17,000	
	Cr Stock		17,000
31. 12. 03	Dr Exchange loss – profit & loss	277	
	Cr Debtors (53.376m ÷ 2,250/£1 =		
	23,723 − 24,000 = 277 loss)		277
7. 2. 04	Dr Bank (53.376m ÷ 2,306/£)	23,147	
	Cr Debtors		23,147
7. 2. 04	Dr Exchange loss - profit & loss	576	
	Cr Debtors (23,147 − 23,723)		576

This is a normal trading transaction and should be disclosed under the appropriate headings of sales, cost of sales, and gross profit. The debtor must be restated at the exchange rate at the year end as it is monetary in nature and the loss of £277 must be written off to the profit and loss account in 2003. The subsequent loss of £576 is caused by an event which occurred after the year end, and is thus non-adjusting. It would only be disclosed in the notes if it is regarded to be material, and necessary to give the user a proper understanding of the financial statements.

Transaction D

		£	£
25. 5. 03	Dr Bank (426,000 rolads ÷ 1.5/£1)	284,000	
	Cr Loan		284,000
11. 11. 03	Dr Loan	284,000	
	Cr Bank (426,000 rolads ÷ 1.8/£1)		236,667
	Exchange gain		47,333

Although this is not a trading profit it should be written off in the profit and loss account under the heading 'other interest receivable and similar income'.

Transaction E

		£	£
9. 11. 02	Dr Investment (196,000 krams ÷ 7.3/£1)	26,849	
	Cr Loan (15,000 nidars ÷ 0.56/£1)		26,786
	Bank		63
31. 12. 02	Dr Investment (196,000 krams ÷ 6.9/£1 =	1,557	
	28,406 − 26,849 = 1,557)		
	Cr Exchange gain		1,557
	Dr Exchange loss	2,060	
	Cr Loan (15,000 nidars ÷ 0.52/£1 =		2,060
	28,846 − 26,786 = 2,060)		

The exchange loss of £2,060 can be offset against the exchange gain of £1,557. The excess loss of £503 must be charged to profit and loss under 'other interest payable and similar expenses'. The offset of £1,557 is carried out within the reserves (SSAP 20, Para. 51).

		£	£
31. 12. 03	Dr Exchange loss	2,273	
	Cr Investment (196,000 krams ÷ 7.5 =		2,273
	26,133 − 28,406)		
	Dr Loan (15,000 nidars ÷ 0.54 = 27,778 − 28,846)	1,068	
	Cr Exchange gain		1,068

The exchange loss of £2,273 on the loan is offset against the exchange gain in the reserves, but only to the extent of £1,068. The excess loss of £1,205 would be charged to the profit and loss account as in 2002.

Transaction F

Branch current account (head office)

		Rolads	R/£1	£			Rolads	R/£1	£
1. 1. 03	Balance b/d	638,600	1.6	399,125	2003	Bank	207,300	1.7	121,941
2003	Net profit	423,400	1.7	249,059		Exchange			
						loss			98,893
					Dec.	Bal c/d	854,700	2.0	427,350
		1,062,000		648,184			1,062,000		648,184

Composition of exchange losses

		£
Exchange loss on remittances		
207,300 ÷ 1.7/£1 average		121,941
207,300 actual		116,727
		5,214

		£
Retranslation loss		
Opening balance	638,600 Rs ÷ 1.6/£1	399,125
	638,600 Rs ÷ 2/£1	319,300
		79,825
Net profit restated		
	(423,400 − 207,300) 1.7/£1	127,118
	(423,400 − 207,300) 2/£1	108,050
		19,068
		98,893

The exchange loss of £5,214 should really be treated as a trading item and should be written off as an 'other operating expense'. The retranslation loss is unrealised and has no impact at present on cash flow. This loss should therefore be taken direct to reserves.

The second example investigates the choice between the two methods of translating foreign subsidiaries – the temporal and closing rate – and provides an illustration of how to translate a reporting entity using the temporal method.

Example – Benburb Plc

Benburb plc acquired 2,100,000 ordinary shares of Kroner 1 in Kevlavik Ltd on 1 January 1985 when the reserves of Kevlavik Ltd were Kr1,500,000 and the exchange rate was Kr10 to £1. Goodwill was eliminated against the consolidated reserves on 31 December 1985.

The profit and loss accounts of Benburb plc and Kevlavik Ltd for the year ended 31 December 2003 were as follows:

	Benburb £'000	Kevlavik Kr'000
Turnover	9,225	94,500
Cost of sales	6,027	63,000
Gross profit	3,198	31,500
Distribution cost	1,290	7,550
Administrative expenses	1,469	2,520
Depreciation	191	2,100
	248	19,330
Dividends from subsidiary	315	–
	563	19,330
Tax	195	7,570
Profit on ordinary activities after tax	368	11,760
Dividends paid 30. 6. 93	183	4,200
Retained profit for the year	185	7,560

The balance sheets of Benburb plc and Kevlavik Ltd as at 31 December 2003 were as follows:

	Benburb £'000	Kevlavik Kr'000
Fixed assets		
Tangible assets	1,765	38,500
Investment in Kevlavik Ltd	305	–
Current assets		
Stock	2,245	3,675
Debtors	615	1,750
Cash	156	9,450
	3,016	14,875
Current liabilities		
Trade creditors	(2,245)	(4,375)
Creditors falling due after more than 1 year		
Loan	(1,230)	(8,680)
	1,611	40,320
Capital and reserves		
Share capital in £1 ordinary shares	600	
Share capital in Kr1 ordinary shares		3,500
Profit and loss account	1,011	36,820
	1,611	40,320

The tangible assets of Kevlavik Ltd were acquired 1 January 1986 and are stated at cost less depreciation.

Stocks represent six months' purchases and at 31 December 2002 the stock held by Kevlavik Ltd amounted to Kr4,760,000.

Exchange rates were as follows:

	Kr: £1
I January 1986	10
30 June 2002	10.5
30 September 2002	10
31 December 2002	9.5
Average for 2003	8
30 June 2003	8
30 September 2003	7.5
31 December 2003	7

In determining the appropriate method of currency translation, it is established that the trade of Kevlavik Ltd is more dependent on the economic environment of the investing company's currency than that of its own reporting currency.

Suggested solution – Benburb Plc

Why the trade of Kevlavik is more dependent on the economic environment of Benburb plc

There are two methods of foreign currency translation – the temporal and the closing rate methods. The former must be adopted where an overseas entity is more dependent on the currency of the parent than on its own currency. Often it has been set up purely as a selling agency or sub-assembly operation. It is in reality a 'direct extension' of the parent's own business into that country. The foreign entity would be unlikely to survive without the parent company's support.

SSAP 20 sets out some criteria that should be investigated but these should all be looked at together before finally deciding on the most appropriate method to adopt. The factors that should be considered include:

(1)   the currency in which most of the transactions are carried out, i.e. sterling or foreign currency;
(2)   whether the overseas entity is buying and selling goods in its own right;
(3)   whether the financing is mainly sterling and the extent to which the cash flows of the overseas entity have a direct impact on those of the parent company;
(4)   the major currency to which the foreign operation is exposed in its financing structure, i.e. sterling.

Preparation of consolidated profit and loss account and balance sheet using the temporal method of translation for the year ended 31 December 2003

Consolidated profit and loss account of the Benburb Group for the year ended 31 December 2003

		£
Turnover	(9,225 + 11,812.5)	21,037,500
Cost of sales	(6,027 + 7,725.375)	13,752,375
Gross profit	(3,198 + 4,087.125)	7,285,125
Distribution costs	(1,290 + 943.75)	2,233,750
Administrative expenses	(1,469 + 315)	1,784,000
Depreciation	(191 + 210)	401,000
Exchange loss		281,809
Profit on ordinary activities before tax		2,584,566
Tax	(195 + 946.25)	1,141,250
Profit on ordinary activities after tax		1,443,316
Minority interest	(40% of 1,390.316)	556,126
Profit for year attributable to ordinary shareholders		887,190
Dividend		183,000
Retained profit for year		704,190
Profit and loss at 1. 1. 2003		*2,451,810
		3,156,000

*Benburb plc (1,011 − 185 = 826) + Kevlavik (60% × 2,709,684 = 1,625,810)

Consolidated balance sheet of the Benburb Group as at 31 December 2003

		£'000	£'000
Fixed assets			
Intangible assets	(305 − 60% × 500 = 5 less amortised 40%)		3
Tangible assets	(1,765 + 3,850)		5,615
Current assets			
Stock	(2,245 + 490)	2,735	
Debtors	(615 + 250)	865	
Cash	(156 + 1,350)	1,506	
		5,106	
Creditors falling due within 1 year			
Trade creditors	(2,245 + 625)	2,870	
Net current assets			2,236
			7,854
Creditors falling due after more than 1 year			
Loans	(1,230 + 1,240)		2,470
			5,384
Capital			600
Reserves (3,156 − 2 [goodwill])			* 3,154
			3,754
Minority interest	(40% of 4,075)		1,630
			5,384

* Benburb plc 1,011 + 60% × 3,575 = 3,156 − 2 [goodwill] amortised

Workings

1. Translation of Kevlavik Ltd balance sheet as at 31 December 2003

	FF'000	Rate	£'000	
Tangible assets	38,500	10	3,850	historical
Stock	3,675	7.5	490	historical (3 mts. av.)
Debtors	1,750	7	250	closing
Cash	9,450	7	1,350	closing
Trade creditors	(4,375)	7	(625)	closing
Loan	(8,680)	7	(1,240)	closing
	40,320		4,075	
Share capital	3,500	10	350	historical
Profit and loss account				
Pre-acquisition	1,500	10	150	historical
Post-acquisition	35,320	bal.	3,575	bal. fig.
	40,320		4,075	

2. Translation of Kevlavik Ltd profit and loss account for the year ended 31 December 2003

	Fr'000	Rate	£'000	
Turnover	94,500	8	11,812,500	average
Opening stock	4,760	10	476,000	historical
Purchases (bal. fig.)	61,915	8	7,739,375	average
Closing stock	(3,675)	7.5	(490,000)	historical
Cost of sales	63,000		7,725,375	
Gross profit	31,500		4,087,125	
Distribution costs	7,550	8	943,750	average
Administration expenses	2,520	8	315,000	average
Depreciation	2,100	10	210,000	historical
Exchange loss			281,809	
	19,330		2,336,566	
Tax	7,570	8	946,250	average
Profits after tax	11,760		1,390,316	
Dividends paid 30. 6. 03	4,200	8	525,000	
Retained profit for the year	7,560		865,316	
Profit and loss brought forward	27,760		2,709,684	(see W4)
Profit and loss carried forward	35,320		3,575,000	

3. Exchange differences

	Kr'000
Opening net monetary liabilities	
Fixed assets (closing 38,500 + depreciation for year 2,100)	40,600
Opening stocks (given)	4,760
	45,360
Less total net assets at start (40,320 closing − retained profit for year 7,560)	32,760
	(12,600)

		£
(12,600) translated at 9.5 (opening rate)		1,326,316
(12,600) translated at 7 (closing rate)		1,800,000
Exchange loss		(473,684)

Transactions for the year			
Retained profit	7,560,000		
Depreciation	2,100,000		
Decrease in stock	1,085,000		
	10,745,000	@ 7 closing	1,535,000
		@ 8 average	1,343,125
Exchange gain			191,875

Net exchange loss – profit and loss   (281,809)

4. Opening balance sheet of Kevlavik as at 31 December 2002

	£
Non-monetary assets (45,360 ÷ 10)	4,536,000
Net monetary liabilities (12,600 ÷ 9.5)	(1,326,316)
	3,209,684
Less share capital and pre-acquisition reserves	500,000
Opening post-acquisition reserves	2,709,684

Calculation of inter-company stock profits

(i) Closing rate method

		Profit and loss	4
Dr		Profit and loss	4
	Cr	Stocks	4

Elimination of inter-company stock profits

		Sales	14
Dr		Sales	14
	Cr	Purchases	14

Elimination of inter-group purchases and sales
Stocks are valued in the overseas subsidiary at the closing rate, i.e. £14,000 ÷ 7.5 = 105,000Kr, then divided by 7 = £15,000; thus stocks will have to increase from the original cost of £10,000 to £11,000 to reflect the exchange movement.

(ii) Temporal method

The same two journal entries would appear as above but with no adjustment to the value of the stocks as they are retained at their historical rate in the books of the overseas subsidiary; thus stocks remain at £10,000.

Applications in published accounts

A number of accounting policy notes are provided to illustrate when the temporal method might be adopted (CeNeS Pharmaceuticals plc), the use of hedging, and details of the principal foreign exchange rates (Kingfisher plc) and, finally, a straightforward note on the adoption of the closing rate method and how to deal with hyperinflationary conditions (British American Tobacco).

CeNeS   **Year Ended**   **Pharmaceuticals**
Pharmaceuticals Plc   **31 December 2002**

Notes to the Financial Statements (Extract)

f) Foreign currency

Transactions in foreign currencies are recorded at the rate of exchange at the date of the transaction. Monetary assets and liabilities denominated in foreign currencies including long-term liabilities, are translated into sterling at rates of exchange ruling at the balance sheet date. All exchange differences on these monetary assets and liabilities are dealt with in the profit and loss account. This treatment is required by SSAP 20 *Foreign Currency Translation* in order to give a true and fair view of the group's results. Compliance with SSAP 20 overrides Schedule 4 Para. 12 of the Companies Act 1985 which states that only profits realised at the balance sheet date should be included in the profit and loss account.

The results of overseas operations are translated at average rates of exchange during the period and their balance sheets at the rates ruling at the balance sheet date. Exchange differences arising on translation of the opening net assets of overseas operations are dealt with through reserves except as explained below. All other exchange differences are included in the profit and loss account.

The joint venture undertaking, CeNeS (Bermuda) Limited, is accounted for under the temporal method. Transactions are accounted for as if they were entered into by CeNeS Pharmaceuticals plc directly. Consequently, all transactions are translated at the rate ruling at the transaction date. Monetary items are translated at the closing rate at the balance sheet date. Non-monetary items are translated at the exchange rate ruling at the date on which the initial transaction to recognise them is made and not retranslated at each balance sheet date. All exchange gains and losses, including those arising on the retranslation of opening monetary items, are taken to the profit and loss account for the year.

Kingfisher Plc   **Year Ended**   **Home Improvement;**
                     31 January 2003   **Electrical Retailing**

Notes to the Accounts (Extract)

1 Accounting policies

Foreign currencies
Transactions denominated in foreign currencies are translated into sterling at contracted rates or, where no contract exists, at average monthly rates.

Monetary assets and liabilities denominated in foreign currencies which are held at the year end are translated into sterling at year-end exchange rates. Exchange differences on monetary items are taken to the profit and loss account.

The balance sheets of overseas subsidiary undertakings are expressed in sterling at year-end exchange rates. Profits and losses of overseas subsidiary undertakings are expressed in sterling at average exchange rates for the year. Exchange differences arising on the translation of opening shareholders' funds are recorded as a movement in reserves, and are reported in the Statement of Total Recognised Gains and Losses (STRGL).

The group's share of net assets or liabilities of associated undertakings and joint ventures is expressed in sterling at year-end exchange rates. The share of profits or losses for the year are expressed in sterling at average exchange rates for the year. Exchange differences arising on the retranslation of opening net equity are recorded as a movement on reserves.

Exchange differences arising on borrowings used to finance, or provide a hedge against, the group's net investment in foreign subsidiaries are recorded as movements in reserves to the extent of exchange differences arising on the equity investments. Other exchange differences are taken to the profit and loss account.

Principal rates of exchange

Euro	**2003**	2002
Year-end rate	**1,531**	1,642
Average rate	**1,583**	1,614

British American Year Ended 31 December 2003 Tobacco Tobacco

Accounting Policies

4 Foreign currencies

Turnover, profits and cash flows expressed in currencies other than sterling are translated to sterling at average rates of exchange each year. Assets and liabilities are translated at the end of the year. For high inflation countries, the translation from local currencies to sterling makes allowance for the impact of inflation on the local currency results.

The differences between retained profits of overseas subsidiary and associated undertakings translated at average and closing rates of exchange are taken to reserves, as are differences arising on the retranslation to sterling (using closing rates of exchange) of overseas net assets at the beginning of the year, after taking into account related foreign exchange borrowings. Other exchange differences, including those on remittances, are reflected in profit.

Sundry accounting standards

11.1 FRS 4 *Capital Instruments* (December 1993)

Background

The 1970s and 1980s were periods of fundamental change in the financial services sector, with the traditional high street banks and the building societies starting to compete with each other in each other's territory, e.g. banks started to offer mortgages and building societies, normal banking facilities.

As part of that process the financial institutions began to offer their clients the opportunity of raising monies from capital instruments which would have the least damaging effect on the key performance ratios of earnings per share and gearing. In particular, capital instruments were offered which in some cases cost zero per cent interest and at the same time disclosed only a fraction of their total repayment value on the balance sheet, as a liability. The financial statements clearly could no longer provide a true and fair view.

The financial institutions also offered their clients the possibility of raising finance from a number of hybrid financial instruments (i.e. partly debt and partly equity) such as convertible loan stock. Often companies would classify these as mezzanine finance and therefore outside the definition of debt and thus excluded from gearing, on the assumption that the holders of these instruments would eventually convert their loans into shares.

Key issues

Balance sheet classification

Capital instruments, under FRS 4, must now be clearly classified as either debt or equity. Nothing must 'sit on the fence'. If an instrument meets the definition of a liability then it must be classified as debt, i.e. if there is an obligation to transfer future economic benefits as a result of a past transaction or event.

All other capital instruments must then be classified as equity. However, the ASB does recognise that some of the equity is really in the nature of debt in that a fixed dividend will be paid annually as well as the share having a preferential right to repayment. In those cases, where there is any form of restriction on the shares, then the instruments should be classified as non-equity but still recorded within the capital and reserves section of the balance sheet.

The amount recorded for non-equity on the balance sheet should include not only the share capital but any reserves attached to those shares, e.g. share premium.

Convertible loan stock should be classified as debt until such time as the loan stock is actually converted into shares. It should no longer be treated as a 'hybrid'. The balance sheet should be treated as a picture of the business at a particular point in time and not as a predictor of the future intentions of loan holders. They may never actually convert if the conditions are not to their satisfaction!

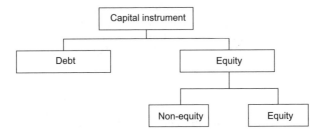

Profit and loss charge

The second main objective of FRS 4 is to ensure that a fair charge is allocated to profit and loss on an annual basis to reflect the true cost of borrowing over the life of the capital instrument. Finance costs will incorporate the following:

(i)   annual interest or dividend payments;
(ii) any premiums/discounts on redemption; and
(iii) any direct issue costs.

The finance costs are defined as 'the difference between the net proceeds of an instrument and the total amount of the payments that the issuer may be required to make in respect of the instrument'.

Finance costs should, however, be charged to profit and loss at a constant rate on the outstanding amount. The straight-line method is not permitted.

EXAMPLE
ABC plc issued a deep discount bond of £100 par value for £64. It will be repayable at a premium of £10 in 5 years' time. Interest is payable at 2 per cent per annum and the company has incurred direct issue costs of £4.

SOLUTION

	£	£
Total payments over the life		
repayment of capital		100
premium on redemption		10
annual interest (£2 × 5 years)		10
		120

Net proceeds		
gross proceeds	64	
direct issue costs	(4)	
		60
Total finance costs		60

Sum of the digits $5(5 + 1)/2 = 15$

Year	Opening	Finance		Interest paid	Closing
	£	£		£	£
1	60	4	(1/15)	2	62
2	62	8	(2/5)	2	68
3	68	12	(3/15)	2	78
4	78	16	(4/15)	2	92
5	92	20	(5/15)	112 (incl. principal)	–
		60		120	

Minority interests

Should be analysed between equity and non-equity interests, both in the profit and loss account and on the balance sheet.

Scrip dividends

If a company proposes to offer to its shareholders a choice between taking up a cash dividend or shares, the following procedures must take place:

(i)   The full cash equivalent should be provided as a proposed dividend in the profit and loss and as an accrual on the balance sheet.

(ii) At the time of the payment of the dividend, those wishing to be paid cash will be paid out but opting for the scrip dividend instead should result in a reversal of the previous accrual.

(iii) On the day that the shares are issued the fair value of those shares should be taken out of the profit and loss reserve, with the nominal value of the shares being credited to share capital and the premium to the share premium account.

The example below shows how to calculate the total finance cost for redeemable preference shares and how to spread that cost under FRS 4 through the profit and loss account to produce a constant rate of return on the outstanding liability. The required disclosure on the balance sheet is also covered:

Example – Ardglass Plc

On 1 October 1998 Ardglass plc issued 10 million £1 preference shares at par, incurring issue costs of £100,000. The dividend payable on the preference shares was a fixed 4 per cent per annum, payable on 30 September each year in arrears. The preference shares were redeemed on 1 October 2003 at a price of £1.35 per share. The effective finance cost of the preference shares was 10 per cent. The balance sheet of the company on 30 September 2003, the day before the redemption of the preference shares, was as follows:

	£m
Ordinary share capital (non-redeemable)	100.0
Redeemable preference shares	13.5
Share premium account	25.8
Profit and loss account	59.7
	199.0
Net assets	199.0

Ardglass Plc – Suggested solution

The finance costs to be allocated to the profit and loss account should be governed by the rules in FRS 4 *Capital Instruments*. In particular, FRS 4 requires the difference between the total payments during the life of a capital instrument and the net proceeds received initially, to be recorded as finance costs in the profit and loss account. The finance costs should be allocated to profit and loss to ensure that the total finance cost of any preference shares issued are allocated at a constant rate on the outstanding amount over the life of the instrument. This will require the adoption of a sum of the digits or actuarial approach for allocation. A straight-line method would not be acceptable. The preference shares will increase by the finance cost each year and be reduced by any dividends paid or payable. The finance cost should be reported in the profit and loss account as part of the finance cost or interest payable and recorded after operating profit. The preference shares are legally part of capital and reserves but they have the nature of debt and thus FRS 4 insists that they still be included within capital and reserves but, in addition, must be recorded separately as non-equity on the balance sheet – to indicate that they have priority over ordinary share capital in relation to both repayment and dividend receipt. The charge to profit and loss account needs to be backed up by a detailed 'interest payable' note which details the break-up of the charge to profit and loss.

Calculation of the finance cost for 5 years ended 30 September 2003

Total payments	£	£
Dividends payable 4% × £10m × 5 years		2,000,000
Repayment 10m shares at £1.35		13,500,000
		15,500,000
Less net proceeds received		
Gross proceeds	10,000,000	
Less finance costs	100,000	
		9,900,000
Total finance costs		5,600,000

	Opening carrying amount	Finance costs (10%)	Net liability	Cash flow	Closing carrying amount
	£m	£m	£m	£m	£m
1999	9,900	990	10,890	(400)	10,490
2000	10,490	1,049	11,539	(400)	11,139
2001	11,139	1,114	12,253	(400)	11,853
2002	11,853	1,184	13,037	(400)	12,637
2003	12,637	1,263	13,900	(13,900)	–
		5,600			

The effective cost of preference shares was given as 10 per cent. Under the sum of the digits approach the finance cost would be $5(5 + 1)/2 = 15$, i.e. 1/15, 2/15, 3/15, 4/15 and 5/15 each year for the next 5 years (373, 747, 1120, 1494 and 1866).

Balance sheet of Ardglass plc as at 1 October 2003

	£m	
Capital and reserves		
Ordinary shares of £1 each, fully paid up	100	
Share premium account	25.8	135.8
Capital redemption reserve (0 + 10)	10	
Profit and loss account (59.7 − 10.0)	49.7	
	185.5	
Net assets (199 − 13.5)	185.5	

On redemption of the preference shares these must be replaced by either a new issue of shares or a transfer out of distributable reserves into a 'locked-up' capital redemption reserve (nominal value).

The double entries were as follows:

			£m	£m
Dr		Redeemable preference share capital	13.5	
	Cr	Bank		13.5
being the repayment of preference shares at a premium of £1.35 per share				
Dr		Profit and loss account	10	
	Cr	Capital redemption reserve		10
being the transfer from distributable reserves to maintain capital				

Financial Reporting Review Panel

Securicor Group Plc (February 1996)

This case involved a failure to properly analyse shareholders' funds between their equity and non-equity components under FRS 4, in this case for participating preference shares. The directors agreed to amend future financial statements.

Newarthill Plc (March 1996)

The company's accounts for the year ended 31 October 1994 had been qualified by the auditors because the recognition of the financial cost of redeemable convertible preferences shares was not in compliance with the requirements of FRS 4. The Review Panel discussed this with the company and the company agreed to issue revised accounts, which were subsequently audited and given an unqualified auditors' report.

Alexon Group Plc (May 1996)

The main matter at issue was the conformity of the analysis of shareholders' funds between equity and non-equity interests under FRS 4. After discussions with the Panel the group restated their analysis of shareholders' funds at 28 January 1996 to accord with FRS 4 and reduced their ordinary funds by £18m along with a similar increase in its non-equity funds. The directors also provided a fuller explanation of the rights of the company's cumulative preference shares and of its deferred shares. The auditors, Price Waterhouse, were referred to the ICAEW's disciplinary committee following the review.

Ransomes Plc (June 1996)

The main concern of the Review Panel was the conformity of the analysis of shareholders' funds between equity and non-equity interests under the provisions of FRS 4. The company agreed to include in its 1996 interim accounts a restatement of the analysis at 30 September 1995 conforming with FRS 4 and the directors confirmed that the analysis would be included in the final 1996 accounts in conformity with the standard, together with some additional information about the rights of the non-equity shares.

Application in published accounts

HMV has appropriated dividends and a redemption premium through its profit and loss account as required by FRS 4 but it has also credited these back to reserves, as a reserve movement.

HMV Plc   52 Weeks Ended 28 April 2001   Music Retailing

Accounting Policies

Change of Accounting policies

The financial statements have been prepared on the basis of the accounting policies set out in the group's Report and Accounts for the 52 weeks ended 28 April 2001, other than in respect of FRS 19 *Deferred Tax* and FRS 4 *Capital Instruments*.

In adopting FRS 19, the group was in a deferred tax asset position as at 28 April 2001. As a result the comparative taxation charge in the profit and loss account for the 52 weeks ended 28 April 2001 and the net asset position disclosed in the balance sheet as at 28 April 2001 have been adjusted as disclosed below.

In accordance with the provisions of FRS 4 *Capital Instruments*, the company has appropriated through the profit and loss account dividends and redemption premium in respect of its Senior and Junior Preference Shares. As permitted by FRS 4, the appropriations have been credited back to the profit and loss account reserve, with the cumulative amount appropriated included as an element of non-equity shareholders' funds, together with the issue price of non-equity share capital of £216,640,000. This represents a change of accounting policy, as in earlier periods the cumulative dividends and redemption premium charged were accrued as a liability on the balance sheet.

The adjustments to the prior period's profit and loss account and net assets were:

	2001 Taxation charge (credit) £000	2001 Net assets (liabilities) £000
As previously reported	2,336	(534,330)
Effect of change in accounting policy: deferred tax	(3,529)	8,365
Effect of change in accounting policy: dividends and redemption premium	–	102,793
As restated	(1,193)	(423,172)

The impact on the reported net assets as at 27 April 2002 of not adopting the new accounting policies would have been to reduce net assets by £154.6 million (FRS 4 £145.0 million; FRS 19 £9.6 million).

11.2   FRS 13 *Derivatives and Other Financial Instruments*: *Disclosure* (September 1998)

Background

This is one of the more complex of the accounting standards as well as the longest. It applies to all listed companies with an instrument traded on the stock exchange as well as all banks and financial institutions. It has arisen due to the collapse of Barings Bank by the speculative behaviour of a derivative dealer, Nick Leeson, in bringing the bank into liquidation. The standard is split into three sections:

1.   Part A: reporting entities other than financial institutions;
2.   Part B: banks and similar banking groups;
3.   Part C: other financial institutions.

Objective

There are basically two different types of investors recognised in the standard – the average private investor and the more sophisticated institutional investor. The former in actuality wants to be aware of the broad strategies and policies chosen by the company whereas the latter would require, in addition, more detailed numerical back-up.

Narrative disclosure

This would normally be incorporated in the operating and financial review at the front of the annual report. Entities must disclose the following for all financial instruments (defined as a financial asset in one set of books and a financial liability in another).

1. The overall strategy for primary financial instruments, e.g. using loans, borrowings, etc., to finance the business and for using derivative products, e.g. to manage the overall risk profile of the entity;
2. Whether or not derivatives are being used for speculative purposes or purely for managing risk;
3. An overall discussion of how the entity copes with the specific risks faced by the reporting entity. Normally this would lead to a discussion of liquidity, foreign exchange and interest rate risk.

    Interest risk – this may include a discussion of the break-up of financing between own capital and outside finance and what policy the company may adopt in relation to the percentage of floating rate debt.

    Exchange risk – this may include a discussion of the extent to which the company avails itself of forward foreign exchange contracts and the use of hedging techniques for investments.

    Liquidity risk – this may include a discussion of the overall policy of how much finance should not be due for repayment for 5 years or a discussion of detailing scheduling of the liquidity repayments.

Numerical analysis

Reporting entities also need to prepare detailed numerical analysis to back up the narrative disclosure. This can take up to three to four pages in the notes to the financial statements. The following detailed back-up notes are normally presented:

Interest rate risk

Detailed analysis of total amounts borrowed and invested should be analysed by major currency and details provided of the total amount split between fixed and floating rate liabilities, the weighted average interest rate for each currency and the length of time for which the rate is fixed.

Exchange risk

Detailed analysis of foreign currency exposures by currency is required.

Liquidity risk

A detailed maturity analysis of the financial liabilities split between the amounts due within 1 year, due between 1 and 2 years, due between 2 and 5 years and the amount payable in over 5 years, is required. Details of undrawn borrowings facilities expiring within 1 year, between 1 and 2 years and those expiring after 2 years.

In addition to the above, reporting entities should also provide a fair value table in which are set out both the book and the fair values of primary and derivative instruments side by side. Fair values would normally be based on current market values or discounted cash flows. FRED 30 will eventually introduce IAS 39 into UK reporting and these fair values will ultimately appear in the primary financial statements themselves. Finally, entities should prepare a table listing all unrecognised gains and losses on hedging operations.

FRS 13 requires reporting entities to disclose, in narrative form, a sensitivity analysis, to outline the extent to which small changes in a key variable could have on reported profits or net debt. An example would be to estimate what a 1 per cent increase in interest rates or exchange movement would have on profitability. Centrica plc even provide a note detailing the impact of a small change in temperature on their profitability – weather risk. It is very popular to include this note in the Operating and Financial Review rather than in the notes to the financial statements.

The Financial Reporting Review Panel (FRRP) in April 2001 criticised reporting entities for failing to comply with FRS 13, particularly in relation to disclosure of primary financial instruments, and they may investigate companies over the next few years to see whether or not notice is being taken of their comments.

FRED 23 *Financial Instruments: Hedge Accounting* (May 2002)

FRED 23 was published in May 2002 to establish principles for the use of hedge accounting. In particular, it sets out to introduce both hedge criteria that must apply as well as hedge effectiveness requirements, which should have the effect of tightening up hedge accounting so that it is only adopted in genuine hedge situations.

The hedge relationship criteria are:

(1)   At the inception of the hedge there is formal documentation of the hedging relationship, the entity's risk management objective and its strategy for undertaking the hedge, including identifying the hedging instrument and the hedged item as well as how the entity will assess hedge effectiveness;
(2)   Effectiveness can be reliably measured; and
(3)   If a forecast transaction is hedged, then it is highly probable that it will result in a cash flow exposure that could affect profitability.

The hedge effectiveness criteria are:

(1)   The hedge was expected at the outset to be highly effective in achieving offsetting changes in fair values/cash flows consistent with the original risk management strategy;
(2)   The hedge has been assessed on an ongoing basis and determined to be highly effective.

Provided that the criteria are met for a foreign hedging situation then any effective hedge gains and losses should be reported in the STRGL but any ineffective part in profit and loss.

FRED 23 is implementing part of the financial instruments project that was formerly contained in SSAP 20 but not in IAS 24 so that hedging rules are still kept on the books of the ASB.

FRED 30   *Financial Instruments: Disclosure and Presentation, Financial Instruments: Recognition and Measurement* (June 2002)

The IASB has two standards on financial instruments, IAS 32 *Financial Instruments: Disclosure and Presentation* and IAS 39 *Financial Instruments: Recognition and Measurement.* FRED 30 sets out both standards and also proposals to withdraw FRS 4 and FRS 13.

The main proposals can be summarised as follows:

(a) *Recognition* – There will be no change to existing UK regulations for the time being.
(b) *Measurement and hedge accounting* – UK standards should be amended from 2005 so if an entity chooses to use fair value accounting it will be required to adopt IAS 39's fair value model.
(c) *Presentation* – If presentation requirements in IAS 32 are not further amended before 2005, UK standards should be amended from 2005 in full. FRS 4 will be withdrawn at the same time.
(d) *Disclosure* – From 2005, the existing UK standards on financial instruments (FRS 4 and 13) will be replaced by a UK standard implementing IAS 32.

The effect of the proposals will be that:

(a) the requirements of revised IAS 32 will be implemented in the UK for all listed entities and all banks from 1 January 2005;
(b) the presentation requirements of IAS 32, but not the disclosure, will be implemented in the UK for all unlisted entities from 2005/06;
(c) although the recognition and derecognition requirements of revised IAS 39 will not be implemented in the UK, all the other provisions of IAS 39 will have to be followed from 1 January 2005 by those entities adopting fair value accounting.

Changes are required to companies' legislation and FRED 30 assumes these will take place for accounting periods starting on or after 1 January 2005.

Main changes proposed to existing UK requirements

Measurement

Main accounting requirements are contained in the Companies Act 1985 and allow companies a fair degree of complexity although:

(a) liabilities are required to be measured at cost-based amounts;
(b) only in limited cases can unrealised gains be recognised immediately in the profit and loss (e.g. financial instruments held by banks) but in all other cases such gains must be recognised in the STRGL.

The ASB understands that, by 1 January 2005, the Companies Act is likely to be amended to permit companies to adopt an alternative fair value regime. Companies should measure certain financial assets and liabilities at fair value and recognise changes in those fair values immediately in the profit and loss account.

FRED 30 proposes to introduce requirements setting out how the fair value accounting rules should be applied if an entity chooses to adopt them. In particular, such companies are required to:

(a) measure at fair value all derivatives, all financial assets and liabilities held for trading and all 'available for sale' financial assets;

(b) measure at cost all financial assets held to maturity and all financial liabilities that are neither derivatives nor held for trading except that an entity can elect to measure any of these at fair value and recognise changes in fair values immediately in the profit and loss;

(c) recognise in the profit and loss immediately all changes in the fair value of financial instruments, except that changes in fair values of available for sale financial assets are recognised immediately in the STRGL.

These requirements are the same as those in revised IAS 39 but there are some detailed differences explained later.

The measurement proposals will have no direct effect on accounting practices of reporting entities not covered by the fair value accounting rules.

If the Government decides not to require IFRSs for unlisted entities or for individual statements of listed companies, FRED 30 proposes that the position post-2005 for such entities should be the same as the pre-2005 position. Thus IAS 39's measurement rules would only apply if the fair value accounting rules are adopted.

Hedge accounting

Existing UK requirements mainly cover hedge accounting for foreign operations. FRED 23 was published in May 2002 but will be replaced in early 2005 by a standard covering all types of hedges and containing restrictions on the availability of hedge accounting.

The draft requirements in FRED 23 are the same as some of the hedge accounting requirements in IAS 39. The effect, from 1 January 2005, is that those adopting the fair value rules should comply with a UK standard that implements almost all of the other hedge accounting requirements in IAS 39. Those requirements further limit the availability of hedge accounting and prescribe exactly how hedge accounting should be applied.

From 2005, listed entities are required to adopt IAS 39's hedge accounting in consolidated accounts. FRED 30 suggests that UK standards should require IAS 39 to be complied with by unlisted entities and individual financial statements of listed companies but only if fair value accounting rules are adopted.

Presentation

Under the Companies Act, financial instruments are classified as either 'shareholders' funds' or 'liabilities' and the former split between equity and non-equity. All dividends should go to profit and loss.

It is expected that, before 1 January 2005, those requirements are likely to be amended as follows:

(a) The categories will change to 'liabilities' and 'equity' to accord with their substance. Preference shares will become liabilities.

(b) Income payments on redeemable preference shares will be treated as interest and the overall effect will be to increase the interest expense in the profit and loss. Ordinary dividends will no longer be reported in the profit and loss.

FRS 4 currently requires convertible debt to be classified as a liability but FRED 30 will require convertible debt to be split into an equity and a liability element known as 'split accounting'.

FRS 5 restricts the offset process of assets and liabilities but FRED 30 will replace this with the provisions in IAS 32. This will permit balance sheet debits and credits to be off-set more often than at present.

Disclosure

Currently UK entities are required to provide a range of narrative and numerical risk disclosures. FRED 30 will replace IAS 32 disclosures. IAS 32 disclosures mirror the broad thrust of existing UK rules but are less detailed. The main effect will be to provide greater flexibility as to the form of the disclosures they provide.

At present, the main UK disclosures apply only to banks and listed entities that are not insurance entities. FRED 30 proposes that listed insurance companies and groups should be brought within the scope of the disclosure requirements.

The following example provides a short insight into the impact of adopting fair values for an entity's financial instruments, when FRED 30 is finally adopted as a full accounting standard:

Example – Lecale Plc

Lecale, a public limited company, issued a 3-year £30 million 5 per cent debenture at par on 1 December 2003 when the market rate of interest was 5 per cent. Interest is paid annually on 30 November each year. Market rates of interest on debentures of equivalent term and risk are 6 per cent and 4 per cent at the end of the financial years to 30 November 2004 and 30 November 2005 (assume that the changes in interest rates took place on 30 November each year).

Show the effect on 'profit' for the 3 years to 30 November 2006 if the debenture and the interest charge were valued on a fair value basis.

Lecale Plc – Suggested solution

Fair value reporting – AX plc

	2004	2005	2006
	£'000	£'000	£'000
Historical cost – interest (5%)	1,500	1,500	1,500
Adjustment to fair value	–	267	(288)
Effective interest	1,500	1,767 (6% × £29.45m)	1,212 (4% × £30.29m)
(Gain)/loss on change in fair value	(550)	571	–
Net charge to profit	950	2,338	1,212

Fair value of debenture at 30 November 2004		Fair value of debenture at 30 November 2005	
Interest £1.5m × discount rate of 6%	=£1.42m	Capital and interest 30. 11. 2006 (£31.5m × 4%)	= £30.29m
Capital and interest 30. 11. 2006 (£31.5m × 6%)	= £28.03m		
	£29.45m	Fair value (£29.45 + 0.267m)	£29.72m
		Loss on fair valuation	(£0.57m)
Capital at nominal value	£30.00m		
Gain on fair valuation	£0.55m		

Application in published accounts

A good example of both the narrative and supplementary numerical analysis required by FRS 13 has been provided by CRH plc. Like many companies the narrative has been incorporated as part of its Finance Review at the front of its report.

CRH Plc   Year Ended 31 December 2003   Aggregates and Building Materials

Finance Review (Extract)

Financial risk management
The group uses financial instruments throughout its businesses: *borrowings* and *cash and liquid investments* are used to finance the group's operations; *trade debtors and creditors* arise directly from operations; and *derivatives*, principally interest rate and currency swaps and forward foreign exchange contracts, are used to manage interest rate risks and to achieve the desired currency profile of borrowings.

The board of directors sets the treasury policies and objectives of the group, which include controls over the procedures used to manage financial market risks. The major financial market risks borne by the group arise as a result of foreign exchange and interest rate movements. The group accepts currency and interest rate exposures as part of the overall risks of operating in different economies and seeks to manage these in accordance with the policies set out below. The group does not trade in financial instruments nor does it enter into any leveraged derivative transactions.

Interest rate and debt/liquidity management
The group's policy is to fix interest rates on a proportion of the group's medium- to long-term net debt exposure in individual currencies. In recent years, the group's target has been to fix interest rates on approximately 50 per cent of group year-end net debt. Underlying borrowings are arranged on both a fixed rate and a floating rate basis and, where appropriate, the group uses interest rate swaps to vary this mix and to manage the group's interest rate exposure. At the end of 2003, 48 per cent of the

group's net debt was at interest rates which were fixed for an average period of 5.2 years. US dollars accounted for approximately 45 per cent of net debt at the end of 2003 and 47 per cent of the dollar component of net debt was at fixed rates.

In September 2003, the group completed a US$1 billion Global Bond Issue, which substantially extended the maturity profile of the group's net debt. The issue raised US$700 million of 10-year money and US$300 million due for repayment in 30 years. This Bond Issue, which is rated BBB+/BAA1/A−, was significantly over-subscribed and followed the successful US$1 billion 10-year Global Bond Issue completed in March 2002.

The Group finished the year in a very strong financial position with 97 per cent of the group's gross debt drawn under committed term facilities, 88 per cent of which mature after more than 1 year. In addition, at year end, the group held €638 million of undrawn committed facilities, which had an average maturity of 2 years.

Based on the level and composition of year-end debt, an increase in average interest rates of 1 per cent per annum would result in a decrease in future profit before tax of €12.1 million per annum (2002: €8.3 million).

Currency management
CRH's activities are conducted principally in the local currency of the country of operation resulting in low levels of foreign exchange transaction risk. The primary foreign exchange risk is translation-related arising from the fluctuating euro value of the group's net investment in currencies other than the euro. The group's policy is to spread its net worth across the currencies of its different operations to limit its exposure to any individual currency. This is consistent with the group's desire to have a balance and spread of commercial operations. CRH believes that this is an appropriate policy for an international group with international shareholders. In order to achieve this, the group manages its borrowings, where practicable and cost-effective, to hedge its foreign currency assets. Hedging is done using currency borrowings in the same currency as the assets being hedged or through the use of other hedging methods such as currency swaps.

The bulk of the group's net worth is denominated in the world's two largest currencies − the US dollar and the euro − which accounted for 50 per cent and 36 per cent respectively of the group's net worth at end-2003.

The strengthening of the euro during 2003 resulted in a negative €523 million currency translation effect on foreign currency net worth mainly arising on US dollar net assets. This negative effect is stated net of a €243 million favourable translation impact on net foreign currency debt.

A strengthening of the euro by 10 per cent against all the other currencies the group operates in would, when reported in euro, reduce the group's year-end 2003 net worth by an estimated €277 million and year-end 2003 net debt by €144 million.

Credit risk associated with financial instruments
The group holds significant cash balances which are invested on a short-term basis. These deposits and other financial instruments give rise to credit risk on amounts due from counterparties. Credit risk is managed by limiting the aggregate amount and duration of exposure to any one counterparty primarily depending on its credit

rating and by regular review of these ratings. At year end 2003, 96 per cent of the group's cash and liquid investments had a maturity of 6 months or less. The possibility of material loss in the event of non-performance by a counterparty is considered unlikely by management.

Note 20 to the financial statements provides a detailed breakdown of debt, cash and capital employed by currency together with additional treasury-related information.

Notes on Financial Statements
20 Treasury information

The interest rate and currency profile of the Group's net debt and net worth as at 31 December 2003 was as follows.

	Euro €m	US dollar €m	Pound sterling €m	Swiss franc €m	Other €m	Total €m
Weighted average fixed debt interest rates	3.6%	7.3%	6.9%	3.6%	7.6%	5.8%
Weighted average fixed debt periods – years	2.8	8.9	0.1	1.4	1.8	5.2
Fixed rate debt	(371.6)	(485.4)	(42.9)	(97.0)	(101.9)	(1,098.8)
Floating rate debt	(761.1)	(963.7)	(289.9)	(276.3)	(216.3)	(2,507.3)
Cash and liquid investments – floating rate	408.5	421.8	238.4	190.7	38.6	1,298.0
Net debt by major currency	(724.2)	(1,027.3)	(94.4)	(182.6)	(279.6)	(2,308.1)
Loans to joint ventures	60.9	–	1.1	0.3	–	62.3
Deferred acquisition consideration falling due after more than 1 year	(0.1)	(95.3)	(1.1)	–	–	(96.5)
Net financial assets and liabilities (excluding short-term debtors and creditors)	(663.4)	(1,122.6)	(94.4)	(182.3)	(279.6)	(2,342.3)
Capital employed at 31 December 2003	2,305.8	3,497.4	435.8	248.4	627.1	7,204.5
Minority shareholders' equity interest	(7.5)	–	(0.5)	(5.4)	(77.2)	(90.6)
Capital grants	(12.3)	–	(0.4)	–	–	(12.7)
Shareholders' funds (net worth) At 31 December 2003	1,712.6	2,374.8	340.5	60.7	270.3	4,758.9

PS The same information is provided for the comparative data for the year ended 31 December 2002.

The amounts shown above take into account the effect of currency swaps, forward contracts and other derivatives entered into to manage these currency and interest rate exposures.

Floating rate debt comprises bank borrowings and finance leases bearing interest at rates fixed in advance for periods ranging from overnight to less than 1 year largely by reference to inter-bank interest rates (US$LIBOR, sterling LIBOR, Swiss franc LIBOR, Euribor).

Cash deposits and liquid investments comprise cash deposits placed on money markets for periods up to 6 months and high-quality liquid investments such as commercial paper and bonds.

As explained in the finance review on pages 28 to 31, the group's policy is to spread its net worth across the currencies of the countries in which it invests. Interest rate swaps are entered into only for the purpose of managing the group's mix of fixed and floating rate debt. Currency swaps are entered into only for the purpose of managing the group's mix of fixed and floating rate debt by currency to ensure that the group's debt funding sources match the currency of the group's operations. In line with group policy, all derivative contracts are entered into with highly rated counterparties. Gains and losses arising on the re-translation of net worth are dealt with in the statement of total recognised gains and losses.

Transactional currency exposures arise in a number of the group's operations and these result in net currency gains and losses which are recognised in the profit and loss account. As at 31 December 2003, these exposures were not material.

Fair values of debt, cash and liquid investments

A comparison by category of book values and fair values of all the group's financial assets and financial liabilities (excluding short-term debtors and creditors) at 31 December 2003 and 31 December 2002 is set out below.

	Gross debt	Derivative contracts Gains	Losses	Cash and Liquid invest- ments	Other financial instru- ments	Total
	€m	€m	€m	€m	€m	€m
2002 book value	(3,152.4)	10.3	(101.0)	1,533.2	(114.1)	(1,824.0)
2002 fair value	(3,490.2)	324.5	(119.4)	1,533.2	(114.1)	(1,866.0)
Unrecognised gains and losses as at 31 December 2002	(337.8)	314.2	(18.4)	–	–	(42.0)
2003 book value	(3,428.9)	18.4	(195.5)	1,298.0	(34.3)	(2,342.3)
2003 fair value	(3,679.0)	225.7	(205.3)	1,298.0	(34.3)	(2,394.9)
Unrecognised gains and losses as at 31 December 2003	(250.1)	207.3	(9.8)	–	–	(52.6)

Reconciliation of movement in unrecognised gains and losses

At 31 December 2002	(337.8)	314.2	(18.4)	–	–	(42.0)
Portion recognised in 2003	97.8	(85.7)	8.4	–	–	20.5
Arising in 2003	(10.1)	(21.2)	0.2	–	–	(31.1)
As at 31 December 2003	(250.1)	207.3	(9.8)	–	–	(52.6)

Of which, expected to be recognised

in 2004	(111.5)	91.3	(6.8)	–	–	(27.0)
after 2004	(138.6)	116.0	(3.0)	–	–	(25.6)
	(250.1)	207.3	(9.8)	–	–	(52.6)

Other financial instruments comprise loans to joint ventures and deferred acquisition consideration due after more than 1 year.

Most of the fair value of derivative contracts arises from interest and currency swaps. A small portion arises from contracts to hedge future energy costs.

The book value of fixed rate debt and fixed rate swaps is the outstanding principal value of debt/swaps. The fair value of swaps and fixed rate debt is the net present value of future interest and capital payments discounted at prevailing interest rates. When the fixed interest rates on debt and swaps differ from prevailing rates, fair value will differ from book value. The fair value of floating rate instruments approximates book value.

As the group has a policy of fixing interest rates on a portion of net debt, the fair value of such debt will be above book value when prevailing interest rates are below the fixed rates being paid by the group.

At both 31 December 2003 and 31 December 2002, interest rates were generally below the fixed rates being paid by the group. As a consequence, the fair value of the group's fixed interest rate instruments included a net unrecognised loss of €52.6 million (2002: €42.0 million).

11.3   FRS 8 *Related Party Disclosures* (October 1995)

Background

A number of recent scandals has brought to light the need to have clear transparency between a reporting entity and certain closely related parties. The Robert Maxwell affair and the problems with the Mirror Group pension scheme, in particular, exemplified the problem. If there is a close relationship between two parties then it is argued to be more likely that transactions will be carried out between those parties at other than arm's length to the detriment of other parties. It is therefore important that reporting entities not only be, but also be seen to be, as open and independent as possible.

FRS 8 has therefore been published to ensure that financial statements contain sufficient disclosure so that attention is drawn to the possibility that the reported position and results may have been affected by the existence of related parties and by material transactions with them.

Who are related parties?

There are three separate sets of definition provided in the standard:

(i)   General definition;
(ii)   Deemed set of related parties;
(iii)   Presumed set of related parties.

(i)   General definition

This set of definitions has been drawn up to ensure that a relationship which might escape the more specific sets of definitions, is included. They are:

(a)   where one party has direct or indirect control of another party;
(b)   where both parties are subject to common control from the same source;
(c)   where one party has influence over the operating and financial affairs of the other so that it prevents the other from exercising its own separate interests;
(d)   where the parties are subject to influence from the same source to such an extent that one of the parties has subordinated its own separate interests.

(ii)   Deemed set of related parties

The following are deemed to be related parties and material transactions between them must therefore be disclosed:

(a)   Directors and their close families (i.e. members of family or household who may be expected to be influenced by the director);
(b)   Associates;
(c)   Pension funds;
(d)   Companies in the same group; but there are exemptions for intra-group balances eliminated on consolidation and for parents and 90 per cent or more subsidiaries provided the information is disclosed in the group accounts.

This is the key set of definitions and 90 per cent or more disclosures are currently emerging from here.

(iii)   Presumed set of related parties

The third set of definitions is presumed to be in respect of related parties but this may be rebutted by the reporting entity:

(a)   Key management and their close families (see above);
(b)   A major shareholder (i.e. controlling more than 20 per cent of voting rights);
(c)   An entity managed by the reporting entity via a management contract;
(d)   Each person acting in concert to exercise control or influence over the reporting entity.

What is a related party transaction?

It represents the transfer of assets or liabilities or the performance of services by, to or for a related party irrespective of whether or not a price has been charged.

What information must be disclosed?

The reporting entity should disclose all *material* transactions between itself and its related parties and the following should be disclosed:

(a)   Names of the related parties;
(b)   Description of the relationship between the parties;

(c)   Description of the transactions;
(d)   Amounts involved;
(e)   Amounts due from/to related parties at the balance sheet date and any provisions for bad and doubtful debts;
(f)   Any other elements of the transactions necessary to understand the financial statements;
(g)   Any bad debts written off during the period.

The information may be aggregated unless it is necessary to disclose a particular transaction separately in order to understand the impact of the transaction on the financial statements or it is required by law.

Materiality is defined slightly differently for directors/key managers/major shareholders in that a transaction must be disclosed if it is material not just from the reporting entity's view but also from the individual director/manager, etc.'s, view. It is therefore strictly essential to be aware of the individual's own personal financial position!

Disclosure of ultimate controlling party

When the reporting entity is controlled by another party the FRS requires disclosure of the name of that party and, if different, the name of the ultimate controlling party. If the ultimate controlling party is not known then disclosure of that fact is necessary.

This disclosure is required irrespective of whether or not there are any related party transactions between the parties.

Exemptions

There are a number of specific exemptions from disclosure:

• Providers of finance in the normal course of business;
• Public utilities;
• Government departments and agencies; and
• Customers, suppliers, franchisers, etc., with whom the reporting entity has a significant volume of business, i.e., the economically dependent factor.

FRED 25 *Related Party Disclosures* (May 2002)

As part of the convergence process, next Spring the ASB will implement the international standard, IAS 24 *Related Party Disclosures*, which will involve some relatively minor changes to the current FRS.

The definitions of related parties are broadly similar, although by focusing on key managers the FRED does not distinguish between key types of management. The FRED will continue to demand disclosure of the name of the controlling party or, if not known, a statement to that effect.

The most difficult aspect of FRS 8 is actually making the decision as to whether or not a particular relationship should be classified as a related party. The example below provides an insight into that decision.

Example – Portavogie Plc

Portavogie plc, merchant bankers, have a number of subsidiaries, associates and joint ventures in their group structure. During the financial year to 31 October 2003, the following events occurred:

(i) The company agreed to finance a management buyout of a group company, Cloughy, a limited company. In addition to providing loan finance, the company has retained a 25 per cent equity holding in the company and has a main board director on the board of Cloughy. Portavogie received management fees, interest payments and dividends from Cloughy.

(ii) On 1 July 2003, Portavogie sold a wholly owned subsidiary, Millisle, a limited company, to Comber, a public limited company. During the year Portavogie supplied Millisle with second-hand office equipment and Millisle leased its factory from Portavogie. The transactions were all contracted for at market rates.

(iii) The pension scheme of the group is managed by another merchant bank. An investment manager of the group pension scheme is also a non-executive director of the Portavogie Group and received an annual fee for his services of £25,000, which is not material in the group context. The company pays £16m per annum into the scheme and occasionally transfers assets into the scheme. In 2003, fixed assets of £10m were transferred into the scheme and a recharge of administrative costs of £3m was made.

Portavogie – Suggested solution

Are the following events related party disclosures under FRS 8?
FRS 8 gives express exemption from disclosure of the normal financing arrangements between a company and its bankers. However, in this case the merchant bank holds 25 per cent of the shares in the entity and could possibly be classed as an associated relationship. If this were the case then all material transactions would need to be disclosed between the two parties. In addition the merchant bank would appear to exercise significant influence over the entity as it has a member of its own on the board of directors of Cloughy. However, the 25 per cent holding and membership on the board would not be sufficient to ensure an associated relationship. The bank must also take an active part in the operating and financial policies of the other entity. It could be, for example, that the other 75 per cent of the shares are held by another party and thus clearly the bank has little influence. Also, merchant banks often do not regard their investments in other companies as associates but merely investments. FRS 9 *Associates and Joint Ventures* says that if the business of the investor is to provide capital to the entity accompanied by advice and guidance then the holding should be accounted for as an investment rather than an associate.

If the relationship is deemed to be associate then the company would need to disclose all material transactions and that would include disclosure of all management fees, interest, dividends, etc., as well as details of the terms of the loan.

One of the main exemptions permitted by FRS 8 is the elimination of all inter-group transactions and balances on consolidation. The transactions that need to be disclosed will be limited to those that were incurred when Millisle was not part of the group (i.e. between 1 July 2003 and 31 October 2003) but not those that occurred prior to 1 July 2004. There is no related party relationship between Portavogie and Comber as it is simply a business transaction unless there has been a subordinating of interests when entering into the transaction due to influence or control.

Pension schemes for the benefit of the employees of the reporting entity are related parties of the entity. The requirements of FRS 8 were largely introduced to quell the discomfort felt after the Mirror Group pension scheme fell insolvent at the time of the Maxwell affair. However, FRS 8 expressly exempts the contributions paid from disclosure but it does insist on disclosure of other transactions with the group. The transfers of fixed assets of £10m and the recharge of administrative costs of £3m must be disclosed, but not the £16m of contributions paid.

The investment managers of the pension scheme are employees and would not normally be regarded as a related party of the reporting company. However, a related party relationship would exist if it can be demonstrated that the investment manager could influence the operating and financial policies of the reporting entity through his/her position of non-executive director of the company. Directors are deemed to be related parties under FRS 8 and, although the management fees of £25,000 may not be material from the reporting entity's perspective, FRS 8 insists that materiality (in the case of individuals) should be considered in the context of individual directors as well and, if material, should be disclosed. It would certainly be the case that £25,000 would be significant in this context and the fee should therefore be disclosed.

Applications in published accounts

There are four examples provided of related party disclosures. The first (Fuller Smith & Turner plc) shows a typical disclosure note regarding transactions between a company and its directors. The second example (Kerry Group plc) refuses to name directors as these are mainly farmer directors and the information could be regarded as sensitive so only the aggregate purchases and sales are disclosed with no names released. The third example shows a typical plc (BAE Systems plc) which has a number of joint ventures and the detailed sales, purchases and debt owed to and from the company. The final example, and the most detailed, provides very extensive information about key shareholders and the company, particularly the fact the group (Associated British Foods plc) is effectively controlled by a family trust.

Fuller Smith & Turner Plc   Year Ended 31 March 2003   Brewers

Notes to the Financial Statements (Extract)

26 Related Party Transactions

During the year, the Company paid £65,000 (2002: £95,000 on two properties) rent on a property leased from Hammerson plc on an arm's-length basis. R R Spinney, a Non Executive Director of the Company, is the Chairman of Hammerson plc. The lease was entered into prior to Mr Spinney joining the Board of Fuller's.

Kerry Group Plc   Year Ended 31 December 2002   Food Industry

Notes to the Financial Statements (Extract)

29 Related Party Transactions

In the ordinary course of business as farmers, directors have traded on standard commercial terms with the Group's Agribusiness Division. Aggregate purchases from, and sales to, these directors amounted to €872,000 (2001: €1,290,000) and €328,000 (2001: €393,000) respectively. The trading balance outstanding to the group at the year end was €46,000 (2001: €81,000).

BAE Systems Plc   Year Ended 31 December 2003   Aerospace Industry

Notes to the Financial Statements (Extract)

31 Related Party Transactions

The group has an interest in a number of joint ventures, the principal ones of which are disclosed in note 12. Transactions occur with these joint ventures in the normal course of business. The more significant transactions are disclosed below:

	Sales to related party £m	Purchases from related party £m	Amounts owed by related party £m	Amounts owed to related party £m
Related party				
Airbus SAS	139	1	23	169
AMS NV	9	96	73	87
Eurofighter Jagdflugzeug GmbH	170	4	22	–
Flagship Training Limited	–	–	–	10
MBDA SAS	38	11	29	526
Panavia Aircraft GmbH	82	74	12	1

Associated   **Year Ended**   **Food Industry**
British Foods Plc   **13 September 2003**

Notes Forming Part of the Financial Statements

31 Related Party Transactions

The group's related parties, as defined by Financial Reporting Standard 8, the nature of the relationship and the extent of the transactions with them, are summarised below:

	Sub Note	2003 £'000	2002 £'000
Management charge from Wittington Investments Limited (see note 30), principally in respect of directors and secretarial staff of ABF paid by Wittington		–	190
Charges to Wittington Investments Limited in respect of services provided by the Company and its subsidiary undertakings		35	53
Amounts owed to Wittington Investments Limited		281	269
Dividends paid by ABF and received in a beneficial capacity by:			
(i) Trustees of The Garfield Weston Foundation	1	4,103	3,593
(ii) Directors of Wittington Investments Limited who are not trustees of the Foundation		720	618
(iii) Directors of Wittington Investments Limited who are not trustees of the Foundation and are not directors of Wittington Investments Limited	2	7	4
(iv) A member of the Weston family employed within the ABF group	3	400	344
Sales to fellow subsidiary undertakings on normal trading terms	4	7	5
Amounts due from fellow subsidiary undertakings	4	–	–
Sales to joint ventures and associates on normal trading terms	5	52	33
Purchases from joint ventures and associates on normal trading terms	5	1	1
Amounts due from joint ventures and associates	5	4	2
Amounts due to joint ventures and associates	5	2	1

Sub notes

1. The Garfield Weston Foundation ('The Foundation') is an English charitable trust, established in 1958 by the late W. Garfield Weston. The Foundation has no direct interest in the company, but as at 13 September 2003 held 683,073 shares in Wittington Investments Limited representing 79.2% of that company's issued share capital and is, therefore, the company's ultimate controlling party. At 13 September 2003, Trustees of the Foundation comprised four of the late W. Garfield Weston's children and one grandchild and five of the late Garry H. Weston's children.
2. Details of the directors are given on pages 32 and 33. The beneficial interests, including family interests, in the company and its subsidiary undertakings are given on page 45. Directors' remuneration and share options are disclosed on pages 40 to 43.

3. A member of the Weston family who is employed by the group and is not a director of the company or Wittington Investments Limited and is not a Trustee of the Foundation.
4. The fellow subsidiary undertaking is Fortnum & Mason PLC.
5. Details of the group's principal joint ventures and associates are set out on page 79.

11.4 FRS 20 *Share Based Payment* (April 2004)

Background

Share options have become a common feature of employee remuneration in recent years and they can also be used as compensation to suppliers rather than paying cash. Until FRS 20 was published there was no accounting standard on the subject and standard setters throughout the world were concerned about the failure in world accounting to disclose a fair cost for employing their labour force.

Three different types of share based payment are covered in FRS 20:

- equity settled transactions;
- cash settled transactions; and
- transactions in which an entity receives or acquires goods or services and the terms permit the entity or the supplier a choice between settling in cash or by issuing equity.

Key issues

The main purpose of FRS 20 is to ensure that a fair charge is recorded in the profit and loss for any share based payment issued by the entity as well as providing sufficient disclosure so that users can understand the impact on future profitability. The standard requires entities to recognise the fair value of the goods and services received as both the expense and the increase in equity/liability associated with the share option. If an entity cannot measure the goods and services reliably then it must value the cost of goods and services indirectly by reference to the fair value of equity instruments granted.

Fair value must always be measured at the date of grant. The fair value must be based on market prices taking into account the terms and conditions upon which those equity instruments were granted. If market prices are not available, e.g. unlisted or listed companies with thin markets, then a valuation technique should be used to estimate the price of equity. Option pricing models such as the Black-Scholes-Merton and Binomial models may be adopted.

Equity settled transactions

Employee share options must be measured at the fair value of equity instruments granted as it is not possible to reliably estimate the fair value of employee services received. However, for parties other than employees, there is a rebuttable presumption that the fair value of goods and services can be reliably estimated. If, rarely, that is not possible then fair value of equity is substituted measured at the date the entity obtains the goods or the other party renders service.

Example – Equity Settled Share Based Payment Transactions

An entity grants 100 options to each of its 500 employees. Each is conditional on the employee working for the entity over the next 3 years. Assume the fair value is £15. Based on weighted average probability, 20% of employees will leave during the 3-year period and thus forfeit their rights. The total fair value of options granted = 500×100 options $\times £15 \times 80\% = £600,000$.

The entity also estimates that the departures will occur evenly over 3 years.

Application

Scenario 1

If everything turns out as expected		Cumulative	Expense
Year 1	50,000 options × 80% × £15 × 1/3 year	200,000	200,000
Year 2	50,000 options × 80% × £15 × 2/3 years	400,000	200,000
Year 3	50,000 options × 80% × £15 × 3/3 years	600,000	200,000
Total over 3 years			600,000

Scenario 2

During year 1, 20 employees leave; then the entity revises its estimate of total departures from 20% to 15%.

During year 2, 22 employees leave; then the entity revises its estimate of total departures from 15% to 12%.

During year 3, 15 employees leave; thus 57 in total forfeited their rights leaving 443×100 options vested.

		Cumulative	Expense
Year 1	50,000 options × 85% × £15 × 1/3 year	212,500	212,500
Year 2	50,000 options × 88% × £15 × 2/3 years	440,000	227,500
Year 3	44,300 options · × £15 × 3/3 years	664,500	224,500
Total over 3 years			664,500

Vesting conditions, other than market conditions, are not considered when estimating the fair value of the options but they are considered in adjusting the number of equity instruments included in the measurement of the charge to profit and loss to ensure that eventually the charge to profit and loss is based on the number of equity instruments that actually vest.

Example – Equity Settled Share Based Payment Transactions (Performance condition – vesting period varies)

Background

At start of year 1 an entity grants 100 shares to 500 employees conditional on staying for vesting period.

Shares vest at end of year 1 if earnings increase by more than 18%.

Shares vest at end of year 2 if earnings increase by more than an average of 13% p.a. over 2-year period.

Shares vest at end of year 3 if earnings increase by more than an average of 10% p.a. over
3-year period.

Fair value at start of year 1 is £30 per share and no dividends are expected over the 3 years.
   End of year 1: earnings increased by 14% and 30 employees left – expect earnings to
increase similarly in year 2 and thus vest at end of year 2. However, a further 30 employees
are expected to leave.
   End of year 2: earnings increased by only 10%. 28 employees left during the year; expect
a further 25 to leave during year 3. Earnings are expected to rise by a further 6% and thus
achieve an average of 10% p.a.
   End of year 3: 23 employees left and earnings rose by 8% – an average of 10.67% over
3 years. 419 employees received 100 shares at the end of year 3.

Application

		Cumulative	Expense
Year 1	440 employees × 100 shares × £30 × 1/2 years	660,000	660,000
Year 2	417 employees × 100 shares × £30 × 2/3 years	834,000	174,000
Year 3	419 employees × 100 shares × £30 × 3/3 years	1,257,000	423,000
Total charged during the 3-year period			1,257,000

Cash settled transactions

FRS 20 requires an entity to measure the goods and services acquired and the liability
incurred at the fair value of the liability. Until settled, the entity is required to remeasure
the fair value of the liability at each subsequent reporting date and at the date of settlement
with any changes being reported in the profit and loss for the period.

Example – Cash Settled Share Based Payment Transactions

An entity grants 100 cash share appreciation rights (SARs) so long as an employee stays
3 years.

During year 1, 35 employees leave and the entity estimates that a further 60 will leave dur-
ing years 2 and 3.
During year 2, 40 employees leave and the entity estimates a further 25 will leave during
year 3.
During year 3, 22 employees leave and at the end of year 3, 150 employees exercise their
SARs, another 140 at the end of year 4 and the remaining 113 at the end of year 5.

Year	Fair value	Intrinsic value
1	£14.40	
2	£15.50	
3	£18.20	£15.00
4	£21.40	£20.00
5		£25.00

Application

		Cumulative	Expense
Year 1	Expense for services received and consumed, and the year end liability (500 − 95 employees × 100 SARs × £14.40 × 1/3)	194,400	194,400
Year 2	(500 − 100 employees × 100 SARs × £15.50 × 2/3)	413,333	218,933
Year 3	(500 − 97 left − 150 exercised × 100 SARs × £18.20 × 3/3)	460,460	
	150 exercised × 100 exercised × £15	225,000	
		685,460	272,127
Year 4	150 exercised × 100 SARs × £15	225,000	
	140 exercised × 100 SARS × £20	280,000	
	(500 − 97 left − 290 exercised × 100 SARs × £21.40)	241,820	
		746,820	61,360
Year 5	150 exercised × 100 SARs × £15	225,000	
	140 exercised × 100 SARs × £20	280,000	
	113 exercised × 100 SARs × £25	282,500	
		787,500	40,680
	Total charged over the 5 years		787,500

Transactions with choice of cash or equity

The terms of the arrangement sometimes provide the entity or a supplier with a choice of settling in cash or by issuing equity. In these cases, the entity must account for that transaction as a cash settled share based payment but only if, and to the extent that, the entity has incurred a liability to settle in cash or as an equity settled transaction if no such liability has been incurred.

Example – Share Based Payment Arrangements with Cash Alternatives

An entity grants employees a choice – 1,000 phantom shares (cash) or 1,200 shares conditional on 3 years' service. If choosing the latter, shares must be held for a further 3 years after the vesting date.

Grant date: share price £50 and at end of years 1, 2 and 3 – £52, £55 and £60 respectively.

No dividends are expected to be paid out during the 3 years.

After taking into account effects of post-vesting transfer restrictions the entity estimates that the grant date fair value of the share alternative is £48 per share.

At the end of year 3, the employee chooses (1) cash or (2) equity.

Application

Fair value of arrangement is £57,600 (1,200 shares × £48)
Fair value of cash is £50,000 (1,000 phantom shares × £50)
Fair value of equity component of compound is £7,600

			Cumulative Liability	Cumulative Equity	Expense
Year 1	Liability	(1,000 × £52 × 1/3 year)	17,333		17,333
	Equity	(£7,600 × 1/3 year)		2,533	2,533
Year 2	Liability	(1,000 × £55 × 2/3 years)	36,666		19,333
	Equity	(£7,600 × 2/3 years)		5,066	2,533
Year 3	Liability	(1,000 × £60 × 3/3 years)	60,000		23,334
	Equity	(£7,600 × 3/3 years)		7,600	2,534
Total expense under both scenarios					67,600

Scenario (1)

End year 3	Paid	(60,000)	
		Nil	

Scenario (2)

End year 3		(60,000)	60,000
		Nil	67,600

Disclosure

FRS 20 prescribes various disclosure requirements including:

(a) the nature and extent of share based arrangements that existed in the period;

(b) how the fair value of goods and services received or the fair value of equity instruments granted was determined; and

(c) the effect of share based payment transactions on the entity's profit and loss for the period and on its financial position.

11.5   Urgent Issues Task Force Abstracts

The following are the extant abstracts as at 31 March 2004, all of which must be complied with in order to provide a true and fair view of the financial statements.

Abstract 1   Convertible bonds – supplemental interest/premium (*July 1991*)

Superseded by FRS 4.

Abstract 2   Restructuring costs (*October 1991*)

Superseded by FRS 3.

Abstract 3   Treatment of goodwill on disposal of a business (*December 1991*)

Superseded by FRS 10.

Abstract 4   Presentation of long-term debtors in current assets (*July 1992*)

Disclosure is required on the face of the balance sheet where the figure for long-term debtors is so material in the context of net current assets that a reader could misinterpret the financial statements without separate disclosure of that amount. In the majority of cases, however, the information may be adequately disclosed in the notes to the accounts.

Abstract 5   Transfers from current assets to fixed assets (*July 1992*)

Assets must be valued at the lower of their cost and net realisable value prior to any transfer to fixed assets and only subsequently may the rules of SSAP 12 (now FRS 15) and the Companies Act re fixed assets apply.

Abstract 6   Accounting for post-retirement benefits other than pensions (*November 1992*)

Superseded by FRS 17.

Abstract 7   True and fair override disclosures (*December 1992*)

Superseded by FRS 18.

Abstract 8   Repurchase of own debt (*March 1993*)

Superseded by FRS 8.

Abstract 9   Accounting for operations in hyper-inflationary economies (*June 1993*)

The abstract permits the adoption of one of two methods of adjusting the local currency financial statements to today's prices prior to its translation for consolidation purposes. The first method adjusts the local statements for general price inflation by price indices, e.g. CPP accounting, and the second permits the adoption of a relatively stable currency, e.g. US $, as the currency of measurement.

This will be superseded when FRED 24 implements IAS 29 *Financial Reporting in Hyper-inflationary Economies* in 2005 or 2006

Abstract 10   Disclosure of directors' share options (*September 1994*)

The only voluntary abstract to date. It requires disclosure of the number, prices and dates of options in relation to each director as well as providing the market price of the shares at the year end and the range of prices during the year.

Abstract 11   Capital instruments: issuer call options (*September 1994*)

The abstract insists that the amounts payable on the exercise of an issuer call option be written off immediately and not treated as part of the finance costs to be spread over the instrument's life.

Abstract 12   Lessee accounting for reverse premiums and similar incentives (*December 1994*)

If a company receives a reverse premium to encourage the taking up of a new tenancy, this should be spread on a straight-line basis over the lease term or over the period to the review date on which the rent payable is expected to be adjusted to the prevailing market rate.

Abstract 13   Accounting for ESOP trusts (*June 1995*)

Under FRS 5 the abstract treats an ESOP trust as no more than an extension of the sponsor's business and therefore proposes that shares held by the ESOP be treated as current assets of the sponsoring company and valued at the lower of cost and net realisable value.

Superseded by Abstract 38.

Abstract 14   Disclosure of changes in accounting policy (*November 1995*)

Superseded by FRS 18.

Abstract 15   Disclosure of substantial acquisitions (*January 1996*)

This is a *status quo* abstract following changes to the Stock Exchange rules re 'substantial acquisitions'. The abstract requires reporting entities to disclose the same information post, as prior to, the change in the rules in relation to detailed disclosures of these acquisitions.

Abstract 16   Income and expenses subject to non-standard rates of tax (*May 1997*)

Superseded by FRS 16.

Abstract 17   Employee share schemes (*May 1997*)

If a company offers shares to its employees it must now charge the fair value of those shares to its profit and loss account and credit both its share capital and share premium. The only exception to this rule are SAYE schemes. In addition, in the case of long-term incentive plans (LTIPs), these should be charged to profit and loss throughout the period to which the performance criteria relate, on a straight-line basis and based on the market price of the shares at the date of the initial award.

Abstract 17 was amended in December 2003 to reflect the consequences for profit and loss of the changes in the presentation of an entity's own shares held by an ESOP Trust. It requires that the minimum expense should be the difference between the fair value of the shares at the date of award and the amount that an employee may be required to pay for the shares (i.e. the intrinsic value of the award). The expense was previously determined either as the intrinsic value or, where purchases of shares had been made by an ESOP trust at fair value, by reference to the cost or book value of shares that were available for the award.

Abstract 18   Pension costs following the 1997 tax changes in respect of dividend income (*December 1997*)

Superseded by FRS 17.

Abstract 19   Tax on gains and losses on foreign currency borrowings that hedge an investment in a foreign enterprise (*February 1998*)

Where foreign currency exchange differences are taken to reserves under the hedging rules of SSAP 20 then the tax charges/credits must also be taken to reserves and both reported in the Statement of Total Recognised Gains and Losses.

Abstract 20   Year 2000 issues: accounting and disclosures (*March 1998*)

Withdrawn July 2000.

Abstract 21   Accounting issues arising from the proposed introduction of the euro (*March 1998*)

The abstract insists that these costs should be expensed immediately to profit and loss except where the reporting entity already has a capitalisation policy for software and the expenditure clearly enhances the asset beyond that originally assessed. These are also regarded as exceptional costs. The abstract also insists that exchange differences written off previously to reserves should remain there and should not therefore be transferred to profit and loss.

Abstract 22   The acquisition of a Lloyd's business (*June 1998*)

On the acquisition of a Lloyd's managing agent, the identifiable assets and liabilities to be recognised include all profit commissions receivable in respect of periods before the acquisition, including those relating to years not yet closed.

Abstract 23   Application of the transitional rules in FRS 15 (*May 2000*)

Prior year adjustments, on first implementation of FRS 15, should be restricted to the elimination of any provisions for repairs and maintenance and to the creation of smaller components from major assets such as ships and aircraft but it does not include changes to the useful economic lives or residual values of fixed assets.

Abstract 24   Accounting for start-up costs (*June 2000*)

Start-up costs should be accounted for as assets if they meet the criteria for recognition as assets under FRS 15, FRS 10 or SSAP 13. Otherwise, they should be recognised as expenses when incurred.

Abstract 25   National insurance contributions on share option gains (*July 2000*)

Provision should be made for NIC contributions on outstanding options that are expected to be exercised. It should be calculated at the latest NI rate applied to the difference between the market value of the underlying shares at the balance sheet date and the option exercise price and allocated over the period from the date of grant to the end of the performance period. If no performance period exists, full provision should be made immediately. All amounts should be charged to the profit and loss account except for staff costs capitalised under other accounting standards.

Abstract 26   Barter transactions for advertising (*November 2000*)

Turnover and costs for barter transactions for advertising should not be recognised unless there is persuasive evidence of the value at which the advertising could be sold for cash in a similar transaction.

Abstract 27   Revision to estimates of the useful economic life of goodwill and intangible assets (*December 2000*)

On initial implementation of FRS 10, where estimates of the useful economic lives of goodwill or intangible assets are revised, the carrying value should be amortised over the revised remaining useful economic life, including an infinite life to one of 20 years or less.

Abstract 28   Operating lease incentives (*February 2001*)

Lessees should recognise the aggregate benefit of incentives as a reduction of rental expense and it should be allocated over the shorter of the lease term and the date when the prevailing market rental becomes payable. The allocation should be on a straight-line basis over the period. Lessors should allocate the costs in a mirror treatment over the same period.

Abstract 29 Website development costs (*February 2001*)

Website planning costs should be expensed immediately to profit and loss but design and content development costs should be capitalised, provided that they meet similar criteria to those in SSAP 13. Any subsequent enhancement or maintenance expenditure, however, should be written off immediately. The useful life of any capitalised costs should be relatively short.

Abstract 30 Date of award to employees of shares or rights to shares (*March 2001*)

An award to an employee of shares or rights to shares that is subject to shareholders' approval is not made until that approval is obtained.

Abstract 31 Exchanges of businesses or other non-monetary assets for an interest in a subsidiary, joint venture or associate (*October 2001*)

Where company A transfers assets into a new joint venture, etc., and company B also introduces assets, then in company A's books the assets transferred in should be valued at book value while the assets introduced by the other party should be valued at fair value in A's consolidated accounts.

Abstract 32 Employee benefit trusts and other intermediate payment arrangements (*December 2001*)

When an entity transfers funds to an intermediary, there should be a rebuttable presumption that the sponsoring entity has exchanged one asset for another and that the payment itself does not represent an immediate expense.

Abstract 33 Obligations in capital instruments (*February 2002*)

If a capital instrument contains an obligation that can be settled at the issuer's discretion and there is no genuine possibility that it will be exercised it should be treated as a liability. Where there is a genuine possibility then the instrument should be reported as part of shareholders' funds. If neither applies then the instrument should be treated as a liability if the number of equity shares that would be needed to settle the obligation will vary with changes in their fair value so that the total fair value of the shares issued will always equal the amount of the obligation.

Abstract 34 Pre-contract costs (*May 2002*)

Pre-contract costs should be expensed, except that directly attributable costs should be capitalised when it is virtually certain that a contract is expected to result in future cash inflows to the entity.

Abstract 35 Death-in-service and incapacity benefits (*May 2002*)

The cost of providing death-in-service and incapacity benefits should be accounted for in accordance with paras 73 and 74 of FRS 17 except where the benefits are not wholly insured, in which case the uninsured scheme liability and the cost should be measured by applying the principles in paras 20 and 22 of FRS 17.

Abstract 36   Contracts for sales of capacity (*March 2003*)

Telecommunications and electricity companies often sells rights to use capacity on their networks. There are three issues:

(i)   Should a contract for the right to use capacity be reported as the sale of an asset or whether income from the contract should be recognised over its life. A number of criteria, based on FRS 5, must be met for transactions to be reported as sales.

(ii)   Where sale criteria are met, UITF 36 sets out the limited circumstances where the proceeds should be reported as turnover rather than as a disposal of fixed assets.

(iii)   In exchanges of capacity, turnover should only be recognised in rare circumstances where the assets or services provided have a readily marketable value.

Abstract 37   Purchases and sales of own shares (*October 2003*)

This abstract requires a holding of an entity's own shares to be accounted for as a deduction in arriving at shareholders' funds rather than being recorded as assets.

Abstract 38   Accounting for ESOP Trusts (*December 2003*)

This abstract supersedes Abstract 13. It changes the presentation of an entity's own shares held in an ESOP Trust from requiring them to be recognised as assets to requiring them to be deducted in arriving at shareholders' funds. Transactions in an entity's own shares by an ESOP Trust are similarly recorded as changes in shareholders' funds and do not give rise to gains or losses. This is in line with Abstract 37.

Draft Abstract Emission Rights (*May 2003*)

Within Europe a 'cap and trade' model has been launched to introduce tradeable polluter licences across the Community. In the United Kingdom an Emissions Trading Scheme was launched in 2002 in which participants accept a cap on their carbon dioxide emissions and receive tradable emissions allowances equal to their cap. The draft abstract proposes that entities recognise an asset (equal to emission allowances held), a liability (for the obligation to deliver allowances for emissions made) and a Government grant (where allowances are allocated by Government for less than fair value).

However, commentators are concerned about its proposals and it is likely that major amendments will still emerge before finalisation.

Index